HIDDEN EMPIRE OF FINANCE

MICHAEL GOLDMAN

HIDDEN

HIDDEN EMPIRE

EMPIRE OF

OF FINANCE

FINANCE

HOW WALL STREET
PROFITS FROM OUR
CITIES AND FUELS
GLOBAL INEQUALITY

DURHAM AND LONDON
DUKE UNIVERSITY PRESS
2026

Project Editor: Livia Tenzer
Designed by Matthew Tauch
Typeset in Warnock Pro by Westchester Publishing Services

Library of Congress Cataloging-in-Publication Data
Names: Goldman, Michael, [date] author.
Title: Hidden empire of finance : how Wall Street profits from
our cities and fuels global inequality / Michael Goldman.
Description: Durham : Duke University Press, 2026. | Includes
bibliographical references and index.
Identifiers: LCCN 2025026142 (print)
LCCN 2025026143 (ebook)
ISBN 9781478033004 (paperback)
ISBN 9781478029557 (hardcover)
ISBN 9781478061762 (ebook)
Subjects: LCSH: Urban economics—History—21st century. | Cities and towns—
History—21st century. | Real estate development—Finance. | International
finance—History—21st century. | Global Financial Crisis, 2008–2009.
Classification: LCC HT321 .G64 2026 (print) | LCC HT321 (ebook)
LC record available at https://lccn.loc.gov/2025026142
LC ebook record available at https://lccn.loc.gov/2025026143

Cover art: Unfinished apartment building, Bengaluru, 2016.
Photo by Pierre Hauser.

FOR RACHEL,
WITH LOVE,
FOREVER

CONTENTS

ACKNOWLEDGMENTS

As we who do research know so well but don't often admit, all knowledge production is social, relational, and conjunctural. My long and circuitous journey has been all of the above. One of the benefits of being a slow researcher and thinker is that I have been able to study change over a lengthy period, leaving me with the gift of being able to sustain incredible friendships. This project has drawn me to many nurturing places around the world. It all started with a sabbatical year during which my family (Rachel, Nadia, Eli) and I lived in Bangalore.

At first, on a Senior Fellowship from the American Institute of Indian Studies, I was invited to affiliate with the Institute for Social and Economic Change, generously hosted by Professors Gopal Karanth and Supriya RoyChowdhury. Later, shifting to the National Institute of Advanced Studies (NIAS) on the Indian Institute of Science campus, I was bigheartedly hosted by Professors Carol Upadhya, A. R. Vasavi, and Narender Pani. Both institutes are vibrant sites of great significance in the national and city landscape. Both supported me and organized a number of academic and public workshops that allowed me to present and learn from so many people in-the-know, key actors and observers of the rapid changes occurring in Bangalore/Bengaluru. From one fruitful workshop at NIAS, we produced a special issue of the Delhi-based public journal *Seminar* (2017), together with scholars, planners, government officials, artists, filmmakers, and activists.

Back at the University of Minnesota, soon after I arrived, we started a collaborative reading group with PhD students and professors. This group took on many forms and eventually settled down with a core group that received funding from the university's many institutions, such as the GPS Alliance, the Institute for Advanced Studies, and the Interdisciplinary Center for the Study of Global Change—great incubators of intellectual work. With limited start-up funds, we began to build a larger network of scholars through a series of international gatherings, in

Minneapolis (2010), Jakarta (2012), and Shenzhen (2013), with smaller and more intensive workshops in Bengaluru (2016) and Jakarta (2017). The organizers of the 2012 Jakarta event, funded by the Urban Studies Foundation, included an amazing crew of intellects—Helga Leitner, Vinay Gidwani, Eric Sheppard, Ananya Roy, Anant Maringanti, Maliq Simone, and Dean Jo Santoso and his colleagues at Tarumanagara University.

Influential to the conceptualization of my early findings was the 2008 workshop "Inter-Referencing Asia: Urban Experiments and the Art of Being Global," funded by the Social Science Research Council (SSRC) and hosted by the Dubai School of Government, United Arab Emirates (UAE). Coordinators Ananya Roy and Aihwa Ong turned those papers into a widely circulated book, *Worlding Cities* (2011).

While I continued to conduct research in India, I was also spending time elsewhere in the world, conferring with scholars, officials, and activists at meetings, offices, universities, and public forums, as well as in homes. Most influential to my thinking were my experiences living in Valencia, Spain, in 2012, as well as spending a week in Rio hosted by Professor Carlos Vainer and his inspiring colleagues from across Brazil, who were developing new curricula on global urbanism from a Latin American perspective, at the Federal University of Rio de Janeiro (2015). I also learned much from a series of talks and engagements with scholars and activists across Turkey: At Koc University for the SSRC conference "Inter-Asian Connections" (Istanbul, 2013), with wonderful feedback from Professors Ching Kwan Lee and Cetin Celik; then as the keynote speaker at the International Urban Studies Congress, at Anadolu Universitesi (Eskisehir) in 2015, and with faculty and students at Bilgi, Boğaziçi, Mimar Sinan Fine Arts universities (Istanbul) and Adnan Menderes University (Izmir). Special thanks to my former PhD students, now all reputable professors and brilliant scholars, Serife Genis, Emin Adas, Yildirim Senturk, and Sinan Erensu.

An early version of chapter 5 was presented at the workshop "Land Dispossession in China and India," funded by the American Council of Learned Societies (ACLS), hosted by Singapore Management University and organized successfully by Professors Michael Levien and Joel Andreas, from which emerged a journal special issue (2021) and an edited book (2020). Professors Sophie Gonick and Thomas Sugrue (New York University) organized a generative workshop at that university's campus in Florence, Italy (2017), where early versions of chapters 2 and 3 were first, clumsily, introduced. Later, I spent a week in residence at the WZB Berlin Social Science Center, hosted by Professor Dieter Plehwe where I presented an early version of the Introduction. Over multiple invitations, I engaged with Paris-based scholars hosted by Cermes3 Institute, Centre National de la Recherche Scientifique-Paris, the University of Paris, the Natural Science Museum-Paris, and the Centre for South Asian and Himalayan Studies, particularly Dominique Pestre, Lorraine Kennedy, Ozan Karaman, Veronique Dupont, Pierre Benoit-Jolly, and Ludovic Halbert.

My most profound and lengthy set of interactions emerged from a multiyear research grant from the National Science Foundation, with co-principal investigators Professors Vinay Gidwani, Helga Leitner, Carol Upadhya, and Eric Sheppard. We worked as an intensely generative and creative team that sponsored extensive research on Jakarta and Bengaluru, working with and training many dynamic researchers and collaborators. Helga Leitner and Eric Sheppard spearheaded a series of panels over two annual meetings of the American Association of Geographers on the theme of speculative urbanism, which was so generative for our collective thinking and produced a journal special issue (2023). It also spawned a marvelous book, *Chronicles of a Global City* (2024), that was co-researched and cowritten with some of our talented young colleagues, working in an inspired experiment in knowledge production. Vinay Gidwani and Carol Upadhya, dear friends as they are, performed miracles to produce this book, driving the unique project with their masterful creativity and commitment to distilling our analytics into an expressive narrative, picking up my responsibilities when I was emotionally unable.

Thanks to our creative postdoctoral leader, Professor Hemangini Gupta, as well as Kaveri Medappa, Sachinkumar Rathod, Jawairia Mehkri, Priyanka Krishna, Anuradha Sajjanhar, B. Manjunatha, Revathi Kondor, Harpreet Kaur, and Deeksha Rao. Their insights and dogged research skills were so instrumental in our collective research, some of which spills into these pages. We also worked closely with a number of talented colleagues with expertise in business economics, mapping and GIS, and real estate and finance dealmaking—Amay Narayan, H. S. Sudhira, and Sanjiv Aundhe. My childhood friend, now a famous photographer, Pierre Hauser, accompanied us during three periods of research and produced a catalog of incredible photographs, some of which adorn these pages.

One standout who offered me so much expertise, wisdom, and friendship is Vinay Baindur, my first and longest-standing research colleague and friend, an expert in so much about this complex city, introducing me to so many actors, from key legislators and judges to displaced villagers and farmer advocates, as well as an expert in landmark *dhabas* and bookstores. People who were so generous with their time, knowledge, and friendship were P. Rajan, B. Manjunatha, Leo Saldanha, and Bhargavi Rao and their courageous Environment Support Group staff, Solly Benjamin, R. Bhuvaneswari, Devika Narayan (and her loving family), Diba Siddiqi, and Vinay Sreenivasa and the dedicated Alternative Law Forum staff, Lalitha Kamath, and Sharadini Rath. Leo and Bhargavi and their staff are remarkable scholars, activists, advocates, communicators, and organizers, doing what few have been capable of, which is to shine a bright light on the injustices occurring across the city and countryside, bringing expertise on environmental and social dimensions to the crisis of the global city. They teach youth, scientists, legislators, and judges, as well as leading numerous campaigns to regenerate the lakes, rural commons, wetlands, truly sustainable farming, and, most important, old and new forms of grassroots democracy. My heart goes out to Leo and his family as he works with and through a heartrending health crisis.

Four eminent scholars—Professors Supriya RoyChowdhury, A. Vasavi, Janaki Nair, and Carol Upadhya—helped me understand and navigate the multiple layers of city and rural life, in more ways than I can possibly acknowledge. Carol was, and continues to be, an amazingly gifted interlocuter and friend, without whom I could never have established myself in this enthralling but dauntingly complex social environment of the city.

My PhD students along the way were, and continue to be, remarkably helpful and supportive: Wes Longhofer, Sinan Erensu, Snigdha Kumar, Kriti Budhiraja, Devika Narayan, Anuradha Sajjanhar, and two undergrads, Ross Abrams and Jake Carlson (who is now a professor).

Down the final tortuous stretch, and during the two most difficult years of my life, dear friends stepped up and supported me in immeasurable ways—in the final editing process as well as in my well-being—for which I am eternally grateful: Ron Aminzade (who offered his unflagging intellectual, editing, and joke-telling skills over countless drafts—and meals and cultural events), Karen Ho, Vinay Gidwani, Kriti Budhiraja, Snigdha Kumar, Eric Sheppard, Helga Leitner, and Carol Upadhya. You all helped me enormously in the final stretch.

My non-book-related friends who supported me with succor and love amid grief include Rebecca Skoler and Steve Stovitz, Trisha Barry and Sean O'Driscoll, Maree Hampton and Corey Brinkema, Sue and Tom Trondson, Julie Pringle Garner, George Henderson and Rachel Breen, Diyah Larasati, Divya Karan, MJ Maynes, Awa Abdi, Rachel Bergman, Bruce Braun and Morgan Adamson, Ajay Skaria and Shiney Verghese, Tom Wolfe, Serra Hakyemez, Danielle Dadras, Evelyn Davidheiser, Kathy Hull, Allison Pugh and Steve Sellers, Karen and Miles Rhein, Andy Nash, Paul and Barbara Schurman, Josh Schurman and Kate Dunnigan, Monica and Mark Abrahams, Vivian and Steve McClure, David Goldman and Dalia Nevo, and our WRITE! Group (which includes Devika, Kriti, Snigdha, Michelle Lee, and Niharika Yadav). And, of course, the (now-adult) kids, friends, and partners of my own kids who loved Rachel as their auntie and who supported me these last years like few adults could ever imagine. And especially to my life inspirations, my dearest Nadia and Eli, awe-inspiring spirits of love and care and creativity. An amazing generation: Watch out, world!

The Duke team has been remarkable, especially editor Elizabeth Ault, who had faith even with such uneven initial reviews; Ben Kossak; and the two stalwart reviewers who stuck with me until the bitter end, including reviewer 1, who beat me over the head until I came up with a coherent analytic and methodological framework in which the data actually fit, and vice versa. Thank you.

When the family lived in Bengaluru, we lived on a lane in which the homes to the west of us were built close to the ground and crammed with working-class families, while the homes to the east had been recently rebuilt as two stories and spread out like eagles across an enlarged footprint, inhabited by IT professionals. At the far end of that side, a ten-story residential building was being built, the first in the neighborhood; at the opposite end of the lane was a series of crudely constructed shanties, with a handful of roaming pigs and tied-up goats. Every morning, we watched as men and women trudged down the lane with the simplest of tools, coming from their handmade homes and heading to the construction site. At night, they walked back down our lane, exhausted, through the neighborhood kids' makeshift cricket pitch, to light their fires and make their meals. As the building on the far end became complete, the homes on the other end were unceremoniously bulldozed, and the community of workers disappeared from the lane. Perhaps they joined the multitude of itinerant laborers who would build the next multistory building at another site, or perhaps on their own demolished plot—first a home, then a graveyard, then real estate.

Learning what and why all of this was happening before our eyes—its incomprehensibility and normalization—could occur only within an entangled supportive web of people, noted above, helping me every step of the way. I am eternally grateful to all; this book is a product of all those social insights, exchanges, and friendships. Just as this book focuses on the importance of social networks of care and concern, so too have networks of friends nurtured me through these tough times. But no web or network or community could ever match the love and support from my dear Rachel, who in the last two years battled with the nastiest of cancers. She did it with strength and love and laughter and wisdom. She confronted it all head on, like the "Schurman tank" that one of her father's best friends used to call her when she was a youth. More life was packed into those two years than one could possibly imagine. She not only strengthened her bonds with people around her but also became besties with the staff at National Institutes of Health's National Cancer Institute and Dr. Steven Rosenberg's miraculous team. Anyone who says government spending is a waste knows nothing about the intense work of people experimenting with immunotherapy to save lives, more every day.

But in an instant, all her vitality disappeared. In moving through death as powerfully and gracefully as she moved through life, Rachel taught us that there is no such thing as a full life without its final stage, that there is no love without grief. She taught us to be unafraid, clear-eyed, and in full acceptance of the inevitable and the natural—all of which our culture, or some cultures, refuses to acknowledge, embrace, or prepare us for. Her values and love continue to blossom in our two kids and animate the lives of so many people in our inner circle as well as others around the world. This book was fueled by Rachel's vivaciousness and her endearing and powerful sense of curiosity, commitment, analytics, anger, caring, love, and gratitude. For Rachel, forever.

INTRODUCTION

THROUGH THE LOOKING GLASS

OF GLOBAL-CITY MAKING

> Organizationally, *haute finance* was the nucleus of one
> of the most complex institutions the history of man has
> produced. —Karl Polanyi, *The Great Transformation:*
> *The Political and Economic Origins of Our Times*, 1957
>
> They might give us money, but they will never give us
> land. Land is the new money. —Dalit slum activist, 2019
>
> It's quite simple: No one invests without an exit strategy.
> —Upper-caste investment banker participating in a
> global summit in Delhi, 2016

Not so long ago, at the dawn of the twenty-first century, a strong desire erupted to build global cities (Shatkin 2017; Ananya Roy and Ong 2011). Ambitious world leaders heeded a call for "world-class" infrastructure. They imagined a string of their own branded metropolises, brimming with new business districts, sleek skyscrapers, and state-of-the-art metro systems linking IT and biotech industrial parks with multiuse gated residential towers. These cities would be bejeweled with luxury malls and recreational facilities that would put to shame anything found in the aging cities of the twentieth century, such as London, New York, and Paris. Driving innovation and an endless virtuous cycle of large-scale capital flows—financiers with their trillions of dollars of liquid and convertible capital—would make the whole city-to-city system thrum, from the Arabian Sea to the foothills of the Himalayas.

In Dubai, dueling projects with bombastic names competed for scope, scale, and euros and dollars. At The Universe project, Dubai's major developers promised to convert private and state capital into an offshore real estate extravaganza: an artificial archipelago in the shape of the cosmic Milky Way. Not to be outdone, The World project offered another artificial archipelago but with many more newly created islands of dredged sand and imported rock, all in the shape of the world's map of nations. Rumors swirled of billionaires and rock stars racing to secure their favorite nations, with Rod Stewart snatching up Ireland and Brangelina claiming Ethiopia. Lindsey Lohan, gossip revealed, purchased her own island—to be named Lohan, naturally—crowing that she would "out-Trump Trump!" Like Brangelina, however, these wild, ambitious headline grabbers would stall out. Amid the cataclysmic 2008 financial crisis, real estate values along Dubai's glittering coastline dropped 75 percent as capital took flight. Several high-profile fraud indictments hit the courts. One investor committed suicide. And yet, as I write, plans have resurfaced to revive, if not the whole world map, at least the European bits, luring tourists with destination sites, year-round snow skiing in the Arabian Desert, and luxury-goods stores that only accept euros.

China's Belt and Road Initiative, announced in 2013, is grander still—and hitting several of its benchmarks. The government project, which the Communist Party in 2017 dubbed the Twenty-First-Century Silk Road on its inclusion in the Chinese Constitution, is scheduled for completion in 2049. It would urbanize parts of Asia, Europe, and Africa into a single colossal, massively surveilled grid. The Chinese state imagines a hundred global cities comprising a multitrillion-dollar empire of infrastructure stretching across seventy countries, together representing a bid to reorient the global economy. Many declare, "If anyone can do it, China can," but coming down from these atmosphere-high aspirations, things look troubling at ground level.

There have been no environmental assessments to anticipate the effects of all this tar, concrete, steel, and glass on ecosystems, nor social assessments regarding what might happen to the many millions of villagers being shunted into an urbanized economy, ecology, and life where they may suffer from marginalization and intolerance. Investors and politicians radiate optimism, overlooking that China's rural landscape has already become littered with ghost cities, built-but-empty metropolises, and dams so enormous that scientists believe they may have realigned the earth's rotation (Shelton et al. 2018). Smaller investors have lost bundles of money in these speculative schemes, yet the Chinese construction industry rolls forward to its next state-led projects, elsewhere around the globe.

The land on which these speculative desires are built is not in some barren nowhere disconnected from essential ecosystems and social lives (Goldman et al. 2024). The land comes from somewhere and someone, such as land-based communities embedded in specific forms of use, exchange, and governance (Benjamin and Raman 2011; Benjamin 2008). Yet the proponents of these urban dreams claim they are built on a universal object of value—cheap and transferable land. Consequently, this same phenomenon of unbridled global urban expansionism heralds massive protest movements by the dispossessed, many of whom are focused on retaining their land and dignity.

Scholars and activists alike have weighed in on these momentous and disruptive trends (Bonizzi et al. 2019; Brenner and Schmid 2015; Brenner 2014). I identify the rise of *global finance capital* (or what I refer to as *Wall Street* or just *finance*) and its collective intrusion into the productive sectors of national economies as a major culprit. It invents opaque financial tools that few around the world understand, such as initial public offerings, mergers and acquisitions, interest rate swaps, real estate investment trusts, collateralized debt obligations, securitized bonds, and derivative hedges and contracts. By 2021 global asset managers were playing with more than $100 trillion worth of assets, up from $31.5 trillion in 2003, with the biggest spike in growth occurring *after* the 2008 global financial crisis, and with Asia being the highest-growth region (Boston Consulting Group 2021).[1] Historically, this form of capital would have flowed into familiar financial assets like stocks/shares and bonds. However, in the decade leading up to the 2008 financial crisis and afterward, the most aggressive large investors put their money into what is called *alternative assets* (i.e., alternatives to traditional banking that avoid banking regulations and use tools and strategies to keep their capital liquid and mobile, as much as possible), such as real estate, housing, and urban infrastructure. The brilliance, or conniving, of this clique of financiers is reflected in the ways they would convert what appears as illiquid and fixed, such as urban infrastructure (e.g., luxury residential complexes, shopping malls, rail and road projects), into something that *becomes* liquid in their savvy hands and for their near-exclusive benefit. This sublime trick of the imagination, as Ian Baucom noted in *Specters of the Atlantic* (2005), is the focus of the analysis here.[2]

Housing investments entered the lived spaces of rental apartments, public or social housing, single-family homes, nursing care facilities, and mobile homes, while infrastructural investments flowed into transport (e.g., toll roads, parking lots), energy (wind farms), telecom (transmission towers), office campuses and shopping malls, food production (farmland), and social infrastructure (schools, hospitals). These alternative assets act very differently than how we typically perceive that finance works, with the prevailing assumption being that these investments will enhance productivity and growth (Ward and Swyngedouw 2018; B. Weber et al. 2016).

"Forty years ago," Brett Christophers writes, "it would have been more or less unthinkable that we would buy our gas from, make our parking payments to, or rent our home from a company like [the giant private equity firm] Blackstone. But today, for growing numbers of people around the world, such is the social reality" (2023, 7). We have entered a brave new world, a reality that Christophers calls "asset-manager society," denoting that so much of the financial world's profits come from rents extracted from the routine "social functioning and reproduction" of our lives. Over the past decades, unbeknownst to most of us, finance capital has turned these social goods, if not essentials, into liquid assets tradable on global markets. The largest of alternative investors—called *private equity firms*—now have portfolios that are profoundly reshaping our lives, as suggested by the title of Christophers's 2023 book, *Our Lives in Their Portfolios.*

By 2023, this segment of the global financial world, called the "shadow banking system" by conservative institutions such as the Federal Reserve and the IMF (International Monetary Fund) for its ability to remain largely untraceable, untaxable, and unregulated, controlled more than $250 trillion of assets, which is almost 50 percent of the world's total financial assets (Financial Stability Board 2023). The two riskiest, most aggressive, and most profitable arms of the shadow system have grown by leaps and bounds. Hedge funds have grown at twice the pace of traditional banking and manage fifteen times as many assets as they did in 2008. Private equity funds have grown by 170 percent over the past decade (McKinsey 2022).

The business model of private equity runs on the piling up of debt on the acquired firms, extreme cost cutting, the firing of workers, and the selling off of the most valuable assets of any acquisition (such as the land under retail chain stores or the iconic downtown buildings of local US newspapers). These are common strategies that enable them to extract maximum profits from these short-term investments before exiting. Whatever the merits and demerits of such a slash-and-burn business model, which can make record profits for investors and suck dry the productive potential of the investment, one key concern is that most people have absolutely no idea how this new financial world works. Is anyone watching or regulating it? The CEO of Brookfield Asset Management explained its management of $825 billion in assets across five continents as follows: "What we do is behind the scenes. Nobody knows we're there" (quoted in Christophers 2023, 9). What kind of trouble have such secretive and powerful entities produced by infiltrating arenas that were once commonly the purview of governments? What is the impact of this increasing influence of financial logics, motives, tools, and strategies—what we call *financialization*—of public goods, services, and infrastructure, including residential spaces, roads, water/sewerage systems, hospitals, and care facilities? If more of the infrastructure that comprises city life is owned and controlled by a handful of major financial firms based outside the borders of local governance, with the sole goal of maximizing profits for their (also remote) investor clients, we need to ask how private equity's ascendency into these arenas affects democracy and governance. How does it affect people's livelihoods and societal patterns of inequality? How does it transform the conditions of city life? Why are these world-altering practices opaque to the public, and how can they become transparent and be tamed, if not reversed? These are some of the key questions addressed in this book.

Finance Capital in the Twenty-First Century

There are several dimensions to this sprawling financial sector of the twenty-first century. Finance capital promises high returns for their high-net-worth individual clients as well as for their institutional investors, such as Vanguard (managing $8.5 trillion); large insurance companies like Allianz (worth $100 billion); workers' pension funds (e.g., New York State Common Pension Fund alone handles $250 billion of workers' pensions); and sovereign wealth funds such as the Norway Oil Fund and Abu Dhabi Investment Authority (which manages more than $1 trillion). In the United States, the 1970s marked a dramatic turn in the regulations and rules governing finance, insurance, and real estate (FIRE) industries. The linchpin of the rise of neoliberal politics during this period was the privatization of pension funds and the deregulation of US banks, insurance, investment firms, and real estate companies.

Wall Street firms merged and consolidated into a handful of mega-banks (which included private equity and venture capital managers) and, with the help of the US Congress, took over the management of people's retirement and pension funds, a model that is fast becoming universal. Their capital reserves overflow with steady revenue streams from millions of workers' biweekly paychecks. Where there were once hundreds of small and regional firms across the United States where you could save and borrow, today there are few. The big players include firms such as JPMorgan Chase with $3.31 trillion, the Bank of America with $2.41 trillion, and Citigroup with $1.71 trillion. These behemoths have folded under their corporate wings a string of investment banks, insurance companies, credit card companies, and mortgage agencies. Take JPMorgan Chase as one example: It consists of a conglomerate of Chemical Bank, Washington Mutual, Chase Manhattan, Bear Stearns, Bank One, First Republic, and many more (Parsons and Nguyen 2017). With such consolidation comes corporate power over capital flows and their regulation by the state. In the 2020 US election cycle, Wall Street spent an estimated $3 billion—or $4 million a day—on lobbying government officials (Collins et al. 2021).

One of the investment strategies of the "alternative to banking" sector of private equity is the transformation of firms producing commodities (e.g., cars) and providing services (e.g., health care) into firms that produce asset value increases. These upticks in value can come in the form of higher stock prices and distributed dividends, as well as from selling off key assets from the acquired companies (Ho 2009). During the tumultuous period of the 1970s where the US economy slowed to a halt, Wall Street promoted the idea that major firms had lost their value-generating steam and needed to change by following the stripped-down goal of focusing solely on increasing asset values, period. Pleasing shareholders and investors over consumers and communities would be the ultimate goal of the financialized corporate world.

One exemplary case is the retailer Toys"R"Us: After its Wall Street takeover and initial public offering (IPO) by KKR and Bain Capital, stock prices spiked, but a few years later, after they piled more than $5 billion of debt from the IPO onto Toys"R"Us, the toy megaretailer was paying more than $400 million in interest annually to the purchasers and was unable to fix the prevailing problems that had allegedly spurred the Wall Street intervention in the first place. With such a debt burden, the owners increased their profits beyond the interest and management fees by selling off the most valuable asset remaining: the real estate under their well-placed stores. The result: the popular retailer fell (or was shoved) into bankruptcy in 2017. The cannibalized company left a vast gap in the market that was happily filled by megafirms Walmart and Amazon. More than 800 stores were shuttered and an estimated forty thousand employees were fired, while KKR, Bain Capital, and a third firm made an estimated $464 million from the deal, according to their SEC (US Securities and Exchange Commission) filings (PESP 2018).

Building on this successful business model, private equity's reach today expands into a wide range of service-providing enterprises, including nursing and de-addiction homes, detention facilities, surgery centers, health care providers, and even schools. They raise funds through leveraged buyouts, so called because they purchase a company through the capital raised from loans taken out against the company, leaving minimal risk and debt with the purchasing firm and instead placing the full burden on the purchased company. Following private equity logic, that debt and risk burden is a natural market exchange for a company being "rescued" and the savvy firm doing the rescuing. Private equity firms rarely use their own capital reserves, and if they do, they use their investor clients' capital, minimizing the firm's own risk and liability.

Private equity's new business strategy has often thrown the rescued company under the bus with a debt burden that leads to bankruptcy and requires selling off their valuable assets, such as real estate and specific units within the company with the highest revenue-generating capabilities. In most cases, these buyouts trigger layoffs and deep cuts that affect the firm's clients—the elderly at nursing homes, the health-fragile in de-addiction centers, hospital patients, low-income renters in apartment complexes, and so on. Such cuts also affect the remaining employees in these firms—the ill-paid and underinsured staff at nursing homes, the nurses and support workers at hospitals. A few decades of numerous value-extracting deals have left workers and service receivers much worse off, while private equity firms and banks have boasted record profits (Christophers 2023; Gottfried 2022; Robertson and Wijeratne 2021).

Scholars, tell-all memoirs, and even Hollywood movies have portrayed this late twentieth-century financial world as swimming in massive personal wealth, inhabited by cocaine-infused Wall Street traders' jet-setting on private jets and oversized yachts. Less understood, however, is the way finance is encroaching on other aspects of our everyday lives, to create a brave new world of the financialization of everything in city life (Langley 2020).

Following the Money: The Two-Way Traffic
Between Global Speculative Urbanism and
Bengaluru's Transformation

In this book I explore the themes discussed above through extensive qualitative research on what I call global-city making (Sassen 1991). I initially started my project by tracking the making of a global city in Bangalore/Bengaluru, India, through the practices of its water and sewerage agency.[3] Everyone needs water, and its scarcity and abundance can reveal a lot about how a city works and how the discourse of global-city making shapes the interplay between expansionary urban infrastructure and people's lives. At the time (2006–7), the water agency, called the Bangalore Water Supply and Sewerage Board, happened to be caught in a crossfire between the World Bank and Asian Development Bank's efforts to privatize the water agency and the street protests of the urban majority, who lacked basic access to potable water and were fearful of having to pay fees for water distributed by a private European corporation. The powerful antiprivatization campaign succeeded in pushing back on these development banks' mandates and global water firms' wishes (which included France-based Suez and Veolia as well as interested financial backers at Goldman Sachs and Deutsche Bank). Although I started my research in the water agency with its water tanks, pipes, and channels, my field site soon slid into the murky world of foreign debt, as the mounting debt of the water agency had become a major drain on city government coffers. Once it was clear that the debt could not be repaid from the relatively paltry sums collected from water user fees, the city government realized it had to find another way to generate revenues. Government agencies thus entered the shadowy world of the land market and began selling off government land. One summer early in my research, I watched a patch of water agency land next to my apartment building become a fancy for-hire wedding facility.

Meanwhile, an illegal market for water began to flourish as the public sector failed to deliver water to the urban majority. These local entrepreneurs (colloquially labeled the *water mafia*, suspected to be backed by politicians linked to the land mafia) needed access to rural land to tap the underground water aquifers, so they, too, jumped into the land market. The ensuing flurry of activity, along with a palpable sense of excitement, fear, and uncertainty around land and real estate, led me to consider the sinewy relations of water, land, and finance in urban space making differently (Ranganathan et al. 2023; Anand 2017; Ranganathan 2014).

By the time the 2008 global financial crisis hit, my attention was already shifting from the specifics of water infrastructure to the enigmatic world of finance that drove it. Clear explanations existed as to why water infrastructure successfully delivered water to elite quarters and not to the rest of the population, but people were much foggier on the role and actions of the financial actors undergirding these infrastructural processes. Although more everyday experiences in the city were being mediated by new financial arrangements, the latter remained a mystery. Yet the business media and politicians alike expressed excitement when Wall Street firms like Blackstone, BlackRock, and Goldman Sachs began arriving in town in the 2000s. And when investors pulled their money from unfinished projects a few years later, earning large profits for themselves while leaving the city without sufficient funds, elite journalists and politicians insisted that Wall Street's success reflected the city's success. Why would profiting from the abandonment of the city be construed as success? Little of this made sense to me or my local interlocutors—not the disruptive financial dynamics, nor the discursive consensus on extracted profits as a positive for city life, nor the deepening of anxiety-ridden speculation that spread across the city.

Displacement from speculation occurs in many forms. Senior water engineers expressed to me their concerns about the accumulated debt from loans piled on their agency and its effects on their ability to provide water to the urban majority, who had to look elsewhere for water resources (Goldman and Narayan 2019). Young IT professionals told me of their parents' distress at developers' plans to replace their single-family homes with high-rises as home and land prices skyrocketed, inviting in new investors from around the world to take over prized neighborhoods of the city. This burgeoning professional class is the fastest-growing community in Bengaluru to buy new apartments to house themselves and/or their elders, and often a second place as an investment with promised value appreciation (Upadhya 2016). But the

I.1 Welcome to Bengaluru IT Park, 2019. Many years after the dispossession of farm, village, forest, watershed, and commons land, very little construction or production has occurred. Photo by Pierre Hauser.

weight of such risk-taking for the young is substantial, as is the impact on their elderly parents, who are moved out of their tight-knit communities just so they can stay in the city.

Most other city denizens, however, do not have the capital to buy, nor the luxury to speculate in this manner. Street vendors, barbers, and shoe cobblers have been judged by the middle class and city officials as too unsanitary and dangerous to ply their trades on footpaths adjacent to these newly valorized residential complexes. Where else could they go? Small farmers on the city's periphery were pressured to sell their land quickly so that land could be aggregated and sold as large parcels to developers. In these transactions, caste, class, and gender play an outsized role in determining how much compensation a farmer could get for their parcel and where they could expect to move, as I show later in the book. On the city's circumference, a gold rush for farmland in the 1990s put many small and large farmers in the difficult position of having to decide whether to sell (and at what price), speculate on land elsewhere, or try to hold out (figure I.1). Though one might assume that these decisions could be based on some clear economic calculation, small farmers (typically from lower castes) face a world of uncertainty and are up against powerful interests. Making such decisions represents a burden for those most likely to lose out and reflects the wide range of speculative risks forced on people with few resources already shouldering too much risk in their lives (Upadhya and Rathod 2021; Gururani 2020; Balakrishnan 2019; Cowan 2018).

Throughout this period, street protests decrying this growing power over land and water were becoming more common. They reflected the raw collective angst of people experiencing the tumult of speculative city life in Bengaluru, India. Housing and rents had become too expensive for the urban majority. Land prices had gone crazy. In one pivotal example, the siting of the new international airport and adjoining special economic zones (opening in 2008) in vast rural terrain just north of the city gave elite insiders with advance notice the opportunity to buy land. This speculative land grab caught this region of lower-caste small producers by surprise. As they began to organize and seek protection from government courts and other agencies, farmers learned too quickly that these instruments of the state were in fact working hand in glove with investors to take advantage of rising land values rather than defend villagers from unscrupulous brokers.

Elsewhere in Bengaluru, politicians and developers promised a stream of pipe dreams, including a Formula One raceway to draw in big spenders from abroad, a Japanese-financed monorail to fly over congested streets, and self-managed private townships with heliports and living quarters that promised a more luxurious life than one could find in Singapore or Dubai (Buckley and Hanieh 2014). These speculative dreams transformed city life by "rendering urban space an object of investment," even if rarely realized as imagined (Nowak 2023, 472). This encouraged city leaders to build world-class infrastructure to "catch up" in the hypercompetitive global economy by using finance capital and financial tools that end up extracting and evicting more than they offer in the form of improvements. This phenomenon is not unique to Bengaluru. Its manifestation in India is a deliberate consequence of processes intimately linked to ones occurring elsewhere around the world. Although we are asked to believe that cities and their world-class infrastructure are distinct and self-contained accomplishments (or failures), I argue throughout the book that the financing of these projects is, by design, a multisite global process. They enable global financiers to exert power across different sites to extract value in a quasi-monopolistic fashion. I trace common business tendencies that typically yield high profits for the most powerful firms regardless of whether specific projects in different cities achieve their public goals.

From observing these similar practices and paying attention to what undergirds these projects, I learned what these projects produced for the major investors, what they offered to communities, and why so many projects disappoint in terms of delivering public goods even while they are touted as successes (and indeed are successes for many large investors). Simply put, I immersed myself in the world of finance as it works within one city and across investments globally. Having conducted research in three cities experiencing the immediate and lingering effects of the 2008 financial crisis—Minneapolis (United States), Valencia (Spain), and Bengaluru (India)—I learned how certain private equity firms take over cities and transform them into markets of assets (housing, water, land, roads) in different places similarly. This research also revealed to me how their competitors chose not to compete in these same geographic and sectoral markets, which for us calls into question notions of free and competitive market practices.

Following these cues led me to acknowledge that behind the turmoil around access to water and land was a bigger story of finance capital discreetly moving money across seemingly unrelated projects. For example, Blackstone, a key player in Bengaluru's land and water price explosion, also played a central role in the housing crisis (and its afterlife) in the United States. The research for this book started in India, but it followed the money globally to reveal and explain transnational connections and their volatile multisite effects. By developing an argument that is at once theoretical, methodological, and political, I show that when we trace financial investments and strategies across the globe, we can see how finance reshapes everyday life. This is not an argument that replaces the local with the global; rather, it foregrounds their relationality and shows how different localities play or are played off each other for profit. This approach helps us reveal the mysteries of finance and the power-laden entanglements that shape today's precarious urban condition. It also introduces a way of knowing, a methodology embedded in a theory of history. Along with other scholars, I refer to this methodology as the *relational-conjunctural approach*, and I name this particular twenty-first-century conjuncture, where financialization meets the global city, *speculative urbanism*. The following section provides a short review of scholarship that, along with my empirical findings, brought me to this theoretical and methodological framework.

Thinking Through the Role of Finance in City Life

Scholarship on the growing trend of financializing the city brings together two phenomena that are often seen as discrete: urbanization and financialization. The contemporary version of the term *financialization* refers to the global process that started in the neoliberal era (circa the late 1970s), during which investment capital shifted its strategies of growth in Global North economies to those that could derive profit from the *circulation* of capital rather than from the *production* and sale of goods and services. The latter reflected the dominant business model for manufacturing, construction, agriculture, and services over the twentieth century. This strategy has led to the remarkable growth and consolidation of different sectors of the economy in the subsequent decades, which those in the business community now call "the FIRE sector." The acronym FIRE refers to the close synergistic connections across once-discrete arenas of finance, insurance, and real estate. It also signals the destructive effects that critics decry (Stockhammer 2012).

Critical scholars effectively utilize political-economic analytics and a long-term historical approach to understanding this latest upsurge in the power of finance (Marx and Engels 1997). Geographer David Harvey (2003) refers to what he saw as a Northern capital-led practice of "accumulation by dispossession," an expropriative phase of global capitalism; economist Costas Lapavitsas (2014) calls it "profiting without producing." Sociologist Saskia Sassen (2014) characterizes the effects as global "expulsions," while Jamie Peck (2012) understands the driving political force in city life as "austerity urbanism." Neil Brenner and Christian Schmid (2015) stress a universalizing form of power that they see as "planetary urbanization," where urbanization becomes the driving force for capital accumulation. Greta Krippner (2011) interprets finance's rise in the United States as "capitalizing on crisis," and Karen Ho (2009) and Gerald Davis (2009) explain the historic turn in the logic of capitalism starting in the 1970s as a structural shift in the United States from managerial to shareholder capitalism. This change occurred within large corporations once controlled by in-house managers interested in reproducing and growing their companies (albeit under exploitative labor conditions). More recently, major investors and their largest shareholders have taken over the management of nonfinancial firms (like Toys"R"Us), paying themselves extraordinary management fees (2 percent annually) and performance fees (20 percent of the profit) as standard forms of compensation. In this era of shareholder capitalism, major investors are primarily interested in any short-term spike in asset value for the firm, even if it means selling off its value-creating assets (such as its inventories, real estate, and factories), alienating its customers, and discarding its employees for the good of the shareholder, who has now become the king in this radically refashioned global economy (Ho 2009; Davis 2009). Interestingly, the largest financial firms also tend to be the largest shareholders of nonfinancial corporations' shares.

These scholars stress macroeconomic global forces, their political manifestations and cultural codependencies, and the social fallout affecting the general population. Many argue that since the 1980s, beyond finance's leveraged takeover and revamping of major corporations, the new landscape of profit became *the built environment of the city*. Following David Harvey's (2001) lead, scholars refer to this move as a "spatial fix" for sectors of capital that suffer from shrinking of profit rates earned from their traditional business practices.[4] This major shift into land, real estate, and the physical infrastructure of the city started after the collapse of the Fordist regime of production in the United States in the 1970s and subsequently spread across the Global North.[5] Shifting from a production-led to a finance-led economy has caused significant crises and ruptures with variegated global consequences. For example, many national governments have adopted a neoliberal approach to public and industrial obligations by letting go of the (Keynesian) social contract that asked governments to provide affordable housing, water, electricity, and transit to industrial working-class communities. Now, the responsibility for public investment and industrial strategy has been placed upon the shoulders of investors.

Early on, the city governments of New York, London, and Paris enticed financial firms with tax breaks to set up headquarters as islands of wealth alongside the city's crumbling urban infrastructure, hoping that this concentration of wealth would create positive ripple effects across the city, including in nonelite communities paying inflated fees for public services. Large financial firms were freed up to invest in old and new forms of real estate—producing a new class of office and residential skyscrapers while converting industrial ports and warehouse districts, once part of the productive economy, into high-end amusement and entertainment centers—creating some glitter to urban life that had lost its sheen.

By the 1990s we found a marked shift away from these saturated centers of Northern wealth with new strategies that go far beyond what the scholarship emphasizes under the shareholder capitalism moniker. In this deregulated banking environment, a new branch of unfettered finance capital emerged with its own logics and practices, with a portfolio of interventions from IPOs to new frontiers of investment into urban infrastructure, such as in Global South cities. A fast-growing wing of global finance, private equity, mobilized stockpiles of capital and invented new tools to invest, in ways that kept their capital fairly liquid and mobile: investing in rapidly expanding cities, like Dubai and Shanghai, and in new forms of value-extracting infrastructure, such as World Cup stadia, destination airports, and luxury enclaves for globetrotting elites looking to invest (and launder ill-gotten wealth). These high-profile investments have been touted by some as engines creating a new tier of city formation—world-class or global cities. However, boosters of this approach ignore the rather banal but essential elements of this new landscape of investment: These new forms of wealth generation depend on widespread liquidations, evictions, and dispossessions (Rolnik 2019; Gillespie 2016; Sassen 2014). These financial strategies require "freed-up" land and public space, placing limits on protective government regulations, and the movement of people to create these fantasy-like global-city landmarks (D. Hall 2013). Is displacement necessary for accumulation?

The new scholarship on global cities and their financialization offers us a valuable jumping-off point for an explanatory framework to understand some of the major changes in the global economy that affect city life and vice versa. To build on and enrich inquiries into the workings of global finance, my research brings together a global approach with a more localized set of production sites, seeing them as coconstitutive and generative. That is, by scrutinizing happenings closer to the ground—observing the places and sites of engagement where the mysterious world of globalized finance meets everyday city life—I can unpack the "organic" aspect of a global crisis emergent from long-standing contradictions and tensions alongside the more particular "conjunctural" dimensions that pop up "almost accidentally" from particular clashes and events, as Antonio Gramsci (1971) has suggested in his conjunctural approach to crisis and change. For example, in subsequent chapters I focus on specific clashes around contested land deals that displace farming communities so rural land can become part of the new urban real estate landscape—a disruptive process that has been treated by state and market actors as necessarily good for the economy while also being ignored by many urban scholars (Peck 2017). It is a significant worldwide phenomenon worthy of our scrutiny.

On the periphery of Indian cities, I find that the creation of these speculative land markets has been shaped by divisive social hierarchies: Lower-caste farmers and workers have been forced to give up their fertile land or homes to (mostly) upper-caste real estate brokers, through transactions lubricated by (mostly) upper-caste government officials receiving a cut of the action, so that a global-city project can be built. Thus, I find that the terrain of local transformation is mediated by both local and global practices. Value creation and destruction for global finance capital does not just become real from the rollout of algorithms scripted in Wall Street headquarters or in the back offices of Bengaluru's Silicon Valley—it is actively reconstituted across multiple localized sites.

One of the most startling lessons I learned from interviews with people caught in the crossfire of land sales and evictions is well articulated by Indigenous writer Vine Deloria Jr. in *Custer Died for Your Sins*: "[The US government] took away [Indigenous peoples'] title to their land and gave them the right only to sell" (Deloria 1988, 30). In other words, minoritized communities' right to possess land existed only in the form of the singular right to sell to their oppressor. Historically, these property "rights" (or wrongs) were the basis for systematized expropriation that triggered not only a massive land grab but also new racialized regimes of property, dispossession, and finance (Coulthard 2014). I heard echoes of this portrayal from the most oppressed group of Indian society, Dalits, who repeated to me often that the new global-city airport built on the rural outskirts of Bengaluru created a "Dalit graveyard."[6] Many small farmers and landless farmworkers explained that all they could get in return for the state-led land grab for the benefit of global investors and local developers was a pittance of monetary compensation, money that was value deprived in a land market that would skyrocket in price once the land exchanged hands. This land transfer/eviction left many small landowners and landless users with little means to remain on the land and/or benefit from its newly profitable economy. After many interviews over nearly two decades of research, I determined that their eviction was not an unfortunate by-product of this gold rush; the creation of their graveyard became the foundation for the birth of this speculative land market and the attraction of investors from around the world. Therefore, I think it's more valuable to consider this global-city phenomenon in terms of the main forces supporting it, what I call *dispossession by financialization*, to emphasize the coconstitutive nature of this relationship between land dispossession and financial gain.

But what about the social-hierarchy dimensions to land theft? In his fascinating 2020 book *Theft Is Property!*, political theorist Robert Nichols argues that dispossession has been fundamental to capital accumulation throughout modern history, generating the dual process of "propertization and systemic theft" (98). The consolidation of stolen land throughout the early years of the US nation-state produced a property-based globalizing economy, with the state investing in major infrastructure—like the railways—using borrowed capital from the eastern US banking industry, with liabilities and risks offset by the nascent insurance industry (Sell 2021; Baucom 2005). These nation-producing financial transactions were dependent on and shaped by projects of *racialization*, that is, through the alienation of minoritized and raced populations and the dismantling of the structure of their societies. These social hierarchies enrich some (white elites) and impoverish others (other-than-white subalterns), creating and reproducing an extremely rigid hierarchy of racialized difference—in the case of the early United States, white, red, and Black. The enslavement of Africans and the mass murder of Indigenous peoples for their land are formative practices that produced the racialized social and geographic US landscape and its wealth-producing, slave-plantation- and eviction-based economy. Lessons from these brutal moves were subsequently borrowed by European governments curious to learn how the United States had created such a robust economy through what appeared to be a plantation-based economy on the one hand and frontier expansionism on the other. As scholars have recently revealed, Europe strategically absorbed those lessons for their tool kit of colonial rule in Africa and Asia (Sell 2021; Mamdani 2020).

In sum, many reinterpret the rise of global capitalism as based on theft—from land grabs to body snatching—through the creation of racialized hierarchies of power (Nichols 2020). The concept of racial capitalism reflects this combination and emphasizes the coconstitutive nature of race and capital throughout history (Melamed 2015). Related to my inquiry, Black studies scholar Cedric Robinson (1983) argues throughout his path-breaking book *Black Marxism* that "racial capitalism's historical agency" is the "operational form of financializa-tion" which functions through "scalar hierarchies that animate the dis-tributional order of global finance." In the case of India, Crispin Bates (1995) contends that the concept of race emerged with the early British invaders, who decided that caste reflected a hierarchy of races (hence the relevance of race to caste in global history), mobilizing the racialized notion that upper castes have a strong Aryan/European biological com-position while lower castes are biologically inferior. Similarly, Gajen-dran Ayyathurai (2021) explains that racialization and racial capitalism in Indian history were "situated entanglements of Brahminism, colo-niality, and global capitalism" (see also Cháirez-Garza et al. 2022, 196).

It is important to clarify why I, along with others, use the term *ra-cialization* regarding the historically specific and enduring phenomenon of caste in India. Can caste be reduced to race or vice versa? As Sheetal Chhabria (2023) argues, caste as a violent system of social hierarchy did not persevere because it is deeply rooted in tradition and culture, as advocates of discriminatory casteism insist. Instead, she and others demonstrate that, much like the constitutive role of race in the United States and Europe, capitalist property regimes mobilize caste hierar-chies to help produce the social relations of property and difference, both of which have been important scaffolding for capitalist modernity in India (Yengde 2019; A. Rao 2009). The term *racialization* highlights a set of practices in which ethnic or racial identities are systematically constructed and legitimated, even if the specifics of racial categories change over time. The concept of racialization can signify processes by which elites in power manage resources and people to create both net-works of affiliation for elites and also barriers for nonelites (or subal-terns) to prevent them from mobilizing against powerful interests.

In challenging the key tenet of casteism in India, Dalit leader B. R. Ambedkar rejected racial theories of caste that claimed, spe-ciously, that "untouchables" or Dalits were biologically inferior. Caste is neither a physical obstacle nor a biological truth, as Ambedkar argued, but a state of mind and a tool of violence. Further, he demonstrated how public spaces as well as bodies were racialized in ways that defined who was untouchable and who was Brahmin. In his 1936 treatise "The Annihi-lation of Caste" (2016), Ambedkar argued that only through the destruc-tion of the caste system—and its social, institutional, and psychological dimensions of power—could the unfree ever be free (Cháirez-Garza 2022). I use the theory of racialization as a valuable analytic lens to understand how ideas of social difference—race, color, caste, ethnicity, and so on—are utilized by institutions (and networks) of power on behalf of capitalist relations, class and political power, land grabs, and more.

Specific to the city of Bengaluru today, Malini Ranganathan (2022) demonstrates how twenty-first-century urban space becomes organized along the lines of what she calls environmental casteism, in which Dalits are shoved off their land using the (once British) law of eminent domain. Much as David Chang (2010) writes about US settler colonialism compelling settlers to convert Indigenous usufruct rights into white-owned homesteads, Ranganathan reveals how new governmental categories of ecologies—such as deeming Dalit land as unproductive wasteland and Dalits as a race of filthy wasters—were generated to legitimate the expulsion of lower-caste communities, justifying the taking of their land to benefit a "more productive" class of upper-caste urban elites.[7]

Throughout the book I highlight two features of speculative urbanism: the centrality of *dispossession* for finance's accumulative endeavors and the *racialization* of these institutional practices, which creates opportunities for accumulation. In the globally mediated case of India, they combine to deprive lower classes and castes (including Dalits, Other Backward Classes [OBCs], Muslims, and Adivasis), to the advantage of upper-caste and upper-class networks and communities. I highlight the agentic thrust coming from what I call *the patrimonial regime of governance*—populated by networks of mostly upper-caste and upper-class elites ruling over the transformation of city and economy, and ultimately governance. These elites operationalize their networked power within the economy and state apparatus to racialize (via caste and class fraternal power) dispossession in the financialization process. There is nothing natural, stable, or inevitable about this or any form of dispossession or hierarchy creation for urban development; rather, it shape-shifts as a result of power moves that support rapid accumulation for local and global elites.

A traditional notion of the patrimonial regime refers to an oligarchic regime using state resources to produce wealth and to enlist obedient clients all the way down to the village to access resources and compliance.[8] More recently, French economist Thomas Piketty uses the idea of patrimonial capitalism to show how since the 1970s the Western imperial countries have experienced a "strong comeback of private capital," a return to global finance's influence of the late nineteenth century under European empires (Piketty 2019). This renaissance occurred through the gradual privatization and transfer of public (state-based) wealth into private corporate hands in the neoliberal era. He focuses on the long-term "catch-up of real estate and stock prices" of the financial world since the 1970s, creating favorable conditions for financial firms' wealth accumulation (Piketty 2014, 173, 237, 260).[9]

I extend the notion and adapt it to reflect practices of networking to produce regimes of elite power and specifically the ways they influence financial investment strategies as well as governance structures of the economy and of the state. I argue that the realms of market making and wealth creation emerge from the hard work of elite global networks—that is, Wall Street firms and their affiliates—working together with localized upper-caste patrimonial networks with their own dynamic characteristics. The more that global-city projects affect investment and spending priorities in the city, the more these networks of actors influence the ways cities, people, and ecosystems are governed. I emphasize the dialectical nature of elite networking that encompasses the undercurrents running through three domains: the tight-knit network of rich (mostly) men who run the global financial system, the cadre of elite self-proclaimed experts of global-city making within and outside of the state, and the entangled network of local elites—land brokers, members of parliament, lenders and buyers, state officials, developers—within cities who work closely to orient financiers to their particular interests and pet projects. I demonstrate that the common tendency among these elite networks of power is to use markers of race, class, gender, and caste to determine whose land will be acquired with what types of compensation, and how projects will be designed to benefit elite segments of the population (Mitchell 2002). Whereas some reduce these designs and consequences to the shady realms of corruption or clientelism, I prefer to see it sociologically as a practice embedded in enduring hierarchical institutions of power—caste, class, gender, and race.

Power, of course, is never unidirectional or one-dimensional. We find immanent critique deep within the threads of dispossession. As Indigenous scholar Leanne Betasamosake Simpson explains, "The opposite of dispossession is not possession, it is deep, reciprocal, consensual *attachment*. We [Indigenous peoples] relate to land through connection—generative, affirmative, complex, overlapping, and nonlinear *relationship*. The reverse process of dispossession within Indigenous thought then is Nishnaabeg intelligence, Nishnaabewin. The opposite of dispossession within Indigenous thought is grounded normativity. This is our power" (Simpson 2017, quoted in Nichols 2020, 144).

In the expropriation of land in and around Bengaluru, I argue that the very idea of Dalit justice has been forged in and through modes of resistance to land expropriation, what some scholars call the fight against the possessive logic of upper-caste patriarchy (Pandian 2007; Mosse 2018; Ajantha Subramanian 2019; Viswanath 2014). Caste-based expropriation and oppression are fundamental to the financialization process in India's urban transformation, a process that mirrors larger tendencies in our global economy and society. These power dynamics are central to my analytic framework of speculative urbanism and to my relational-conjunctural approach. I learned more about finance power by understanding how specific firms play urban and rural sites off each other rather than by conceptualizing financial projects and locations as discrete entities with their own particularistic needs and logics. To do so effectively, I trace finance capital wherever it goes, following the money along with its many discursive maneuvers and institutional supports. I follow finance as it undermines Dalit justice while fueling elite regimes of governance. I capture these movements and landings wherever they create trouble.

As noted earlier, I first burrowed my way into the water bureaucracy as a starting point to understanding the rapid urban changes occurring in Bengaluru. It was the bureaucrats themselves who steered me to my topic by emphasizing that their biggest worry was not water allocation but the mounting debt they suffered under. The imperative they faced was to comply with the World Bank, the Asian Development Bank, and Japan's development finance agency (Japan International Cooperation Agency) and package even grander water projects that required much bigger loans with more expensive financial mechanisms—larger dams and more extensive water canals that would draw water from water-scarce neighboring regions. This idea of bigger and riskier went counter to their conservative engineering training and prudent sensibilities. Once the 2008 crisis hit the city, it became clear to me, as instructed by my interviewees, that it was not water and its scarcity but finance capital and its abundance that impinged most on urban and institutional life. So rather than use the most typical metrics of researchers and observers for understanding large projects—that is, in situ success or failure—I decided to instead find answers to my questions by trying to understand the lens used by financiers to see the world, or what Devika Narayan and I call the *optics of finance capital* (Goldman and Narayan 2019).

Tracing Finance Capital Across the Globe: A Relational-Conjunctural Approach

As I demonstrate in subsequent chapters, global finance is rarely interested in one place or city or piece of infrastructure, nor is it nested within a single nation-state with any permanence or allegiance. I show how investment firms can rapidly remake their financial tools and strategies at key moments, such as when the world is rattled by a tsunami of bankruptcies and defaults. A relational-conjunctural approach focuses on large-scale ruptures as they occur across sites in a world of uneven interconnectedness (Hart 2023b; Peck 2024; Robinson 2022; Goldman 2021; Leitner and Sheppard 2021, 2020; Sheppard et al. 2015). It directs us to an appreciation of why relationships across sites matter for finance capital and therefore for our research. These relational dynamics can proliferate at moments of crisis, that is, conjunctures, such as the 1970s collapse of the Bretton Woods monetary system, the 1997 Asian financial crisis, and the 2008 global financial crisis.

The debates on the most propitious method to understand global capitalism as it traverses city life are immense and complex. Here I only profile the thinking to which I am drawn, as it embodies method, theory, and politics equally (Hart 2023b; S. Hall et al. 1978). In brief, the lineage of this methodology starts with the Italian political theorist and activist Antonio Gramsci, in his own work on the rise of Italian fascism in the 1930s. He understood that Italy was a case of something much larger: the uneven rise of fascism across Europe at a cataclysmic moment when capitalism was taking new form and working-class movements were responding by shutting down factories and taking to the streets. Gramsci's instinct was to see this disruptive moment through a methodology that helped locate the volatility he experienced in contemporary Italy within a larger context of diverse but interconnected European revolutions during the previous two centuries. As Gillian Hart argues, "Conjunctural analysis is not simply a 'method' that can be divorced from theory and politics" (Hart 2023b, 136).

While Gramsci was against the notion of empiricism (i.e., research divorced from theory), he nonetheless saw what Stuart Hall (2021, quoted in Hart 2023b, 139; S. Hall et al. 1978) calls the "specificities and the connections" of such a study on the ground (i.e., empirical research) as parts of "the complex unity of structures" (i.e., embedded theory). Seemingly abstract structures, according to Hall (2021, 36, quoted in Hart 2023b, 153) "have to be demonstrated by concrete analysis of concrete relations and conjunctures," Hart (2023b) argues in a seminal article on the method, and Helga Leitner and Eric Sheppard (2020) deftly develop this point in their recent works. Using this stance as my starting point, I argue that theory cannot be "conjured out of thin air" but only through close observation as to how forces, structures, and imaginations work along multiple scales and across sites. Gramsci understood "the relations of forces" (i.e., the powers of the state, the military, and capitalist enterprises) in terms of interconnected processes unfolding across scales and "in constant flux" (Hart 2023b, 149). That is, conjunctures—or moments of crisis that emerge from perplexing and often unpredictable circumstances—create moments of both rupture and opportunity, occurring relationally across sites and practices.

Jamie Peck (2024, 462) summarizes the point in this way: "Conjunctural analysis engages the abstract, the structural, and the historical through the contingent, the concrete, the particular, and the real; it works through the specificity and particularity of situations in part for their own sake, as loci of concern, but also as prisms through which to read, to map, and to situate the systemic, the global, and the 'general.'"

The French sociologist Henri Lefebvre developed his approach through studying the city at a key juncture in history, the late 1960s, which were rife with social turmoil. He focused on what he called *everyday life* as the experiential site of data collection (method), understanding (theory), and politics (Benjamin 2008). From an analysis of the streets of French cities, he not only explored the contradictory relations of production of urban space but also scaled up to broader questions of global forces and change. Gillian Hart reframes Lefebvre's approach as layered analytics: "three dialectically interconnected domains rather than levels: *global conjunctures*, praxis in the multiple arenas of *everyday life*, and projects, practices and processes of *bourgeois hegemony* that mediate between global forces and everyday life" (Hart 2023b, 151).

In this book I build on this approach by focusing on key moments in recent history as points of departure: the 1970s crash of Northern economies, with its entangled political norms, leading to the rise of neoliberalism globally; the 1997 Asian financial crisis, with the shakeup of state-centered economic policies in Asia and the emboldening of international finance institutions; and the 2008 global financial crisis, as the catalyst for a full-throttle financialization of the city. By explaining the historical rise of finance power through the coconstitutive changes in governance over the banking and finance sectors and city public financing in three countries (Spain, United States, and India) preceding and subsequent to the 2008 crisis, I am able to show what precipitated the global crisis as well as what the crisis generated afterward. The conjunctural moment matters, I find, as it reveals how the preceding rise and ensuing consolidation of finance power across countries propelled the financialization process across cities of the Global North and South (Mawdsley 2018; Lapavitsas and Powell 2013). Of course, it was not the crisis itself as some disembodied force or actor but rather the intense relational dynamics within/across capitalist economic sectors, as well as the business classes and state institutions in their support, that catalyzed the urban-financialization process. These corporate and state actors proceeded to collaborate on a new agenda for capital accumulation expressed unevenly in cities around the world (Fernandez and Aalbers 2020). Lefebvre understood such conjunctures as "generative of new conditions," with their "worldwide reverberations" emerging from multiple sites of production that were not "just recipients" but rather highly generative of global processes (Hart 2023a; Lefebvre 1991).

Starting with this conjunctural perspective, I refine this methodological approach by emphasizing the relational nature of such global practices—relations that reveal the problematic portrayal of the city as an isolated site for inquiry and the realm of global finance as its own distinct and discrete galaxy (Hart 2018). I focus on relations unfolding at key historical moments across cities, between the urban and rural, within and among state institutions, and across capitalist sectors and processes—such as the tensions between finance capital and productive capital. Hence, I study the financialization of the city through a relational-conjunctural approach that helps clarify what Gramsci called the "practico-political" possibilities before us. The diagram in figure I.2 reflects the methodology.

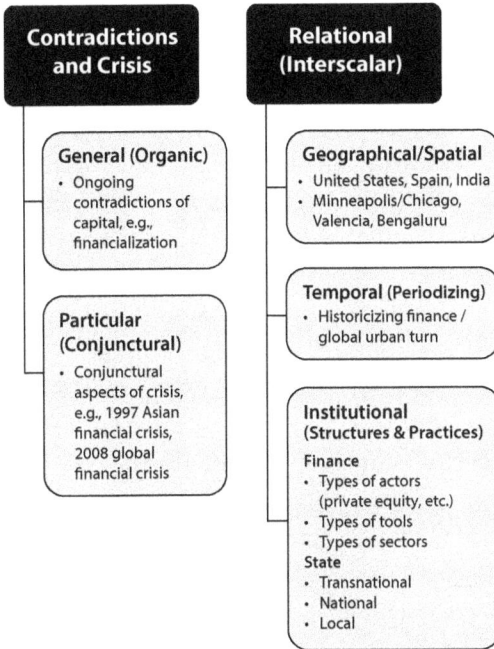

1.2 What is the relational-conjunctural approach? Source: Michael Goldman, Snigdha Kumar, and Devika Narayan.

- **Contradictions and Crisis**
  - **General (Organic)**
    - Ongoing contradictions of capital, e.g., financialization
  - **Particular (Conjunctural)**
    - Conjunctural aspects of crisis, e.g., 1997 Asian financial crisis, 2008 global financial crisis

- **Relational (Interscalar)**
  - **Geographical/Spatial**
    - United States, Spain, India
    - Minneapolis/Chicago, Valencia, Bengaluru
  - **Temporal (Periodizing)**
    - Historicizing finance / global urban turn
  - **Institutional (Structures & Practices)**
    - **Finance**
      - Types of actors (private equity, etc.)
      - Types of tools
      - Types of sectors
    - **State**
      - Transnational
      - National
      - Local

The Relational-Conjunctural Approach and the Key Traits of Finance

Applying this methodological approach helps me discover where the world of global finance meets the everyday of the city. As there are infinite ways to drill down into these interactions, I decided to study the world of finance by learning to see through the lens that finance capital uses when it pursues its business strategies, or what my colleague and I call the *optics* of finance capital (Goldman and Narayan 2021). From this perspective, I found a constellation of notable traits that explain how an important set of global finance actors—private equity firms—perform in cities around the world. I refer to these traits throughout the book as *liquidity, arbitrage, opacity*, and *monopoly*. Here, I offer an initial interpretation of these findings to show how theory and method can generate analytics that help explain the mystifying and multisite world of finance.

My methodological approach reveals how this first trait of *liquidity* works in its paradoxical form. Private equity is a complex and misunderstood asset class of finance (Morran and Petty 2022; Byrne 2016; Davis and Kim 2015; Finel-Honigman 2009; Gotham 2009; Epstein 2005). Compared to mutual funds, stocks, or bank accounts, it is actually one of the *least* liquid for individual investors but potentially the *most* liquid for the financiers of private equity. That is, unlike when investing in a stock or mutual fund, in which you can cash out anytime, when you invest in private equity, you must wait until the asset is sold before you can see your money again. One hopes that the value of that real estate venture or bridge has grown during the time of the investment. But private equity firms make sure that *their* activities and assets remain as liquid as possible. They want to be able to freely exit any investment before the value decreases, sometimes as soon as possible if the winds of risk switch directions. Often their exit itself can trigger a price fall, which never bodes well for average investors holding on to the depreciated share or for the productive thing itself.

To offer one multinational example, when the Australian firm Macquarie owns the United Kingdom's Thames Water or the United States' Chicago Skyway toll road, it owns a monopoly without any competitors. As provided by contract, the multinational firm can raise its monopoly rents as it wishes across countries, thus producing an almost guaranteed consistent—liquid—revenue stream for it to extract and export through its multisite investment portfolio.[10]

In fact, the whole premise behind the world's first stock market was to make shareholding liquid, to enable stocks to be easily converted into cash and securitized—turning "'unliquid capital' into tradeable instruments . . . increasing the mobility and globalization of capital" (Ho 2009, 184, referring to Sassen 1998, xxxv). In the twenty-first century, private equity takes this trait to another level: Its capital accumulates wealth both from cashing out from one deal and through moving capital across national borders (thus avoiding internal tax and regulatory burdens) via tax havens with the greatest of ease (Shaxson 2018). This liquidity premium exists because governments actively unshackle international capital flows by not taxing or regulating them, in hopes that liquidity and mobility will increase economic activity (and therefore prosperity) for their people.

Through this method I establish a second trait of private equity firms, *arbitrage*, which has many dimensions. According to the economics literature, there is regulatory arbitrage, risk arbitrage, cross-border arbitrage, and spatial arbitrage. For us, the term *arbitrage* reflects the technique of leveraging difference and unevenness within and across geographies, projects, and regulatory practices. Sometimes finance works to skirt laws in one place and ask for more attractive rules elsewhere, pitting one set of regulations against another. In all cases, it raises the specter of capital scarcity as its bargaining chip to get a better deal—even when it sits on trillions of dollars of capital. Moreover, finance capital invents opaque tools such as derivatives, swaps, hedges, and more to work in markets that it either tries to corner (i.e., dominate) or helps to create, such as the post-2008 market in nonperforming (i.e., bankrupt) assets.

In many arenas in which private equity invests, it is both a monopoly (a single seller) and a monopsony (a single buyer); it uses arbitrage in these circumstances to convince buyers to offer guaranteed profits just to access the capital it provides. As the historical record reveals, a handful of European financial firms in the mid-1800s convinced the British Parliament to guarantee them an attractive profit rate for lending for the construction of the Indian railways, largely because there were so many British colonies worldwide bidding for scarce money to finance colonial transit structures. As the sole proprietors of capital financing wars and colonial conquests, the Rothschilds and Pereire Brothers (and a few others) were able to negotiate a profitable set of guarantees and commitments (Jenks 1927).

The same monopoly power also exists in the post-2008-crisis period for housing and commercial real estate markets: As asset values plummeted, only a handful of megafinancial firms were equipped and willing to purchase these depressed assets, but they would do so only, of course, under conditions of their own choosing. Financiers could invest in the United States, Spain, or India, depending on the best deal available. That they chose to invest in all directions should have sent a warning flare to buyers that capital is not scarce and thus overvalued. This practice exposes the important role that *monopsony arbitrage*, as I call it, plays in private equity's portfolio, where a single buyer dominates the demand for a service or good simultaneously in multiple markets. Monopsony and monopoly forms of arbitrage allow finance capital to set the prices and conditions of its deals; it signifies the power of finance capital in these times (Christophers 2018).

Through this methodological approach, I intervened into private equity's third trait—its *opacity*—by searching for meaning in its oft-hidden activities. Most people have never heard of the arena of alternative finance and have no idea what hedges and derivatives are, nor interest rate swaps or collateralized debt obligations—even though these collectively represent a multitrillion-dollar industry, and some of the biggest debt obligations our cities now shoulder. Their workings are completely opaque, and the way they profit is mystifying. Gone is the world where a loan means the cash up front plus an interest rate payable over time. Now there are a series of obfuscating gambles set up by the house, in which case the house typically wins. While the business press heralds the huge profits accumulated by global private equity and tantalizes us with the enormous end-of-the-year take-home pay for its CEOS—now up to $1 billion a year—it never digs deep into the contractual obligations to reveal, from the opacity of business deals, how a firm can extract such wealth from mundane services like maintaining roads or commercial buildings.

Moreover, it is unclear who the house, or the financier, is. For example, the Chicago Skyway toll road—a simple, decrepit, and congested highway outside the spread-out city of Chicago—used to be owned by the city. During times of fiscal crisis, the city's financial advisers convinced it to lease the road to a private company based in Australia. As it turns out, Macquarie is the world's leader in highway/toll road deals; the deals are based on a calculation in which they put up a minimal amount of cash up front (i.e., a loan to the city in exchange for a road) to help pay off the worst of the city's existing debts. Macquarie has a global reach, owning similar toll roads in India, Germany, and France. Recently, it shed from its core smaller firms, which include ATLAX, ATLIX, QTPP, Atlas Arteria Holdings, and Green Bermuda Holdings—all of which own a piece of CCPI, the owner of Skyway Concession LLC. What does this complex ownership structure do for Macquarie? And where exactly would a discontented Chicago-based consumer or regulator go to collect money or find solutions to their grievances? Bermuda? Australia? One would need a team of lawyers to find the correct holding company and access their staff. A string of tax-haven-based shell/shadow holding companies as owners of public goods around the world reflects global finance's opacity. In subsequent chapters the value of this opaqueness for the central business strategy of skirting regulations, taxes, and accountability will become clear.

The relational-conjunctural approach to my research enabled me to see private equity's final trait—*monopoly*—as I observed firms collaborating with state agencies to create the conditions for consolidation and market control in multiple sites (i.e., the relational) at critical moments (i.e., the conjunctural). As I will show, the largest financial firms actively avoid competition among themselves in key markets. While industry advocates might call this *specialization*, I find that private equity makes its money from investing in monopolies in two senses: one, they tend to invest in public goods that are in themselves monopolies—like electric and water services, highways, and telecom towers, which are set up as noncompetitive. It is rare to have competing water firms or competing toll roads in the same town (Christophers 2023; Aalbers 2017; Lapavitsas 2014; Ho 2009). But as I explain throughout the book, private equity firms also create new markets in which individual firms can dominate, that is, monopolize. This is one of the most remarkable, opaque, and profitable aspects of their ever-evolving business model.

These four traits—liquidity, opacity, arbitrage, and monopoly/ oligopoly—thrive in tandem. As a heuristic, they teach us to think across institutional domains, such as transnational entities, state agencies, and civil societies. For example, the discourse of finance-led urbanization since the mid-1990s became coherent and legitimate in large part because it emerged from star-studded conversations of eminent experts that included leaders of the World Bank, urban institutes, chambers of commerce, and the heads of PricewaterhouseCoopers and McKinsey (see chapter 1). Their emergent discourse aligned well with what Wall Street firms like KKR, BlackRock, and Blackstone had been calling for: the financialization of the city. Global boosters of urbanization, of regulatory/deregulatory systems of law and governance, and city-based project planners began to invoke a series of mirrorlike policy approaches, plans of action, cost/benefit calculations, and infrastructural projects. Global finance's traits began to inform and be legitimated by the new-normal language of global urbanism (Leitner and Sheppard 2021). Each chapter in this book explains how these overlapping domains of finance, urbanization, global expertise, state action, and public life converge in ways that reveal the contours of this new financial regime of urban governance and how it produces interurban patterns of disruptive change.

In sum, this is a case in which theory and methodology reveal a way of thinking that avoids the more common notion that pivotal events succeed or fail based on the specific characteristics of an individual nation, state, or economy. Focusing instead on the relational and conjunctural in multisite interscalar research allows us to see the intersection of finance and the city in its coconstitutive, messy reality. This zigzagging of capital, discursive framings, global forms of expertise, and state regulatory practices across cityscapes requires such an innovative analytic framework. The typical methodological approach that understands our current urban crises as the products of national cultural problems, such as Spanish overexuberance, American working-class overreach, or Indian corruption, makes even more opaque the workings of global finance and portrays structural problems as ethnic. By contrast, the relational-conjunctural approach has helped me understand this recent convergence of urbanization and financialization as a phenomenon I call *speculative urbanism*.[11]

Speculative Urbanism

From this approach emerges my concept of speculative urbanism. It captures the events and practices I was observing and resonates well with others who have taken up the term and modified it based on their findings and perspectives (see Leitner and Sheppard 2023). The concept comprises a bundle of fundamental characteristics. The first focuses on *the power and instruments of finance working to financialize the city*. Financialization—which intersects with but is different from privatization—denotes the increasing power of the financial sector and capital markets in the nonfinancial worlds of business, land relations, government, and even citizenship (Christophers 2022; Fields 2018; Pereira 2017; García-Lamarca and Kaika 2016; Ouma 2016; Searle 2016, 2020; Sud 2014; Krippner 2011; Aalbers 2008, 2016, 2017). This world-altering phenomenon of financialization works in part because of the oft-changing set of tools and strategies produced by global finance to fit its needs and desires. Because of finance's current power in society, these tools determine the stakes of the game and dictate for the state and private entities the parameters for the provisioning of capital for equity and debt investments.

For example, in the United States, almost half of the gross domestic product now comes from the financial sector, a significant increase from the 1950s, when it was less than 5 percent (Krippner 2011; Wolfson and Epstein 2013). Behind these startling statistics are the daily financial innovations and tools necessary to make this transition happen. Contractual agreements with local developers and municipal governments tell an important story about how these new relationships between global finance and local builders and service providers are forged and to whose advantage. I focus on the specifics of global finance's tool kit of innovative practices and strategies marketed to the world as well as how they are negotiated on the ground and to what effect (Wu 2022, 2021; Aalbers 2019a, 2019b; Searle 2018; Fields 2018, 2017; Moreno 2014). The nuts and bolts of financial practices reveal in the aggregate how finance's rise to power occurred in an atmosphere in which there now exist few alternative strategies for city leaders, builders, and administrators.

The second characteristic of speculative urbanism is captured by the worldwide phenomenon of the *global urban turn*, or the creation and spread of an elite discourse of global-city making, which gained traction in the 1990s and became dominant in the 2000s. It promotes the new common sense that high-risk borrowing from global financial firms will produce world-class infrastructure. This new discourse emerged from twin currents of urban change. The first current was expansive urbanization: At the dawn of the twenty-first century, more people live in cities than in the countryside, a dramatic reversal in human history, with its magnetic force of possibility and innovation. The second current reflects the opposite trend: the crumbling of the infrastructure on which the urban is based. In many parts of the world, the neoliberal era of the 1970s and 1980s produced the *decrepit city*, born from the ashes of the wholesale withdrawal of government support and the punitive/moralistic demand that cities go it alone. Promoters of the global urban turn seized on this opportunity: McKinsey in an Infrastructure Practice and Global Institute report declared, "$57 trillion will need to be spent on building and maintaining infrastructure worldwide between now and 2030 . . . greater than the estimated value of all the world's infrastructure assets today" (Palter and Pohl 2014, 36–39). This audacious claim attracted the attention of governments and business elites alike and produced an extremely risky and expensive game plan to transform budgets and their rationales.

From Singapore to Barcelona, as illustrated in chapter 1, dozens of coordinated events brought together world leaders and thinkers on this question and generated an elite set of expert discourses and experts on global-city making. These elites boldly declared that large-scale investments would offer a tremendous boost to lagging cities whose leaders were eager to catch up to, if not surpass, long-standing global successes like New York and Paris. It didn't take long before industry and financial leaders fully supported this mandate, as did mayors and citizen groups keen to equip their down-and-out cities with much-needed public goods like housing, roads, commercial centers, energy, and water. This dreamscape gained traction as the vise of needing basic infrastructure and the lack of public financing squeezed governments, cities, and citizens alike, making the global urban turn very attractive to those in control of major capital flows. The imagined possibilities of this global urban turn seemed endless, fortifying the new paradigm of finance-led urbanization.

The next set of related features of speculative urbanism focuses on the state and government. One aspect I call *speculative governance* to denote the increasingly prominent role that financiers play in socio-spatial rule and governance. Financiers have increased their sway over the domain of urban public goods and services normally under the governance of local or national state entities. Finance now determines which public goods are creditworthy and can generate increased (and exportable) flows of revenue and which are not worth the investment. As finance capital infiltrates the logic of city government and its budgeting responsibilities, it influences governance-based ethics and responsibilities. Consequently, many of the largest infrastructural investments, such as public light-rail systems, airports, and water/sewage systems, suffer from the weight of onerous debt and rents extracted from the large (and expensive) loans required to build or upgrade them.

Such loans privilege the bottom line of global financial firms at the cost of accessibility and affordability for the public. As the built environment (e.g., concretized land, buildings, infrastructure, housing) is converted into assets (i.e., assetized) and made into something tradeable and liquid on global capital markets, and as state agencies and their regulatory capacities respond and adapt to the needs and demands of finance, we can say that finance, in this speculative fashion, remakes the domain of governance (Swyngedouw and Ward 2024). The fate of, and governance over, large infrastructural projects in one location has become more closely aligned with financial business priorities across nations and borders through the process of fast entry and exits. The liquidation of assets and the rapid circulation of capital has become a common business—and governance—practice with manifold disruptive effects.

I emphasize another dimension of the active participation of the state, which I refer to as the *speculative state*: its role as both a handmaiden to finance capital and a speculative agent that buys and sells land in support of real estate ventures. The roots of this relationship can be traced back to the colonial period, in the formation of the British Empire (Cowen 2020; Mehta 1999). More recently, financial sector reforms have enabled nontraditional financial entities and practices to sprout and thrive in countries that once had banned or heavily regulated them

(Pike et al. 2019; Fumagalli and Mezzadra 2010; Epstein 2005). Some of the most significant reforms have occurred at critical junctures, for example, during the 1997 Asian financial crisis and the 2008 global financial crisis, when states responded by further liberalizing rather than tightening the rules overseeing finance. These reforms often reflected the tough-love conditionalities of the International Monetary Fund (IMF) and the World Bank and their debt relief/loan packages, which mimicked calls by global urbanists to open cities to the creative powers of finance (World Bank 2015; BlackRock 2015; Fischer 1998).

Alongside these reforms, national and municipal governments have liberalized their approach to providing key public goods and services by disinvesting from public land, housing, and infrastructure. They have shifted the authority over them onto capital markets while playing the role of intermediary speculators and brokers, and they have invited international investors to enter local markets and establish financialized urban landscapes.[12] Consequently, it is becoming more difficult to separate out the functioning of the state from the workings of finance capital. The state has become a broker and guarantor of public assets, while finance capital has inherited the role of architect and benefactor of public initiatives.

These state-finance alliances are closely connected to another dimension of state relations, what I call *speculative governmentality* (Goldman 2011). It refers to the question of how to be a governable state subject and citizen under these speculative-urban forces. Governmentality, a concept first articulated by French philosopher Michel Foucault, captures the rise of an orientation of government that is less about the state itself than about how we conduct ourselves as state subjects and how we choose to govern ourselves, govern others, and seek to be governed (Lucarelli 2010; Foucault 1991). As Laura Bear and her colleagues suggest, the term *speculation* borrows from the Latin origins of the term *speculari*, meaning to watch, spy, and observe, and from *specula*, a lookout or watchtower surveilling the populace (Bear 2020, 2017, 2015; Birla 2015; Bear et al. 2015a, 2015b).

Speculative governmentality reflects the types of conduct, rationalities, and subjectivities that emerge from the tensions of risk-taking and future-divining, albeit within the context of the burgeoning power of finance. Such dispositions are necessary for urban denizens to keep up with spiraling global-city ambitions and rents in the context of dwindling state provisioning of public goods, services, and spaces. As the ability of governments to provide services and goods becomes contingent on external capital flows, access to public services is threatened when these currents run dry or reverse course. To survive the tumult of city life under speculative urbanism, people must typically embrace the risk-laden strategies of world-class city making and management championed by government and corporate entities. They must find their own way in this dangerous chaos of speculation, which is largely determined by power relations in society that place differentially weighted risk on different shoulders, based on caste, class, gender, and other factors. Crucial to this aspect of the concept, dispossession and risk-taking have become normalized and shape one's subjectivity as part of twenty-first-century urban survival.

Speculation encompasses the city's elite and nonelite residents, taking different forms with differing effects. One manifestation is the way many people participate in "chains of rentiership" (Leitner and Sheppard 2020) whereby large-scale projects trigger a cascading set of possible speculative opportunities, with different life chances emerging along the chain (Upadhya and Rathod 2021; Gururani 2020; Balakrishnan 2019; Cowan 2018). Some farmers take their compensation money and try their luck in the city. Others expand their village homes into dormitories for transient construction workers, and some end up on the street with inadequate payments for their land to jump-start a new livelihood. Government rationalities see such displacements and risk-taking as natural and necessary for the process of producing wealth, citizenship, and governance in cities that must become economically and globally competitive (Foucault 2004).

A final and underlying feature of speculative urbanism is the transformative effect of rapid urban and rural transformations on the environment, which colleagues and I conceptualize as *speculative ecologies* (Gidwani et al., 2024). Throughout the book I highlight the significance of water, land, and the public commons as necessary conditions of production and reproduction that are being directly threatened by the financialization of the city (O'Connor 1988; Goldman 1998). Societies across the planet are being confronted with cataclysmic weather conditions—unexpectedly struck by multiple and entangled environmental crises, from flooding to water scarcity, to deadly fires and air pollution, to loss of biodiversity and species extinctions. While some cities suffer from extreme drought and heat, Bengaluru faces destructive floods as well as a life-threatening scarcity of drinking water. The rapid expansion of this city in just a few decades—gobbling up villages and towns as well as floodplains, forests, pastures, watersheds, underground aquifers, lakes, and drainage channels—is based on the expectation that the IT and biotech revolutions would transform the city's wealth and future. Yet the IT/biotech corridor was built atop precious life-supporting wetlands. Lakes and channels were paved over with water-sucking residential complexes and bejeweled with high-end shopping malls and five-star sporting and leisure complexes, concrete motorways, and fossil-fuel-driven heliports. Just like so many urban landscapes being remade in the likeness of a global city, the dream of transforming Asia's Silicon Valley into a well-managed global city is now faced with the implosion of the ecological foundation on which the city and countryside had been built over earlier generations (Angelo and Wachsmuth, 2015).

The relationship among all these elements of speculative urbanism can be summarized like this: The global urban turn succeeded as a discursive-material set of practices at a particular juncture in which neoliberalism's material limits were transformed into an opportunity for finance capital. This accomplishment required a concerted effort by elites, working with an attractive discourse in hand and a set of political, social, and cultural institutions to rally behind it. The global urban turn enabled elite patrimonial networks to mobilize the financialization tool kit and become the new governance regime for city life, affecting people's subject positions and the ways they could conduct themselves within the changing parameters of city life and space. These local and transnational networks have joined forces to devalue and thus undermine the social-natural dynamics that once sustained life for and in the city. The urban and ecological commons are now being converted into assetized collateral whose value is free to circulate globally through capital circuits while destroying essential ecological resources. These characteristics combine to create the new reality of speculative urbanism.

I tell this story through a transnational, historical, and dialectical lens. It starts with a series of chapters (1 through 3) that focus on the intersection of financialization and urbanization, followed by chapters (4 through 6) that drill down into its manifestations as seen from the city of Bengaluru, but always making clear that each chapter reflects an interconnected and interscalar piece of the puzzle. The conclusion recounts the critical voices running through the book as a multivocal articulation of a postspeculative future.

You might wonder what the roots of the book's title, *Hidden Empire of Finance*, are. It comes from my reading of a fascinating history of the

British Empire that focuses on the quiet but powerful role of global finance in making and unmaking empire. Here is the last paragraph from Leland Hamilton Jenks's 1927 classic study:

> There was a curious unreality in their conception [of the British Empire as the geographic extension of the British Isles]. For while they spoke of an empire of fidelity to the Queen, and strove to bring new areas within its bounds, they lived their economic life in *another empire*, which did not, could not wholly coincide with the Queen's. The economy which owned London for a metropolis was at once more broad and more restricted than the empire which praised Victoria as the pattern of all the virtues. That economic empire was even more essential to the people of the stocks-and-bonds and to the people who earned them dividends. It did not yet in 1875 exist; but its elements were in being. And as the migration of British capital proceeded, and from the mechanisms that moved it, the structure of that other empire grew. (336, emphasis added)

Jenks's words suggest a proposal: Amid the pugilistic struggles of European powers, there emerged a *shadow or hidden empire* ruled by the ruthless efficiencies and violent practices of non-state-based finance capital. Alongside the oceans of imperial blood and sweat, empire was built on the speculative-financial technologies of power that elevated an increasingly wealthy but vanishingly small global elite class (Gilbert et al. 2023). He clearly demonstrates that wealthy financiers did not act alone, nor did states ambitiously conjure imperial power abroad without the necessary support of global finance, coming from many banking nodes across Europe (Hobsbawm 1987). Although this book focuses on the twenty-first-century challenge of how to convert the city into a financial asset, we should not lose sight of the fact that this is not the first time global finance has ruled with such awesome power—or fallen so hard from grace, as it did in the late 1920s and 1930s.

What I Did and What Comes Next

I started this project in late 2006 by living in Bengaluru and conducting interviews with local researchers and scholars, journalists, and local "people in the know," that is, the oral historians who have a breadth of knowledge as to how government works, how local deals are brokered, how elites often work in stealth, and how working-class people respond to cycles of opportunities and challenges. Some of my best interlocutors were school principals and real estate consultants, farmer advocates, and remarkably talented researchers, all of whom introduced me graciously to their networks and explained to me how things worked in their niches of the city and countryside. As I became known through these networks, I received invitations to meet a wider range of people immersed in the many local controversies. Some interlocutors helped me get invited to official and unofficial meetings where questions of land and lake grabbing were discussed, and evidence presented. I attended discussions between lawyers/advocates and their clients and became integrated into public debates on city- and countrywide concerns (Upadhya et al. 2017).

From 2009 to 2018, I spent from two to six months each of these years conducting participant observation and in-depth formal and informal interview research—more than two hundred interviews by the end. I worked closely with research assistants who were embedded in city and country life, equipped with intimate knowledge of and expertise in different aspects crucial to my questions. I worked closely with various nongovernmental organizations (NGOs), including one well-regarded environmental organization that has close relations with present and former legislators and judges overseeing legislation. They worked on cases to stop the most egregious illegal mischief related to land grabbing by senior officials in Bengaluru and New Delhi. I also spent considerable time over the years interviewing—and hanging out with—financial elites, some of whom invited me to exclusive conferences where frank discussions transpired among foreign and Indian investors, government officials, and city managers. I made sure to follow up on conversations with attendees in their offices back in Delhi, Mumbai, and New York City.

I started out as a visiting American Institute for Indian Studies scholar at the Institute for Social and Economic Change (ISEC) in Bengaluru, later became an adjunct professor at the National Institute for Advanced Studies (NIAS), and then returned to ISEC as the endowed Dr. V. K. R. V. Rao Chair Professor from 2016 to 2018, where I gave keynote addresses and short courses for their excellent PhD students. All these opportunities enabled me to engage with scholars and researchers working on elements of the questions I was pursuing.

In 2016 Professors Carol Upadhya (NIAS-Bengaluru), Vinay Gidwani (University of Minnesota), Helga Leitner (University of California, Los

Angeles [UCLA]), Eric Sheppard (UCLA), and I received a multiyear research grant from the National Science Foundation (NSF) for the research project "Speculative Urbanism: Land, Livelihoods, and Finance Capital." We jointly hired several research assistants to conduct ethnographic research, and we hired consultants from the real estate industry to explain the inner workings of contract negotiations and deals, a geospatial expert to analyze public data and turn them into impressive visual images, and a photographer to document our research experiences. Whereas most of my research on financial maneuvers, land deals, and dispossession for this book focused on the airport region in the northern reaches of Bengaluru, the research for the NSF project focused on two other important regions in the center and east. This collaboration with my NSF colleagues informs my analysis here as well as corroborates what I found.

Pre-1990s Bangalore was a quiet, small, and verdant city. Retired upper-caste bureaucrats whom I interviewed waxed nostalgic about the old days in which they would ride their bicycle home from their government jobs in the Vidhana Soudha office complex at lunchtime, eat with their families in the outlying neighborhood of Koramangala, and then ride back to finish the workday. Such an excursion is now impossible by bicycle and takes up to three hours one way by car. Environmental activists were school buddies with parliamentarians, and high-court judges were childhood friends with now big-time real estate developers. Those connections, though thinning like their hairlines, still exist. An office visit to a retired judge often led me via a quick phone call to the otherwise inaccessible, heavily secured offices of the leading "land bankers" in town. Of course, these social networks are closely tied to caste- and class-based communities. I found similarly strong ties within the lower-caste, lower-class, and Dalit communities and their advocates, researchers, journalists, land brokers, farmers, and wage laborers. They, too, had compelling but vastly different stories about local transformations. Although the city is now bursting at the seams with more than fourteen million people, many denizens were able to construct astute historical, sociological, and ecological analyses, the sorts that would be the envy of any prestigious university around the world. I try to capture their insights in my writing.

The chapters on the global project of financialization of the city are based on research conducted in India (Bengaluru), the United States (Minneapolis), and Spain (Valencia), where I conducted expert interviews and monitored, with the assistance of local scholars and activists, the ways in which finance capital created a newly financialized landscape of unfinished projects and public and private debt (Christophers 2023; Derickson et al. 2021). Living in these cities in the wake of the financial crisis, I found that the same private equity firms working in Bengaluru were also mobilizing similar strategies and tools in Valencia and Minneapolis, albeit with some differing effects. My relational-conjunctural tool kit helped me recognize how finance works across sites, using strategies of arbitrage and monopoly to get the most out of their investments.

To immerse myself in the intricate debates on urban markets for finance before and after the 2008 crisis, I attended exclusive finance sector conferences in New York City, New Delhi, and Bengaluru and global urbanization events in Goa, Bengaluru, and Barcelona; scrutinized their annual reports and white papers; and, with my NSF grant colleagues, co-organized scholarly conferences on these topics to learn from others, hosted in Minneapolis (2008), Shenzhen (2010), Jakarta (2012), and Bengaluru (2016).

The rest of this book is divided into two. In the first part, chapter 1 presents the construction of a discourse of global-city making, based on data collected from my participation at a series of global insider meetings from 2007 to 2019, a time span long enough to observe big shifts in strategy and expansive dispersion. Among the many organizations comprising this newfound elite network are the World Bank, UN-Habitat, the United Nations Development Programme (UNDP), the McKinsey and PricewaterhouseCoopers consulting firms, C40, the Cities Alliance, high-tech "smart cities" firms such as Cisco, and infrastructure firms such as Siemens. I show how the idea of high finance for urban infrastructure became a global imperative for these prominent elites.

In chapters 2 and 3, I explore the forces that set the stage for financialization in three countries—Spain, the United States, and India—from the mid-twentieth century to the present. My argument emerges from research conducted in, and on, three cities—Valencia, Minneapolis, and Bengaluru—as well as from secondary data sources. I highlight their historical differences before the 2008 crisis in chapter 2 and the various convergences occurring postcrisis to create a financialized urban landscape globally in chapter 3. Over time, state–finance sector relations became increasingly similar globally, reflecting a new form of global urban governance.

In the second part of the book, chapters 4 through 6, I present how the intersection of financialization and urbanization affects and is shaped by processes occurring in the city of Bangalore/Bengaluru. In this way, I explicate how these arguments play out in one place, fully cognizant that this one place is constituted by translocal practices. Once establishing in part I how exactly the world is changing, we can then see more clearly in part II how the city becomes an important generative site of transnational processes and events. Like many metropolises, Bengaluru bustles with tens of thousands of migrant construction workers building a city they cannot afford to live in for people who have little intention of inhabiting many of the luxury homes built for speculation.

Chapter 4 digs into the city's history to set the context for our understanding of successive rounds of change in the making of the city, from colonial times through the postindependence era of big state-driven projects, what India's first Prime Minister Jawaharlal Nehru referred to as India's "modern temples." The chapter documents changes occurring up to the 1970s period of state fiscal crisis and retrenchment. Chapter 5 lays out the next phase of urban development, a process of converting rural land and ecologies into urban real estate, with their dispossessive and opportunistic effects, eventually becoming a system of dispossession by financialization. Chapter 6 tells the story of what happens when the bottom falls out of twin markets of capital and real estate. It explores the negotiations between foreign capital and local developers and documents how this rollercoaster ride of uncertainty and tumult creates a debt-ridden, precarious city landscape on which only a small cadre of well-networked elites (local and global) can capitalize.

The book's conclusion sheds light on the relationship between the power of finance and responses to it by millions of people in India and around the world who are working to envision and make real a postspeculative alternative to the crazy world of speculative urbanism and financial dominance. As the late Indian scholar Kalyan Sanyal (2007) observed, the distance workers travel between the *commodity-based economy* and the *need economy* is the space where we should focus our attention to imagine and develop an alternative politics. Under speculative urbanism, the volatility of city life quickens to the point of crisis, which creates new opportunities for more than speculative accumulation, including new forms of resistance, solidarity, and alternative modernities. This book, and the last chapter in particular, features some of these voices and articulations of hope.

I will end this introductory chapter with a suggestion for a thought experiment: When reading the rest of this book, consider how the dominant realms of money, finance, and credit were created and normalized, and then consider how they could (just as easily) be different—more fair, more ecologically protective, more socially just. What if the money needed to build housing or water infrastructure were handled by people and institutions that were *not* profiting from every transaction but were instead democratically chosen for that task? What if investment in our cities and towns were not dictated by the circulation and accumulation demands of finance capital but were debated and determined deliberatively by people concerned with meeting real social needs and ensuring future ecological survival? These what-if questions are so important during times of inhumane volatility, widening inequality, and ecological collapse. They allow us to envision a world in which decisions about public investment are not made in the backrooms of private capital but in the open spaces of the public commons. They can open our imaginations to a nonexploitative, ecological, and democratizing way of making our world socially just and overflowing with care for humanity and the environment.

Currencies are called US dollars and Indian rupees for a reason; they are printed and backed by the full power of the state and legitimated by the nation. So why give up the power of the state and the nation to a bunch of self-interested bankers and self-appointed elites and expect them to act on the public's behalf? Pay attention throughout this text to how the definition of the public good evolves in the hands of finance capital. Read the narratives in the chapters that follow and see how the foundational claims of modern capitalism—the notions of capital neutrality, the efficiencies of private property, and the invisible hand of the market, so cherished among economists and bankers—melt away when scrutinized.

The material presented in this book illustrates how money becomes abundant at certain moments in select places, and scarce elsewhere. Financiers depend on the muscular game of arbitrage to dangle huge sums of money before the eyes of developers and government officials to entice them to build big, and promises of substantial profit to individual speculators whose salaries alone cannot keep them without jeopardy in the city. Yet that surfeit of money and promises can miraculously vanish when it comes time to provide essential public goods like potable water, affordable housing, life-enriching employment, public education, public health, and climate-mitigated ecologies. An abundance of money can suddenly reappear when it comes time to build bullet trains and exclusive gated communities. Why and how does money work in this fashion? Why has it unfolded this way recently but not in the mid-twentieth century? Why does it shift over time?

Finally, why do we bail out those controlling the invisible hand of the market when a global financial crisis hits, yet fear the visible hand of elected community bodies that could, if pressed, create conditions for lending that directly benefit the people, for the public good? The following chapters describe the making of cities during the past forty years of the dominance of finance capital. It is up to us to imagine and work toward its unmaking. As we hear from those who challenge the hegemony of finance today, borrowing the words of the poets, with dreams come responsibilities. Those responsibilities could be ours.

PART I

In October 2012 the mayor of Barcelona kicked off the Re-thinking Cities: Framing the Future conference, at the Fira de Barcelona convention center, organized by the World Bank and Barcelona government agencies and sponsored by many attending corporate leaders (figure P1.1). He started boldly with "Welcome: You have come to Barcelona to challenge the whole world to rethink the city." To make his point, he projected on a large screen a photo of congested Cairo—a city he described as chaotic, unmanageable, and unworkable, with poverty and pollution, traffic gridlock, collapsing buildings, exposed electrical wires, and too many people. He contrasted this image with a photo of the sleek and modern Barcelona conference center complex, built in the 1930s, just below the 1992 Olympics stadium, as one of Europe's premier exposition sites. Today Barcelona is the global city par excellence, he touted. Once he had juxtaposed underdeveloped Cairo with cosmopolitan Barcelona, the mayor then offered us a clear message: Everyone can make a Barcelona! This before-and-after trope was raised by other keynote speakers to exemplify the simple truisms of their claims. One presenter showed an image of the immigrant tenements of Lower Manhattan in the early 1900s juxtaposed with the sparkling marvel of its skyscraper skyline today to convey the point about urban transformation: *Even* Global North cities had their Southern/underdeveloped moment.

At one point in the mayor's speech, his triumphant voice was drowned out by chants, whistles, and clatter from a maddening crowd in the streets. Some of us darted to the lobby windows to watch a parade of protesting police and fire officers and their families chanting while marching with

P1.1 Rethinking Cities: Framing the Future, Barcelona, 2012. One of many global investor and development conferences generating elite consensus on the global urban turn. Photo by the author.

placards down a major boulevard, stopping traffic and drawing hundreds of onlookers and supporters. They marched to protest the austerity policies that slashed their salaries and pensions, residual effects of the 2008 global financial crisis and its draining of the city budget. Many government employees hadn't been paid in months.

On the next day of the Rethinking Cities conference, the exterior noise pulsated again through the halls as Barcelona's protesting students and teachers also blocked the city's main arteries while marching. The protest was supported by hundreds of people lining the streets, clapping and cheering, backed by live music and dance. The striking educators and students demanded that the city end its sizable cuts from the university and its dramatic increase in tuition costs. How ironic that citizen outrage at the draconian austerity politics of the postfinancial crisis era had shut down the world's most famous global city, which was being marketed inside. But the political cries from the streets did not puncture the fantasy-scape conjured inside the conference hall.

Soon after the inaugural speech, the next speaker defined the mission of the conference attendees in unequivocal terms. The former mayor of Barcelona, Joan Clos, who presided over the transformation of the city from an industrial to a high-end services-based city, spoke on this day as the director of UN-Habitat, the UN agency set up to sponsor housing schemes in the Global South. "We are in an exponential phase of urbanization." Waving his hands with great enthusiasm, he declared, "There will be more infrastructure built in the next thirty years than has been built in all of human history!" He paused so that his words could be absorbed. (Wait . . . in all human history? In the next thirty years?) He spoke of the need for private-public partnerships to raise the trillions of dollars of capital and produce the necessary ambitious projects that would fuel this growth and bridge the "infrastructure gaps" from which the world currently suffers.

He paused to shake his head with theatrical flair and added:

> Many a rural minister would come to me wanting to make the old argument that much of the world's population is rural and we, too, need major infrastructural investment. And I say, OK, yes, you need lots of infrastructure. True. But you must understand that world-class infrastructure is very expensive. How do you expect the rural to pay for it? Even our urban slums—whether in Spain or India—are more productive than your rural! It's obvious: The world needs to support not spontaneous growth but infrastructure-led growth. We will have three billion people moving to cities soon. It is not a question, it's a fact. Only our growing cities can afford the costs of new infrastructure, and it only makes sense to build there. Our decisions today will affect human history for the next one hundred to two hundred years!

Could this be true? There were, of course, no rural ministers, farmers, or pastoralists in the audience to question this hyperbolic claim that the global rural is somehow a burden and the global city is our only hope. Sitting alongside me instead were well-heeled European managers from Siemens, Cisco, the world's major banks, Wall Street firms, representatives from global construction and materials firms,

UN agencies, and several invited big-city mayors. His words seemed to be music to their ears.

At another elite global-city conference—this one named the Global Summit on Urban Infrastructure, in New Delhi—presenters struck a different tone. A prominent British fund manager who represents pension funds from North America and Asia began his keynote address by challenging some basic assumptions about Global North–Global South dynamics. He started on a speculative note by arguing that India is *the* new place to invest, placing his advice within the context of a new investment strategy: "It's no longer a question of a world divided between developed [i.e., the Global North] and emerging [i.e., Global South] markets, in which the latter is too risky for investors. US and European cities are now seen by Wall Street as *declining* and Global South cities are the new growth markets *overflowing* with opportunities for high returns." He asked with a sly smile, "Who is still willing to invest in the dying markets of the North?" He continued, "Large pension funds from California, Texas, and Ottawa, and sovereign wealth funds from Abu Dhabi and China, have plenty of capital and are eager to invest, albeit under the condition that city governments are willing to offset the huge risks of global-city projects with guarantees of attractive financial returns."

A corporate representative jumped into the fray, referring to how we need to rethink the world of governments competing among themselves in the same market regime of urban financialization: "We need new forms of governance in order to get access to sovereign wealth funds and pension funds sitting on trillions of dollars. So the real question of the day is: How do we innovate our governance models? There's plenty of capital available, but the public sector needs to rethink its governance models to access the capital."

Whether in India or the United States or Spain, since the late 1990s elite leaders have been promoting a form of discursive arbitrage in which the future of our cities is presented in terms of comparative advantage for global financiers to choose from, never privileging one city over another unless a city can meet certain criteria laid out by the financial world.

It was as if they were refining the rules for a reality TV bachelor competition in which global finance would get to choose the most attractive potential groom. By the 2010s this worldview, or optics, of the authority of the financial world melded itself seamlessly into global debates on the future of our cities, focusing on how governments, citizens, and corporations need to respond to, and accommodate, a consolidated and emboldened singular market of finance capital.

The next three chapters capture the arc of this new discourse as well as its material and political consequences. Chapter 1 explains the rise of this discourse that naturalized the need for and logic of financializing our cities to overcome late twentieth-century urban stagnation and strife. Chapters 2 and 3 demonstrate how policies and practices in three countries—the United States, Spain, and India—evolved through political-economic ruptures specific to their national trajectories *before* the 2008 financial crisis (chapter 2), and how the twin processes of urbanization and financialization converged globally *after* the crisis (chapter 3). These chapters illustrate the discursive and material conditions for the growth of a twenty-first-century global process of speculative urbanism.

French philosopher Michel Foucault (1979) offered an insight into the dynamic of discourse and government developing amid the rise of neoliberalism: "The market must tell the truth (*dire le vrai*); it must tell the truth in relation to governmental practice" (1979, 32). Since the 1970s neoliberalism's birth has been rooted in an epistemology that viewed markets as truth, becoming the authority directing how governments and populations should govern or self-govern accordingly. So what truth is the world of finance capital telling us, and how can we discern fact from fiction now that they have invested in, and invaded, so many aspects of our everyday life? These are the questions and themes that motivate part I.

THE MAKING OF THE
GLOBAL URBAN TURN

TRANSNATIONAL POLICY NETWORKS
REDEFINE THE CITY

In 2007 European executives first rendered the idea of the global city to Indian elites at the EuroIndia Forum. They brought together European experts on global urbanization with sets of newbies to the hobnobbing scene—Indian mayors, bureaucrats, and state ministers—to promote this brand of global-city making. The event was called "Investing in the Future of Indian Cities, Leveraging European Expertise for Their Renewal," and it was hosted at a fifty-six-acre five-star resort and spa in Goa along a pristine private beach. It offered a swimming pool that flowed through the grounds like a lagoon but with cocktail bars, as well as a human-sized chessboard, golf course, catered meals from different regions of Europe, an open bar, and entertainment that included a fashion show, a classical European concert, and a Bollywood dance and sing-along.

As European executives mingled and chatted about everything from privatizing public services to building skyscrapers, I noticed that many Indian officials were quite new to the idea and clearly hesitant to imbibe the notion of converting their historic and culturally distinct city into a so-called global one. Some explained to me that they were already knee-deep in debt and struggling to fund basic needs such as sewers, drinking water systems, and affordable housing. The PricewaterhouseCoopers executives who invited me to attend were also skeptical that this sales job could work on Indian city managers. Back in early 2007, the newness of the idea was reflected in the pondering of one mayor who presented at the event but also in his willingness to consider this urban turn for his city. I paraphrase here from his speech before the full plenary:

Thanks to these types of meetings and experiences and conversations, I have begun to see my home city differently. When I look out from Jaipur's main railway station, I can see makeshift huts with women cleaning dishes and children playing and grazing their animals, the dhobis washing clothing, the small food carts setting up for the day, people meeting the call of nature.

I have always seen this as a typical city scene in India, the way it has been and will always be. But why couldn't we build right along the station a line of nice hotels, corporate centers, and shopping malls? Now I can imagine that Jaipur, too, can become a world city that can generate jobs and money and bring in tourists and make the city and its people much more productive. From this view, our cities are full of untapped value and potential, making them a very exciting place to be.

Through his participation in these high-profile events, he acknowledged the possibility of incorporating in his own city these turbocharged expectations and imaginaries. He was beginning to see the light.

Once disparagingly represented as megacities with intractable megaproblems, Global South cities are now praised as leaning toward global-city status, beacons of a new regime of urbanism, smart cities, and planetary sustainability. Over the past twenty-plus years, a new discourse of global-city making has emerged that focuses on the vital need for large-scale infrastructural investments, the crucial role of private finance to support this transition, and the attendant need for city governments to reduce the private sector's economic risk and create an enabling environment for these financial investments.

In this chapter I illustrate how a set of actors collectively constructed a new discourse, which I and others call *the global urban turn,* and highlight how different discursive logics converged to propose a particular problem while also solving it. That is, this elite network collectively chose to see Global South cities' overarching problem as *the lack of world-class infrastructure* and its particular solution as *the need to attract global private finance* (World Bank 2012, 1994). This global-cities discourse did not come out of thin air but from the peripatetic hard work of a transnational policy network (Goldman 2005, 2007) that emerged just before the turn of the millennium and grew in scope and degree of alignment over the next quarter century. While initially led and funded by global development and financial institutions such as the World Bank, the Asian Development Bank, and UN-Habitat, this transnational policy network (TPN) came to encompass the global consulting industry, many city mayors and planners, large institutional investors, hedge and derivative funds, global infrastructure-building firms, elite nongovernmental organizations (NGOs), and climate change strategists.

As this disparate group of individuals and organizations interacted over time—often through a lavishly funded and widely attended progression of global fora and other convenings—they converged on a discourse that prioritized large-scale infrastructure investments and the importance of finding global financial partners to finance them. While each set of actors came into the conversation with its own agenda, making distinct contributions to what became this shared common sense, the most powerful actors in the network ultimately defined its parameters, ensuring that it would reflect and serve their interests.

The chapter is organized as follows. First, I introduce the most important instigator, funder, and promoter of the new global-cities discourse—the World Bank—noting how it played key roles as funder of the network building and content provider of the discourse. I show how over the 1980s and 1990s, the world's most powerful development institution shifted its funding priorities from a thirty-year focus on rural-based productive sectors to addressing what it saw as the growing problems of so-called Third World cities. It defined these problems as overcrowding, the growth in urban slums, and a dearth of adequate housing and municipal water supplies. Before and after the 2008 global crisis, the World Bank's funding and discursive emphasis shifted again, to embrace the importance of building state-of-the-art infrastructure as a means of attracting new investment and stimulating economic growth in the world's major cities.

Yet the World Bank's role in promulgating the new urban turn did not end there. It established and spun off a handful of new organizations that comprise a vibrant TPN on global urbanization. This network produced a shifting agenda, from identifying basic urban ills to fulfilling the desires of the world's largest financial institutions, ranging from Wall Street's private equity firms to nation-based sovereign wealth funds. None of these big-time investors had dabbled in city planning, nor had they worried about the needs of city dwellers until these arenas were translated into bankable business opportunities.[1]

The World Bank: Seeing the City Through the Optics of Development

Prior to the 1980s, the World Bank and its sibling international financial institutions (IFIS) generally considered the idea of lending to Third World cities absurd.[2] From the 1950s through the 1970s, these development policymakers and project lenders found their mission *outside* the cities, in the rural-based sectors that produced economic "value," such as energy, mining, industry, agriculture, and transport. From their perspective, it was the failure of the rural, where most people in the Global South lived, that caused urban problems, as cities became a refuge for rural migrants in search of work. As the economists and engineers staffing the World Bank saw it at the time, the solution to the failed Third World city was to finance large-scale fixed-capital projects beyond the urban chaos and congestion. Obsessed with a US-centered geopolitics agenda, Robert McNamara (World Bank president from 1968 through 1981) pushed for capital infusions that would propel the so-called green revolution of agriculture and agro-industry, which also could stem the tide of the red rebellions and revolutions in the countryside of such ex-colonies as Vietnam, Indonesia, and Cambodia (McNamara 1981; Goldman 2005).[3]

McNamara justified these rural investments to his staff and clients as contributing to overall economic growth and reducing the stress on cities from rural-urban migration, but he had a much more difficult time selling the idea of lending to cities directly. The World Bank was dominated by neoclassical economists with a Wall Street business sense who wanted something concrete to invest in that produced measurable forms of output and value, such as energy development or mining. So the prickly question became: On what grounds could the Bank justify lending money to cities? As political scientist Edward Ramsamy (2006, 83) explained it, the World Bank needed to find the urban equivalent of "a targetable population that could be the recipient or direct beneficiary of productive investments, not simply welfare transfers," to justify such spending.

Under the rubric of basic-needs programming, in the 1970s the Bank cautiously started to finance small schemes for what they called urban slum "upgrading."[4] It also helped create UN-Habitat in 1978, a marginally funded United Nations (UN) agency focusing on city development to complement the many UN agencies working on rural development. The belief was that if cities could improve housing and access to water and sewerage services, the poor could have their basic needs met, enabling them to participate as healthy laborers in the economy rather than being a hindrance to the urban good life. Most urban loans during this early period of urban lending were channeled through the Bank's program of Sites and Services, which included housing upgrades and hookups of sanitation and water (Turner and Fichter 1972). A World Bank retrospective titled *Thirty Years of World Bank Shelter Lending: What Did We Learn?* (Buckley and Kalarickal 2006, 9) describes the early years: "At the time, many slums were located in city centers and served as temporary bases for poor (rural) migrant families, where they could secure a job before moving to what were essentially illegal settlements to build more permanent shelter."

The whole idea of lending for the urban sounded unfamiliar to most Bank economists and quite different from lending for easily measurable investments such as energy or mining. As one Bank official reported, "Some people in the Bank were making jokes that next we are going to have suburban development, or an outer-space development program" (quoted in Ramsamy 2006, 83). Another senior Bank official stated, "I am surprised that urban poverty should be regarded as an important topic for McNamara's speech. None of these social problems, including this one, can really be resolved except in the context of economies which have a reasonable rate of growth," that is, are benefiting from productive investments (quoted in Ramsamy 2006, 83).

When McNamara insisted on launching an Urban Department, he met so much resistance to the idea that staff quietly merged the Urban Department into the Transport Department—the city as a transit site?—and they left it to languish for a while. McNamara did, however, cultivate allies in the US Congress, where he articulated an explicitly political angle. An early report from a Senate subcommittee noted, "Social and political unrest and Communism are natural consequences of squalor conditions. The actions of these large masses of underprivileged and ill-housed people can wipe out all the gains from economic assistance in these countries" (quoted in Ramsamy 2006, 73). McNamara often used the political volatility of the Third World poor as one of his rhetorical weapons to stimulate financial and political buy-in. As he noted in a 1975 speech given in Washington, DC, "Historically, violence and upheaval are more common in cities than in the countryside. Frustrations that fester among the urban poor are readily exploited by political extremists. If cities do not begin to deal more constructively with poverty, *poverty may begin to deal more destructively with cities*" (quoted in Ramsamy 2006, 87).

The Bank's urban lending patterns changed significantly over the subsequent two decades. Whereas 70 percent of its early urban loans were channeled to upgrading housing conditions in working-class neighborhoods and slums, by the 1990s the Bank was directing as much as half of its urban loan portfolio to financial institutions promoting home mortgages—a category of lending that had barely existed in most Global South cities. In short, the focus of the Bank's urban lending changed from attempts to upgrade housing for underpaid workers to a focus on the corporatization of mortgages. In this way, the Bank kicked off the process of financializing the housing sector of its Global South borrowers, much to the delight of Northern investors. The Bank continued to refer to these as pro-poor policies even though the world's poor typically weren't allowed into banks and had no collateral against which they could borrow money.

The Bank mobilized its capital and influence to help create new nationwide home mortgage markets, seeing the US housing model as the most efficacious for spreading globally the private-home model of urban progress.[5] Because finance requires collateral, and land is the most attractive form, the unfettering of land markets became a precondition for investment. Once land and homes could become privately owned assets, and not just inhabited places with ambiguous (or locally negotiated, informal) ownership rights, they could be used as collateral. The Bank therefore urged countries to adopt national land-titling campaigns, which formally encoded legal rights to land while disadvantaging those without the power to navigate either government bureaucracies or so-called land mafias. In effect, the Bank's urban policy evolved into supporting private property ownership in cities and home mortgage lending and debt rather than public and social housing schemes. One sympathetic observer summarized the Bank's thinking as follows: "Most of the poor already possess the assets they need to make a success of capitalism. . . . But they hold these resources *in defective forms*. . . . They lack the process to represent their property and create capital. . . . They have houses, but not titles. . . . It is the representation of assets in legal property documents that gives them the power to create surplus value" (Mammen 2001, 2–9; see also de Soto 2000).

This push to document property rights created vast new opportunities for bankers, private investors, and finance capital, who could now cash in on the multitude of new titling policies, mortgage streams, and household borrowing required to own a home in cities across the Global South.

Both these trends—allocating more loans to low-income housing im-provements and supporting the creation of a home mortgage market—were limited by the jarring conjuncture of the 1980s debt crisis and the imposition of neoliberal structural adjustment programs (SAPS) across the Global South by the World Bank and International Monetary Fund (IMF). As the literature has exhaustively documented, SAPS represented a punitive approach that forced borrowing countries to impose auster-ity programs to balance their budgets and pay off their debts (Naiman and Watkins 1999). As a precondition to receiving some debt relief and future capital lending, the Bank and IMF insisted that governments slash social expenditures and public employment, sell off their public enterprises at bargain-basement prices, privatize municipal goods and services (including water, electricity, transportation, and housing), and impose user fees for access to these services. This led to what many refer to as the "lost decades" for many African and Latin American countries, reflected in dramatic falls in indicators for national-level health, life ex-pectancy, income equality, and per capita gross domestic product (GDP) growth during the 1980s and 1990s in those countries where the Bank and IMF held sway (Weisbrot and Ray 2011; Ismi 2004).

The hardships imposed by SAPS catalyzed widespread social pro-tests across the Global South, as the populations of Latin America, Africa, and Asia reacted to the sharp decline in their living standards (Walton and Seddon 1994; Structural Adjustment Participatory Review International Network [SAPRIN] 2004). Protesters took to the streets, particularly in urban areas where residents had become accustomed to a certain level of public services and were deeply angered by the impact of the SAPS imposed by the IFIS. In response, the Bank canceled many of its nonperforming loans to cities. Rather than acknowledging that its policies had such draconian effects, it blamed local mismanagement of public services for these loans' failure.

Conjuring the Twenty-First-Century City:
"The Future Is Urban, and We Must Be There"

Coterminous with its imposition of SAPS, the World Bank began to adopt a more ambitious approach to the well-being of cities, as the organization's urban division staff realized that they needed to think more broadly about the urban.[6] A 1991 policy paper largely authored by

Michael Cohen, then chief of the Bank's Urban Development Division, identified the limits of the Bank's earlier interventions. It posited that "the World Bank should move toward a broader view of urban issues, *a view that moves beyond housing and residential infrastructure*, and that *emphasizes the productivity of the urban economy and the need to alleviate the constraints on productivity*" (World Bank 1991, 3; emphasis mine). Among the constraints Cohen and his colleagues identified as limiting "the productivity of firms and households" were major infrastructure deficiencies, government regulations that stifled private investors, weak municipal institutions, and "inadequate financial services for urban development" (15; see also 7). Elaborating on this final constraint, the report noted, "Poorly developed financial sectors constrain investment in infrastructure, housing, and other urban economic activities. Weak financial systems are unable to mobilize private savings and lead governments to use public resources to finance housing. The links between the financial sector and the urban economy go in both directions, as pressure for financial subsidies in housing can have macro-financial effects" (8).

At the Bank these innovators believed that they had developed a new urban agenda that would address global issues of urban poverty and environmental degradation in one fell swoop (World Bank 1991; interviews with Bank officials and consultants, 2014–16). But Cohen and his colleagues were a lone voice that for several years fell on deaf ears elsewhere in the Bank.

By the turn of the millennium, the World Bank's position shifted away from the punitive disciplinary policies of structural adjustment to a more "productive" focus on cities as growth machines. This would both support global finance's expansion into the realm of the urban and resuscitate the Bank's own fading reputation as stagnant and irrelevant. The Bank was undergoing considerable internal and external turmoil in the 1990s. Countries in Latin America had elected progressive parties to power that had campaigned on explicitly anti-Bank sentiment, promising to sever their cumbersome, if not imperial, relationships with the IFIS. Some countries minimized these relations with the IFIS by establishing their own development-oriented financial institutions and sovereign wealth funds. For example, the Brazilian government started the Banco del Sur in 2009, promising an alternative to the IFIS that included a redistributive policy to better fit the needs of poor Latin Americans.

Focusing on the urban seemed to offer the World Bank a way out in this context of declining global legitimacy. By the late 1990s, through major reorganizations and consolidations, the Bank reemerged as a leader by supporting the global urban turn. To kick-start this new focus, the Bank ran a series of conferences and in-house meetings, from which emerged a major report in 2000 on the growing importance of cities, called *Cities in Transition: World Bank Urban and Local Government Strategy* (World Bank 2000). Its authors outlined the contours of a new strategy for a rapidly urbanizing world, pointing to the Bank's ability to rebound from its past mistakes and generate business for itself and its clients. As the report's executive summary put it:

> Fostering rural-urban synergies and well-integrated national and city strategies to help countries realize the promise of urbanization represents *a prime opportunity* for the Bank to pursue a new "comprehensive development framework," as expressed by President Wolfensohn at the 1998 Annual Meetings of the World Bank and the International Monetary Fund. *Renewing the Bank's commitment and capacity to assist effective urban development therefore makes sense as a corporate strategy. It is also good business for the Bank*, as national and local government clients increasingly seek knowledge and financial support to improve the economic performance of cities and to translate national policy directions into daily realities on the ground. (3; emphasis added)

Yet becoming a global leader in sustainable urban development, as the World Bank called it, required more than just a newly articulated Bank strategy and increased funding for its urban department. It also necessitated the creation of a broad network of partners, collaborators, and influencers who would see urban growth in the Global South with new eyes: as a dynamic development arena. As the World Bank publication *Cities in Transition* noted:

> The new urban and local government strategy does more than simply retool the urban development portfolio or seek stronger performance from it, although both are required. Rather, it argues for the Bank to recognize cities and towns *as a dynamic development arena* where the convergence of sectoral activities, and *collaboration among communities, levels of government, and other private and public sector institutions*

can create a microcosm of sustainable development for the country. . . . The strategy therefore calls for a commitment by a wide coalition of forces within the institution and among external partners to working together in new ways on the urban frontier, with a newly empowered set of clients. (World Bank 2000, 6; emphasis added)

Such a wide coalition of forces had to be created, of course. One way the Bank did this was to establish several new organizations with which it could work and that could help it achieve its agenda. In 1999, for instance, the World Bank coordinated with the Japanese and UK governments, USAID, and donors from a handful of European governments to create the Public-Private Infrastructure Advisory Facility (PPIAF). The mandate was to "support the legal and regulatory environment conducive to private sector participation in infrastructure in developing countries" (PPIAF, n.d.). Over its first twenty years, PPIAF claims to have leveraged $17.4 billion for infrastructure projects, helped raise close to $1 billion more for subnational infrastructure projects, trained over nineteen thousand officials to become better managers of infrastructural projects, and crafted 146 policies and regulations to improve "enabling environments" (World Bank 2020). Seemingly independent, the organization is physically embedded in the Bank, where its linkages to this and other multilateral development agencies help PPIAF enjoy a global reach (PPIAF, n.d.). This TPN has become one of the World Bank's key partners on global-city making. This TPN has become increasingly focused on large-scale infrastructural investments, which is precisely the PPIAF's bailiwick.

Another Bank program supporting its new urban agenda was its ambitious City Creditworthiness Initiative, which aims to help municipal and local governments access financing for urban development. This started in 2013 with the training of officials in the fundamentals of creditworthiness and municipal finance at City Creditworthiness Academies. These short courses train officials to take the next step and utilize what the Bank calls market-based financing transactions for its "climate-smart" infrastructure projects (World Bank 2020). According to Patrick Bigger and Sophie Webber (2021, 45), "The academies are training courses for bureaucrats to assess their city's capacity to issue debt on regional or international capital markets." These courses are then followed up with "implementation programs [which] are long-term, in-depth, technical assistance programs to rectify impediments to creditworthiness that were identified at the academies."

Two other important nodes in the global-city TPN organizations are the Cities Alliance and the Global Platform for Sustainable Cities. In late 1999 the Bank partnered with UN-Habitat to create the Cities Alliance as a trust fund to finance projects in two arenas: slum-upgrading programs and city development strategies. The Cities Alliance describes its own history as reflecting "a vision shared by the stakeholders of the city of the future and a programme 'setting out priorities for improving city management performance and the investments required to improve the city's infrastructure and services,' while forging closer links between local authorities and communities, the private sector and finance" (Development Planning Unit, 2002, 2).

The World Bank also partnered with existing organizations, some of which had long focused on urban issues, whereas others were in the process of expanding their activities to include the challenges of rapid urban growth. These organizations joined the network with their own agendas, such as climate change, green growth, or urban poverty. For example, C40, founded in 2005 by Ken Livingstone, then mayor of London, has the stated purpose of uniting mayors from the world's major cities to combat climate change.[7] Working with mayors in nearly one hundred cities, C40 has become one of the most prominent organizations involved in urban development. Another key TPN participant is the World Resources Institute, a large, mainstream NGO with headquarters in Washington, DC. Historically, its central focus had been the environment and natural resources, but in 2014 it created a multimillion-dollar division dedicated to cities, called the Ross Center for Sustainable Cities (World Resources Institute Ross Center for Sustainable Cities, n.d.).

From the mid-2000s, the World Bank cosponsored a seemingly endless series of international conferences, meetings, workshops, and training courses on urban development. These meetings, typically held at swanky hotels and premier conference venues around the world, brought together representatives from national, regional, and local governments; financial firms; international development agencies; global consulting companies; and concerned NGOs to discuss the importance of global urban growth. Animated through these encounters, this disparate set of actors began to converge around a singular discourse that emphasized the importance of investing in world-class infrastructure as *the* central tenet of global-city making. Another group of players has been key to constructing this global discourse, building the network, and, ultimately, establishing the idea of a global infrastructure gap: the global corporate consulting industry, to which I now turn.

Getting in on the Action: The Global
Consulting Industry

Keenly aware of their clients' ever-changing interests and motivated by their desire to develop new arenas of expertise to secure additional revenue flows, the largest global consulting firms began working on cities around the mid-2000s. Sometimes hired as consultants by the World Bank, a regional development bank, or a city government, and sometimes working on their own, these firms—including Pricewater-houseCoopers (PwC), KPMG, the McKinsey Global Institute, and Deloitte—produced and circulated report after report, identifying what they viewed as the key challenges facing the world's major cities and offering specific solutions to these problems. Simultaneously functioning as "policy entrepreneurs" (Ball 2012) and "network conduits" (Munro 2017), these consulting firms played critical roles in bringing certain ideas to the fore and connecting actors across a variety of organizational locations and interest areas.

In 2004 PwC entered the scene as one of the earliest participants, establishing a City and Local Government Network that sought to "bring together city leaders . . . [to] share the experience, knowledge and insights that they have gained and to develop their ideas and strategies for the future" (PwC 2005, 1). In its 2005 *Cities of the Future* report, PwC used the collective *we* to promote its perspective on cities (as well as its products): "We need new perspectives on cities, their dreams, knowledge, creativity and motivation in order to find new ways to develop strategic city management. Therefore PricewaterhouseCoopers (PwC) will develop a new arena for dialogue with leaders in cities as a tool for strategic development and knowledge sharing, resulting in added value for people in cities, organisations or companies" (1).

The report included a graphic in the form of five concentric circles representing five *forms of capital* deemed necessary for cities of the future: (1) intellectual and social, (2) democratic, (3) culture and leisure, (4) environmental, and (5) technical capital. Notably, these were all bound together within one encompassing circle titled *financial capital*. Without financial capital, PwC suggested, none of the other forms of capital could be fully realized.

New platforms feeding on such bold ideas started spreading like mushrooms through international conferences and meetings, widely circulated reports, and snappy-looking websites, fertilized with similar ideas and talking points. The global consultancy firms that specialized in spinning a persuasive tale of future success generated a lot of talk and attention through these platforms—on such topics as smart cities and cities as the future—helping to facilitate the global urban turn. During the 2000s, McKinsey, KPMG, PwC, and Deloitte each initiated discussions focusing on the significance of large cities (Farrell et al. 2006). The frequency of such reports on cities increased swiftly, and their tone shifted. Whereas initially the reports simply described the process of urbanization and its business implications, soon the emphasis morphed into a more prescriptive approach to urban development.

These consultancy firms began to present cities' growth as necessary for achieving several Millennium Development Goals, reflecting the terrain of development that the World Bank, the UN, and development NGOs inhabit. The message that we would be entering the urban century became an oft-repeated cliché, with an ever-widening set of actors portraying cities as key to fighting poverty, confronting global pandemics, and even reversing global climate change. This was a troubling reinvention of the discourse of sustainability, given that unbridled urbanization was once the primary critique of global environmental NGOs.

But ideas have evolved. This new global mindset insists that the best way to reverse poverty and climate change trends is through a new trajectory of urban growth. The World Bank reimagined the world as a "system of cities" that would "[harness] urbanization for growth and poverty alleviation." As a 2009 Bank publication framed it:

> Urbanization is a defining phenomenon of this century, and the developing world is the locus of this demographic transformation. Nearly two billion new urban residents are expected in the next 20 years, and the urban populations of South Asia and Africa are likely to double. Much of the growth will be in small and medium-sized cities; even today more than half the world's urban population resides in cities smaller than 500,000. This raises questions about managing urbanization and delivering World Bank assistance for urban development in the coming

decade. With cities accounting for some 70 percent of global Gross Domestic Product (GDP), recent economic thinking is reshaping the Bank's approach to urbanization. (World Bank 2009, 3)

The idea of consciously urbanizing the planet spread like wildfire: The Bank began aggressively pushing it, with its appeal seeping into other actors' agendas. But to these global urbanists, the main concern evolved into the question of who would finance it.

PricewaterhouseCooper's publications captures well this ideational progression.[8] When PwC launched its annual report *Cities of Opportunity* in 2007, it ranked cities by metrics such as financial clout, the number of Fortune Global 500 company headquarters, and cost competitiveness (PwC 2007). Over the years, however, PwC's reports became increasingly prescriptive and introduced new measures of city progress. In its 2019 report, *Creating the Smart Cities of the Future*, PwC lays out "the way forward for government and the private sector": as purchaser of services from the private sector; as co-investor/co-participant with the private sector in smart city solutions; and as regulator and protector of the public interest, both overseeing and facilitating smart infrastructure—including aspects such as the permitting/regulatory environment, tax increment financing (TIF) and other economic incentives" (13).

Meanwhile, the global consulting firm KPMG jumped right into advocacy for urban infrastructure. The following excerpt emphasizes the importance of urban infrastructure for corporate profitability: "Senior executives are concerned that the current infrastructure inadequately supports their businesses. Indeed, only 14 percent believe that infrastructure is 'completely adequate' in this regard. Infrastructure will become more important over the next five years and 7 percent of business executives surveyed fear *there will not be enough infrastructure investment to support the long-term growth of their organizations*" (KPMG International 2009, 13; emphasis mine).[9]

While arguing that infrastructure is necessary for corporations to run smoothly, KPMG does not recommend an increase in public funding through taxes or floating safe and inexpensive municipal bonds as a potential solution. "Eighty percent of executives believe governments should partner *with the private sector to finance* major infrastructure projects" (KPMG International 2009, 5; emphasis added).

For many TPN actors, the question was not how to *contain* urbanization and its rapid expansion but rather how to *capitalize* on it. An emergent consensus found the solution to be clear: Let's figure out ways to raise global capital resources to finance urban infrastructure.

Promoting the Global Infrastructure Gap

These innovative ideas on the city circulated not just through high-profile reports by global consultants but also through a multitude of summits held annually in such places as Dubai, Singapore, Shanghai, London, and Chicago. One of the largest is the annual World Cities Summit, held in Singapore, which is supported by the Singaporean government, the National University of Singapore, the Asian Development Bank, and numerous corporate sponsors. Its inaugural summit in 2008 ran in conjunction with the East Asia Summit Conference on Livable Cities and alongside the Singapore International Water Week (a water industry conference and trade show); the 2010 summit also incorporated the World Urban Transport Leaders' Summit "to reap synergistic benefits" (World Cities Summit 2010).

The discourse emanating from these global events and reports focused on a specific concern: the infrastructure gap—the disparity between the amount of capital needed to invest in indispensable infrastructure and the public funding currently available. Spokespeople in the TPN argued that this gap would require large-scale corporate financing, which could take several unique forms. In addition to traditional bank borrowing, they promoted a variety of vehicles to mobilize capital: private-public partnerships, land value capture, asset monetization, asset sales and land development, green bonds, and debt financing.

Three formerly discrete portfolios within the IFIs' repertoire, namely, the urban, the financial, and infrastructure, congealed around one project: financing urban infrastructure. At a high-profile event in 2009, amid the collapse of the global economy, World Bank President Robert Zoellick ceremoniously launched the World Bank-Singapore Urban Hub and the Infrastructure Finance Centre of Excellence with these words:

> *Infrastructure* is a cornerstone of the World Bank Group's recovery strategy for the global economic crisis. These investments can create jobs today and higher productivity and growth tomorrow. . . .

The needs are huge: an estimated 880 million people still live with-out safe water; 1.5 billion people without electricity; 2.5 billion without sanitation; and more than one billion without access to an all-weather road or telephone service. The world's urban population is expected to increase from 3.3 billion to five billion by 2030—with Africa and Asia doubling their urban populations—creating new infrastructure de-mands for transport, housing, water, waste collection, and other ame-nities of modern life.

. . . These infrastructure choices will shape cities and lifestyles for many decades or even a century to come. (Zoellick 2010)

Simultaneously, KPMG mobilized the concept of the infrastructure gap in its 2009 *Bridging the Global Infrastructure Gap* report, published in collaboration with the Economist Intelligence Unit. The McKinsey Global Institute picked up the theme in its 2011 report *Urban World: Mapping the Economic Power of Cities* (Dobbs et al. 2011) and further developed it in a 2013 report, *Infrastructure Productivity: How to Save $1 Trillion a Year* (Dobbs et al. 2013). Other network actors adopted the same terminology as it became widely used to refer to the idea that pri-vate financing must dramatically increase to ensure adequate new infra-structure for rising urban populations, to increase GDP, and to confront the challenges posed by climate change. What remained unclear was the precise definition of private financing and the rules of engagement that would apply to the rapacious Wall Street financiers who had begun to express interest—private equity, hedge, and derivative fund managers. Discussions of the infrastructure gap extend far and wide: from the annual *Financing for Development* report series, published by the UN starting in 2016, to the 2019 Davos World Economic Forum report *The World Is Facing a $15 Trillion Infrastructure Gap by 2040. Here's How to Bridge It*, and many more (World Economic Forum 2019).[10]

As these new ideas popped up and gained traction, one might assume that they represent a vast world of diverse actors generating a variety of new ideas to help cities innovate. The term *global civil society* might imply that these ideas come from many of the 195 different countries across the globe, reflecting many sectors of civil society and their varied world-views. Yet a closer look reveals the lack of a diverse landscape. This particular domain of global civil society is quite narrow and remarkably self-referential, populated by many of the same people, and effectively saturating the space of open global dialogue on the future of our cities.

Transnational Policy Network: It's a Small World After All

Both McKinsey and PwC are members of the Coalition for Urban Transitions (CUT), as are many other organizations participating in this global-cities conversation, including the aforementioned World Resources Institute and the C40 Cities Climate Leadership Group. Reports by the CUT are cited in the reports of these consultancies and in writings from the Davos World Economic Forum's Global Future Council on Infrastructure. The CUT was directed by Andrew Steer, whose career followed a classic revolving-door pattern, from the World Bank to the World Resources Institute and then to the directorship of the Cities Alliance. In turn, the CUT works closely with the Global Infrastructure Facility of the World Bank. It is no coincidence that these entities, working closely with other entities in the network, envision the problem and its solution similarly. They are mostly funded by the same agencies, peopled through the same elite network, and proposing similar solutions.

Making cities investable—that is, requiring them to adapt to the needs of finance capital—has become the mantra of many of these reports and forums and experts. In this TPN it is hard to find any voices of concern arguing that global finance itself needs to adapt to the ground realities of our cities and to the struggles of the urban majority in search of affordable housing, living wages, and accessible education and health care. Although one might expect such a concern when considering the complex ground reality of India and its urban woes, this is not the case. In *India's Urban Awakening* (Sankhe et al. 2010), the McKinsey Global Institute argues that urbanization—once the bane of global consultants' representations of India—is critical to India's development and inclusive growth. McKinsey mobilizes development to endorse the central role of large-scale infrastructure investment and the finance needed to underwrite it. It will require India to "unlock" buried and undertapped value streams. McKinsey identifies four funding sources: monetizing land assets, collecting higher property taxes and user charges that reflect costs, engaging in public-private partnerships, and relying on highly restrictive "formula-based" government funding (Sankhe et al. 2010, 19). Failing to demonstrate any deep knowledge of India's geographically diverse urban concerns or specific Indian policy alternatives and solutions, the authors claim that India "will not be able to bridge the gap between demand for services and their provision" unless it dramatically increases external capital flows (19).

Instead of prescribing that the global infrastructure sector devise solutions best suited to India's situation, they advise, "As investors, companies therefore have *an obligation to demand urban transformation* as a prerequisite for investment—and lobby a great deal more vigorously than they have in the past to drive change. At the same time, they can help transform India's urban landscape by bringing their expertise and capacity to execute the opportunities *unlocked* by reforms" (32; emphasis mine). The *right* to demand national reforms as a prerequisite to foreign investment looms large in the discourse, as does the promise that it can unlock hidden values buried in the public commons of Global South cities that advocates believe are somehow invisible to the naked eye of India's population. In this ahistorical and culturally problematic account, there is never a word about the lingering effects of what ex-colonies inherited from the colonial era of violent expropriation in the form of old infrastructure built for resource extraction to Europe or of the imperial financing behind expropriation benefiting foreign entities.

A second question emerges as a vital theme circulating across these platforms: Is public capital more efficacious than private capital? This issue was of prime importance to ex-colonies in the early years after independence, when governments developed a response to the devastation of colonialism by nationalizing economies and building up state capacity to revitalize an eviscerated public sector. The TPN experts twist this postcolonial sensibility, however, by redefining the meanings of *public* and *private*:

> It is often assumed that public capital is cheaper than private capital, but in practice the two are difficult to compare. In order to attempt the comparison, it is important to distinguish between the cost of debt and the true cost of capital. The true cost of public capital is higher than the cost of debt (i.e., private finance capital) because of a hidden risk premium in the form of implicit government guarantees ultimately borne by taxpayers (for example, revenue guarantees, or the implicit assurance that a government will continue to provide an essential service, regardless of the financial implications). (Sankhe et al. 2010, 24–25)

One might think that it is cheaper to use (not for profit) public financial resources to self-finance public infrastructure and services, but the TPN argues that in fact it is cheaper to borrow from external capital markets. Even though Wall Street firms have generated outsize profits from such investments, it is still deemed cheaper to rely on their financial tools than the public sector's. These corporate boosters have a simple remedy for certain public goods that governments could provide. According to the McKinsey Global Institute, "Governments can partially allay the financing challenge by exploring alternative sources of funding. A broad range of funding tools is available to governments, including various forms of taxes, user fees, and divestitures. Here we focus on those that have traditionally been under-exploited—road pricing, property value capture, and capital recycling" (Dobbs et al. 2013, 26). Further, "roads are arguably the *greatest untapped source of user fees*," and road tolls are an ideal way to finance new infrastructure (26; emphasis mine).

Another financial tool is *property value capture*, where a government can lease or sell the area around an infrastructure project after it is completed (Peterson 2008). A third is *tax increment financing*, much used in US cities (see chapter 2), where governments capture anticipated future increases in property or tax revenues, using these anticipated revenues as collateral to finance infrastructure. Finally, the report advocates for *capital recycling*, whereby the sale of public infrastructure to global finance can generate newer infrastructural deals. Shifting liquid capital across assets is precisely the modus operandi of today's largest financial firms. They become the new global arbiters of public finance while also meeting their own needs by keeping their investment capital as liquid and mobile—and of course profitable—as possible.

The McKinsey Global Institute report *Bridging Global Infrastructure Gaps* (Woetzel et al. 2016) clearly illustrates some of the main points of the discourse of TPN actors. Stretching far beyond the mandate of building roads, the authors insist we fill the gap with new forms of governance (e.g., globally standardized regulatory reform and transparency in principles and actions) and new types of investment opportunities, giving private capital the freedom to conduct business across borders, without constraints.

The economic assumption here is that private capital is inherently scarce and therefore must be distributed with great efficiency (as defined by lenders); at the same time, TPN experts argue that there is a plentiful supply of capital waiting to be spent. As evidence, McKinsey (Woetzel et al. 2016, 23) lists the following sources:

- Banks: $40 trillion in assets;
- Investment companies (including investment banks, asset managers, wealth managers, family and multifamily offices, investment trusts, and investment companies): $29 trillion;
- Insurance companies and private pensions: $26 trillion;
- Public pensions and superannuation plans: $11 trillion;
- Sovereign wealth funds: $6 trillion;
- Infrastructure operators and developers: $3 trillion;
- Infrastructure and private equity funds: $3 trillion;
- Endowments and foundations: $1 trillion.

In other words, the discourse suggests that while there is definitively no shortage of capital, they calculate a whopping $120 trillion just sitting on the table waiting to be tapped, sadly none of these actors can imagine investing without government intervention to reduce the risks associated with investing in the public sphere. "To attract these investors, governments and other stakeholders need to develop their project pipelines, remove regulatory and structural barriers, and build stronger markets for infrastructure assets" (Woetzel et al. 2016, 23).

PwC offers a similarly prescriptive agenda in its report *Increasing Private Sector Investment into Sustainable City Infrastructure* (PricewaterhouseCoopers and Global Infrastructure Facility 2020), produced in conjunction with the World Bank's Global Infrastructure Facility. Here PwC argues that cities need to present themselves as *investable* with preconditions relating to the fiscal, regulatory, legal, and institutional environments. "These environments should be underpinned by a strong vision and leadership from the city accompanied by a long-term strategic infrastructure plan including a pipeline of investable projects which will provide an acceptable return level capable of attracting private sector investors" (3).

Conclusion

To summarize, the prospect of investing in Global South cities started with great apprehension, expressed in numerous questions: Is it feasible? Is it worth shifting our capital from safer investments in the United States and Europe? With what government guarantees? How do we exit these investments on a schedule suitable for our shareholders and clients? What happens if currencies devalue, and political regimes change? What if governments decide to nationalize public infrastructure, as many do under popular pressure? How can we turn a profit investing our dollars in economies based on local currencies such as the rupee or the peso, and how do we exit with the higher (Northern) currency values intact? The emergent discourse of global-city making frames the answers to these questions in a way that highlights potential opportunities and obstacles for global financiers. In their numerous global forums, workshops, platforms, reports, and websites, this TPN on global urbanization purports to offer persuasive answers. These answers speak to international financiers' interests and concerns, inducing them to gradually abandon their initial reluctance to invest in urban infrastructure in the Global South by creating lucrative new opportunities for generating high profits.

This chapter has documented the discourse and practice of the global urban turn from the perspective of TPN experts who used their networking prowess and political connections to help create an urban-financialization project that they and their shareholders could imagine as feasible. Beginning in the early 2000s, when the World Bank saw the potential in the world's cities and asked the premier consulting firms to help bring together investors, lenders, and country officials, a TPN emerged, grew, and solidified. Initially funded by the World Bank and its affiliates, this network's nodes and hubs started in capital-saturated cities such as London, New York, and Singapore but soon spread to cities across China, India, and Brazil. The new organizations comprising the network were led by senior officials from the IFIS, consulting firms, infrastructure-related firms, and a few well-heeled urban planners and UN elites. Their events reflected a tight-knit community, with their voices, within a decade, becoming one. Today the world's largest and wealthiest private equity firms and pension funds have major stakes in the investment landscape that this network originally promoted.

Working at a different scale and register, powerful global institutions such as the World Bank and IMF—struggling with their own declining legitimacy and perceived value—strove to mobilize networks of experts and knowledge producers to muster new types of data and interpretations of reality to translate their own failures into the basis for their next interventions and experiments. This chapter has documented the various actors who helped to build and propagate a new discourse of the global city and facilitate the global urban turn. The World Bank and its affiliates and consultants sit perched ready to reemerge as the global arbiter of the next era. This time it is under the rubric of urban transformation.

One of the great silences of this postcolonial era concerns the way dominant discourses of development focus on the workings—and so-called failures—of the Global South, while ignoring the roles of Northern elites and the practices of global capital. This vision of a world in which the Global South can improve itself through smart ideas, hard work, and greater integration into the global economy hides the motivations and workings of IFIs and global finance and their collective push for a major transformation in the realms of governance and access to "untapped" public resources (Ghertner 2015; Gidwani and Baviskar 2011). The dominant discourse of the urban turn fails to acknowledge that financiers capitalize not just on the promises and guarantees surrounding new construction and provisioning but also on the collapse of those commitments, a crisis that can spawn new opportunities for finance capital—a peculiar phenomenon explained in subsequent chapters.

As speculative engines of financial capital revved at a feverish pitch around the world, with stock markets, financial firms, and real estate deals experiencing once-in-a-lifetime profits, the global economy suddenly reversed itself and collapsed. The year 2008 completely redefined any notion of growth or progress of the city and its purported rights, protections, and guarantees. To understand the push to grow the city without limits, we need to appreciate its contribution to the financial crisis and the global economy's afterlives. The next chapter focuses on the exhilarating experiences of urban speculation, inspired in part by this TPN discourse, as it played out across three continents.

THE GATHERING STORM

URBAN TRANSFORMATION ACROSS
THREE CONTINENTS

The discourse of the global urban turn gained traction around the world in the years leading up to the financial crisis of 2008. This chapter explores the period preceding the crisis in the United States, Spain, and India. Very different national and economic regimes operated in each case to shape the process of converting city space into apparatuses of financial power. These divergent national paths to financialized urban landscapes set the stage for what would be a new opportunity for the finance industry in the wake of a global crisis. For each country case, the chapter first lays out the relational-conjunctural conditions for the rise of urban financialization. In the United States, for example, it was largely attributable to the structural collapse in the 1970s of both the mid-twentieth-century era of Fordism (manufacturing-focused production with mass consumerism) and Keynesianism (high-value state-driven supports to economy and society), which brought about new opportunities for the rise and consolidation of national banking-and-finance sectors. But the story is very different in Spain and India, with a variety of nation-based factors and forces contributing to the rising power of finance in cities. The chapter highlights the public policy maneuvers and corporate innovations that helped empower finance capital. It explains finance's remarkable run of wealth creation from city-based assets, effectively growing right up to the 2008 financial crisis. By offering an overview of the rise of finance in three different countries, I argue for the importance of understanding the diverse contexts and conditions in which such power and authority gets manufactured across nations.

The rise of finance across these nations is not a result of universal or natural laws of capital or politics but materializes from an elite consensus at moments of crisis: Actor networks of finance, the state, and chambers of commerce come together to negotiate a path forward for capital accumulation. In this case, they together envisioned how arenas that were once the purview of the state—the distribution and maintenance of public infrastructure, goods, and services—could become converted into drivers of profitability for the banking-and-finance sector. This drive for corporate profit would then spur, they argue, a surfeit of public benefits, such as rising incomes and improved services. But scholars have well documented earlier attempts to re-engineer the public sphere: The 1970s fiscal crisis in the US produced what Keeanga-Yamahtta Taylor (2019) calls "predatory inclusion." Building on Taylor's insights, I argue that these elite networks brought into the realm of accumulation and exploitation historically excluded and minoritized urban communities in life-altering ways. This chapter establishes the conditions of finance's rise and expansion leading up to the 2008 financial crisis, while the next chapter explains the period after 2008, when the industry shifts gears and creates a new set of relational dynamics in and across these countries. These two chapters provide the global and structural dimensions to the book's argument and the context in which the case of Bengaluru arises.

The United States: Neoliberalism Hits the City

The economic and political crises of the 1970s in the United States generated a raft of new legislation and policies to deregulate the financial sector and create new arenas for investment in once-protected domains of public city life. New financial tools were created: special tax districts cordoned off from city cores to produce white middle-class suburbs using new inflows of capital for infrastructural improvement; new tools such as tax increment financing for neighborhood redevelopment projects; mortgage-backed securities for the housing sector; and interest rate swaps for indebted cities willing to gamble to borrow expensive cash now to keep the city running. These policy and economic interventions were pivotal in injecting financial expertise, tools, and profit making into city governance structures. They also created the institutional apparatuses to channel more revenue streams away from city budgets and into the hands of financial firms, which, in turn, contributed to the increased influence of the financial sector in city life, but austerity for the public. This early period of abundant accumulation produced the destructive conditions of the 2008 financial crisis.

The financial turn in the US economy started with the economy's contraction during the 1970s due to a constellation of factors. The US war in Southeast Asia drained the state coffers of resources at the same moment that manufacturing in the United States declined, with many of its once-prosperous cities devolving into the nation's rust belt. Meanwhile, more competitive economies around the world cut into US corporate profits and contributed to a deepening feeling of political malaise. Europe and Japan lost confidence in the United States and its dollar currency and chose to invest elsewhere. As Gerald Davis and Suntae Kim (2015, 206) note, after two decades of phenomenal postwar economic growth, the United States faced three types of crises: a *fiscal* crisis, due to the yawning gap between government spending and revenues; a *social* crisis, with growing demands from diverse social groups for equitable access to public resources as state revenues plummeted; and a *legitimacy* crisis, because of declining trust in government and the economy. The simultaneity of these crises inspired a political movement calling for the dismantling of the welfare state and the state's withdrawal from the market so that the market's natural forces could, unleashed, flourish.

This call echoed political and structural trends unfolding across Europe. Austrian economist Friedrich Hayek and University of Chicago economist Milton Friedman worked industriously from the late 1940s on to cultivate a transnational fraternal network of like-minded elite Euro-American economists—the Mont Pèlerin Society—conceived of in a Swiss mountain resort. They propagated the belief that the only way to combat postwar Keynesian thought and policies, as well as counter pro-public and even communist philosophies worldwide, was through a neoliberal agenda of limited government and maximum market-actor freedom (Mirowski and Plehwe 2015).

As these ideas percolated, they were translated into US policies on a few fronts: Anti–property tax campaigns of the 1970s (which catapulted the actor Ronald Reagan into power) meshed with the antiregulation campaigns of the 1980s to create the basis for an unfettered banking sector that would consolidate previously siloed sectors of insurance, real estate, and finance. Their collective power was driven in part by new financial tools designed for big urban projects at a time (circa the 1970s) when cities like New York City were declaring bankruptcy, and the federal government was retreating from its long-standing commitment to support its cities through grants and low-interest loans. Consequently, US mayors increasingly had little choice but to turn to financial firms for capital to run their cities. The largest financial firms responded with a set of tools that required cities to increase and redirect existing revenue streams (e.g., taxes and user fees) as well as create new ones to pay back financial firms for both the borrowed capital and the high interest and management fee rates slapped onto each loan. The aggregate of these transactions led to a sizable flow of capital from cities to a handful of the most powerful financial firms and their privately controlled capital markets (Gotham 2009; Hackworth 2007). Separating city management from its finances was a major step toward generating a new regime of financialized urban governance (Hildreth and Zorn 2005).[1]

The US government's retreat from its urban responsibilities occurred during a time of crisis and conjuncture. In the 1970s cities were hit hard by a series of cascading events. The disappearance of manufacturing left vacant, decaying infrastructure and empty wallets. In 1978 California ushered in a major tentpole of the neoliberal revolution via Proposition 13, or the ballot initiative popularly known as the People's Initiative to Limit Property Taxation. This amendment to the state constitution substantially reduced urban tax revenue generation and inspired similar political campaigns across the nation. Soon after, the US savings and loans collapsed, after which the Glass–Steagall Act was repealed, no longer preventing the isolated sectors of finance, insurance, banking, and real estate from consolidating. These shifts inspired a new political economy that left cities on their own to find capital resources in the unregulated open marketplace (Fligstein and Habinek 2014; Fligstein and Goldstein 2010; Epstein 2005; Harvey 2007, 2005). Through sagging urban economies and rising neoliberal policies, the practices of financial firms and city management became more closely linked.

For example, the newly consolidated banking-and-finance sector across the country was no longer obliged to lend locally or keep reasonable capital reserve ratios, thus introducing extra risks into cities' borrowing practices. City managers and redevelopment agencies were urged by financial consultants to create special tax districts that would offer tax breaks to businesses willing to set up shop as a way to revitalize neglected neighborhoods. Another financial tool introduced by Wall Street was tax increment financing (TIF) and its various offshoots. Starting slowly in California in the 1950s, but exploding across the country by the 1990s, TIFs basically are a value-capture revenue tool that uses municipal bonds and the taxes from anticipated future gains in real estate values to pay for new infrastructure improvements today (Pacewicz 2013). Cities use tax incentives and subsidies to lure developers and investors to a yet-to-be-gentrified area of the city, with the belief that those projects would not have come without incentives and subsidies and that once they come, they will generate ample tax revenues in the future to be shared with the rest of the city.

The evolving and consolidating financial industry, in the wake of California's monumental Proposition 13 vote, created terms for borrowing that transferred control away from city councils and into these financialized mechanisms (Moser 2013, 2012). By the end of the 1980s, 90 percent of spending on public works in California had shifted from federal to local and state governments, and then from local and state governments to special districts and special funding mechanisms (Kirkpatrick and Smith 2011; Campbell 2010). Wall Street's new tools weren't merely mainstreamed in California's outsize economy (the fifth-largest in the world if it were a country); they were positioned as the sole option for city finance (Lefcoe and Swenson 2014).

Soon, TIFs and special tax districts caught on nationally. As many of the TIF redevelopment projects did not produce additional revenues for the city as promised by financial analysts and boosters, cities then had to pull financial resources from other neighborhoods and essential public services to foot the bill for these TIF loans and bonds. This shifting of essential resources from much-needed areas to risky real estate ventures plagues cities across the country. The developers and city politicians who agree with their financial prognosticators are not held liable for the mistaken impression of future revenues. The risk creates a regressive tax on marginalized communities and their public services.

By 2006 California boasted 4,778 special tax districts, offering a quasi-private array of public goods, services, and infrastructure based on $68 billion in outstanding long-term bonds and reflecting a substantial chunk of the $2.7 trillion municipal bond market (Kirkpatrick and Smith 2011).[2] These special districts, and their investors, received a sizeable portion of tax receipts originally managed by local governments to distribute to the whole city. Consequently, governments—and their public schools and social services—are left being ruled by contractual obligations to repay bondholders and their underwriters first.[3]

Shifting from Public to Corporate Financing
of Urban Redevelopment

Nationally, the Tax Reform Act was passed in 1986, and by 1991 the municipal bond market swung from "a placid environment" to "a frenetic and arcane market" with dramatic growth of "private activity bonds," promoting "securities where the proceeds are utilized for a project or a purpose that benefit[s] a private entity" (Campbell 2010). From the Depository Institutions Deregulation and Monetary Control Act (1980) to the Tax Reform Act to the Gramm–Leach–Bliley Act (1999; also known as the Financial Services Modernization Act), which repealed the 1933 Glass–Steagall Act, national legislators brought down the walls once separating a multitude of discrete financial institutions such as credit unions, savings and loans, banks, Wall Street firms, and insurance companies. The rush to corporate mergers birthed megafinance institutions that are no longer beholden to depositors for access to their capital, nor restricted from designing new tools and strategies for high-risk speculative behaviors. Many cities were lulled into believing they could revitalize their moribund downtown or decrepit waterfront with a world-class "renaissance center" or towering central business district, in cities emptied of well-paid manufacturing and well-secured public sector jobs.

Among the most popular emerging financial techniques for US cities were TIF deals. They offered cash, up front, to finance construction and redevelopment in what were initially described as blighted urban sites. These TIFs financed projects from opera halls to the development of peri-urban farmland by borrowing against expected future property tax revenues from the completion of these urban improvements. Most states allow TIFs, but the score sheet is bleak for TIFs' success at generating more revenue than what is owed. The tourist-magnet and wealth-generating real estate development of Hudson Yards in New York City is one recent example that is considered a TIF success by the real estate industry but had cost taxpayers at least $2.5 billion of increased taxes by 2022 (B. Fisher and Leite 2020; Hudson Yards Infrastructure Corporation 2017; New York City Independent Budget Office 2004). Across the city, New York allows for $10 billion per year in tax exemptions for firms that promise economic development. Hudson Yards promised "much-needed" office space even though by 2024 more than 20 percent of New York's office space remained unoccupied; meanwhile, Hudson Yards is an extremely prosperous enterprise that offers luxury residences but pays little in property taxes.[4]

These tax exemptions and revenue bonds are negotiated and underwritten by Wall Street firms like Citibank, Goldman Sachs, and Morgan Stanley. They are the underwriters of the Hudson Yards' economic redevelopment bonds, as they are of other needy enterprises like Madison Square Garden and the Yankees and Mets baseball stadiums. Crain's New York Business News (Elstein 2023) called these types of revenue bonds and tax subsidies one of the fastest growing industries in New York.

Chicago is one of the densest sites of TIF districting and TIF-related debt, and most of the city's public resources are funneled to these districts, emptying the city coffers for the rest of the city. Half of Chicago's TIF funds flow into the central business district, the Loop, which houses the city's major corporations but only a tiny percentage of the working population. Much of the rest of TIF financing goes to predominantly white neighborhoods or adjacent BIPOC ones being gentrified by these tax-free investment vehicles. Since 1984, 185 of Chicago's TIF districts have received $5 billion in subsidies and bond funding; yet by 2022, they failed to return that amount to the city in the form of property taxes (Hackett 2023). As many of the TIF promises have soured across the city, a large percentage of revenues from city taxes and fees leave the city for the bond market. The TIF-driven financialization practice is considered one of the foremost reasons that Chicago (and the State of Illinois) landed in such dire economic conditions by 2008 (Luby and Moldogaziev 2014; R. Weber 2010).

Speculating with Mortgage-Backed Securities

At the same time that US cities were caught in the TIF snare, working-class communities of color were given the "opportunity" to pursue the American dream of homeownership: The federal government created incentives for first-time borrowers to jump into the deregulated industry of mortgage lenders, and that market swelled by the early 2000s. With the rapid expansion of the internet at the same time, there was no shortage of new lenders (many internet based) offering guaranteed loans to all who applied. The mortgage industry exploded with a lucrative opportunity for financiers to securitize these new revenue flows, which attracted domestic and international capital. Bundles of mortgages were purchased with short-term finance procured in the US asset-backed commercial paper (ABCP) market by financial firms at very low interest rates, revealing how different market players colluded to facilitate speculative bubbles in mortgages, in mortgage-backed securities, and in the movement of capital across markets around the world.

Whereas a single-home mortgage is an illiquid and tenuous cash flow—a worker's layoff can stop the payments immediately—thousands of bundled mortgages can be more predictable for global financial investors and thus became a desirable asset (G. Davis and Kim 2015). Mortgage-backed securities divide mortgages up into bonds, and within those, they are divided by different risk profiles. The higher the risk, the higher the possible return for bond investors. This type of gambling, on its own, became a multibillion-dollar industry in the early 2000s.

First-time buyers, mostly working-class borrowers, became the new ownership class in the United States. Behind the scenes, the sellers—financial firms with few or no bank deposits or reserves—resold the mortgages as securities to large institutional investors. Each transaction was funded by ABCPs, a type of invented liquid capital that was collateralized by other financial assets from structured investment vehicles that were typically offshore and out of reach of US regulators (Tooze 2018).[5] No regulator, economist, or members of the general public could follow or comprehend the dizzying array of sleight-of-hand maneuvers. All we knew was that there existed a spectacular boom in the housing sector, open, for the first time, to all.

Insiders, however, knew exactly how flimsy the repackaged mortgages were when they hit the market as securitized (sliced and diced) bonds. Lehman Brothers was the largest producer of subprime (i.e., high-risk, flimsy) mortgage securities; at the market's explosive height, Lehman expanded its assets by purchasing two large mortgage firms. But by September 2008, when approximately nine million mortgage holders were fired from their jobs, the US media figured out that something was amiss. The recession hit at the same time as ballooning mortgage interest rates—"teaser" rates of below 4 percent more than tripled. Lehman was no longer receiving its payments and instantly owed hundreds of billions of dollars to its backers. Lehman needed to borrow tens of billions from the government *daily* just to keep up with its commitments. The house of cards was exposed. No one was willing to lend to keep Lehman afloat, as rumors circulated that several other key firms were about to buckle from insurmountable debt. One of them, France's Société Générale, had ironically won the Derivatives Bank of the Year award a month earlier from leading experts in the field unwilling to pay heed to the implosion occurring right under their feet (Fligstein and Habinek 2014).

Gambling on Interest Rate Swaps

US cities did not go bankrupt because homebuyers couldn't pay their mortgages or because Lehman Brothers collapsed. Cities went bankrupt because they were caught in a convergence of financialization hustles. Mortgage-backed securities and TIFs were two of the main financial gambles thrust on cities; a third was an equally mysterious tool that must have amused elite financiers in their back-office conversations—they are called *interest rate swaps.* In an illustrative example of this winner-take-all gamble, Stockton, California, borrowed more than $100 million between 2004 and 2006 to rebuild its crumbling city hall and construct a riverside renaissance commercial center to generate tourist revenue, a seemingly improbable ambition for a city with a reputation for being poor and run-down. But instead of using traditional municipal bonds or federal or state-backed support to raise the money, the city's financial advisers offered Stockton a deal based on the wager that interest rates would soon rise—that is, interest rate swaps. In the real world at that time, with economies struggling to regain their footing, the US Federal Reserve kept rates close to zero. Consequently, Stockton and other cities that rolled the dice and hoped that rates would rise as promised had to pay back hundreds of millions *more* than they had borrowed.

Similarly, the New York City Metro Transit Authority (MTA) needed to raise capital to rebuild dangerously decrepit infrastructure at the very moment capital became scarce; financial firms offered borrowers only these dubious swaps as their lending option. The MTA paid a net $658 million under a series of swap contracts between 2000 and 2011. Under political pressure from public outcry, the transit authority insisted on terminating the interest rate swap contract. Alas, in its fine print, the contract required that MTA pay an additional $1.3 billion to end the deal, which had already led to the layoff of two thousand employees and left New Yorkers with 66 percent higher transit fares.

Between 2006 and 2008, US financial firms held a record $18.4 *trillion* in interest rate contracts, and by 2012 only four firms (JPMorgan Chase, Citibank, Bank of America, and Goldman Sachs) controlled 93 percent of total derivative holdings (Bank for International Settlements 2009). That is, an oligopoly of the largest firms fully controlled a market of lending they themselves had invented. These are just some examples of city finances going south from deals with Wall Street. A pattern emerged that set the conditions for a monumental crisis, the likes of which the United States hadn't seen since the late 1920s, the last time finance capital had effectively wielded such sizable power and high yields.

Finance Capital Becomes the Driver
of the National Economy

Behind the veil of this dramatic set of changes arose what the International Monetary Fund (IMF) calls "the shadow banking system," which is massive in size and scope, largely unregulated, undocumented, and untaxed (Campbell 2010; Kodres 2013; Poznar et al. 2010). By the early 2000s, large financial firms such as Goldman Sachs, Morgan Stanley, and the newly consolidated Citigroup garnered more assets and power and global reach than the traditional banking system could ever imagine.[6] Because of its size, practices, and unregulated nature, the shadow banking system has had an inordinate effect on cities' ability to access capital, and the conditions of such access. The array of mysterious financial tools available from the shadow banking system included collateralized debt obligations (a $30 billion market), credit card debt (a $400 billion market in the United States), the credit default swaps ($60 trillion), and the repo or repurchase market ($12 trillion), which, many scholars argue, were the triggers for the financial crisis (Tooze 2018; Gorton and Metrick 2012; Campbell 2010). When foreign banks, financial institutions, and governments saw the wild profits being raked up in the United States, they jumped into the game, empowering US financial firms to create and spread globally these structured risks in the form of securitized assets based on their own predictions of future revenue flows. Speculative urbanism is being shaped by the shadow banking system's skillfulness at promoting its own superpowers of future divining.

Securitization is a fundamental enabler of financialization (G. Davis and Kim 2015, 207). It mobilizes assets with cash flows—think mortgage payments, toll fees, auto loans, credit card debt, pension savings—and converts them into tradeable securities or bonds. It facilitates the intermediation of finance into the larger economy and institutionalizes the underlying logic of late twentieth-century financial capitalism: maximizing shareholder value by creating opportunities for profit from the most liquid assets coming from the ownership of the least amount of assets. By not owning the physical structure but controlling the cash flow from it, financiers can minimize their risk and yet earn sizable rents from the monopolization of that flow.

A 2024 UK *Guardian* article summarized the "financialisation on steroids" of the UK water system owned by Thames UK and purchased by asset management firm Macquarie: "In the 2000s, investment banks began to realize that there was an opportunity to acquire the water company assets and to put significantly more leverage [i.e., debt] on to those capital structures." Investment banks skewed incentives and created "the predisposition of thinking of water companies as financial assets." Shortly after Macquarie bought it, Thames embarked on a "'whole business securitization' in 2007—a fundraising whose banal name belied its aggressive approach. A previously staid business of pipes and sewage treatment works was packaged into a complex corporate structure, with eight layers of ownership—including a subsidiary in the Cayman Islands, which allowed debt to be layered on debt, like the tiers in a wedding cake" (Pratley 2024).

Of course, this golden rule of the lightest base of assets ran counter to the buildup of the world's most productive and profitable corporations of the mid-twentieth century—making cars, steel, machinery, tractors, tanks, airplanes, and more. Yet it has become the business model of not only the financial sector but the world's largest corporations, which it influences—Google/Alphabet, Amazon, Microsoft, Facebook/Meta, and NVIDIA.

Before the 2008 crash, most urban cash flows had been securitized, adding up to trillions of dollars of investment and paying lucrative profits to the financial firms packaging them. One simple sign that securitizing urban assets was lucrative for finance capital is reflected in the astronomical compensation to their brotherhood of top CEOs. According to Steven Kaplan and Joshua Rauh (2010), the top five hedge managers in the early 2000s earned more than all the CEOs in the top five hundred companies combined. As a second sign of their power, senior managers of alternative finance firms (like private equity) now occupy the majority of the board of directors' seats inside nonfinancial corporations in the United States, signifying a major shift from business and industry experts in those positions to largely Wall Street elites (K.-H. Lin and Tomaskovic-Devey 2013).

Since the 1980s approximately $6 trillion (in 2011 dollars) had transferred from the overall economy into the financial sector, mostly as profitable rents, as delineated above (Tomaskovic-Devey and Lin 2011). This transfer of wealth should not be interpreted as business as usual, nor as smooth sailing for most denizens of US cities. Historically excluded populations were pulled into these speculative ventures, with devastating effects on them and their neighborhoods. I argue that we can best understand this major phenomenon as a product of patrimonial networks of elite actors orchestrating world-altering shifts in capitalist social relations. Major financial firms, business consultants, and leading government officials (including congressional leaders and pivotal city mayors) came together to ignite this new governmental culture of betting on financial tools to pay their bills and provide public services. Furthermore, urban financialization was only possible through multiple forms of active dispossession. These practices not only dragged the excluded into these volatile markets but also enriched the always-included.

If we look beyond this US case, we can see very different origins of the urban financialization process and very dissimilar results.

Global Urbanism in Spain: Overpromising and Overconstructing

The unique trajectory of Spain's urban housing market and the rise of speculative investment markets in the lead-up to the financial crisis help us understand the precrisis origins of national-level speculative urbanism. A relational-conjunctural standpoint positions us to see what happens leading up to the crisis; how the rupture affects the different arenas of finance, property, and government; and how they realign toward a more globalized speculative urbanism. For Spain, the first significant shift in the structure of the housing market occurred in the 1950s, as rural migrants flooded into Spain's cities due to untenable postwar conditions in the countryside. The influx created an urban crisis of migrants living in shanties, even caves and stables (López and Rodríguez 2011).

As discontent spread among the urban working class, General Francisco Franco tried to forestall their demands for socialist-type relations by building state-subsidized, but privately owned, housing and offering urban rent laws to incentivize affordable housing. In a marked departure from most of western Europe, Franco's housing director, José Luis Arrese, proclaimed in 1957, "Let's make a country of homeowners, not proletarians" (López and Rodríguez 2011). The Franco regime hoped to pacify an agitated public by tying the populace to home mortgages. The central state gave developers substantial subsidies and provided workers with cheap loans from its Mortgage Bank. After the devastation of the Spanish Civil War, in a quest to maintain social peace amid great inequality and tension, the dictator pushed an agenda of subsidized home financing and private homeownership (Gonick 2021).

That model of rule lasted until the rupture of the global recession of 1973–75, which hit Spain hard. Although this crisis overlapped with the death of Franco (1975) and a change in power, the political transition to socialist party leadership did not alter macroeconomic policies much. The new Spanish leaders adopted some of the key neoliberal policies of the United Kingdom's Margaret Thatcher and the United States' Ronald Reagan. They reduced state spending for social welfare and public goods, reduced taxes for the corporate sector and elites, sold off and privatized public enterprises, undermined public sector union power, slapped user fees on most public services, and increased the power and authority of finance capital and its new vehicles (e.g., pension funds) for accessing household wealth and governmental resources.

These neoliberal policies transformed social relations of land and property, as well as relations between the government and capital markets, and reintegrated Spain into the postcolonial globalizing economy. By the early 1990s, Spain and eleven other nations formed the European Union with a shared citizenship, a single currency, a common security platform, and a strengthened European Parliament. The steps to full integration of European countries into a single market opened the continent to the much-touted four freedoms of the Maastricht Treaty of 1992 and the monetary union of the eurozone (1999). These included the free movement of goods, services, capital, and people. But what did these freedoms actually mean for the people of Spain?

Isidro López and Emmanuel Rodríguez (2011) interpret this period of transformation as *neoliberal euro-ization*, a three-pronged policy that took the public on a rollercoaster ride of property value boom and bust. First, it produced low interest rates and a fall in the price of credit across the continent. Second, the eurozone monetary union enabled leading European economies (e.g., Italy, Germany, France, England) to shift their capital surpluses to weaker economies such as Spain's, which had lower-valued assets and regions that were off-limits for foreign investment, making it easier to secure higher returns on their investments. Third, the dominant powers of northern Europe pushed for increased privatization of state enterprises with cheaper-valued infrastructure.

Even after Franco's fall, the terms *state-subsidized* and *public* continued to refer to state-assisted private housing; moreover, renting was penalized through the Spanish tax structure (Palomera 2014, 222). By the 1990s, however, backers of the real estate sector pressed for passage of two key acts: Spain's Urbanism and Land Act of 1990 and the 1998 Land Act, jokingly known as the "build anywhere act" (López and Rodríguez 2011). These acts opened previously off-market land for purchase, triggering a frenzy of speculative buying and selling (Coq-Huelva 2013). From 1995 to 2006, Spain created seven million jobs, mostly in low-paying services and construction, and the economy grew at a rapid rate of nearly 4 percent (López and Rodríguez 2011, 5). Although wages were close to the lowest in western Europe, by 2007, 87 percent of families owned homes, the highest rate in Europe (10). With little growth in industrial production, the national economy instead specialized in what elites and firms from northern and eastern Europe desired: sun, property, and asset accumulation. Since exports were down in all categories in the 1990s—except land values and rents—Spanish policymakers decided that it was pointless to compete to produce and export goods in a highly competitive European market when land values could grow so fast and high. Even the country's former trade staples, like ham and car parts, couldn't compete with the promise of value capture from the incredible rise in the real estate market.

The historic introduction of the euro as a unified currency in 1999 sparked a flood of capital flowing into Spain. German, French, and English investors were attracted by Spain's low land values and beautiful coasts, which had previously restricted large-scale real estate development. Spain's regional governments invited European developers to take advantage of relatively cheaper and less restrictive land, labor, and tax regimes and invest in the buildup of its coastline with housing, tourist destinations, casinos, and more. By the early 2000s, Spain was second only to the United States in net foreign capital import, most of which was channeled into land and housing speculation (García 2010). Housing growth greatly outpaced population densities, albeit unevenly, as government resources and foreign investments engulfed coastal areas and a few main cities, draining the economies, populations, and prospects of other parts of Spain. In cities such as Málaga, Murcia, and Alicante, the 102 percent increase in foreign direct investment in real estate between 1998 and 2006 meant that housing units soon outnumbered inhabitants. By 2008 coastal Málaga had roughly forty thousand excess homes. At the national level, more than 6.5 million new housing units were built in nine years, such that the ratio of housing to people hit 1:1.83 in 2008. At its best, Spain's annual housing construction topped one million units per year, more than in Germany, Italy, and France combined (García 2010, 969).

In tourism and real estate industries, Spain emerged as Europe's new playground—a place of leisure and a source of wealth that could compete with Portugal and Greece. Regional governments across Spain were primed to outspend and outbuild each other to entice investors and accommodate the expectations of globally competitive Europe, which demanded world-class football stadiums, international airports, high-speed trains, and privatized toll roads (making Spain's the densest network in Europe). In the 2000s Spain experienced stunningly high economic growth, with credit and real estate bubbles inflated by this unregulated speculative capital in local markets. The 1992 Maastricht Treaty helped reengineer Spain's economy from highly regulated export-oriented industry and agriculture to deregulated services, real estate, and tourism. The latter sectors became far more lucrative—though volatile—because they were based on, and fed, skyrocketing real estate values.

For a brief period, the Spanish economy did well through what Robert Brenner (2006) calls "asset-price Keynesianism," in which banks were incentivized to offer cheap loans and the state provided subsidized money to stimulate investment in the speculative sectors of real estate and the stock market (Norris and Byrne 2015). The rising value of household financial and property assets provided high demand for financial products, and the finance sector experienced incredible profit rates. Reduced social and infrastructure spending by the state created the opportunity for high finance to take over the state's job in providing infrastructure and services. In the 2000s public spending for public goods was down, and wages suffered, but borrowing was high, and asset values soared in this new rentier economy.

The World Bank and bilateral agencies advocated for the global urban turn in lending and urban planning, and a new network of expertise on cities contrived global-city strategies; early on, they focused on Barcelona as a trailblazer in the art of global urbanism. This transnational policy network (TPN) was populated by global consultancy firms (e.g., McKinsey, PricewaterhouseCoopers), UN agencies (e.g., UN-Habitat, the UN Development Programme), international financial institutions (e.g., the World Bank, the Asian Development Bank), and newly organized forums cosponsored by real estate and infrastructure firms, events that were based in Europe (and Barcelona in particular).

In major cities of Spain, a national public campaign worked in solidarity with this global effort to fuel a nationwide shift to speculation. Recent college graduates could walk into the local bank to borrow for their first scooter but come out with a home loan. Knowing their first job would be low paying, young borrowers followed the cautionary note of the labor market and the enthusiasm of the real estate market: Invest in property and watch your assets grow. At the height of the property bubble, between 2003 and 2006, house prices were rising 30 percent *annually* (López and Rodríguez 2011). If, in three-plus years, you could double your investment, securing wealth that your wages would never bring, why not borrow to buy three properties? Europe's major banks followed suit, with Germany's Landesbanks, Barclay's, Deutsche Bank, and ING rushing to invest in Spanish banks, mortgage pools, and murky real estate deals. At the height of the bubble in 2007, 25 percent of Spaniards owned two or more homes for speculative purposes, all built on a sandy heap of cheap credit and a bounty of hope.

The lofty domain of finance capital infiltrated not just wealthy neighborhoods and business logics but also the world of the urban poor. In his ethnography of Barcelona's so-called run-down immigrant neighborhood of Ciutat Meridiana, Jaime Palomera (2014) found housing prices soaring at the same phenomenal rate as the rest of expensive Barcelona. With only 1.5 percent of housing being public in the sense of state-subsidized rentals, and an abundance of empty investment homes, the poor feared they would be put out into the streets unless they bought before prices rose even higher. Credit was offered for as much as 120 percent of the price of the home, in the buoyant expectation that home prices would always rise. Urban residents, from fruit merchants to hairdressers, borrowed on easy credit to purchase homes. Many became liaisons to banks to bring in new customers, especially in their network of arriving immigrants. One million of Spain's six million new foreign migrants became homeowners before the crash. According to Palomera, the long-standing culture of the established immigrant community providing for newcomers until they found their footing was rapidly converted into a financialized relationship. Every new migrant became a potential renter, one who could help bail out those laden with ballooning mortgage payments. One of Palomera's informants, a Latin American fruit seller, explained that at the height of the market, she sold more apartments than apples. Barcelona's immigrant urban poor speculated to survive. Like in the United States, predatory inclusion was a central dynamic of speculative urbanism in Spanish cities.

Meanwhile, the ongoing infrastructure campaign had each region of the country attempting to outdo the other by building world-class airports, football stadiums, tourist spectacles, casinos, and high-speed trains. Valencia, for example, spent more than $730 million in 2007 on a Formula One racetrack, charging more than $300 per ticket for elite Europeans to be amused by precision driving while it displaced a long-standing fishing community. Valencia also built the priciest European tourist attraction of the decade, the City of Arts and Science (figure 2.1). It cost more than $1.5 billion to build, plus a rumored $750 million bonus to the local star architect. Locals were unwilling and unable to pay the exorbitant entry fees, and local street protests occurred repeatedly, but city leaders insisted that it was a success story. While the arts complex remained unprofitable for the city, it was only one of a series of white elephants planned in the first decade of the 2000s. Valencia's second international airport remained empty and unfinished for more than a decade, and its third football stadium was half-built and bankrupt.

In Barcelona the model of urban development was a manifestation of the social neoliberalism common in many western European cities. In this model, unlimited building construction was matched with basic commitments to continue to provide public goods and services. In the late 1980s, the socialist Barcelona municipal administration struck a compromise with the more conservative-nationalist provincial government of Catalonia. They agreed to maintain open and interlinked public spaces but under the conditions of a state-subsidized explosion of private real estate development. The Barcelona model had multiple phases, which shifted as the local economy grew in fits and starts. The mega-infrastructure phase started with winning the 1986 bid for the 1992 Olympics, which required the city to clear out working-class

2.1 City of Arts and Sciences complex in Valencia, Spain, built between 1996 and 2009 at an enormous public debt of more than $1.5 billion and visited primarily by elite tourists who can afford the expensive price of admission.

communities and sites to build formidably priced edifices of sports, housing, and tourism. The Barcelona model of mega-event infrastructure traveled far and wide as an enviable success story. Barcelona's city leaders, meanwhile, evolved as high-paid globe-trotting consultants, spreading the gospel of finance-driven urbanization abroad.

Some of the most transformative changes in Barcelona included the gutting of the old industrial area, the Poblenou of the so-called Catalan Manchester. It was replaced with the Olympic Village of sports, cultural and residential complexes, and the reopening of the city to its four-mile coastline, once marred by a high-polluting industrial port that bustled from the late nineteenth century until the 1970s. These Olympics-driven transformations perpetuated the Franco-era obsession with destroying history and heritage, in this case a rich industrial heritage and working-class neighborhoods, seen as obstacles to positive change. This produced a "programmed 'amnesia' . . . the aim being to erase the city's working-class memory by demolishing popular and cooperative centres, old social housing and factories" (Montaner 2010,

CHAPTER TWO

53). The project did not include in its grand plans the construction of much-needed social housing for the many residents who were displaced and priced out of the new real estate–driven paradigm of city living. Although Barcelona was somewhat unique in the amount of new public space and public culture created, it elbowed out local populations from city spaces remade to privilege international tourists and the resulting high-rent marketplace.

After Olympian infrastructural changes, the city underwent a property boom that lasted until the global financial crisis of 2008, when the Spanish economy, like so many other economies around the world, collapsed under the weight of speculative finance. The limits to the Barcelona model became apparent to those who experienced it as a "city of [high] rents" (Charnock et al. 2014). The roots of the spectacular boom and collapse can be traced to three entangled processes: first, the passing of major land and banking reform policies that opened wide swaths of land for speculation driven by cheap loans; second, the 1990s European monetary integration with the euro and the maintenance of cheap credit and low or negative interest rates; and, third, the globalizing trend toward financialization of urban assets that attracted global investors to Spain but provided no guarantees the capital would stay in Spanish cities. These investors often wrote the rules of the game, which allowed them to remain only for the short term and to exit without penalty and without obligations to contribute positively to city life (Goldman and Narayan 2021; Charnock et al. 2014, 203).

Amid signs of increased volatility after the Olympics (post-1992), city leaders tried to prop up economic growth and attract new investors by converting the more lethargic areas of the city, profit-wise, into knowledge districts driven by the notion of a knowledge-based economy. In this second phase of the Barcelona model, city officials converted public land and buildings into reclassified zones with increased-density rights, to create the environment for what is called *private value capture* and to build up incubators of IT innovation with infrastructure supplied by the public. The 22@ project is one example of this in the heart of deindustrialized Barcelona. As late as 2007, just prior to the crisis, the investment arms of Credit Suisse, the Spanish bank BBVA, the German fund Difa, and the French fund AXA were acquiring new office towers forecasted to have "good capital appreciation" (Charnock et al. 2014, 206). But few of the innovative value-adding IT firms arrived; instead, the torch of innovation was replaced with already existing real estate firms and tourism-related businesses. The romantic notion of twenty-first-century knowledge as a vehicle for transforming undervalued districts was undermined by a lack of interest from the global productive sector. Instead, some of the most common renters in these incubator sites were low-end, low-wage, low-rent call centers, something one might expect in cities in Bulgaria and the Philippines rather than in the European beacon of the twenty-first-century global city.

The Spanish case reveals important differences compared to the United States. As discussed earlier, economic downturns in the United States due to deindustrialization and intensified international competition in the productive sectors (which include manufacturing and mining) were translated by elite policy networks into opportunities for finance capital. Neoliberalism's promoters sold the idea that deregulating the FIRE (finance, insurance, and real estate) sector was fundamental to the promises of economic revitalization and individual freedom, and unfettered financial firms consolidated and expanded by extracting financial rents from arenas once deemed pedestrian types of income flow, like home mortgages, toll road fees, and so on. As more income streams were channeled profitably into the financial sector, very little infrastructure improvement or modernization occurred. At the peak of this post-1970s phase of urban financialization, US cities were left in debt and infrastructurally feeble, with, in many cases, increased social inequalities between minoritized people of color and white populations.

The Spanish case offers us a very different view. After the fall of Franco's regime, the circulating neoliberal agenda steered the Spanish government to build big across its major cities and link them with state-of-the-art transit systems that could take people (and new investors) to every point within the Spanish territory. By the early 2000s, the financial sector had consolidated and transnationalized, with the business model of seeking out new revenue streams to control and securitize, such as construction and home mortgage loans. The ambition, which became a national obsession of hope and risk, was to harness European speculative real estate desires and pave the beautiful and once-protected coastline (and the outlying areas of major cities) with unlimited second and third homes for locals and internationals. By 2006 this form of speculative urbanism had radically altered the physical and social-psychological landscape of Spain. By 2008, for both the United States and Spain, their speculative bubbles burst with the global crisis, producing a reconfigured financial world that became more deeply interconnected, profitable, and powerful.

The next section highlights the case of India and its contributions to the global urban turn. I focus on the main initiatives engineered to stimulate a revolution in how Indian cities would be financed and governed. The trajectory was different from those of the United States and Spain, yet we can see how global patrimonial networks worked to prime Indian elite institutions and networks to become an equally important contributor to the global phenomenon of speculative urbanism.

India: The Advent of Neoliberal Reforms and the Transformation of Urban Finances

India's late twentieth-century history is, of course, starkly different from Spain's and the United States', and yet there are similar transformative processes in play. The tensions surrounding India's shift to liberalization in the 1980s were extremely high. A hornet's nest of activity engulfed city managers and midlevel bureaucrats during these times. Using state debt and economic stagnation as leverage, consultants and high-level officials everywhere pushed for an array of fast-changing priorities to convert Indian cities into economic machines. These new models of financing urban infrastructure meant the abandonment of decades of postindependence accomplishments, including import-substitution industrialization, India's semiautonomy from the Global North, and local forms of democratization.

One of the key tenets of India's liberalization was to privilege India's corporate sector while at the same time encouraging foreign corporate investment. It was a difficult but necessary dance, according to political elites, that included the revoking of the postcolonial import-substitution economy that was premised on the political commitment to replace all British-imposed imports with indigenously produced alternatives. To make this monumental move, the national government began to deregulate and privatize the vast public sector that ruled the productive economy. It was a juicy bone offered to both foreign and domestic corporations (Kundu 2013; Zérah et al. 2011).

The ecosystem of corporate financial institutions also made inroads in the national agenda, although more slowly, through the promotion of major policy shifts concerning land conversion and urban change. Corporate finance worked to promote the grand promise that India's best hope for becoming a player in the global economy was to build world-class infrastructure and replace the bad image it had around the world—the well-publicized sordid life of India's "chaotic and unsanitary" cities (World Bank 2015; Sankhe et al. 2010). During India's neoliberal period, foreign and domestic finance capital and its allied policy network pressured the Indian state to liberalize access to land, weaken labor protection laws, and allow for greater access to off-limits markets, such as banking, insurance, finance, and real estate (Ruparelia et al. 2011; Breman 2013, 2010). As early as the 1990s, policy and corporate circles focused on the questions of who would pay for these ambitious capital-intensive infrastructural projects and what compromises would be made to attract wary foreign investors to what the West perceived as risky India (Goldman 2011). Some early initiatives included the idea of building a system of national toll roads that would link and inspire a series of luxury private townships and special economic zones (SEZs) to house new industries.

For India, the late 1980s and early 1990s were a pivotal and disruptive period. By 1990, though always small in size and reach, foreign direct investment (FDI) had almost completely exited India. There was no inflow of capital as the economy had free-fallen due to a series of global events, topped off by the US wars in Iraq and Kuwait, which had cut India off from its essential supply of gasoline and crucial dollar remittances from Indians working in the Gulf. The central government had relied on those dollars to repay external debt and keep investable money flowing through the public banks and into the economy. The early 1990s marked a time of major discontent in India, stirred up by what some activists called the *LPG crisis*— the combined forces of liberalization, privatization, and globalization.[7]

In January 1991, when the United States invaded Iraq and Kuwait, India's foreign reserves fell to less than $1.2 billion. By June it was only half that amount, with reserves estimated to last twenty days. The government was on the knife edge of complete default on its payment commitments to the World Bank and Asian Development Bank, as well as to importers of India's essential resources, such as gasoline, chemicals, and food. Most painfully, it had to pledge as collateral its precious gold reserves. Early in the year, the government airlifted two-thirds of its gold to the Bank of England and one-third to the Union Bank of Switzerland as promissory notes on the loans that these banks were willing to offer to keep the economy from total collapse. As if the whole experience wasn't humiliating enough for the government, the minister decided to transport the gold to the airport in the middle of night to avoid media attention, but, as if to symbolize spectacular defeat, the van broke down en route. News traveled fast, and amid widespread public outrage, the government fell. The new government, led by P. V. Narasimha Rao, started with a major shake-up: a transformative liberalization campaign, designed by Oxford-trained and UN-employed economist and new Finance Minister Manmohan Singh. Together with the IMF, the government enacted policies to open India's borders to foreign companies and dramatically reform the tangled regulatory system (commonly known by its derogatory nickname, the License Raj), as well as initiate a major disinvestment campaign to sell off many public sector industries, most of which were based in cities.

The groundwork to liberalize the economy had the full support and guidance of the IMF, the World Bank, USAID, the Japan International Cooperation Agency, and the Asian Development Bank. Together they negotiated a series of technical assistance grants with the central and state governments to promote private financing and the delivery of public services through privatization. This helped to catalyze a cultural shift in government, driven by the liberalization/privatization wave. However dismal the scene on the ground—with bank runs, food shortages, and cattle famines—the economic collapse offered a great opportunity for those advocating liberalization inside and outside India. The IFIS worked closely with an emergent lobby of elite bureaucrats, politicians, business leaders, and consultants to open avenues for foreign capital investment and accumulation. At the national level, trade and capital restrictions were abandoned, public sector industries were opened to international tie-ups and state disinvestment, and the Eighth Five-Year Plan (1992–97) introduced draconian steps of cost recovery into municipal finance systems. This was reinforced under the Ninth Five-Year Plan (1997–2002) with a "substantial reduction in budgeting allocations for infrastructure development" (Baindur and Kamath 2009, 16).

In 2006 the Infrastructure Leasing and Finance Services company was set up with a thirty-billion-rupee fund, named the Urban Infrastructure Fund. This fund created a new financial tool—the Pooled Municipal Debt Obligation financed in large part by the World Bank, the International Financial Corporation, and the Asian Development Bank. It tasked municipal and state governments to pool their resources and borrow together. In that way, they could collectively defray some of the risks for potential investors, acknowledging that individual cities alone were ill equipped to start borrowing from IFIS and private capital markets.

Meanwhile, USAID had been working behind the scenes on a three-phase program, the Finance Infrastructure Reform and Expansion-Debt (FIRE-D), that offered models for market financing of local government projects.

Subsequently, a raft of changes occurred. The government of India's influential *India Infrastructure Report* (Government of India 1996) delineated how cities must finance their work. The Ministry of Urban Development initiated a seven-year, sixty-four-city $20 billion program that directed cities to replace central government subsidies and guarantees with borrowed capital from the market and to implement user fees to increase revenues (Ministry of Urban Employment and Poverty Alleviation and Ministry of Urban Development 2005). In 2004 the Twelfth Finance Commission recommended in the starkest terms that cities be denied substantial shares of central government funding as a way to compel them to undertake development through borrowing from the market, a tactic reaffirmed in the Asian Development Bank report *Managing Asian Cities* (2007) and in the main strategy of USAID in India. The new discourse of global urbanism echoed throughout the words and deeds of India's major policy organizations during this tumultuous period of change. Meanwhile, the international consulting firms endorsed these actions, as captured in pivotal reports such as PricewaterhouseCoopers's *Cities of the Future* (2005) and *Cities of Opportunity* (2007) and McKinsey's report *Vision Mumbai* (Bombay First–McKinsey 2003).

At the EuroIndia Forum in Goa (2007), the keynote speaker, the CEO of Lafarge Paris, a major construction firm, declared enthusiastically that "the disastrous response to Hurricane Katrina and the Asia Flu shows us how important the private sector could be if the public sector would step aside." The director general of the Reserve Bank of India, in his "Policies for Accelerating Urban Growth" presentation, argued that "urban stagnation" is a direct result of an overly rigid and antiquated urban land policy, with its regressive landownership ceiling policies from the 1970s and rent control since the 1940s. He emphasized two key points. The first was the government's failure to adequately charge residents fees for public services; he expressed frustration over recent victories by Indian city dwellers who stopped the government from selling off their municipal water systems to European conglomerates. Second, he highlighted the government's failure to sufficiently liberalize restrictive land laws: "There is huge value *locked up* in urban land, money that could be used for urban infrastructure. Think of how many jobs get generated—and not just profit—from selling public land" (emphasis added).

That same year, I heard similar calls by senior officials in Bengaluru to accept this globalizing tide. At a public meeting in a middle-class neighborhood (February 2007), the city commissioner brashly declared what he considered necessary to convert Bengaluru into a European-style global city: "Clear the city of its slums and bring in world-class amenities like pubs and theaters." Elsewhere, city commissioners called for massive investments to convert crowded and run-down parts of town into entertainment complexes by transforming under-valued public spaces into privatized value creators that would benefit the new cosmopolitan citizen. For finance capital, these new ventures represent revenue streams or rents that can be securitized and circulate far and wide. These statements and notions reflect more than discrete individual confessions, revelations, and logics. One finds them articulated within Indian bureaucratic and elite circles—in PowerPoint presentations from PricewaterhouseCoopers staff, in bureaucrat training courses subsidized by the World Bank, in urban planning exercises, international fora on urban futures, and in Asian Development Bank loan portfolios (J. Robinson 2011).

The period of 2005–10 brought on a flurry of major reforms that eased access to land markets and real estate deals for foreign and domestic capital and increased sevenfold the inflow of FDI equity from that of the previous five years. This FDI flowed into manufacturing (21 percent), finance (19 percent), construction and real estate (17 percent), mining (0.8 percent), energy (4.5 percent), and agriculture (a measly 0.2 percent, even though farming is the sector in which most of India's population works). Thus, 36 percent of all FDI funneled into real estate and finance. Simply put, the race to invest in India during the exuberant phase prior to the 2008 crisis had largely focused on the sectors of finance, insurance, and real estate. Fifty percent of this foreign capital originated in Mauritius, and 11 percent in Singapore, with a total of 70 percent flowing from these and other tax havens that benefit foreign capital firms with double tax-free rules, enabling risk-averse investors to make money from the movement of capital across borders, currencies, and economies. These capital-flow earnings have become a substantial source of profit for financiers as well as a necessary risk-mitigating strategy for their investments that might fail to generate profit once they land within the volatile urban economy.

For Indians, the career of a professional involved in the global urban turn can be summarized as follows. First, according to my interviews with government officials, the trajectory of an ambitious administrative civil servant changed in this period, such that it became imperative that one's résumé include training programs run by the World Bank and the Administrative Staff College of India's Urban Management program in Hyderabad, originally designed by the World Bank Institute. These TPNs sought to train Indian professionals in the global art of the financial deal. For example, a 2009 workshop on strengthening urban management, cosponsored by the Administrative Staff College and World Bank Institute, featured modules such as "Creating Creditworthy Cities and Urban Systems," "Good Urban Governance and Decentralisation," and "Public Private Partnership in Urban Infrastructure and Service Delivery." Financialization was the main theme, and "strengthening urban governance through financialization" was the message.

Second, whereas previously only national government ministries could expect to borrow foreign finance capital from the IFIs, and the ministries in turn would offer grants to state governments and municipalities, both would now gradually be cut off from central government grants for basic urban services. State governments and cities would have to bid for international finance loans and grants, offering local governments new powers but also new risks as small service-providing bureaucracies had to negotiate directly with global investment firms and consultants. This required a whole new cultural engagement and finance-minded skill set that most local and regional administrators lacked. Loans from IFIs compelled municipalities to pivot away from central government grants and instead turn to capital markets for funding and advice. Aided by consultants from firms ensconced in the transnational arena of global-city making, local governmental agencies were asked to follow the prescriptions of TPN actors promoting this worldview of global urbanism.

Third, the central government of India initiated its own global-city investment strategy, the J. Nehru National Urban Renewal Mission (JN-NURM), which was initially created with support from USAID. Between 2005 and 2014, it channeled more than US$20 billion to sixty-two cities that made bids for project funding but with policy conditionalities. It encouraged forming corporate partnerships between foreign service providers and public goods managers in state agencies, borrowing capital from international markets and financing debt through municipal bonds, and converting municipal bureaucracies into competitive and "responsibilized" agents (Rose 1999) infused with new financial governance norms. India's major global-urban stimulus package of JNNURM sat precariously between the old no-strings-attached policy of central loans and grants and the new risk-filled (and disciplinary) policy of requiring participation in the power-laden and vertically integrated international marketplace of credit and debt.

An assessment of JNNURM implementation within the state of Karnataka, which contains the two large cities of Bengaluru and Mysore, reveals that four-fifths of the money was channeled to projects that financialized new and old urban infrastructure. Most of the money landed in these two large cities, not in the many smaller, infrastructure-poor cities. Approximately half of the infrastructure money was spent on transportation projects, such as ring roads, highways, airports, and the Metro system in Bengaluru—all of which have substantially negative climate effects and require the acquisition of large land tracts and therefore various forms of displacement. Although JNNURM advocates claim that the program directed money to "basic services to the urban poor," very little of this money flowing into Karnataka targeted low-income citizens, rural or urban (Pani and Iyer 2013).

A nationwide assessment of JNNURM explains how the program mirrored the TPN's global advocacy campaign (Baindur and Kamath 2009). The authors found that most of the policy reform objectives of the World Bank and Asian Development Bank in India were identical to the ones JNNURM ultimately required from state and city agencies.

As the JNNURM's mandates mimicked IFI directives and TPN advocacy, together they reflected the demands of international and domestic finance capital. As these rules and policies cohered, they percolated down to city planners and managers. Together with consultant-derived master plans, local consultant-driven private and public meetings, staff training courses, and the general expectation of city leaders that India's major cities would conform to these new global standards, local leaders began to visualize their cities anew. In a short time, one could hear leaders in public venues speak of the transformation of their old city markets into central business districts, of clusters of small shops and street-vending locales replaced by downtown shopping malls, and of irrigation tanks (small lakes) and village fields becoming sites of glass and steel corporate campuses for the new Googles of the business world.

Global Finance's Welcome to India

Back in 1990, annual foreign financial flows into India were $1.66 billion and hardly grew through 1999 (K. Rao and Dhar 2011). Then the boom came. Between 2000 and 2005, the annual average foreign investment jumped to nearly $3 billion, surging in the next five years to hit $20 billion in 2010, before it briefly collapsed in 2011. In other words, foreign capital flows more than doubled early on and then quadrupled by 2010. In 2011 capital vanished (temporarily), two years after its disappearance from US and European markets. In those two years, expectations rose dramatically as to what could be accomplished in India. High volumes of capital flowed into India and elsewhere in Asia precisely when financial institutions in the United States and Europe complained they had no capital to invest and required bailouts to survive, manipulating governments and public opinion to their advantage.

In this precrisis boom period, most foreign financial capital flowed into the Indian stock market, real estate/construction, and telecommunications. A large percentage of foreign capital was invested in mergers and acquisitions, creating short-term share price spikes, and a new financializing strategy for India. Less than 20 percent of this new capital flowed into manufacturing. This reflected a worldwide trend: According to Organisation for Economic Cooperation and Development (OECD) reports, across developing countries, between the 1980s and the 2000s, the proportion of foreign capital flowing into the financial sector grew from 6 percent to 21 percent, while capital flowing into manufacturing continued to decrease over time (OECD 2009, 2002).

It took until 2002 for finance capital to gain access to Indian real estate as an investment, and even then investments were restricted to what the government labeled socially productive endeavors, such as a new private township (of more than a hundred acres) built to ostensibly satisfy the nation's high demand for housing and jobs. It is important to note that the township's original minimum size requirement of a hundred acres was imposed as a deterrent to speculative investors who profited from short-term investments, extracting surpluses within short periods and then exiting, taking advantage of their ability to capture monopoly rents. In 2004, following China's lead, India opened SEZs to foreign capital, encouraging much-needed investment in the attenuated manufacturing sector, with the idea that FDI flows onto large swaths of rural or peri-urban land would ignite a renaissance in industrialization, followed by housing.

Even though the government sweetened the pot by promising to provide land and services, such as roads, water, and electricity, gratis, and adding multiyear tax breaks, most investors were uninterested in the slow returns of manufacturing. Instead, investors willing to enter India were drawn to the more lucrative and short-term economy of the land under these imagined factories, especially *if* they could also receive the land for free or at a drastically reduced price. Although SEZs started out as part of a postindependence policy to incentivize manufacturing and commodity production and produce high-value land, well-paid skilled jobs, and an invigorated Indian economy, by the 2000s SEZs became prime sites for global-city speculation and profit by finance capital.

Whereas Spain had its beachside resorts and luxury complexes on which to speculate, and the United States less glamorously had its decrepit infrastructure and neighborhoods that inspired new markets in lucrative debt financing and rent extraction, India had its SEZs as lures for high finance. Teams of international consultants drew up plans for massive national infrastructure projects that would link New Delhi in the north with Kolkata in the east, Hyderabad and Bengaluru in the South, Mumbai and Ahmedabad in the west, and back up to Delhi. Notions of a twenty-first-century India teeming with a world-class infrastructural network seamlessly linking new city expansion via state-of-the-art transport corridors of bullet trains and monorails occupied the elite imagination, harkening back to the imperial dreams of British finance capital. "Out-Shanghaiing Shanghai" was the slogan of spirited political leaders.

In 2005, as soon as Parliament and national leaders rewrote restrictive investment and land laws, foreign private equity began to trickle into India's real estate sector. Under pressure from chambers of commerce, real estate, and finance interests, SEZs across the country transitioned from industrial to real estate purposes, from productive to financial enterprises. In the first sixteen months of the 2005 SEZ Act's passage, nearly five hundred sites were approved. In contrast to the Chinese model, in which the government developed the zones for export-oriented industries, the Indian government's sole job has been to acquire land (what critics call land grabs), leaving the capital accumulation possibilities to financial investors.

On the cusp of the financial crisis, of the three countries, India was least shaken. Its banking sector was still largely immune from the high-risk gambles that were pervasive in large parts of Europe and North America. But the ground had been laid for a dramatic inflow of finance capital to help implement the lofty dreams of political leaders and the corporate sector. While the financial crisis unfolded in the United States and Spain, those same firms that cried scarcity at home were quietly but eagerly initiating new infrastructure investment funds for many parts of Asia, especially India.

Conclusion: Three Paths, One Direction

For each country case, this chapter presents the relational-conjunctural conditions for the rise of urban financialization, with its myriad opportunities, financial tools, public policy maneuvers, and corporate interventions. I demonstrate how finance's phenomenal run of wealth creation in the 1980s was based on a shifting discursive and corporate terrain that introduced the idea of newfound city-based assets. It was a phenomenon that expanded and intensified right up to the 2008 financial crisis. The rise of finance power occurs in these three countries differently, with distinct financial tools, objects of speculation, and elite political-discursive appeals. But by taking a relational-conjunctural approach, we see how these diverse contexts and conditions produce, over time, forms of power and authority for finance capital that eventually converge and consolidate. Conjunctural crises create new opportunities rooted in practices that work across sectors, cities, and time zones. When we look closely at patterns within countries, we see the multitude of ways finance capital creates the conditions for its growth and power.

This chapter highlights the convergence of discrete forces that propelled these countries into crisis. It also explains how the subsequent rupture shaped the worlds of finance, property, and government; and how they realigned toward a more globalized speculative urbanism. Chapter 3 explores in greater depth how finance capital took advantage of the 2008 crisis to create new opportunities for consolidation as a muscular sector with newfound power and authority over urban governance institutions across nations and continents.

CHAPTER 3

"THE BUBBLE ON
A WHIRLPOOL OF
SPECULATION"

AFTERLIVES OF THE FINANCIAL
CRISIS AND THE NEW URBAN
IMAGINARY

> Speculators may do no harm as bubbles on a steady stream
> of enterprise. But the position is serious when enterprise
> becomes the bubble on a whirlpool of speculation. When
> the capital development of a country becomes a by-product
> of the activities of a casino, the job is likely to be ill-done.
> —John Maynard Keynes, *The General Theory of Employ-*
> *ment, Interest and Money*, 1935

In stark contrast to Spain, India, Brazil, or Turkey, infrastructure in the
United States has been crumbling, and collapsing, since the 1980s. For
decades, the notion of infusing massive state funds into nationwide
infrastructure—especially when linked to climate crisis mitigation—
has faced serious roadblocks from market fundamentalists who instead
suggest that we impose toll roads and user fees and let the users pay
for infrastructure investment and repair. If market mechanisms fail to
generate adequate revenues, say these fundamentalists, then let cities
borrow from Wall Street, as that will always be more efficient and apo-
litical than any government investment or loan program.

Yet, as I have shown, and highlight in this chapter, Wall Street's loan
programs have become quite inefficient and highly political for many
cities around the world. Turning to speculative investors, or casino capitalists, to fund public and private infrastructure has been disastrous for

most cities and highly rewarding for investment firms. The term *casino capitalism*, used by scholars such as John Maynard Keynes and Susan Strange (1997), refers to hyperspeculative investing that produces a wild ride for bettors at the casino. It describes how the betting table, that is, the market to which the metaphor refers, is controlled by the house, in this case, global financiers and their partners in the patrimonial state.

In the aftermath of the 2008 financial crisis, cities were compelled *not* to reboot and go back to the calm days of public finance with relatively stable and long-term municipal bonds backed by the government. In the face of bankrupt infrastructure and indebtedness, city governments were obliged to transfer even more power to corporate finance to maintain public infrastructure and deliver public goods, such as housing, roads, parking meters, parks, government buildings, and health care clinics. Financiers create contracts that minimize the risks of their investments while creating hazardous conditions for the public by selling off the rights to future public revenue streams. What happens to the city when public officials let the market resolve the problems of a low tax base, crumbling infrastructure, and a shortage of affordable capital? What emerges with respect to the ethics of city living and the new urban economy? The answer to these questions, suggested by the data presented in this chapter, is that the historical (and commonsense) meanings of *the public* and *the public good* as they are served by public infrastructure—thus fulfilling the needs of the urban majority and reflecting their collective right to the city—dissolve into smoke.

This chapter continues the discussion of the United States, Spain, and India by exploring trends in global urban transformation that developed in the aftermath of the financial crisis. It shows how arenas of urban life—home and neighborhood, health care and the care economy, local media—became financialized and alienated from public service provisioning. The previous chapter demonstrated varied national-level paths to the global urban turn and its financialization. I found an explosion of cross-city and cross-national firm-based relations fueled by financial innovations and expropriations, supported by overlapping state policies and discursive shifts.

This chapter highlights how the relational-conjunctural approach to the 2008 crisis reveals an intensification of finance's power (figure 3.1). Finance capital capitalized on the new opportunities emerging from the moment's debt-ridden and cash-short detritus, which unfolded unevenly in multiple sites across the financialized map. We can learn more from

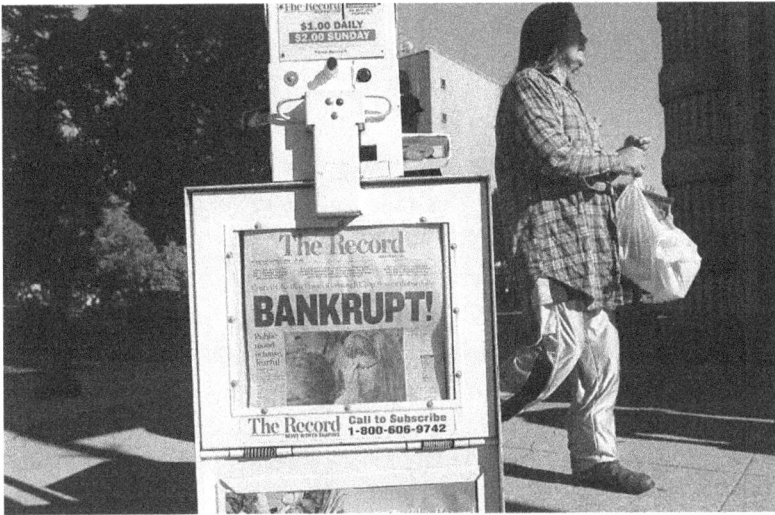

3.1 Stockton, California, newspaper headline, declaring the city broke in 2012.
Source: Getty Images.

studying these transactions as they occur along capital's circulatory path rather than treating countries as discrete sites of rent seeking. Finance capital also took advantage of, and got support from, patrimonial regimes of governance (within and outside of the state, national and global) to create the conditions for more sophisticated financial manipulations shaped by the dark arts of opacity, liquidity/mobility, arbitrage, and monopolization. The chapter concludes by situating the convergences of urban financialization within the larger frame of twenty-first-century capitalism and diminished mechanisms of democracy. It marks the end of part I, in which I have focused on the global-structural context, and leads us into part II, where the attention is on the local-experiential dimensions of the hidden empire of finance in the city of Bengaluru.

The Aftermath of the Crisis in the United States: Metering Urban Space in Chicago

Let's start with the famous parking meter scandal in Chicago as the first of a few examples of postcrisis ploys by finance capital to transform public infrastructure, including toll roads and parking garages, into liquid revenue streams to export. The subsequent sections highlight incursions of finance capital into two other domains of postcrisis city life in the United States—health care and local media.

With the crisis came huge deficits for city managers. The same financial consultants who led city governments down the path of bankruptcy also tended to be the ones selling new financial solutions to the postcrisis blues. In this case, the leaders of the second-largest city in the United States, Chicago, agreed in 2009 to lease thirty-six thousand parking meters for seventy-five years to Morgan Stanley and the Abu Dhabi Sovereign Wealth Fund (M. Fisher 2010). It was a life jacket thrown to city leaders: an offer of a big cash loan up front to help make the city's most onerous debt payments in exchange for the leasing of a public good with a steady flow of revenue—parking meters. The deal was negotiated by the city's patrimonial elites, led by Mayor Richard M. Daley, son of the infamous city Mayor Richard J. Daley, who ruled Chicago like his own fiefdom for twenty-one years in the late 1950s and 1960s. After the dust of the deal had settled, the press discovered that a key player on finance's team was the mayor's nephew William Daley Jr., Morgan Stanley's public finance chief.

As soon as the deal was signed, a public outcry erupted over claims that the city had been ripped off. The mayor responded that it had been the best bid on the market, much better than the second-highest bid ($1.15 versus $1.0 billion) (Spielman 2020). As more details leaked out over time—a typical occurrence when public deals are made in secret by a close network of friends—the public learned that the second bidder, the Australia-based financial firm Macquarie, happened to be the highest bidder on Chicago's main toll road, the Skyway, just ahead of Morgan Stanley.[1] The fact that the same two firms repeatedly surface as the top two bidders for rights to urban infrastructure here and elsewhere challenges the neoliberal claim that such deals are made in a fiercely competitive, and therefore price-sensitive and efficient, marketplace. Instead, the two firms crafted an attractive market shaped by their duopoly power, orchestrating the conditions in which they have relatively equal shares of the global market in urban (road and parking) infrastructure.

After control was transferred from the city to this newly created consortium of large institutional shareholders, downtown parking fees more than doubled: from $3.00 per hour in 2008 to $6.50 per hour in 2013 to $7.00 per hour in 2022 (Spielman 2022; R. Weber 2015; Ashton et al. 2020). The contract the city signed gave the local holding company, Chicago Parking Meters (CPM), extensive control of the parking system

(Byrnes 2022). Hours of operation were extended, and the firm exerted pressure on meter readers to give out more tickets for violations. The contract also required that the city pay CPM for street closures that would prevent it from collecting parking fees, required that it keep at least thirty thousand CPM parking meters on the streets each year, and forbade the city from removing meters without fully compensating CPM for the loss (Byrnes 2022). Consequently, CPM earned back its initial payout by 2020. The remaining sixty years of the lease would provide the two main partners, the Abu Dhabi Sovereign Wealth Fund and Morgan Stanley, with pure profit. This arrangement successfully rerouted approximately $11.6 billion out of Chicago's public coffers to finance the $1.15 billion initial payout to the city (Dumke 2015). To add insult to the city's injury, the dealmaker at Morgan received a dealmaker-of-the-year award and a standing ovation at a New York City private equity conference I attended.

The revenues Morgan Stanley earned from Chicago flowed into deals with the cities of Indianapolis, Sydney, and Seoul, all of which were securitized (i.e., repackaged as derivatives) on the global bond market. In other words, Chicago used the up-front loan from Morgan Stanley to pay off some of its biggest debts, which did not catalyze an increase in productivity, employment, or public goods. For Morgan Stanley and its investors, by contrast, the deal earned them record profits. As icing on this cake, Morgan Stanley won a $61 million lawsuit against the city for lost profits due to road work, street closures, and handicapped parking placards, all of which reduced its daily parking revenues from Chicago residents. A Morgan Stanley–led group also won the contract to privatize four downtown parking garages in Chicago, netting them an additional $293 million in nine years.[2] They later filed a successful suit against the city for building a new parking garage downtown, since it was deemed illegal based on the details of the no-compete contract signed by the mayor. A quarter of a billion dollars was paid to financiers to run parking garages, and the city wasn't allowed to build any new spots to accommodate new demand from residents.

According to the *Chicago Sun-Times*, "Chicago's parking meters raked in $138.7 million in 2019. All told, private investors have earned $1.6 billion. That's nearly $500 million more than their initial, $1.16 billion investment—with 64 years' worth of parking meter revenues to go," perfect evidence of "what a great bit of business that deal was for the private investors, who hail from as far away as Abu Dhabi." The [post-Daley] mayor of Chicago in 2020 called it a "burr under your saddle" that "keeps rubbing and rubbing" (Spielman 2020).

The Chicago meters case brings to light the ways in which the financialization of urban infrastructure is not simply a sale that leads to the more efficient management of public goods. Rather, the real accomplishment is the financial-and-governance side of the deal, a proprietary contract that creates a legal channel tapping into the inner workings and rents of the city. It reroutes local revenue streams into the global hub-and-spoke system of capital flows, while the management of physical assets gets outsourced to a local contractor employing nonunion workers without benefits or bargaining power. The losers are also local taxpayers and the public, who are responsible for paying for higher parking fees and extra penalties and lawsuits when the city deviates ever so slightly from the contract. As the new order of financialization takes over, key tools of the trade are mobilized. For example, finance works with local patrimonial bro-culture networks to establish the rules of the game. These rules are typically opaque and are created beyond the public's view through private negotiations with familiar buddies at the table. They produce a contract that enables investors and elite affiliates to benefit from the revenue streams extracted from public goods and resources, often guaranteed even if the project sours. When such *rule by contract* triumphs, democratic accountability disappears, and the powers of city government and its citizens are diminished.

This Chicago example also exposes the shadowy and complex nature of the investor. The Chicago Skyway was leased to an investment consortium led by Cintra-Macquarie, which owns the Skyway as well as many other assets around the world, including the Bristol, UK, international airport. Ferrovial, a Dutch-headquartered firm originally from Spain, owns Spanish-based Cintra as a subsidiary, while the Australian firm Macquarie has spun off several smaller entities that own different infrastructural assets originally in the Macquarie portfolio. These infrastructure-holding firms exist within a spiderweb of opaque relationships that offer tax breaks, greater liquidity possibilities, and liability dodges (Hoang 2022). The Spanish firm Ferrovial moved to Amsterdam in 2023 for the sole purpose of increasing its potential for liquidity through easier access to the US stock market and Wall Street financing.

Back on the streets of Chicago, as metered hours stretched to midnight and included holidays and weekends, citizens expressed their outrage to their elected alderpersons, and metering became a local political issue, fueling the harassment of meter readers. This outrage was amplified when locals realized that the meters would operate on the most sacred holiday in Chicago, St. Patrick's Day, during the annual parade. Angry residents questioned the power and patriotism of the city's alderperson. As the story goes, a local politician contacted Morgan Stanley on Wall Street and demanded the meters be shut down for that one day that many Chicagoans celebrated through the (heavily metered) streets of downtown. When the Morgan manager returned the alderperson's call, after consulting with major investors in New York City and Abu Dhabi, he said the meters could be closed down only if the city repaid investors $60,000 for lost earnings in the downtown corridor, and more than $340,000 if the shutdown would be citywide. The luck of the Irish!

Specifically designed financial instruments and contracts have had a major impact on city finances and planning across the country, affecting a wide range of public services. In Chicago it is the meters, toll roads, and neighborhood redevelopment districts (through tax increment financing); in Pennsylvania, it is several public school districts; in New York City, it is the public transit system; in Detroit, it is the whole city. As the future of city budgets, and hence city governments, becomes increasingly managed by Wall Street investors, we witness the demise of local representative democracy (Fix LA Coalition 2014; DiNapoli and Bleiwas 2012). Government officials become handmaidens in support of finance capital as well as speculative agents facilitating the assetization of public goods and services and the extraction of money from city coffers and citizens. Once-local decisions about public goods become a task of profit-oriented management. As elected officials turn over power to the owners of capital and off-load risks onto the citizenry, urban infrastructure increasingly becomes controlled by a new layer of supranational governance, ruled by legal contracts and capital flows. This vast infrastructural network of assets produces liquid rents that circulate through investment vehicles globally with their own rules and systems of governance.

The new logic of speculative government is based on the premise that cities will pay bills that ensure robust future revenues for investors (Torrance 2008, 2009). Once agreements are made and contracts are signed, city hall no longer has the right to renegotiate the terms unless they're willing to pay an excessive penalty for reneging on the contract, no matter how angry and ready to protest city residents and their elected officials might be. The proprietary contract between the city and finance capital becomes king, while the courts, city council members, and the mayor have little choice (based on how the rules are written) but to acquiesce.

Racialized Dispossession in the United States

Since the 2008 global crisis and collapse of the housing economy, the financial sector has continued to morph, consolidate, and expand its reach. Investors not only search for undervalued assets (like meters and garages) to convert into liquid assets but also seek to actively *undervalue* assets and convert them into new markets under their control. For example, between 2012 and 2014, private equity firms acted swiftly when, due to the financial crisis, millions of people were forced to forfeit their homes to their creditors. They gobbled up streets of foreclosed homes and monopolized micromarkets, especially in low-income and minority communities where housing values plummeted to record lows and residents of poorer communities were pressured to move. Collectively, they spent $20 billion purchasing 130,000 foreclosed homes in those two years and many more afterward. New York–based Blackstone alone purchased more than forty-five thousand highly discounted homes in nine states through its subsidiary, Invitation Homes, spending $100 million *per week* in 2013 on foreclosed or distressed homes. Blackstone's Bayview Asset Management affiliate bought up nonperforming mortgages that were highly toxic or distressed assets at government auctions and repackaged them into short-term bonds for sale. The largest equity firms in this foreclosure marketplace—Blackstone, Cerberus Capital Management, and Colonial Capital—combined to create a new market in loans to small and medium-sized investors who purchased these heavily discounted homes. In a flash, they jumped in and became the largest landlords in US cities such as Minneapolis and Atlanta (Derickson et al. 2021; Call et al. 2014; Strathmann et al. 2014).

In this newly designed specialty market, private equity firms have few competitors. During recent periods of economic crisis, they have used their cash to transform local housing markets into single-family rentals ripe for securitization (Ash 2023). Through Blackstone's subsidiary B2R Finance, investors from as far away as Hong Kong were enticed to buy into the securitized bonds composed of these millions of loans and rent streams (Christophers 2023; Goldstein 2015).

Transformations of life opportunities in US cities have always been driven by racialized class dynamics, but these worsened during and after the 2008 financial crisis.[3] Before the crisis, the wealth gap between Black and white households was perversely broad. Net worth, calculated as assets minus debt, for white households was ten times that of Black households. After the crisis, however, the gap widened to thirteen times, or $142,000 versus $11,000. In Minneapolis the median wealth for Black households hovered around zero. For Black homeowners, the rate of foreclosure in Chicago was twice the city's average (Derenoncourt et al. 2022). In Oakland, California, 93 percent of foreclosures were concentrated in minority neighborhoods (ReFund and ReBuild 2013). In Atlanta "rapid sales of distressed properties in low-income, minority neighborhoods exacerbated already increasing urban inequalities" (Immergluck and Law 2014, 3). Each new financial transaction fortified this racialized infrastructure of social inequality and remade urban and financial landscapes locally and globally.

To capitalize on this value chain of dispossessed homes, global equity firms used their real estate and lending ventures to create a new global market in single-family-rental securitized bonds. Once these homes were foreclosed on by their corporate subsidiaries like Invitation Homes, Blackstone and others in this network created a new type of bond by bundling and securitizing the rental incomes from the homes, which were purchased and rented out (Goldstein 2015). These firms collect and package—securitize—monthly rent checks and discretionary penalty fees into single-family-rental bonds for sale. Unlike the mortgage-backed securities that contributed to the 2008 meltdown of the global economy, these bonds were less dependent on rising home prices for solvency. Instead, they enable investors to profit from monthly rents and fees collected from working- and middle-class families locked out of the home-buying market. As was the case with the mortgage-backed securities model that preceded them, this financial tool transformed urban neighborhoods by creating new circuits of accumulation *through* dispossession. Deutsche Bank has been the lead underwriter for these bonds, originally deploying almost $450 million of its own capital. By March 2015 these equity firms sold more than $9 billion worth of single-family-rental bonds, anticipating that this segment of the bond market based on rents and fees from single-family-rental housing could grow to more than $9 *trillion* within ten years (Anderson 2015). Dispossession and financial sector prosperity go hand in hand.

Although seen as a global expert in this field, Blackstone was completely new to the role of global landlord. "Building a business from scratch without a single employee and buying something like $150 million in homes per week requires a learning process," noted Anthony Myers, a senior managing director of real estate at Blackstone (quoted in Smyth and Gittelsohn 2013). Equity firms were learning while doing: making up the rules of their game, triggering land-price spikes and falls, capitalizing on each trough and peak, and engineering the volatility to their advantage, unfettered by government oversight or regulation. In US urban housing markets, large firms such as Blackstone worked side by side with their so-called competitive rivals, such as KKR and Goldman Sachs, offering new financial products like single-family-rental bonds. These relational dynamics within the financial sector undercut the simple belief that competition keeps markets honest and vital.

The easy profits earned from these collaborations lured major investors from Europe, the Middle East, and Asia to the United States. Less than thirty years ago, most housing markets outside the United States were heavily regulated to maintain public stability and keep nonlocal financial speculators away. However, since the 1990s markets worldwide have been deregulated to allow finance capital to more freely flow into "undervalued" low-income neighborhoods as well as into large government holdings of public and social housing. The spread of speculative urbanist discourses, policies, and practices turned housing stock into liquid assets, platforms for capital accumulation captured by these financial networks and sucked away from local owners.

In 2020, the scariest and deadliest time of the global pandemic, when government officials shut down cities and required people to stay home, the largest corporate landlords were expelling people from their homes. So much for staying home! Although 2020 offered a reprieve from evictions in the United States, as tens of millions of renters, behind on their rents, were protected by a national moratorium, the years before (and after) witnessed a torrent of evictions. One of the leaders in this new vampirish industry, Apollo Global Management (with more than $520 billion in assets), arrived in working-class communities struggling with historical exclusion from banks and offered their version of a mortgage: contracts for deeds. This ploy had stripped many Black households of their money and homes throughout the early and mid-twentieth century by offering repugnant contracts to people whom banks refused to offer mortgages, with rules in which, if one payment deadline was missed, the house could be foreclosed on, the inhabitants evicted, and all equity taken away from the owners no matter how close they were to paying off the loan (Rothstein 2017; Taylor 2019).[4] After years of struggle, these contracts had long been illegal, but Apollo re-introduced their version of them during this postcrisis period, which worsened eviction rates for Black communities. Evictions skyrocketed in the wake of the COVID-19 pandemic: According to the Eviction Lab at Princeton University, 2022 was a record year for evictions across the United States, with holding companies owned by large private firms evicting tenants at rates far higher than the national average.[5]

The firm Equity Group Investments, owned by billionaire Sam Zell, generates more than $95 billion in annual revenues from real estate investment trusts (REITs). Zell coldly describes his firm's strategy as "dancing on the skeletons of other people's mistakes" (Collins et al. 2021, 24). The net income of Invitation Homes, once owned by Blackstone, increased by 340 percent from January to September 2020, at the height of the pandemic, due to its single-family-rental business. It distributed $248 million in dividends to its shareholders that year and spent millions to help defeat the rent control referendum in California. Concurrently, Invitation Homes increased rents during the pandemic and filed for hundreds of evictions from its properties across five states. Such retributive acts were postponed temporarily in many states, which passed legislation to prevent evictions during the pandemic, but returned soon after the pandemic was deemed over.

In Minneapolis, Minnesota, where I live and work, the same firm that became India's largest corporate landlord, Blackstone, became Minnesota's largest single-family-home landlord. Blackstone took advantage of rock-bottom prices resulting from defaults on mortgages by purchasing nearly a hundred thousand homes nationally, including more than a thousand in depressed Minneapolis markets. While Blackstone was making its move, another asset management firm based in the unregulated tax haven of the Virgin Islands—Front Yard Residential—also purchased more than seven hundred homes in predominantly Black neighborhoods of Minneapolis. Not only did this duopoly of home grabs set off record-setting home prices in the poorest neighborhoods—hiking prices at four times the city's average—but these firms also inflicted onerous penalties and fees on home renters, adding substantially to monthly out-of-pocket housing costs (Derickson et al. 2021). Because many urban housing markets had above 90 percent occupancy rates in this period, and minimal regulatory controls, corporate landlords were able to easily raise the rents for new tenants. The profitability of their investment hinges on the perception that these rental bonds are low risk because people will consistently pay their rent in such a tight market. That is, the promise of rising rents and fees will pump up the share value of these bonds and real estate investment funds and demonstrate that these bonds are a great investment.

The housing crisis and its perverse incentives for elite profitability also reveal how the entry of global private equity into low-income neighborhoods exacerbates long-standing forms of housing injustice by driving up home prices, putting the aspiration of buying a home even further out of reach for working-class people of color. All of this is happening in the same neighborhoods where people of color lost homes during the last wave of finance-based expropriation.

In the eviction action complaints filed by these firms in the Hennepin Housing Court of Minnesota, my colleagues and I found that numerous types of fees were being levied on tenants and used as justification for their eviction (Derickson et al. 2021). Fees are imposed for minor infractions, like unmowed lawns, unshoveled snow, or, in the most egregious cases, simply the inability to work the landlord's online portal to pay the rent. In a 2021 report, a tenant explained the predatory fee structure: "They direct you to pay your rent through an online portal where a vendor charges you $10 to $30 each time you process your rent payment" (quoted in Collins et al. 2021). Another tenant pointed out other fees they were charged: "$10 administration fee. $17 processing fee. And a new $12 'HAP' fee—we don't even know what that is!" For these Black working-class renters, such dubious penalties alone comprised up to 10 percent of their monthly rent. As part of this same study, my colleagues and I discovered that in 2019 eviction rates for homes owned by corporate landlords were four times higher than the average in Minnesota. We found a tone of boastfulness in the private equity firms' US Securities and Exchange Commission reports, in which these firms revealed to their investors that their business model relies on rising rents and the imposition of fees to increase the flow of revenues into the future.[6]

The situation in Minneapolis reflects broader national trends. By 2017 two firms, Invitation Homes and American Homes 4 Rent, controlled more than 60 percent of the national market of single-family-home rentals. They used common financial tools, such as mergers and acquisitions (M&As) and initial public offerings (IPOs), to drive up profits without adding value or improving their product: ostensibly, livable homes. Soon after, they invited large investors such as Morgan Stanley and BlackRock to buy shares and received generous subsidies from the US government to expand this market, including a $1 billion loan guarantee from the government's Fannie Mae. By using other people's money to buy heavily discounted houses to rent across the nation, they enjoyed record-setting profits.

On the cusp of, and after, the 2008 global economic crash, the largest private equity firms engineered a spate of new markets cascading one from another. First, there was an enormous market of overburdened mortgage holders who had paid too much for their loans under false promises, which triggered a new market of heavily discounted foreclosed homes, which produced a thriving market in (desperately needed) single-family rentals. These market forces combined to produce the ultimate promise of a multibillion-dollar global marketplace in securitized single-family-rental bonds. Each market phase was more lucrative, monopolized by a handful of the world's largest financial firms working in sync to ensure their mutual benefit.

In the common parlance of liberalism, markets are autonomous sites where buyers and sellers voluntarily interact, with market forces balanced out through market transactions among equal players. By contrast, here we see practices that are clearly engineered by a powerful set of actors—a patrimonial regime of elites—to create so-called markets under their control, using financial tools they themselves invent for their exclusive benefit. Of course, no coconspirators are all powerful, and there are plenty of cracks in the armor of these practices. Nevertheless, it is important to appreciate how these highly effective instruments of wealth extraction are built and sustained amid cries of moral outrage, community pain, and resistance. The next section reveals how these same firms reach beyond the worlds of infrastructure and housing into neighboring domains of urban health care and eldercare that comprise the foundation for healthy social reproduction in our cities. Here we see how sites of care are converted into assets whose exchange value flowed through transnational circuits of capital, sacrificing urban well-being in the process.

Since the crisis Wall Street has muscled itself into the booming health care economy, an arena that witnessed untold misery and death during the global COVID-19 pandemic. Private equity investments in the health care sector spiraled to new heights, with the value of annual deals tripling from $41.5 billion in 2010 to $120 billion in 2019, totaling more than $750 billion during the decade (Brown 2023; Pearl 2023; Schulte 2022; Singh et al. 2022). The number of private equity deals in health care in 2018 alone reached eight hundred in the United States, for a total value of $100 billion, and in 2021 these firms invested $206 billion into more than 1,400 health care acquisitions, according to industry tracker PitchBook (Schulte 2022). One company, KKR, swooped up depressed assets like candy. They spent nearly $10 billion purchasing Envision Healthcare, which operates hundreds of surgery centers across the United States, leveraging the deal by loading $7.7 billion worth of debt onto the company (Bugbee 2022). This then forced Envision to cut costs and eliminate what they perceived as slack, which set off a shareholder value spike that led to record bonuses and fees collected for KKR and high dividend returns for their privileged investors. These practices emptied the coffers of the entrapped health care company. Although KKR, Apollo, Cerberus, and the other largest funds each sat on a boatload of cash (more than $58 billion for KKR in 2020), they took advantage of government-supplied tax breaks, which they used to acquire companies with mounting debt (Kocieniewski and Melby 2020). They also received hundreds of millions of dollars each in pandemic bailout money for the health care companies they had bought and bled (Kocieniewski and Melby 2020). As two *Bloomberg* journalists put it, "The paradox of private equity funds, which profit from tax breaks the U.S. offers on debt, is that even when they're brimming with cash, there is little incentive to use it to prop up their struggling investments. In bad times, the funds can set themselves up for future windfalls by buying new distressed companies and using debt to multiply their profits, even if their current holdings suffer. The pandemic is 'a time to shine,' two Apollo executives said on a call with investors [in late March 2020]" (Kocieniewski and Melby 2020).

Over the past decade, private equity firms such as Carlyle—which is also a big investor in (and we might add destroyer of) India's health care sector—have bought up 1,900 nursing homes for the elderly in the United States. People's well-being necessitates a modicum of compassion and healing, whether it is for health care or eldercare. Yet private equity firms have cut staff and supplies, killed off competitors, and increased prices. In 2020 one-fourth of all COVID-19 deaths in the United States took place in nursing homes, and 40 percent of nursing home deaths occurred in ones taken over by private equity firms (Atul Gupta et al. 2021). Workers willing to speak to the press said they had little access to protective equipment, labored in overcrowded and ill-equipped institutions, worked in more than one nursing home during the week to pay their bills (potentially spreading the deadly virus from job to job), and needed to work up to sixty hours a week to make ends meet. Many who spoke out were fired. Health workers in general were the most likely to get sick from COVID-19 and the most likely to become unemployed. Even before the pandemic, private equity wreaked havoc. According to a National Bureau of Economic Research study, "Private equity ownership of nursing homes both upped their Medicare billings and increased patient mortality by 10 percent—translating to over 20,000 lives lost across [a] 12-year period" (Atul Gupta et al. 2021, 18).

Private equity takeovers of hospitals have also had troubling effects on patient mortality. The units of hospitals that have attracted investors are those that perform expensive elective surgery (i.e., scheduled as opposed to emergency), like knee, hip, and organ replacements (Kannan et al. 2023). These expensive procedures are often paid for by insurance companies or by the vulnerable underinsured. Through all the preventable pandemic deaths, the health care sector revealed itself as a two-tiered system. Emergency rooms, intensive care units (ICUs), and public and university hospitals were overwhelmed with patients, sickness, and death, lacking adequate protective gear and IV fluids. Despite the crowding, hospital wings were shuttered, and health workers were laid off because these businesses were not profitable to run during a health crisis. Many of the country's more than five thousand outpatient surgery centers closed or sharply cut back on the number of elective procedures they performed. One doctor decried this in the press in 2020: "Half of the surgery centers in New York are not doing anything. All these anesthesiologists and nurses who are sitting on the sidelines, they want to help. They don't know how to help. There's nowhere for them to help" (quoted in Anthony and Szabo 2020). The private-equity-influenced health care system is essentially tone-deaf to the needs of the public, disinclined to care for those who lack economic resources, and based on a business model that doesn't allow providers to care properly for their patients.

While the US health industry has always been driven by profits through a class-based system of luxury care for the few and drive-through care for the many, private equity is wringing the industry dry, selling off properties, firing workers, and demanding an entirely new form of fee extraction—dusting off an old playbook exemplified by corporate raiders like Carl Icahn. National Bureau of Economic Research studies reveal that nursing homes and dialysis care facilities under private equity ownership over the decade correlate with worse health outcomes, deteriorating workplace conditions, and higher prices (Atul Gupta et al. 2021). The transformation of US cities extended beyond health care to include a key institution underpinning participatory democracy, local newspapers.

Transforming the US Mediascape:
Local Newspapers Disappear into
Liquid(ated) Assets

Once upon a time, perhaps naively, many imagined local city newspapers as vehicles for local expressions of community, discontent, and hope. Many Americans once viewed the local news as equivalent to the town square, not equally accessible but still a site and mouthpiece for residents (Nicolaou and Fontanella-Khan 2021). Yet by 2021 half of America's daily newspapers fell under the control of private equity and hedge funds. Approximately one in four have closed over the past decade, and thousands remain as skeletal versions of their original selves. One hedge fund alone, Alden Global Capital, has purchased a hundred newspapers and over two hundred publications since the financial crisis (Nicolaou and Fontanella-Khan 2021). The Newspaper Guild reported that Alden had slashed 75 percent of jobs on average across the news enterprises they acquired, selling off equipment and buildings (e.g., their assets) to fuel its profits, bleeding the papers while extracting their wealth. It's unjust but completely legal (NewsGuild–Communications Workers of America 2020).[7] Although local newspapers have typically been owned by wealthy families and, more recently, by national newspaper chains, the takeover of local news organs only to shutter them is a practice, along with other transactions, that further undermines local democracy and community spirit in cities across America while creating wealth for a handful of Wall Street investors.

Since the crisis of 2008, entire neighborhoods, health care and eldercare facilities, and local media outlets have fallen under the sway of private equity's financialization activities. The effects are devastating and society wide. Cities have been left with few alternatives but to borrow from Wall Street, however badly they get burned from repeated cycles of expropriation and humiliation. But this isn't solely a local or even national problem. Large investors purchasing foreclosed homes in the United States have had a keen eye on other markets around the globe at the same time. "When we looked at the situation in Spain," a Blackstone executive explained in the press, "we thought we could see something similar, where we could replicate a lot of the systems and technology that we created in the U.S." (quoted in Smyth and Gittelsohn 2013). Indeed, since the 2008 crisis, a handful of financial firms have come to dominate the urban housing, health care, and infrastructure markets globally.

The empire of finance has spread rapidly across the US economy since the crisis. Private equity grew from $700 billion in global assets in 2000 to $6 trillion by 2023. It also has a controlling ownership interest in more than eight thousand companies, which is more than twice the number traded on public stock markets. As Karen Ho (2009) and others have documented, finance has taken over and now dominates many nonfinancial sectors of the economy, including manufacturing, retail, and services (Stiglitz 2019). The global reach of finance capital is documented in the following section on what has happened in Spain since the 2008 crisis. This European case further reveals how finance capital has turned seemingly immovable urban property and infrastructure into globe-trotting liquid assets.

Finance Capital in Spain: After the Crisis, the Deluge

In Spain, speculative urbanism prompted the rapid expansion of expensive, finance-driven infrastructure and housing ventures; this unsustainable surge was accompanied by growing debt for small investors, regional governments, and urban developers alike. As the fragility of the system cracked from the overwhelming pressure of debt and the inability to pay,

3.2 Crisis-produced ghost towns are found across Spain, including this unfinished row of empty residential buildings in Madrid, 2008. Source: CNBC, Bloomberg via Getty Images.

Spain precipitously devolved from Europe's raging bull into one of its peripheral PIIGS (i.e., bankrupt Portugal, Ireland, Iceland, Greece, and Spain) (Rodrigues et al. 2016). The expansion cycle slowed to a grinding halt, and highly indebted investors tried to sell their assets to pay off some of their debts. Home prices suddenly fell, banks stopped accepting assets as collateral, and the housing and credit markets abruptly collapsed.

From 2008, the urban landscape across Spain shifted, from a reflection of the hopes that came with a skyline full of active building cranes to the desolation of unfinished housing clusters and empty toll roads leading to nowhere (figure 3.2). Spanish household debt rose from 61 percent of gross disposable income in 1997 to 139 percent by 2012, significantly higher than that of other major European economies (Álvarez 2012). Banks went belly up, with thousands of bank branches closing. Four of the largest banks fell into such trouble that the government nationalized them, bailing them out to keep the national economy from collapsing. Nonfinancial corporations experienced even greater indebtedness, with much of this debt linked to construction and real estate. In 2012 debt in the Spanish economy had reached over 150 percent of the gross domestic product (GDP), evenly distributed across nonfinancial firms, banks, households, and the government (Álvarez 2012). By 2011 Valencia's provincial government had to take out high-interest bank loans just to pay its public employees and maintain the city's basic functions, a highly unsustainable proposition (Tremlett 2012).

Investments in toll roads, airports, and fast trains also went sour since they depended on real estate expansion for their economic viability. The largest infrastructure firms were able to use state or European Central Bank bailout money (approximately €100 billion) to extricate themselves from these losses. The central government claimed it was contractually obliged to refinance these failed investments, as there were guarantees written into the contract for minimum usage fees, below which the government would be held responsible. These proprietary contracts reflect the insidious ways finance capital can take control of democratic institutions of governance (Coq-Huelva 2013; García 2010; López and Rodríguez 2011). Some toll roads were at 10 percent capacity, while others were never completed. Many of Spain's precrisis speculative schemes—in which a local patrimonial network of local *cajas* (regional savings banks) had been lending liberally for (dubious) projects, backed by regional politicians and their supporters in the corporate sector—were deemed too big to fail. Financial firms therefore received bailouts with few strings attached.

As Spain's largest banks absorbed the worst-performing private banks and government-owned and smaller *cajas*, they took advantage of both the European Central Bank bailout and their newly accumulated, heavily discounted assets to make strategic investments outside of Spain, particularly in Latin America, which was also hit by a series of financial downturns that could be turned into opportunities for the largest handlers of capital. In 2014 Santander Bank earned 20 percent of its profits from Brazil and only 14 percent from Spain, while another major global bank based in Madrid, BBVA, earned 40 percent of its profits solely from Mexico. These two banks did not compete for these assets in the same countries (Amaral 2010; Buck 2013, 2014; Chislett 2014). By 2014 the four major Spanish banks had absorbed over sixty of Spain's bankrupt private banks and government-owned *cajas* and yet emerged with substantial profits from their large Spanish sovereign debt bond holdings (Buck 2014). As a banker at Credit Suisse noted, the mergers and acquisitions gave the Spanish banking sector an "oligopolistic profile," a description equally appropriate for postcrisis banking in the rest of western Europe (Zuloaga 2014).

Already heavily invested in Spanish banks and real estate, Germany's Deutsche Bank doubled down and purchased nonperforming assets from BBVA and distressed Spanish banks like the government company Sareb. Sareb was set up by the government in 2012 to manage and sell the troubled assets of government-rescued banks. Deutsche Bank also invested in real estate deals that had gone bad at dirt-cheap prices and purchased debt collection agencies at a time when debt had emerged as a hot commodity for large investors. They did so at record low prices, reflecting enormous discounts.

As the financial world consolidated, plans to borrow and speculate on and across cities globally proliferated. Since 2008 Brazil has borrowed money to build world-class infrastructure for the high-profile World Cup of 2014, held in twelve Brazilian cities, and the 2016 Olympics, held in Rio de Janeiro. By 2011 its projects were behind schedule and underfinanced. What better deal than have Spanish and German banks bail out these projects? Finance had the power to temporarily abandon indebted regions of Europe for investments elsewhere, which they did across Latin America and the United States with higher margins. After creating capital scarcity in Europe, firms chose to return to purchase heavily devalued European infrastructure and housing. According to Isidro López and Emmanuel Rodríguez (2011, 22), the sovereign-debt crises in Greece, Ireland, Portugal, and Spain provided "an enormous business opportunity for the big European—German, French, and British—banks, the main holders of the European countries' sovereign bonds." The grip of finance on governmental power tightened through these indebted high-profile projects and through the power to circulate its capital anywhere. It affected governing bodies all the way down to Spain's municipal councils. These local government entities became dependent on private real estate revenues for their social expenditures, the nuts and bolts necessary to keep cities running and people out of deep poverty (Coq-Huelva 2013).

Profligacy for the largest firms translated into austerity for the public. After the crisis the Spanish government, under pressure from the International Monetary Fund, European Union, and European Central Bank, worked to pay off these debts through draconian austerity programs rather than force the financial institutions to cover their huge losses (Coq-Huelva 2013). Government's austerity measures forced massive layoffs and pay cuts, strangled labor rights and pension systems, and deepened cuts to public expenditures. More than 50 percent of Spain's youth became jobless, and huge popular protests (*manifestaciones*) occurred frequently. By 2013 the national budget had endured

€40,000 million in social expenditure cuts as interest payments increased to €38,600 million (Coq-Huelva 2013). Even with drastic public spending cuts, public debt (much of it owed to private banks) continued to grow.

While the precrisis flow of speculative capital into finance and real estate in Spain (and the other PIIGS countries) was already considerable, *after* the crisis the liquidity flows intensified. Between 2009 and 2012, foreign direct investment (FDI) zigzagged across borders and sectors, pulling out of equity deals and switching to debt and distressed sales, flooding the finance, insurance, and real estate (FIRE) sector and disappearing from manufacturing. Investment in Spanish finance and insurance shot up 42 percent, while manufacturing investment fell 38.5 percent. With the state retreating, finance capital created conditions of scarcity in crucial employment sectors and emerged flush in other markets, a volatility that could be assetized. The largest surviving firms consolidated to become multinational conglomerates, purchasing their rivals in the postcrisis period.

Between 2007 and 2013, Spanish property values fell 40 percent, and more than three million homes sat empty. Replicating the investment strategy it employed in the US housing market, Blackstone moved into the Spanish housing market. In one fell swoop in 2013, Blackstone spent $7.5 billion to buy forty thousand homes in Spain, including eighteen large apartment complexes in Madrid alone (Smyth and Gittelsohn 2013), with 1,860 government-subsidized units among them. State-owned Sareb sold $1.5 billion worth of repossessed housing at bargain rates. Blackstone bought a Spanish residential loan portfolio for €6.4 billion and transferred it into their Spanish asset securitization fund. Blackstone wasn't the only financial firm attracted to the Spanish housing market. Goldman Sachs outbid Blackstone on twenty-two complexes, all rentals, including a low-income housing portfolio (Dowsett 2014). Goldman Sachs has since added luxury housing to their portfolio.

As of 2025, approximately 185,000 rental properties remained in the hands of global financial firms, half of which were based in the United States; three US firms (Blackstone, Cerberus, and Lone Star) purchased four hundred thousand privately owned homes (Cunningham 2025). Blackstone has utilized almost thirty different Spain-based funds and subsidiaries to buy the country's social and private housing, a move that has circumvented legislative acts to limit foreign financial firms from purchasing Spanish homes. Meanwhile, foreign hedge funds have swept up 15 percent of Madrid's indebted and heavily discounted social (i.e., low-rent public) housing. "Spain has one of the smallest stocks of social housing in Europe, but as Madrid's authorities cut their budgets, they have sold what they can at fire-sale prices" (Dowsett 2014). Many of the renters who had once received rent reductions of up to 40 percent, provided by the housing agency, lost this benefit after global equity firms bought these properties. Rents and home prices have skyrocketed between 2015 and 2025; Prime Minister Pedro Sánchez named the investors "so-called vulture funds" and accused them of having distorted national markets and ruthlessly converted housing into a financial asset (Cunningham 2025, 8).

A major player in policymaking, the global consulting firm PricewaterhouseCoopers, released a report advising Madrid to sell these public housing assets, claiming that the public housing agency was not sustainable, even though it kept many people out of poverty and in homes, instead of sleeping on the streets. Plataforma de Afectados por la Hipoteca (or the Platform for People Affected by Mortgages [PAH]) estimates that 2.5 million people have been evicted from their homes since 2008 (PAH n.d.; García-Lamarca 2022). One media website in Madrid decried these evictions as "state violence and institutional theft" (Pattem 2021).

As finance capital circulates through cities, receiving postcrisis bailouts here and triggering new sell-offs there, and as city budgets struggle, a similar pattern emerges. Governing strategies become oriented toward the promotion of large-scale, ambitious projects that require freeing up more public land, goods, space, and labor, initially as a subsidized input and later as collateral, to entice developers to build and private equity firms to invest. Despite the persistent rhetoric of free and competitive marketplaces, this could happen only through conditions manufactured by a close alliance of select politicians, bankers, and corporate elites. They comprise the Spanish patrimonial regime of governance intimately tied to these speculative urban impulses. The aftermath of the 2008 Spanish crisis unfolded across three intertwined domains: public infrastructure, public government/budgeting, and the housing market. Seeing them as relational and transnationally linked reveals that both the crisis and its afterlife had deep structural foundations. Governments, political parties, banks, and corporations collectively helped to create the problem, and they collaborated in addressing the effects in ways that benefited the empire of finance and hurt the majority of urban residents.

In sum, as public assets fell into the hands of financial firms, the sector solidified around their wealth-generating financial tools. Markets were created from the detritus of the crash because the united power of private financial institutions left few alternatives for public housing agencies, public banks, and municipalities. Governments acted as if they were powerless, with no choice but to offer public assets at bargain-basement prices. By selling off assets, governments enabled private equity firms to dominate once-public spheres, to manipulate housing rents and prices, and to secure infrastructure revenues and fees through the firms' oligopolistic hold on local markets. Revenues from these purchases serviced cutthroat arbitrage elsewhere around the globe. Large amounts of finance capital still flow into Spain, one of Europe's largest economies, but not in the same diffused and decentralized form it had taken three decades ago. Today it takes the form of an aggressive handful of global hedge and equity funds converting local goods and property through the deployment of risky financial tools that successfully extract rents to enrich their burgeoning global portfolio.

This postcrisis power of finance capital evident in Spain also thrived in India. Across Indian cities, new financial tools were deployed to convert goods into rent-extracting assets, commanded by a tight-knit patrimonial network of governance.

The Rise of Rentier Capitalism in Postcrisis India

India's particular manifestation of speculative urbanism evolved coterminously with new forms of what geographer Brett Christophers (2020) calls *rentier capitalism*, an umbrella term that includes but also stretches beyond the idea of financialization. This section of the chapter presents a bird's-eye view of the Indian economy stemming from the relational conjuncture of the 2008 crisis. It introduces the gamesmanship of global finance as it engages a national-level patrimonial set of actors in government, commerce, and consultancy. The key argument is that, like in the United States and Spain, the crisis created an opportunity for global finance to reenter India with a new business model of rentier capitalism that includes forms of financialization. Whereas chapter 2 demonstrated the different paths leading up to the global crisis, this chapter shows the postcrisis convergences unfolding within and across countries. I offer a very brief overview of the transforming Indian economy with examples from the health care sector and the rentierist elements of trademarks, patents, and copyrights that have mattered so much, postcrisis, for foreign corporations in India. The section does not discuss housing, real estate, urban infrastructure, and public space since those are the main topics of part II of the book.

The best place to start this overview is the election of Narendra Modi and his Hindu-nationalist Bharatiya Janata Party (BJP) in 2014. The BJP took power promoting an economic policy of Make in India, using a hyped-up media campaign targeting Modi's voters as well as foreign capital and promising the transformation of India into a global manufacturing hub. The Make in India initiative promised to increase the manufacturing sector's growth rate to 12–14 percent per annum, to create 100 million additional manufacturing jobs in the economy, and to ensure that the manufacturing sector's contribution to the GDP would increase by 25 percent in eight years, later revised to eleven years (S. Roy 2020).

Central to the initiative was FDI reform that reflected a sea change in India, starting in the postindependence era. Such investment was at first considered a necessary evil in some restricted sectors of the economy that the British had stripped of their technical support. Since the late 1990s of India's neoliberal turn, and fast-tracked after 2104, FDI has become a fundamental pillar of India's twenty-first-century position in the global economy. The BJP government has hoped that an open-door policy would entice large flows of capital into manufacturing sectors, invigorate technology transfers, and encourage joint ventures with domestic firms to trigger accelerated growth in high-skilled employment. Yet these pie-in-the-sky desires are what every nation hopes for from global capital and speculative urbanism. In return for bringing your advanced manufacturing technology, magical financial instruments, and innovative corporate culture to us, we will offer subsidized public space, cheap resources, and low-wage labor to help you gain a competitive edge while enabling us to generate new forms of prosperity nationally.

What is ignored by this imaginary is the reality that corporate capital does not—historically or today—follow these ideal business practices, especially not in the ascendant phase of speculative urbanism amid the larger phenomenon of rentier capitalism (Christophers 2020). In the case of India, large segments of global capital have invested in acquiring assets from which they can accrue rents, rather than investing in making things and, in the process, sharing technologies, patents, and know-how so that others can (also) prosper. Indeed, this era of global rentier capitalism is precisely about making corporate profits through holding exclusive ownership over assets—from land and housing to radio waves and telecom towers to intellectual property rights (Lapavitsas 2014). The business model is precisely to hoard assets—to have them and profit from their exclusive ownership, that is, to corner markets, whether it's a parcel of land (ground rents) or control over the flow of finance capital (financial rents). Sharing technologies and transferring expertise without charging a (typically usurious) fee is unproductive if not anticapitalist in this era, unless sharing is done in exchange for access to data from which new rents can accrue.

For example, some of the biggest nonfinancial firms these days earn a large share of their profits not simply from making and selling things (if they do that at all) but from the steady flow of rents they receive from branding their products, patenting software that they rent out, collecting data to sell to insurers and advertisers, and lending money to consumers so they can purchase their and others' products. Car companies, for instance, earn a sizable amount of their incomes from providing car loans to their customers. Global fast-food corporations such as McDonald's and Subway make their profits largely from renting out thousands of real estate spaces to local franchise owners and from the fees they charge franchisees to purchase their branded and copyrighted food packaging and supplies. Local franchisees must then work to keep up with costs after paying these rents to corporate headquarters. With or without a global pandemic, war, or economic collapse, rents still must be paid, which is why these global chains are so profitable for shareholders, no longer reliant on the number of hamburgers flipped for their revenue during slow times.

The world's most profitable firms—Apple, Microsoft, Google, Amazon, IBM—make their planet-sized profits from owning the cloud from which most firms, governments, and households rent space. More than half of Amazon's enormous profits come from cloud computing, not from delivering packages (D. Narayan 2022). Thus, the recent fad in promoting smart cities is a rentier's dream. Every piece of smart (i.e., data-collecting) infrastructure requires an undergirding of finance capital that cities in the North and South do not readily have. Hence, not only are cities filled with people who rent their homes, but the city itself rents (in other words, borrows) capital to keep up with citizen and corporate demand for services and goods that municipalities need or want to provide. Of course, borrowing is not inherently a problem; it depends on the conditions of borrowing and the way those conditions are conducive to positive relational dynamics or manipulated to exploit (Graeber 2011).

Precrisis flows of FDI into India reflected spectacular growth in a short period. As noted earlier, most barriers for foreign capital were lifted by 2005 so that global firms could acquire majority stakes in Indian companies after decades of postindependence reluctance. The last obstacle fell when the ruling BJP government allowed for 100 percent foreign ownership within the highly protected and secretive state defense sector. After the 2008 crisis, and short lulls of uncertainty, India experienced a 25 percent increase in FDI from 2014 to 2015, followed by an infusion of $55 billion in 2015–16, the largest flow of any single year up to that point. It even surpassed China for new greenfield investment projects. In 2016–17 FDI increased again, to $60 billion, which was an impressive feat (K. Rao and Dhar 2018, 31). The sectors attracting the most FDI were services—a category that includes finance, banking, insurance, telecommunications, and computer hardware and software (36).

A closer look into the figures reveals that much of that capital flowed into already existing subsidiaries of multinational firms, and a significant fraction of the revenue earned flowed *back* to the parent company abroad (i.e., Toyota, Samsung). In their study of foreign capital in India during the first two decades of the twenty-first century, K. S. Chalapati Rao and Biswajit Dhar (2018, 31) found that "equity inflows were sustained mainly by a substantial increase in acquisitions of Indian companies[,] displacing the existing shareholder." This led them to point out that "acquisitions replace existing investors without adding to the equity base of the investee companies" inside India (32). A sizable chunk of the nation's insurance industry was acquired by various global firms once insurance was liberalized by the government. The same was true for telecom, transport industries, construction, and, most recently, retail and e-commerce (think Walmart and Amazon) (32). This period marks a rise in the ratio of repatriated capital to annual inflows, such that by 2018 repatriations and disinvestment (or sell-offs) had reached as high as 47 percent of inflows. In other words, almost half of the FDI capital that came into India in 2018 flowed back out to the original investors. If capital does not park itself in India, it's hard to consider it productive for the Indian economy and city.

For example, China developed a foothold in Indian manufacturing by purchasing a share of US-based General Motors car production in India, and General Motors earned substantial revenues from the rents collected from the use of its brand and its patented technologies and services in India. The car sector in India pays heavy royalties to its foreign parents for the right to produce and sell GM, Suzuki, Ford, Volkswagen, BMW, and Toyota vehicles. Maruti Suzuki India Ltd. paid out $3.5 billion of rents for royalties and technical know-how patents to Suzuki in Japan from 2009 to 2017 (K. Rao and Dhar 2018, 41). Bosch of Germany invested $62 million in Bosch Starter Motors Generators Ltd. in India in 2016 and paid back to the German company $35 million in dividends soon after. Cisco, Facebook, Microsoft, Google Capital, Uber, HP, and Oracle all acquired Indian firms in this period and yet *added* very little in productive investments or jobs in India. The financial act of acquisition across currencies and borders has accrued profits for multinational firms without leaving much on the table for their Indian partners. Meanwhile, with consistent state support, they muscle out competition from local entrepreneurs and businesses, leading to monopoly status.

India's key productive sectors of telecom, defense, pharmaceuticals and medical devices, health care, transport and auto, and civil aviation all experienced mergers and acquisitions during the postcrisis period and a general transformation of their production-focus business model to a financialized one. This achievement for the world of finance is reflected in both the rising inflow of foreign capital into the Indian economy and the substantial outflow of rents back to the parent companies. Rather than creating a diversified and high-salaried Indian economy underwriting the improvement of urban infrastructure and the well-being of city residents, this rentier business model has financialized the economy in ways that contribute to its monopolization by global firms. It has made the local economy more vulnerable to external priorities and has transformed local firms from productive entities to rent-paying ones. A financialized economy tends to be dominated by rent-seeking practices that are often out of reach and above the rule of local governing bodies.

Pandemics and Profits in India's
Health Care Industry

Before many could absorb the significance of the problem, the global COVID-19 pandemic infected city life. Rooted in the intimate entanglements of natural and human worlds, and the rapid expansion of the urban into rural and wilderness environments, the virus traveled from wild to domesticated animals, seeped into the process of industrialized animal slaughtering, and wreaked havoc around the world within weeks. As early as March 2020, all bets were off for any ambitious new speculative urban projects. After India's notable GDP growth over the previous decade (albeit accompanied by intensified social inequalities), more than 200 million people fell back into poverty, earning less than the minimum wage of $5 a day (Azim Premji University 2021). The middle class, defined as those who made between $10 and $20 a day, shrank alarmingly. During India's first lockdown, without much international notice, many millions of migrant laborers, who had come hundreds of miles from their rural homes to find urban jobs, were required to return home and yet were stuck without transport or provisions. By mid-2021 an estimated five million Indians had died from the virus, though official estimates are much lower. There are no official numbers as to how many migrants died on the road trying to get back home during the lockdown. When there's no slack in public infrastructure, a global pandemic can undermine whole communities, as even the middle class experienced when most Indian hospitals ran out of oxygen during the height of the pandemic.

Wall Street firms made highly profitable investments in health care in India right before, during, and after the suffering of the pandemic (Sriram 2023). One news article headline proclaimed in June 2023, "Indian Hospitals Set Investors' Pulses Racing in Post-COVID Boom" (Sriram 2023), and another in 2019 stated, "Indian Hospitals in ICU, Private Equity to the Rescue" (Khanna 2019). As the latter reporter noted, "Despite persistent misgivings, private equity's love affair with healthcare in India continues. Last fortnight, global investment firm KKR-backed Radiant Life Care picked up a 49.7% stake for $293 million in Max Healthcare, extending an investment spree that took off in 2012. In June last year, another private equity (PE) major, General Atlantic, invested $130 million to pick up a minority stake in KIMS Hospitals, one of the largest corporate healthcare groups in southern India, with seven multi-specialty hospitals across the region."

The financial data analytics company Preqin indicated much the same enthusiasm: "Despite a global slowdown in 2020, private equity-backed buyout activity trended upwards in India. More than 100 deals were transacted, worth a combined $20bn, up from 83 deals worth $7.0bn in 2019" (Lee and Blaisdell 2021). The authors continued, "The largest proportion of buyout deals in India tracked by Preqin in 2020 were healthcare deals, spanning the pharmaceutical, chemical, and biotech industries. Some $2.4bn was invested across 31 healthcare deals in 2020, up from $1.1bn invested across 24 deals in 2019" (Lee and Blaisdell 2021). The health pandemic clearly didn't faze those who were interested in investing in upscale and private health care in India; indeed, it seems to have excited them.

India spends the lowest amount of almost any country per capita on health care, less than $17 per person per year. This is less than 1.6 percent of GDP, less than Laos or Ethiopia spend proportionately. These numbers pale in comparison to what private equity spent on elite health care assets in India, especially enterprises that catered to health care tourism for retired Americans and Saudi elites. Little of this surfeit of capital was used to purchase much-needed oxygen, ICU beds, or COVID-related medicines for much of the population, which depends on public hospitals and clinics for their well-being, as well as survival.

What Comes Next: A World of Finance and Speculative Urbanism in Bengaluru

In the previous chapter, we saw how key policy and legal changes associated with the embrace of neoliberal ideas in the 1980s and 1990s, together with the finance industry's creation of new strategies that took advantage of these changes, created the conditions for the financialization of the US, Spanish, and Indian economies. This phenomenon was not limited to these three contexts but was echoed in many other countries around the globe. While each country charted its own course to financializing its economy, the end result was largely the same: the growing role and dominance of finance capital—and with it, a rentier form of capitalism—within the economy. At the global level, we now live in a world where finance is king, and governments often act as its handmaiden.

For cities, the core subject of this book, this process led to speculative urbanism in both discursive and material forms. It began to take shape before the new millennium and became more pronounced and acquired new features after the 2008 financial crisis. In part II, I dive into these trends and their repercussions in one city, Bengaluru, and its surrounding countryside, over a longer period and in greater depth. Chapter 4 explores earlier cycles of city making and infrastructural development, revealing key conjunctures and emphasizing the overwhelming importance of ecological, social, and financial relations in the making of the city. As Bengaluru was built on a high and dry plateau, its survival and expansion required the persistent work of rural communities to build up a complex water catchment and delivery infrastructure of hundreds of water tanks and spider-like channels. They fed the underground aquifers, nourished the soils, and provided year-round supplies of water for plant life, animal life, human well-being, and the potential for a complex city to be built. These dynamics become significant for our understanding of sustainable city life when conditions are good and when things go awry, as they do when this vast infrastructure and set of social relations become ignored, subverted, and eventually converted into speculative urban real estate.

Chapters 5 and 6 together focus on twenty-first-century city expansion, examining the close interactions among local developers, government officials, and foreign finance capital. Chapter 5 reveals the centrality of rural land and the rural majority's dispossession to the whole enterprise of jump-starting urban land markets and land speculation. We hear from small farmers and their advocates working to survive the mad rush for rural land and high rates of return. We also learn about the highly differentiated caste- and class-based positions they are thrown into as most must *move to survive* but with insufficient compensation and support to thrive in the new urban landscape.

Chapter 6 focuses on the most recent cycles of speculative urbanization, with an abundance of finance capital flowing into the city rooted in a completely different business model than local developers anticipated. We hear from financiers and developers on their differing goals and ambitions as well as the outcomes of finance's rapid-fire movements and business decisions. They explain how these financial ventures are based on a few key characteristics supported by finance's global reach and power. But they are also supported through the cultivation of global and local patrimonial regimes of governance—a concept that is developed in the next two chapters.

In sum, we will take a journey through the history of the city to show how old and new tensions among global financiers, government officials, and local developers—in Bengaluru and around the world—have profoundly affected social and ecological relations in city life, leaving its future in uncharted and volatile territory.

PART II

PREFACE TO PART II

[Imperias] offers a lifestyle of unquestionable quality and unrivalled elegance. Extravagant in scale, finishes and cutting edge electronics, the sleek and stylish living spaces feature an expansive backdrop of Bengaluru's iconic cityscape and the calm waters on Varthur lake. The exquisitely decorated and supremely luxurious apartments boast a range of impressive features and world class amenities. —Imperias (pseudonym), sales brochure, 2019

The sales brochure for Imperias's latest construction project on the outskirts of Bengaluru made no mention that this residential tower abuts a dusty and congested farming village, with none of the urban services that one would expect to come with "unrivalled elegance," like paved roads. I participated in a sales tour of this partially finished apartment complex. The building vibrated and echoed with construction, such that I had to squint and imagine what the place would look like beyond the rubble and sounds of jackhammers. "Imagine" became the glue that held together the narrative being woven for the potential buyer.

"See, over there," the Imperias salesman says, pointing out the window to a cluster of palm trees. "Imagine buying your home now at this price, and in a few years, right there will be a major highway which will link to the national quadrilateral highway system, connecting us to Delhi and Kolkata and the rest of the country. Imagine what this apartment would be worth once those are built." This is the perfect spot, he explains: "Everywhere your busy life takes you." I follow his gaze out the window to clogged and unpaved village roads, dust, tractors, palm groves and grainfields, and a host of meandering animals. I strain to imagine better.

The young, well-groomed salesman answers my question as to why a high-tech professional would buy here and take the risk that the village might not just roll up and disappear so that new urban amenities can move in, to the tastes of an urban professional. "Look," he says, "let me explain where this village fits into the larger scheme of the urban master plan." He flips over the price list and draws a series of circles starting from the center of Bengaluru, what is now called the central business district, which is encircled by new highways linking eight rural towns many miles apart and away, bisected by his drawn lines like a wagon wheel's spokes. Circling out from the center are two rings called peripheral ring roads. The first ring road has been built, and further out from the center is one drawn in tentative dashes, hitting the farming town of Varthur just a mile to the east of us. Although this next major highway has yet to be built, and the acres of farmland have yet to be acquired, it would run just a few hundred yards from this apartment complex. He asserts this future scenario with the confidence of a politician right before an election.

"Will we still be around to see it?" I ask jokingly, as we watch a farmer tangle with an unruly draft animal. "Yes, sure, maybe not tomorrow, but maybe tomorrow," he chuckles, "India is changing fast." In any event, he tells us, these homes are going like hotcakes. He gestures toward the horizon, where Prestige Lakeside Habitat—a massive twenty-four-tower, twenty-nine-floor, 102-acre complex in the middle of a whirlwind of brownish construction dust—is being completed. It's best for investors like me to get in now, he advises.

Do I really want a highway right out my window? What will happen to the farming community when it is paved over? Will there be a wall of high-rises perched along a smoggy highway? Isn't this the coveted green belt of the city, protected by numerous laws forbidding nonfarm activities? Haven't water levels in the aquifers dropped precipitously? All of this may be true, says the sales manager who took over once I started asking uncomfortable questions about the future's uncertainty. He admits that my skepticism is reasonable. But he insists that I could easily sell my place, just like the estimated 70 percent of buyers of new homes in the urban periphery.

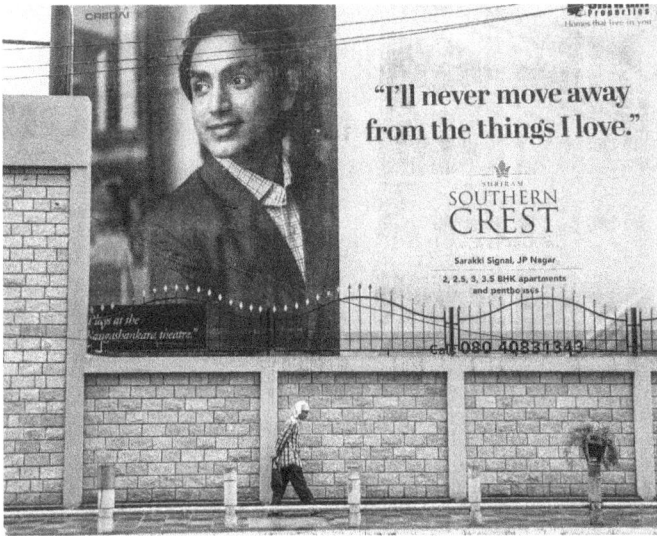

P2.1 A working-class pedestrian passes a billboard in front of a construction site for a luxury residential complex in downtown Bengaluru. Despite the advertisement's message, many new homes in Bengaluru are bought as investments, not permanent residencies, while most locals must move repeatedly to find affordable homes. Photo by Pierre Hauser.

Most people who visit the villages to scout out a deal are buying an asset, speculating on its future value, he explains; they are not primarily interested in the value of a home to enjoy. Maybe that's why the cracks and peels and wobbly guardrails may not matter to other prospective buyers, I think.

He recites from memory the rate increases of every major apartment complex in the vicinity, the buy-early price and the sell-later price difference, which tempts many buyers. You don't have to love it, he suggests, or believe in the charm of the narrative or care if the highway comes or not: You buy low and sell high and move on to the next venture. It's speculative urbanism with guarantees, for those with investment capital. Whether or not the highway comes, whether or not the water supplies dry up, whether or not the building is subpar, asset values are destined to increase. This intimate elite sensibility of risk and reward drives these village-city speculative dynamics (figure P2.1).

Part II of the book follows this speculative logic by focusing on the city of Bengaluru and its major changes over time. Arising from key historical conjunctures and new relational dynamics across the local-global spatial spectrum, the city became an important site for the growth of the global urbanist paradigm. The next three chapters probe the practices that actively disrupt the local and agrarian, replacing them with semblances of the global—the plunge pool within the luxury apartments, the Latin name, the optional "Italian marble in living room," the stylish criteria one can now find in luxury projects in Doha, Luanda, Palembang, Beihai, Valencia, and New York City. I show how this orientation of a global city became common sense, so quickly, in this village and beyond, and I document the multiple effects in the realms of finance capitalism, speculative governance, and speculative ecologies.

Part II reveals how an inquiry into the multiple lives of the city of Bengaluru helps us to see the coconstitutive and multisite nature of the processes of discourse production, dispossession by financialization, and the strengthening of ties across local-global patrimonial networks of power. Bengaluru becomes a key entrepôt site for the circulation of ideas and finance capital, and an experimental site for new innovations in speculation, finance, and governance.

"A PICTURE OF
THE FUTURE"

URBANIZATION AND THE
CHALLENGES TO DEMOCRACY
IN BENGALURU

> Bangalore, as I said, more than any other great city of
> India is a picture of the future. —Prime Minister Jawa-
> harlal Nehru, July 17, 1962, address to the Bangalore
> Municipal Corporation at Vidhana Soudha

Peering from a carriage as she toured the outskirts of Bangalore, Mrs.
L. Bowring, British wife to the British chief commissioner of Mysore,
"marvel[ed] at the sight of the many sheets of water."[1] It was November 1868—the British Raj barely a decade old—when she recorded her
Orientalist observations in a later-published travel diary: "The sugar-
cane and rice crops looked most flourishing in the low wet land under
the great tanks, which have all the appearance of natural lakes. Many
of these have been skillfully constructed, giving proof that the natives
knew something of engineering, long before English rule and public
works were thought of" (quoted in Mathur and da Cunha 2006, 95).

Indeed, as early as the sixteenth century, it was engineering and
skilled labor that enabled Bangalore to flourish. The design, building,
and maintenance acumen of local experts had carved out and built up
a complex water infrastructure, sufficient to sustain city life three thousand feet above sea level. Their gravity-driven system festooned the Deccan Plateau with more than a thousand tanks (later called *lakes*), linked
by contoured water canals, that percolated and drove the monsoon rains
into aquifers and geographically dispersed irrigation tanks. Settlers, able
to fish, plant trees, irrigate crops, raise cattle, and grow food, became

city dwellers. Mrs. Bowring's colonial peers were amazed by the infrastructure, as well as its results: Bangalore's flocks of migratory birds; the horticultural, sericultural, and floricultural specialists growing the region's finest produce; and the production of precious silks sought after by the royals of Asia and Europe. Praise for India's paradisiacal garden city would, by the new millennium, disappear, replaced by dire warnings about the impending death of the city and the end of its water supply. In 2017, when Bangalore was saddled with the *Guardian* newspaper's nickname for it—"the City of Burning Lakes"—few could deny the article's unsettling announcement that scientists feared Bangalore would be wholly "uninhabitable by 2025" (Bhasthi 2017).

The land of a thousand lakes brimming with majestic arbor-lined streets that provide crisp evenings, enveloped by the calls and flaps of migratory birds and a lush green countryside, was no more. Bangalore's largest lake, Varthur, repeatedly caught fire. It nabbed international headlines when it spewed huge quantities of toxic foam into the city's streets. The BBC reported that Bangalore was second only to Cape Town in the dubious global race to run out of drinking water (BBC News 2018). Boosters who had trumpeted the city as Asia's IT center and India's twenty-first-century metropolis were being drowned out by persistent chatter of crisis. Were ecological, financial, and social collapse imminent?

This chapter explores the historical shifts associated with Bangalore's urban development and governance in the lead-up to the global urban turn and the rise of speculative urbanism. I have organized this history into three periods: the colonial period, the postindependence period of the 1950s–1980s, and the liberalization period in the 1980s–1990s. In its ebbs and flows, the city's development can be traced through the overlapping roles of successive governance regimes and the communities of artisans and producers building the city with the ever-present need to attend to water—its infrastructure, availability, provision, health, cost, and more—and the struggle to ensure access for all. There would be no city without water and its perpetual management, and there would be no urban speculation without the water-nourished land. Hence, it is worth discovering the entangled histories of water, land, the ecological commons, and governance shifting over time that have made, and have rapidly undermined, city life.

The first section introduces the early days of the city, with fisherfolk, shepherds, farmers, herbalists, priests, and laundry washers, all of whom worked the tanks and their environs. In the long-standing land-grant system, rulers offered land to warrior groups, priests, and middle-ranked communities who served the kings/maharajas and later became dominant landowning castes such as the Vokkaligas (otherwise called the Gowdas) and the Reddys. By contrast, the out-caste Dalit community received no lands and were primarily agricultural laborers (D'Souza 2024, 2014; Shah 2008). This monarchical system was formally abolished in the 1950s, but its practices remained culturally salient and set the stage for the British colonial era, starting in the 1750s, in which Britain's ambitions, appetites, and norms reshaped India, from its rural districts to its growing cities (Goswami 2004). Considering the idea of the public city and its public works as an imperial project allows us to scrutinize the notion of urban governance under foreign rule.

The second section introduces the postcolonial independence era and the rise of India's socialist-tinged, capitalist-structured public sector. The industrial revolution of this period included widespread housing developments and new urban infrastructure, generating what a local urbanist refers to as a *multinodal urbanism*. New high-profile, high-tech industries (for example, producing radars and electric motors), along with research and education institutions, made midcentury Bangalore a technology-led public city. Yet access to and distribution of public goods continued to privilege upper-caste and upper-class communities.

The final era set the stage for the rise of speculative urbanism in this region and involves the international finance institutions (IFIs), including the World Bank, Asian Development Bank, and Japan International Cooperation Agency (JICA). They become governance actors affecting the financing and functioning of local, regional, and national government agencies overseeing goods like water, land, and housing. As the IFIs intrude, burdening developing cities with international (but non-collateralized) debt, Bengaluru begins its transition to a global city, the focus of chapters 5 and 6.

Throughout, I will return to water and its interrelational social dynamics in the establishment of the city's ecological and social flourishing. It may seem obvious, but there can be no city without the countryside and its multifarious ecology: Urbanites would have no water without the labor of villagers maintaining infrastructure and stewarding the wetlands and fertile soils that cleanse water and grow food, livestock, forests, and pastures. None of this built environment is inevitable, nor could it exist without the commingled and interdependent inputs of land, water, labor, and the oft-unequal social institutions that manage them (Nagendra 2016). Still, rapid changes have swiftly washed these basic truths from the imaginations of global-city boosters. When, in the race to build, expand, and valorize the city, land and water become primarily valued as liquid, salable assets, as collateral with future revenue potential, their roles as foundational are alarmingly forgotten. Urbanization can be a creative and fruitful social-ecological endeavor if these critical ecological and social conditions, often erased from the story of urban history, are recognized and nurtured through equitable social relations.

The First Period: From an Engineered Monarchical to Colonial Habitat

Some of the earliest settlements recorded in the Bangalore region date back to the ninth century. Even then, when there were only a few permanent structures, there is ample evidence of well-maintained water tanks. They were crucial: the Deccan Plateau simply could not be settled without people creating the conditions for, and maintaining, forested wetlands within its undulating, rain-shadowed arid landscape. Archaeologists find evidence from the 1500s of a small, secluded town, surrounded by a moat and water tanks further afield. The large-scale tanks surrounding what is still the old city's center were initiated by Kempe Gowda I (chieftain in the Vijayanagara Empire) in the 1530s and dubbed Sampangi, Karanji, and Agrahara tanks (Mundoli et al. 2018). These water catchments were carved out and maintained throughout the year, sometimes drying up during the dry season and then filling up during the monsoons; they encompassed a range of uses and went by various names—lakes, irrigation tanks, reservoirs, canals, ponds. Some tanks cover areas as large as 1.7 square miles and replenish water supplies for aquifers and numerous villages and towns.

The tanks that store monsoon rains to nurture human settlement were, in short, a vital and necessary commons under community management throughout the sweep of Bangalore's settled history (Mathur and da Cunha 2006). Overlapping political, cultural, and religious rules and norms evolved around supporting the infrastructure that allowed the city and its carefully planted and cultivated forests and pastures (go-mala) to flourish. Until quite recently, Bangalore was a destination for birders, who noted more than twenty thousand migratory species in a wetlands census taken in the 1970s. Researchers lauded this significant habitat as a stopover for ducks hailing from northern Central Asia, waders from near the Arctic Circle, and sandpipers from northern Asia (Environment Support Group 2007).

Under the authority of kings and their representatives, locals practiced ecological stewardship for many centuries—albeit typically through forced labor and mediated by the changing social hierarchy of caste. Overseen by political authorities, laborers managed the water infrastructure; sanctions ensured that many water tanks would be protected as religious artifacts, and forests as protected shrines (*gundu thopes*). Typical village water-use practices limited irrigation for food crops to regulate the tanks' recharge capacities (Mundoli et al. 2016, 2018). Planted crops were commonly low water consumers. This managed rural landscape created the possibility that a city could bloom.

But of course, this notion of ecological balance and bounty should not suggest an equally harmonious humanity. As historian Esha Shah (2012, 509) argues from her close reading of medieval Indian folk literature, the period was marked by "social anxiety, uncertainty, and violence," forced labor, and devastating droughts and famines. Today's crises extend from the conditions under which Bangalore was, in a sense, created.

Though the conditions were in place for the establishment of an urban settlement, the idea of building a city here arose out of a military defeat. When the nearby Vijayanagara Empire collapsed in 1565, artisans and traders rerouted their commerce through Bangalore. For about 140 years, its urban space grew within the boundaries of four towers, yoked by walls to protect the trading post. Existing water tanks were expanded as needed to keep the city livable. Then, with the collapse of the Mughal Empire in 1707, local leaders contested control of Bangalore; military actions under figures like Haidar Ali and Tipu Sultan brought uncertainty. Yet, by the late 1700s, Bangalore became Mysore state's thriving commercial capital. It manufactured the military's armaments, produced food crops and pressed oils, and exported volumes of fine cotton, wool, and silk textiles. The British Empire took notice.

In 1799 George Cornwallis led the British East India Company in the overthrow of Tipu Sultan, ruler of Mysore. Bangalore's riches and its strategically valuable location had proven too tempting a colonial target. A five-year-old Hindu child was installed under the grandiloquent title King of the Princely Mysore State (Krishnaraja Wodeyar III), and the British conquerors set their new Indian subjects to the work of building Bangalore's water catchment, tank, and channel infrastructure to accommodate increased settlement, economic expansion, export, and exploitation.

Ecology scholar T. Ramachandra calls the resulting ecosystem a "wetlands treasure" of maintained forests, admired up until the late twentieth century as India's garden city (Ramachandra et al. 2016). It did not come about by happenstance. When the British first took over the city, for instance, the military settled in its own cantonment, which was sustained by gravity-driven water from forests, water catchments, and farmlands in the north, flowing into channel-linked water tanks in and around the city. This system was successful for rather a long time, but a series of failed monsoons (i.e., droughts) and a devastating famine in 1875–77 forced the British to expand the urbanized water system again. They dammed the Arkavati River and added a major reservoir called Hesaraghatta Lake to the city's northwest. With 1,110 acres of surface area, twenty-nine square miles of catchment, and 174 water tanks linked by channels, Hesaraghatta's water was filtered naturally as it moved into the city center and onward to a series of lakes in the south and east. The largest of these lakes, Varthur and Bellandur, still exist, although today they are contaminated with toxic effluents and wastewater discharge. This system promised to deliver a then-impressive ten gallons of water per person per day. It still wasn't enough for the entitled colonialists living in the British cantonment, however, so they rationed—and racialized— water usage by the Indian community (not their own) and took up new water projects in the countryside.

H. S. Sudhira, a geospatial scientist who set up Gubbi Labs to map the region's contemporary and historical water infrastructures, has used survey technologies to uncover what lies beneath existing roads and buildings: a dense, intricate infrastructure (Sudhira n.d.). The old Indian marketplace (*pete*) dated back five centuries, yet the British changed its name to the pejorative Blackpetty, distinguishing it from their own military cantonment, which they labeled the white town. The cantonment was divided racially by a large park, an expansive military parade grounds, and a racetrack—as well as the strict reservation of access to resources and colonial wealth, amenities, rights, and privileges. Colonial Bangalore was built by water, in a sense, but more directly by the invisibilized work of lower-caste Indians (particularly the Neergunti), who constructed and maintained the channels and tanks, and Dalits, who did the dirty, arduous work of desilting the system and removing animal carcasses. A racialized order created by the British fueled its imperial project in India and abroad.

Throughout the early period of colonial rule, the British were building up an export-oriented industrial landscape. They taxed local artisanal craft systems, disallowed local trade, and eventually destroyed most of Bangalore's artisanal production. The British Raj refused to let Indian domestic production compete with exported finished goods from England: It sought an entirely captive market of colonial consumers as it was threatened by the South Indian economy of artisans who produced the world's finest silk and cotton textiles, supplying fashions all along the Silk Road and across the Indian Ocean to the royal tailors of Europe and Asia. And so the British intentionally undermined indigenous industrial production, flipping India's export-to-import ratio to its own economic benefit (Naoroji 1888). By the 1850s half of Bangalore's looms had closed, and the city's population dropped by 30 percent (Nair 2005, 41).

Like all colonies, the value of India to its colonizers involved the relative abundance of various resources. Water was in short supply on the plateau, but gold and land offset that inconvenience. As British gold reserves dwindled—a problem in a global economy involving primarily gold-backed currencies—production from Bangalore's Kolar gold mines was exported to England. This imperial gold grab was of enormous significance to both England (and its wealth and power in the global economy) and India (and its subjugated status and impoverishment). Had India controlled its own gold supplies, one can imagine how different the British Empire's trajectory might have been. The British Raj legitimated its land (and gold) grab in India by passing the 1894 Land Acquisition Act, which allowed for the seizure of farmland, forests, bodies of water, and the like for the purposes of building British residential areas and government offices for the colonial apparatus, which was perversely described as being for the public good. Entire neighborhoods were demolished and replaced with colonial homes served by roads and sewers, as well as telephone and electrical systems. In central Bangalore, eminent domain laws were mobilized to raze the supposedly unruly and unhygienic working-class neighborhoods, seen by the British as racialized incubators of the bubonic plague that killed a sizable percentage of the population in the closing years of the nineteenth century.

From the start, the British noted that the life pulse of Bangalore flowed through its sophisticated water infrastructure and land governance systems. By harnessing the water supplies, they could build up the geography and economy, and with military force, they could control the population to their liking. Alongside the expropriated mines for which they had a captive labor force to dig, and the roads and railways they created to truck the valuable resources off to export markets, the British built small hydro dams that provided electricity—making Bangalore the second city in Asia to electrify. This was a critical moment in the city's transformation. But let us be clear: Within what was ostensibly a process of generating *public* works for *local* urban development, the electrification of Bangalore was an international effort of exploitation. The US-based firm General Electric built the hydro plant, and its first customer was Britain's John Taylor and Sons—the company that tapped the electricity to fire up the highly remunerative British-owned Kolar Gold Fields. And when Englishman Standish Lee became the city's chief public engineer, he also held the position of CEO of the private, steam-powered Bangalore Woolen Factory and staffed it with Indians incarcerated at the Bangalore Jail. All these entrepreneurial activities occurred under British officiating, to benefit British private investors and clients; moreover, the public investment loans were paid off with tax revenues (and land and labor) extracted from the Indian populace. Bangalore's racialized economy and geography grew in all directions, but the benefits flowed in just one: toward the white British imperial economy.

As we can see, the idea of *the public* is rife with contradiction and colonial trouble, yet freely used in common parlance as a false binary with the idea of the private. With Bangalore, and Indian cities in general, this version of the idea of the public became a discursive creation of the British, a tool of intervention mobilized to justify expropriative colonial endeavors. In the next two chapters, where I show how international development agencies consider India's failure to provide essential public goods as an opportunity to intervene, we will return to this question of public and private. From the Global North, observers tut, *Why can't they manage their poor better? Why can't their cities function properly, especially with all this transfer of technology and expertise under the British, who, after all, brought backward India into the global economy?* The tidy representations of the divisions between state and market, domestic and foreign, public and private, and rural and urban ignore their obviously coconstitutive, relational, and conjunctural—in this case, colonial—nature.

Reading Bangalore's history reminds us that the urban typically emerges from the nonurban. Cities are a visible manifestation of the

work of rural grain producers, pastoralists, sericulturalists, horticul-
turalists, herbalists, hydrologists, foresters, hunters, fisherfolk, brick-
layers, mud workers, tank builders and tenders, and spiritualists. But
cities like Bangalore also emerge from the imperial encounter: When its
riches and geography attracted British investors and administrators, the
new arrivals—including the British military, insurers, financiers, merchants, and the East India Company—worked doggedly to achieve the
transformations that would render the landscapes ripe for their imperial purposes. With Orientalist and racialized justifications and colonial
business acumen, they produced a harshly disciplinary state that forced
many regions of India to become Britain's workhorse. The tendency
(and discursive practice) remains today to imagine the postcolony as
distinctively *Indian*—an independent Indian nation, a developing economy, a not-yet-modern way of life—as if turning the page on its colonial
chapter can erase history. Instead, we should see this colonial encounter
as context for setting the stage for postcolonial encounters.

The Second Period: The Urban Logic
of Postcolonial Public Governance

Historian Eric Hobsbawm (1987) describes the early and mid-twentieth
century as the Age of Extremes. As Europe was embroiled in two world
wars, its hold on its colonies and the imperial economy loosened, then
finally broke. In Bangalore the early century brought a flurry of autonomous activity from the Princely State of Mysore and its dewan (aka
prime minister), the reputable engineer M. Visvesvaraya. The dewan
chose Bangalore as a prime site for science and technology research
institutes (such as the internationally reputed Indian Institute of Science, opened in 1909) and state-sponsored manufacturing enterprises.
Soon a blossoming industrial landscape was churning out turbines, machine tools, radars, telecom equipment, scented soaps, and watches in
the government-owned and -operated factories that ringed an otherwise
modest and sparsely populated city. In-migration led to construction,
generating an urban landscape grounded in the colonial logic of the
productive economy driven by the state. On the heels of World War II,
the managers and workers in these public sector industries would have
to scramble to create urban planning as an ad hoc effort. Over time, the
independence era shifted toward a nation-building logic that sought to

accommodate workers, managers, and the demands of production. This emerging logic of urban planning focused not only on factory production but also on housing, education, health care, retirement schemes, and public amenities. Independent, nationalist ambitions led Bangaloreans (and Indians as a whole) to try to repair that which had been destroyed by 150 years of colonial rule.

In the late 1940s and 1950s, the Bangalore area enacted Prime Minister Jawaharlal Nehru's policy of national industrial development and import substitution. Production units were set up for manufacturing heavy equipment as well as aeronautics, military, and eventually space equipment, often ringed with housing and amenities-filled campuses. Originally sited in the rural periphery, the campuses sprawled out to accommodate workers and their families. In this boom period, the Hindustan Machine Tools and Bharat Electronics Limited factories alone employed well over eighty thousand workers. Hindustan Aircraft Limited aeronautics boasted more than forty-two thousand. These public sector jobs were typically secure, supported with benefits, and backed by a variety of protective factory acts and labor laws. Employees were represented by an assortment of trade unions, and union leaders filled city council seats and served among political parties' leadership, helping set the city's postindependence political agenda. As the city grew outward, the major industrial townships and public sector campuses grew to hundreds of acres and eventually comprised the city core. The Aircraft Township of Hindustan Aeronautics, once on Bangalore's periphery, sits on three thousand acres of public land. Now central pillars of a densely populated city, these units featured much-needed housing with easy credit for workers, as well as English-language schools, parks, bus service, temples and shrines, subsidized markets, cricket fields, and health clinics.

The public sector factories, to a large degree, crafted life in postindependence Bangalore. Upper-management and professional-class jobs were largely offered to upper-caste Indians, while the service and labor jobs were performed by lower-caste Indians. But unique among many other dimensions of urban life, many public sector facilities—especially the research and education institutes—offered lower-caste and Dalit employees a modicum of union-protected job security and (caste- and class-segregated) subsidized forms of care, from housing to health care to, in some cases, English-medium schools.

This rapid urban expansion affected existing water infrastructure and public lands. The nature of the public sector city was defined in large part by the culture of these enterprises. In a lengthy interview, for example, one retired public sector manager joked that "we managers" spent more time providing housing and credit to staff than on producing the goods that formed their businesses' bottom line. As he described it, the culture of management sounded what he called "people-wise but pound-foolish" in this period: "There was a feeling in those days . . . being a government-owned company, it . . . should . . . act like an ideal employer. [Employees] should be paid well, they should have housing, they should have transportation, they should be fed well. And, you know, the idea was to generate employment; therefore, overstaffing was accepted as . . . one of the responsibilities of public sector. . . . In other words . . . they were supposed to be model employers, but hardly a model company."[2]

What locals called a public sector mindset dominated the formal economy and middle-class life in this postindependence period of national reconstruction. This mindset understood that India's abundance would be shared by all and not just by upper management. The following excerpt comes from a lengthy discussion with a pair of leading Bengaluru urbanists—the adviser to the chief minister on urban affairs (whom I will call Dr. AB) and an urban research consultant (whom I will call Dr. CD). The conversation occurred at Vidhana Soudha, the seat of the state legislature of Karnataka, on June 10, 2010:

DR. AB: The industrial policy of the government in India emphasized the role of the public sector. It was called a mixed economy, where the public sector was to play a major role in the industrialization and the development of the country. The private sector was very weak to begin with, in the early 1940s, as it was destroyed by the British. And it was believed that the basic industries to the nation should all come up within the public sector—electronics, machine tools, telephone, defense, mining, transportation. So, the steel industry came up in the north and in [the] east of India, heavy electricals came up elsewhere, and here in Bangalore, we had BEL, HMT, Bharat Earth Movers, and Hindustan Aircraft Limited. We also had large segments of the defense industry, because it was felt that Bangalore was the scientific and research center and located in the southern part of India, far enough away from our so-called enemies, Pakistan and China.

From the urban development point of view, the significance is that when they all started their setup, these central government–

funded industries were given land by the State of Karnataka and built on the outskirts of the city. And now these sites are the center of the city. Back then, because they were large industries and because they employed a large number of people, they built a lot of the city. They developed what were called *townships* in wide-open spaces so that alongside the factories, housing was built for their employees, social facilities like schools and hospitals, playgrounds, and parks. Where these large public sector industries started, even today, you can find lots of open green space and plenty of facilities. Even the employees who did not live there but lived elsewhere in the city were able to obtain housing through the credit programs, and the companies arranged transport.

Today we still have the ITI [Indian Telephone Industries, Ltd.] bus, the HAL bus, which go out and pick up their employees for the work shift, and then they change their signs and switch over as buses for the general public for the rest of the day. So, in a way, housing and transport, health and recreation, were felt to be the responsibility of the employer. And the public sector was the employer.

As these townships started to expand from the edges of the city inward, the city began to develop in between and around these sites. Smaller industries came up, producing the gadgets or repairing them, producing the supplies, as need be. In this way, the city developed along the lines of the needs of the public sector industries along with neighborhoods of workers and suppliers and their own small workshops and retail shops. Other [Karnataka] state-level public enterprises developed in these spaces, given land to produce lamps [Mysore Lamps], porcelain, soap [Mysore Sandal Soaps], and many other basic goods. They are landmarks today in the city, beautifully forested plots of land that are being eyed by the real estate sector.

DR. CD: Another aspect that is important to highlight was that the public sector developed in this planned way when the factory came. It was clear that housing would be necessary, so credit unions were set up and plans were drawn up so that employees could borrow money from the employer and use some of their provident [retirement] fund money to purchase a plot for their house. Many candidates applied from across the country through national exams for these sought-after government jobs, so they needed housing upon arrival, even if they had no savings to use. In those days, you borrowed half from the credit facility set up by the employees' cooperative housing and credit societies, and the other half from the employer. For Rs. 7500 you had a house, which you paid off over many years using the money from your work, at very low interest. And the PSUs [public sector units] helped the employees set up cooperative consumer societies as well, so that they could buy food in bulk and offer it at a great discount to everyone who worked there—from janitors, sweepers, clerks, up to high management.

English-medium schools, too, were built. Many of the children—from all work backgrounds—were well trained at the PSU schools and now work abroad or here in IT. Most did well. And why not? That's how the schools were organized.

So that is a form of planning that emerged from the needs of the employees, who, of course, were needed by the employers, producing essential goods for newly independent India. It was the only type of planning that was happening in the city at the time. The city agencies merely played catch-up to the needs of the public sector industries, trying to acquire land from the villages to meet these pressing demands. This was considered a model of life and work. Still today, those who work for HMT or BEL or HAL feel they live well in the city. By contrast, for the rest of the city, no set plan exists. It just exists for the well-off. I think we could call this earlier model of urban development *multinodal urbanism*—one node here, another node there, each supporting the other.

DR. AB: Bangalore in the twentieth century really developed into a thriving city based on productive sectors with well-trained employees. Although their salaries and wages were not considered high, the benefits of a permanent job with the PSUs were the envy of everyone. You were set for life. Life was good for these public workers, and for people who lived in Bangalore, as the city's culture came from these. Today Bangalore can be considered our national technological hub and knowledge center, with the children of the first rounds of public sector unit employees being the new leaders in this IT industry. But does that make Bangalore a world city? [He laughs.] Certainly not for the physical infrastructure.

So we would have to make a distinction between the physical infrastructure and the knowledge hub. We may lead the world in terms of knowledge and IT work but not in terms of urban infrastructure or development.

This conversation captures the city leadership experiencing the growing pains of planning their way through a shift from (what they believed to be) a comfortable, public-sector-dominant culture in the postindependence era toward the much more corporatized, multinational-firm-derived IT city culture. Yet it misses the experiences of those who lost access to resources along the way. Some land users were moved off their land and incorporated into the lower-paid workforce, while others were totally left behind. When, in the late 1980s and early 1990s, a neoliberal agenda directed the government to disinvest from what were being called "sick" state-owned industries, the secure jobs that brought English-language education and subsidized benefits were stripped away. Bombay and Bangalore saw the nation's largest general strikes in the 1980s, as unions organized the workers most likely to suffer under neoliberal disinvestment. The rise of the IT economy and the aspirational rags-to-riches politics of its engineering class occurred in Bangalore because of the historically strong science and technology educational institutions and the accompanying public sector jobs. And yet public sector employment—and its strong state support—began to disappear right as the private IT sector blossomed (Upadhya 2016). Neither industry nor government could build enough housing to meet the needs of the growing population, and so illegal construction and unauthorized layouts became the norm under the watchful eye of the state government agencies in charge. This was a key turn in the city's governance trajectory (Nair 2005, 186–87).

With a notorious land-grabbing chief minister in the late 1980s willing to break the law and with developers given the green light to think big about luxury housing complexes, mega sports sites, and upscale hotels, India's government leaders stretched the meaning of the public good. Often off the record, they distributed government land and seasonally dry lake beds, urban and village commons, to upper-caste developers and brokers in the 1980s. In the 1990s these practices converged with the debt and liberalization era. In the compulsion to turn Bangalore into a high-rent global city, the local meshed with national and global trends.

The Third Period: International Finance and
Parastatal Governance Take Hold

At least two distinct forces converged in Bangalore in the 1990s. On the one hand, lower-caste workers put pressure on political and union representatives to help them overcome their diminished access to housing, safe water, and job security. On the other hand, international finance institutions (IFIS), to which national and state governments were in debt, insisted that the Indian government liberalize the economy—open up, in IFI parlance—to satisfy their expectations of unbridled growth. A city councilor (known locally as a *city corporator*) who also rotated in as mayor of Bangalore in the 1990s recalled the influx of large-scale infrastructure projects and IFI loans as changing the balance of power. He explained to me in a lengthy interview the problem with the IFIS in his jurisdiction: "1994 marked a moment of critical change in governance throughout India, with the passing of the 74th Amendment . . . empowering the third level of government . . . the local, which in our case is the city. But in Bangalore the [Karnataka] state government wouldn't allow for the city to self-govern. The state-level bureaucracy benefits too much from its oversight over city governance."[3]

He continued, explaining that the chief minister of Karnataka headed up the Bangalore portfolio, as well as the Bangalore Development Agency (BDA) and the Bangalore Water Supply and Sewerage Board (BWSSB), the land-development and water agencies through which the bulk of the international investment money flowed. But the chief minister also "takes particular interest in commanding over the city, a task which itself is quite complex. As a result, the city is completely unplanned and unmanaged and is led by big men in power, driven primarily by money-generating projects." Pointedly, using words that would stay with me, he said, "The city gets reduced to a series of financial projects run by a few men."

International visitors came and went; he experienced this foot traffic as a mayor with little power. He ticked off a list of resources no longer under city government control: "The new Metro rail system is managed by the Ministry of Urban Development in the central government. The water and buses are controlled at the state level." He noted that "very little is left for the city government to manage. Waste collection is probably the main area left for us, the mayor and the city corporation, to manage." Thus, "when international delegations would come through, from Japan or Singapore, led by the Asian Development Bank or the World Bank or JICA, we would be treated like figureheads. We'd be introduced, then told to sit over there [pointing to the corner]. We were not in the conversation. And I was the mayor! We didn't know what the conversation was about, why they were in town, what the deals were. The chief minister's office and key bureaucrats run the city, and they run it through these deals."[4]

In other words, government agencies were being retrofitted to handle this new form of capital—largely debt financing in foreign currencies—and they were made responsible for generating local sources of revenue to pay back these loans. And, as always, when local nodal agencies like these become corporatized and financialized, they lose their administrative power and become little more than intermediaries. They become brokers of rents. Local leaders would be sidelined, such that the mayor, the city government (known as the BBMP), and the city corporators elected from all 243 city wards had less substantive power than the IFI-funded parastatal agency charged with these financial obligations, oftentimes for projects not of their choosing or design. Through these measures, democracy becomes reduced to the art of the deal.

Although *parastatal*—part public, part private—is an odd name for a common modality of governance promoted by the IFIs, it resonates with an older governance modality commonly called the *company agency*. This colonial-era innovation is exemplified by the East India Company, then the world's largest private corporation. Part corporate and part public by design, the public in this structure reflected the private firm within the British colonial order but always under state control. When the World Bank and International Monetary Fund were founded in the mid-1940s, they were staffed by Westerners, mostly former colonial officers with experience in the formerly colonized countries in which they would reinvent themselves as IFI loan and policy officers (Goldman 2005). It made sense that they would import the governance structures that had brought the imperial-driven Western world so much success: the intertwining of private business objectives with the risk absorption and public authority of government agencies. Since the 1960s the IFIs have preferred their large loans to run through agencies they themselves helped to create, with a governance structure more accommodating, and beholden, to their policies and priorities. From this history, the category of the parastatal agency was born.

As noted earlier, the agencies in charge of water, electricity, and the municipality of Bangalore were established for and by colonial rule, and so it was understandable that the IFIs and the Indian elite would approach postindependence governance via parastatal agencies. The rationale held that such agencies could be isolated from local political squabbles and petty forms of illegal and patrimonial rent seeking. Nothing could be further from the truth, as we shall see. In the first phase of parastatal establishment in Bangalore, the BDA was created. It happened in the 1960s, when demand for housing far outstripped supply. The BDA was tasked with acquiring and converting land, creating roads, water mains, and electricity infrastructure primed for private developers to build housing and commercial sites. In the 1970s and 1980s, a second phase emerged when the IFIs introduced high finance to the BWSSB, the parastatal agency tasked with building up the water and sewerage infrastructure necessary to accommodate the city's rapid expansion. The third phase of parastatal governance started in the 1990s, when global private finance jumped in with a proliferation of special project vehicles suited for limited liability investments under state-led parastatal oversight. Enormous global-city projects exerted their own pull of gravity. Each phase further distanced democratic procedures from investments in the city until it was entirely financialized, as I describe in more detail below.

The BDA and the Growing Power of Parastatal Agencies

In 1976, building on the state of Karnataka's 1961 Town and Country Planning Act (a modification of the older British Town and Country Planning Act), the BDA assumed the combined roles of urban planning, land acquisition, and the building of housing layouts. As a parastatal agency, the BDA was beholden only to Karnataka's chief minister and to private financiers and developers. Its board included no elected officials, and no locally elected body had any official say in its decisions. With practically no oversight nor legal obligation should it fail to fulfill its mandate—building affordable housing for the majority—the BDA was designed to be more powerful than the elected city council, known as the *city corporation*. Over time, many residents have come to understand the

BDA as a manifestation of what critics call *government by layout*, a reference to the notion that the lucrative business of contracting out the building of housing layouts (e.g., subdivisions) drove government activities and not the reverse. The collection of bribes by the government officials awarding these contracts dominated their work schedules. With the power to acquire land and hire contractors, the BDA had, by the 1990s, become known as the city's most corrupt agency (S. Paul 1998).[5] Gone was the public sector era's managerial governance structure, outlined earlier. Instead, the BDA redefined the role of the state in city life: It was both the most unethical state agency and the lodestar engineering the transformation of Bangalore into India's premier global city.

Both the BDA and its sister parastatal, the Karnataka Industrial Area Development Board, were created amid the population surge of the 1960s. The latter acquired individual plots of contiguous land, assembling them into more sizable layouts for planned infrastructure projects and supplying basic goods such as roads, power, and water for incoming industries (Nair 2005; Murthy 1997). As land prices rose by as much as 1,250 percent between 1970 and 1985, these agencies were increasingly sought after, not only to support rapid urban expansion, but also for employment for those who wanted to benefit from the bribe-driven practices of the parastatals. All dimensions of the economy cut through these agencies, which, in a land-rentier economy, meant lucrative positions for bureaucrats. They operated under an informal pay-to-play logic, staffed with people who could operate with minimal accountability and scrutiny and who reaped maximum reward from their positions (Heitzman 2004, 53; Balakrishnan and Pani 2021).[6]

Ironically, parastatal agencies' power became amplified by their *inability* to provide adequate housing. That is, the BDA failed to keep up with waves of new urban migrants. For sure, the BDA created new housing layouts, but more than half of Bangalore's new stock of housing came from *illegal* housing or building cooperative societies operating beyond official purview (Nair 2005, 132–48). In part, this was the product of perceived necessity, yet it was also the product of BDA staffers who were handsomely rewarded by developers to look the other way while land was taken and built on. These early years of illegal housing development became entrenched, and the BDA became the key nodal gatekeeper controlling the expansion of the land market and land's conversion into real estate. As documented in numerous court cases and commissioned reports, its triumph was that it oversaw and benefited from the growth of both the legal and illegal land and housing markets.

For example, in the 1980s the BDA oversaw the upkeep of nearly four hundred water tanks or lakes within the city. Within a decade, more than a quarter had been illegally filled in for housing layouts—a system that benefited developers and BDA staff alike (Urs 2018; D'Souza 2014; Heitzman 2004, 70).[7] In subsequent years, the BDA was investigated, and a court-appointed commission revealed the agency had broken the law by allowing the sale of substantial chunks of the green belt surrounding the city. Zoned in the 1980s as protected rural and agricultural land, these 324 square miles of greenspace, equivalent to nearly two-thirds the land area of the city itself, were supposed to act as an ecological buffer offsetting city expansion (Nair 2005, 160; Murthy 1997). According to historian Janaki Nair and numerous government commission reports, the BDA illegally engineered developments that engulfed approximately 270 of the 392 villages in the green belt. It expropriated pastureland originally allotted to the landless, mostly Dalits. It allowed sections of the green belt to be turned into luxury international resorts, more than three hundred exclusive residential layouts, and water-consuming sports and entertainment complexes. It was all an open secret, resulting in few prosecutions, largely because a patrimonial network of local, state, and national politicians benefited from the schemes; they protected each other even though in their public presence, they spar as if they are sworn enemies coming from oppositional party affiliations (Nair 2005, 160; author interviews, 2012–17).

Particularly under Chief Minister Ramakrishna Hegde (1983–88), illegal layouts built by private sector developers far surpassed the legal layouts produced by state agencies. The chief minister's office and the BDA led the way, including by conducting some of the "most ruthless slum clearances" of the century via the Slum Clearance Board (Nair 2005, 173). At that time Justice Michael Saldanha of the Karnataka High Court argued that "the courts were choked with thousands of cases" of illegal land seizures and sales, "activities [which] bear the unmistakable stamp of not only collusion but active partnership of the authorities concerned" (quoted in Nair 2005, 174).

Public outcries and street protests, court filings, legislative appeals, and investigative committee reports could not stop the illegal and dominant rent-seeking and expropriative practices established by the parastatal governance of postcolonial Bangalore.

Drought and Debt: The BWSSB and the Shift
in Local Governance

The BWSSB reflects a different form of parastatal governance, more directly shaped by external forces and practices emanating from the IFIs (figure 4.1). The World Bank, deeply rooted in the colonial mind-set, saw parastatals as a cleaner and more effective form of state governance than direct local leadership. Imbued with structural autonomy and little democratic oversight, the parastatals were imagined (at least rhetorically) as existing above politics and beyond corruption. In practice, however, they would become the bane of many people's existence, as aggressive vessels for expansive dollar-denominated IFI loans. They helped to cultivate a parallel economy based on debt-financed incentives, rewards, and punishments. The BWSSB's evolution demonstrates the impulses of India, like many postcolonial states, to shed its public sector city development profile in favor of a more liberalized and subsequently financialized urbanism, rooted in and beholden to IFIs' strategies, norms, and mores.

Let's look at the element of governance oversight over the essential resource of water. If we understand Bangalore's earlier regime of water governance as catchment based, then the 1960s–1980s should be seen, by contrast, as extractive, which, over time, flows into a regime of financialization. Using substantial IFI loans, Bangalore undertook the creation of an expansive and expensive hydraulic system that extracted water by pipe from the Cauvery River, some sixty-two miles from the city and up a half-mile incline (Goldman and Narayan 2019). It was a major shift in the way water was managed and distributed (Mehta et al. 2014; Manor 2007). The burdensome loan requirements and obligations to IFIs and entities such as the Japan Bank for International Cooperation (JBIC) changed the mechanisms of decision-making as well as the role of public infrastructure in the city.

The Cauvery River water delivery project arose during "a public debate . . . raging around the need for alternative water options" as Bangalore's demand outstripped regional supply (Ranganathan 2010, 43). Neither the local system of networked tanks and wells nor the two major reservoirs along the Arkavati River could meet the city's needs, so eyes turned to South India's third-largest river. The Cauvery River has a catchment area of roughly 31,350 square miles and is the region's largest source of aboveground flowing water. But the river water would be very

4.1 New luxury homes require a steady flow of private water tankers for their daily water needs, which drains rural water aquifers. Bengaluru, 2017. Photo by Carol Upadhya.

expensive to pump uphill to the city of Bangalore—alarmingly so.[8] And no one quite knew how the city would cover that energy cost while also maintaining the existing water infrastructure at a price that the city and its denizens could afford.

In 1964 the World Bank agreed to a series of loans on the condition that the state of Karnataka empower the BWSSB as an independent parastatal agency overseeing all five stages of finance and construction for what became known as the Cauvery Water Supply Project. Nowhere in the reams of paperwork and loan contracts, however, did either the World Bank or the BWSSB assume responsibility for maintaining the age-old and once-robust catchment tank–water channel infrastructure, ailing from neglect and yet essential to the livability of the city.

Through the Cauvery Water Supply Project, financed by a multibillion-dollar loan, water became a highly extractive, centralized, and financially burdensome enterprise. It was ruled by just two forces, the BWSSB (detached from public participation and government oversight, beholden to IFIs and loan contracts) and Karnataka's chief minister. Under this centralized regime, water was used as a generative asset. Its real and perceived scarcity required prices that produced revenues to service its loans. Since it was politically and ethically unviable to raise water prices, it conjured a dependency on a constant supply of international lending. Over time, the BWSSB became Bangalore's most powerful—and most indebted—parastatal agency. It borrowed more than US$35 billion from IFIs in 2017 alone, necessitating a focus on debt servicing and cost recovery via increasing water fees, land sales, and other financial moves. This shift in priorities overshadowed the goal of producing an equitable and sustainable city water distribution system, giving priority instead to allocating this scarce resource in the most lucrative ways—generally, to real estate investors unwilling to undertake luxury housing projects without water provision guarantees (Express News Service 2018; Rath 2017).

A longtime researcher-scientist told me a version of the story of the Cauvery Water Supply Project by foregrounding the politics of distribution and allocation, suggesting that power relations were embedded in its very infrastructure. The project, he said, prioritized the city of Bangalore over the rest of Karnataka, and the upper-caste and upper-class neighborhoods of Bangalore over the rest of the city. All this came at the expense of the countryside of middle-caste, lower-caste, and Dalit communities, where, despite the city's growth, the bulk of the state's population still lives. As he put it, "Farmers tended to be the losers":

> Farmers in 2008 actually tried to block water to Bangalore. It was a huge protest. There were [similar] riots in the 1990s. The state aggregates water as a resource, and you can see the disparities in the dynamics of water sharing. Today less than half of Bangalore's water demands are met by the Cauvery project. A lot of the water is allocated to middle- and upper-class areas, which means half of the city's population is tapping groundwater [on their own] to survive, yet groundwater levels have fallen so sharply that many can't live off it. In one neighborhood, after a lot of government petitioning . . . [residents] used dynamite to blow a hole and put in a network of pipes to divert the [city] water.[9]

Indeed, the spatial unevenness of Bangalore's sprawling, urbanized periphery has resulted in middle-class and elite households receiving most of the limited water connections, while poorer communities rely on shared hand pumps or usurious water markets (Merchant et al. 2014; Ranganathan et al. 2009). By 2019 the water utility pumped some 400 million gallons from the Cauvery River every day for an urban population of over ten million people (Rajashekar 2015). Even if this water were evenly distributed, which it is not, residents would still receive less than the international standard for a metropolitan city (Raj 2013a, 2013b). The official measures are unable, of course, to account for the fact that in Bangalore one-third of the population suffers housing precarity, many lack indoor plumbing, and water access can require making large payments to private water sellers and standing in long lines at scarce public taps. Official measures also fail to capture the other extreme: the dedicated pipelines provided (informally and formally) by state officials to industrial estates, including the new airport, the IT corridor, and the many new exclusive gated communities.

As current and retired administrators acknowledged in interviews with me, the Cauvery Project, like others before it, has turned its focus to capital. Its cost-recovery logic privileges large consumers and large loans but excludes small farmers and most city dwellers from the public water grid. Further, though scientists insist the river's volume is decreasing and its flow is becoming less stable, city managers and developers have bet on the increased flow promised by the Cauvery Project lenders and boosters. They have shifted priorities and funding entirely away from the legacy water catchment systems. No longer basing calculations on the limits of the water catchment and lakes infrastructure, the resource brokers have undertaken a riskier speculative calculus that hinges on potential future revenue from potential future water flows while ignoring the combined effects of climate change and overconsumption of water (Patil 2011; Nair 2005).

As a result of encroachment and neglect, under both the BWSSB and the BDA, Bangalore has lost over two hundred of its lakes in the past three decades (Ramachandra et al. 2015). The remainder have shrunk in size and become heavily polluted with unregulated and unfiltered waste from industrial and residential discharge (figure 4.2). Most of the water channels that link the city's lakes are no longer cleaned or maintained, and so they function as ad hoc garbage dumps. They are full of toxic sludge, jammed with waste. In an interview, geospatial scientist H. S. Sudhira stresses the damaging consequences of destroying this system: "Once we started to concretize [i.e., pour concrete over] the city and its

4.2 One of Bengaluru's largest lakes, Varthur, has been catching on fire and emitting large quantities of toxic foam as a result of unregulated wastewater effluents flowing in from upstream water channels and from new luxury apartment complexes nearby. Bengaluru, 2017. Photo by Pierre Hauser.

periphery, and turn our backs on the catchment system in all its complex and fragile components, we began to destroy the carrying capacity of the city."[10]

Like the researcher quoted previously, Sudhira notes that "the farming communities suffered the most." But building over and eroding the catchment system "affects us all." Looking at the time-lapse maps of Bangalore's disappearing catchment network was all the evidence he needs to argue that the city is experiencing a climate crisis of its own making: "Just look at the maps and you can know why when it rains in the city now, it floods instantly. There is no place for the rain to go. We have completely forgotten how this city was built."[11]

Back in 2009, a seasoned BWSSB consultant from USAID explained to me his view of the downsides of the agency's financialization. Context was key: The IFIs had, in the 1990s, undertaken a global push to privatize municipal water systems to leverage borrowed capital via massive government-backed debts. Their mistake was underestimating the public sentiment against that effort. Thus, as an anti–water privatization movement grew in Bangalore, BWSSB's lenders were insisting that the water agency outsource its work to reduce expenses and circumvent the public sector unions, a surreptitious path to full privatization. He explains:

> I can name the ten basic tasks under the BWSSB to run a water utility, and most of these tasks have been outsourced, some to local firms, some to global consultants, all financed by external capital from the IFIS. The planning process itself has been outsourced to [Australia's] AusAid, the financials to a British firm, Operations and Assets such as pumps and filtration plants to German and French firms, maintenance to a local firm, and only meter reading and collection remained with the BWSSB staff itself. [The Japanese] JBIC and the ADB [Asian Development Bank] and the [World] Bank have lent [many] billion[s], and God knows what is happening. The chair insists there is no privatization, and social movements won't allow it, yet it has already happened, as most tasks are outsourced, much of it is financed through debt. The only two tasks that remain internal are the collection of checks from customers and the reading of meters, which are a big source of corruption. That's it.[12]

He continues, "I was hired to study the agency and make suggestions on how to improve service and keep it financially viable. I recommended a public investment of $200 million and the government could deliver clean and ample water within seven years. But it was rejected. Seven years later, BWSSB lined up a $2 billion loan, and it still has no ability to deliver water to the tap for most people."[13] When I ask him why the cost of water delivery became so inflated, he responds:

> This is how I calculated the distribution within BWSSB of these huge amounts of borrowed capital: Typically, 15 percent goes to interest on the loan; 15 percent is guaranteed profit rate for contractors; 15 percent filters into the political party system; 15 percent filters into the bureaucratic system. Management gets paid in euros, and loans are repaid in euros. What does this leave to distribute water to the population? Where is there incentive for the system to work? Because there is no democratic oversight or democratic process, the success is in fact in the distribution of the loans to these constituents, leaving little money or incentives to try to provide water.

In [the coastal city] Mangalore, there was a huge controversy over their IFI-financed water projects that went nowhere. When the city corporators were asked point-blank by a video crew if the project's finances were based on foreign loans or grants, they had no idea it was all loans to be repaid in foreign currency. Once they learned this, they could not explain how the fees generated from their water system could repay such expensive loans.

From his experience, this consultant laid out the systemic incentives that deprioritized the public mission of delivering water and the transparency of the contractual obligation signed with the IFIS. State governments like Karnataka are saddled with huge debts, but there are no negative repercussions to continuing to borrow. In fact, it is amazingly lucrative. The consultant explained that the Japanese government bank JBIC, for instance, would not consider a project for under $250 million. Financial agencies from around the world lend to invest Northern capital in new regions of the Global South, deemed undervalued. They benefit from the guaranteed rates of return associated with government-backed infrastructure projects and from the fact that each loan contains obligations to purchase capital goods from the country packaging the loan. As is the long-standing tradition of the development banks, a healthy percentage of capital goods and services procured for these projects must be purchased from that finance company's home country (Goldman 2005). Much like the arrangements implemented in the British's colonial railways projects in India, investing in India's cities today represents a guaranteed investment that brings returns for Global North firms and financial agencies (Balachandran 2003; De Cecco 1974; Thorner 1950; Jenks 1927).

With pressure from the World Bank, the central government of India no longer guarantees loans from Japan's JBIC; that is, it won't pay up if the local government agency defaults. So JBIC goes directly to the city and requires that the government of Karnataka guarantee these loans. When we spoke in 2009, the water consultant explained that the BWSSB owed more than $20 million for a JBIC loan on the stage IV of the Cauvery Water Project. Since the BWSSB could not afford to repay it, the central government had agreed to repay it but took the capital from the state budget, which took it from the city government. Where will it come from, he asked rhetorically, when the city budget is minuscule and primarily dedicated to schools, health, waste management, and social welfare?

The BWSSB's chairman granted me an interview in which he laid out his own concerns about the loans. In short, it was all about inflation and the consistently falling rupee exchange rate. With the Indian rupee forever vulnerable to the Japanese yen and the US dollar, currency rate fluctuations can create risks that stretch far beyond repayment plans:

> Although many of us have been in Bangalore as engineers for decades, when JBIC or ADB show[s] up with a loan, the central government's project monitoring consultants design a turnkey project along with the Japanese consultants, while we are tasked with implementing it. We get little say. Whenever we meet with IFI officials, we are always asked to inflate by many times our "ask." At the moment, we must borrow at 9 percent interest rate, but because of currency fluctuation and rupee devaluation, the price tag for borrowing ends up rising to 20 percent, making it impossible to repay and at the same time to fulfill the mandate of delivering water to everyone in the city.
>
> They ask us to see water as a commodity, but that's such an odd thing. They want every project to be a "bankable" project, which means they want these to be full-cost recovery. But the consumer will never be able to pay for its true dollar or yen cost. Right now, consumers only pay 10 percent of the true cost of water and sewerage, in rupees. How do we get from here to there?[14]

The agency's managing director had his own concerns on the administrative side, which he explained to me in an interview. Every year, the base of water customers increases, while his agency's staff size decreases. Many hundreds of employees were nearing retirement age. When we toured the BWSSB offices, most were empty—not only of managers and engineers but of stuff. The managing director waved toward a hulking machine covered by a thick, opaque plastic sheet—it was the latest in geospatial mapping and analysis technology, left unused by some high-paid foreign consultants. I asked whether he'd ever sat down to try out the state-of-the-art computer, but he only laughed and offered a humble, obvious point: "We weren't trained in this. I am a civil engineer and will retire in a few years. Who on my staff can learn how to work this?"

Replacing the plastic cover, he seemed dismayed, as the computer was a sore reminder of all that is lost when a public enterprise is dismantled and financialized. When his staff retire, they are not replaced. They take with them the accumulated and shared local knowledge about building and overseeing the underground water infrastructure. "Who will know where the fickle underground pipes or pumps are, what the building concerns are, where to adapt and what to adjust?" He predicted that soon after the agency's complete financialization, the whole city's underground water infrastructure will become a mystery to those overseeing and maintaining it.

The BWSSB's chairman spoke with me about the public controversy over the dedicated pipelines bringing water to the international airport and the IT corridor, right through dense working-class neighborhoods that get none of that public water. The agency was so far in debt, and the demands on it were so great, he explained, that they were forced to bend to their most powerful clients. Once the secretly dedicated pipelines to special clients were no longer a secret, the largest developers demanded that *their* projects also get dedicated pipelines connected to the Cauvery system. Under his watch, the politics of water allocation had changed. "There is displacement by land, but this is displacement by water. With farmers [surrounding the city] losing access to water, and other interests demanding theirs, water has become a serious political issue," the chairman conceded.

With the water agency now responsible for repaying loans for which it cannot generate enough revenues, the governance process has become financialized; that is, more of its daily activity is premised on the need to find more city resources to convert into moneymaking liquid assets. It must continue to borrow more and therefore take on more debt to keep the debt-financed agency alive. A high-risk speculative governance regime emerges from this cauldron of a messy debt-financed water system.

As stated above, the BWSSB is not mandated, either by the state or by the IFI lenders, to manage, protect, repair, or extend the gravity-driven, community-developed water catchment infrastructure and lake system that kept the city and country hydrated for centuries. As it pursues the Cauvery Project with single-minded zeal, the agency has abdicated any responsibility for the existing system on which most of the city's population once depended. The changes that forced the BWSSB into outsourcing, shifted its logic toward borrowing and its obligation to repay debts, and rewarded other countries' firms with lucrative procurement contracts made something as straightforward as water delivery prohib-

4.3 As more of the public commons have been encroached on by developers and plans for global-city projects, the luxury complexes create their own private commons, with surveillance cameras and security guards to ensure privacy and exclusivity. Brigade Gateway complex, Bengaluru, 2016. Photo by Pierre Hauser.

itively expensive. The fundamental goal of a public water agency has become unachievable.

Economist Sharadini Rath sums up the problem of Bangalore's parastatal shift in governance: "All loans to the state are hidden in the parastatals, and they are terrifying. They are like those futuristic monsters in the movies that keep growing and take over the city! BWSSB's debt is so huge, it's crazy. From my study, it is clear that the city and state governments only have land to sell, in hopes of paying off some of its debts. What a way to run a city."[15]

Conclusion: Who Is the Public in the "Public's Interest"?

As Bangalore's water agency became corporatized and financialized, its emerging logic of debt financing challenged the older rationale emanating from the public sector governance structure (figure 4.3). Some of the loudest protests have come from constituents demanding a return to the days of public sector governance, when water was sparse but accessible. There were bountiful lakes and canals from which to access water, and the underground aquifers were close to ground level and easy to tap. Today water levels are more than eight hundred feet down, and the water is mostly contaminated by subsoil minerals and city pollutants. Farmers demand access to water for irrigation, and middle-class housing organizations demand access to public water via the Cauvery water project and/or lower prices for private trucks to bring water in. Working-class neighborhood associations plead for their sewers and canals to be cleaned and their taps to run again. Activists call for an end to negotiations around the further privatization of the BWSSB. But the structural constraints lenders have placed on the city have made water delivery to everyone an unattainable goal. These forces have transformed government priorities and agency culture. As Bangalore's parastatal agencies overseeing land, water, and housing become financialized, their organizational logic and goals move away from the responsibility to supply public goods and toward the responsibility to fulfill the demands of financiers (Iyer 2014).

In the life courses of the BWSSB and the BDA, land, housing, and water are goods that, in their scarcity, create vibrant contraband markets, tradeable liquid assets, and deepening public anxiety. Life might be technically survivable without access to these basic public goods, but it's awfully unpleasant and difficult. At the tail end of the postindependence, public sector era of urban expansion, India's government leaders made choices in line with IFI lending practices that would change Bangalore's trajectory and challenge the idea of the democratic right to the city.

The overarching questions of the next two chapters are: Why did this city become such a desirable site for highly speculative ventures by global investors other than the traditional IFIs noted here? What structural incentives helped to create the markets that global finance finds it comfortable to enter and exit? In a close look at business transactions before and after the 2008 financial crisis, I demonstrate how high-value markets of land, water, and real estate are molded in large part by a closely aligned local network of elites flexing their caste, class, and gender power, strengthened by the authority of finance and working in close alliance with a parallel network of transnational actors. These next two chapters highlight the key features of speculative urbanization as it unfolds in Bengaluru—a case study that reflects practices occurring in other cities that strive to fall under the mystique of the global urban turn.

THE MAKING OF AN URBAN LAND MARKET

DISPOSSESSION, FINANCIALIZATION,
AND THE EMERGENCE OF
BENGALURU AS A GLOBAL CITY

> Justifying a model of economic transformation that does not treat rural citizens as partners in the largest rural democracy in the world may ultimately be a deeper challenge to a substantive notion of democracy than corruption. —Kanchan Chandra, "The New Indian State: The Relocation of Patronage in the Post-Liberalisation Economy," 2015

> We can fight for the right to the *paisa* (money) but never for the right to land. —Dalit advocate, Bengaluru Rural, 2016

It has been a wretched decade for most small farmers in India. After years of distress, drought, debt, and persistent pressure to give up their land for urban real estate deals, hundreds of poor farmers from Tamil Nadu in southern India captured the country's attention in March 2017 as they occupied the streets of New Delhi, 1,370 miles from home. They performed a disturbing spectacle of humiliation and desperation that government ministers quickly tried to stop, realizing how this protest deeply challenged national faith in the Indian growth miracle (*Hindustan Times* 2017). The protesters sat surrounded by dozens of skulls of farmers who had committed suicide, gnawed on live fat rats and snakes, and ran around naked and in women's saris. None of this was in jest. It marked the desperation of millions of rural citizens caught in the crossfire of policies to remove government supports for small farming and increase funding for urban projects that require cheap and plentiful access to rural land and resources.

Three years later, on November 26, 2020, an astounding 250 million people (according to the Indian Farmers' Union) celebrated Constitution Day by launching a general strike that brought the capital New Delhi and other cities to a standstill. If that number is even partially accurate, this would have been the world's largest protest. Tens of thousands of trucks jammed the city's corridors. This nationwide outpouring of grief and outrage was the culmination of protests that started two months earlier when the central government passed three farm bills to end the postindependence Mandi system. This system allowed farmers to sell their output to the government with a minimum price guarantee, offering them some security at planting time, when they typically take out loans and are otherwise extremely vulnerable to price fluctuations. The Modi regime, suddenly and without any public consultation, replaced this system with a so-called free market in which large agribusiness firms have a heavy hand in determining prices for farmers. These 2020 agrarian reforms destroyed any hope among small-scale farmers that the government would support them through market volatilities, drought, and debt. More than 60 percent of India's population—and 70 percent of women—depend on farm employment for their livelihoods. Most female workers in farming are Dalits who do not own land. As one journalist noted, "India's suffering female farmers have the most to lose" from these new farm bills, and "the country's Dalits are already exploited—and know it can get worse" (Dastidar 2021).

The displacement of Dalit farmers to make way for a new international airport project twenty-two miles north of Bengaluru was smaller in scale than the crisis confronting these protesting farmers but equally painful. Landless and penniless, displaced farmers denounced this landmark global-city project with powerful slogans, calling it the place where "the planes are landing on the graveyard of the Dalits!" This sentiment stands in stark contrast to the billboards decorating the airport road, one of which portrayed a future of luxurious high-rise apartment complexes where light-skinned global elites leaned down from their decks while glancing at golf courses, swimming pools, and shopping malls. Above them appeared the slogan "Brigade Exotica: Life Looks Better When Viewed from the Top." This chapter explores these sharply divergent perspectives and landscapes. It focuses on the deceptively simple process of land transactions, in which a government agency facilitates the purchase of low-value farmland to convert it into high-value urban real estate. Government officials see this transfer of land to developers, reportedly the catalyst for India's recent phenomenal rise in land prices, as the primary engine of transformation for this once-sleepy South Indian city. Most small-scale and lower-caste farmers, however, are left out, or pushed out, of this land bonanza.

In and around Bengaluru, according to protesting farmers and their legal advocates, a highly speculative regime of power has come to rule, invigorated by the sizable sums of finance (and politically related) capital flowing into the land market. Although the official discourse of caste claims that caste violence and discrimination disappear once the backward rural transforms into the modern urban, nothing could be further from the truth. In the conversion of the rural periphery into the fast-growing city of Bengaluru, a patrimonial regime of caste power rules over land transactions. Along with the demands of finance, this regime ends up exacerbating existing social inequalities by extracting value from the land of lower-caste communities. It thus turns the terrain into financial assets to nourish and expand local and global patrimonial regimes of power and wealth (T. Li 2014).

In other words, financialization of the city could not happen in Bengaluru in the manner it did without the original move to expropriate vast amounts of rural land at a discount, which required the dispossession of already vulnerable communities. It started in earnest with the designation of vast acreages of Dalit land and public commons twenty-two miles north of the city to put up a new international airport and surround it with state-of-the-art special export zones flush with factories producing high-value IT and biotech goods and services, with exclusive residential gated communities to follow. Or at least that was the premise. This chapter reveals how this major global-city project became the catalyst for speculative urban transformation across this metropolitan landscape and fed into similar socio-spatial disruptions elsewhere.

This chapter looks at the city from the perspective of the social dimensions of land: at what was acquired, converted, displaced, and negated in rural society as a precondition for the emergence of urban real estate and the financialized global city. I call this *dispossession by financialization* since dispossession becomes the key condition and catalyst for state and financial actors to successfully expropriate and transform land and its grounded social relations into liquid assets that circulate through global capital networks. Dispossessed land can take on many forms in these capital networks—debt, equity, revenue streams, securitized bonds, investment trusts, collateral. At the same time as its liquid manifestations can fly away like an eagle, its illiquid manifestations—land as nature, kinship, vitality, community, food, pasture, forest, wildlife home, water tanks and channels, watershed—become diminished, concretized, and isolated from the public commons (Goldman et al. 2024).

Up until the late 1990s, Bangalore was small, occupying only eighty-seven square miles. In the brief boom prior to the 2008 global crisis, it expanded fourfold through incorporating 120 villages and seven towns. Developers had ambitious plans for Bengaluru to become one of the world's largest megalopolises in the next few decades. This global-city expansion plan mobilized local developers and politicians as speculators. True to their hopes, the rural land surrounding the new airport project rose astronomically in value within a decade. In some places, land prices increased by as much as 9,900 percent.[1]

In 2019, after years of a series of escalating land booms, much of the land around the airport and its affiliated zones of development remained undeveloped and yet completely unaffordable for the displaced rural majority. It is populated with a few industrial plants and underoccupied gated communities. As a result of the frenzy of land speculation, thousands of small farmers were either pushed off land they had occupied for decades or forced to sell land to which they held title at bargain-basement prices. How can we fathom this highly profitable yet socially volatile experience? Where did the dream go awry?

Dispossession by Financialization

Scholars of similar land grabs utilize geographer David Harvey's accumulation by dispossession framework to explain how and why elites can capture the appreciating value of land in places where land once had little market value (Fairbairn 2020; Levien 2018; Vasudevan 2008; Harvey 2003). Harvey updates Karl Marx's concept of primitive accumulation (and the process of the enclosure of the commons) by situating it within the context of post-1970s advanced capitalism and neoliberal politics. He and his colleagues emphasize renewed possibilities of wealth accumulation through the expulsion of vulnerable and seemingly underproductive populations, thereby overcoming barriers for capital to expand into new territory and experiment with new and old forms of extraction (Sassen 2014; Banerjee-Guha 2013; Kundu 2010; Sanyal

2007). In India the financial feasibility of large-scale urban expansion projects depends on the acquisition of the rural land surrounding cities, from which small agricultural producers must be displaced, with or without compensation.

Harvey situates the imperatives and logic of dispossession solidly within the terrain of economic class relations and the internal logic of capital to explain how wealth accumulation travels across space (i.e., national borders), using the city as a new place to harbor capital investments. This "spatial fix" helps investors overcome typical obstacles to capital accumulation by moving to fresh sites of exploitation. But as sociologist Michael Levien (2012) argues, Harvey minimizes the constitutive role of "extra-economic coercion" in Marx's theory of dispossessive forms of accumulation by downplaying the critical significance of the state. State actors, Levien argues, *devalue* activities that were carried out on the land before it was expropriated and *revalue* them once that land becomes incorporated into the capitalist mode of production. In other words, states and state actors actively help create the capitalist land markets from which elites primarily benefit.

Levien shows how the making of India's special economic zones (SEZs) on rural farm and commons land in northwestern India, a source of substantial profits for investors, could not have occurred without aggressive state actions to support major urban and industrial projects for which the state lacked financial resources. These activities included deregulating land markets and disinvesting from rural economies and villages, converting rural public land into urban real estate, and offering large tax-free enticements to domestic and foreign investors. According to Levien, India's state restructuring since the 1990s enabled it to become a "land broker for capitalists in a situation where rising demand for land confront[ed] a rigid supply controlled by a large number of small peasants" (2012, 941). This is an apt description of processes in and around Bengaluru. Neither dispossession nor accumulation could have happened without the active participation of state officials and political institutions.

In this chapter I want to take Levien's analysis a few steps further by highlighting the complexity of both concepts—dispossession and accumulation—as they manifest in places like Bengaluru and its surrounding rural landscape. The term *accumulation* tends to be interpreted as a process of capital investment and exploitation within the realm of production. Although new infrastructure projects may appear to be productive investments, on closer inspection they often become debt burdens for the public. Although designed to offer world-class amenities and services, they often become too expensive to complete or run. Thus, many become hosts to financial investors rotating in and out, taking advantage of early revenue projections and then exiting when asset values start to plummet. What appears as something that offers productive economic qualities may actually turn into a financialized asset that primarily benefits those investors, who control supplies of finance capital, rather than the public, who are held over a barrel. While they need the goods and services, such as a highway, housing, or an upgraded water system, they are unable to control financiers' manipulation of contracts to allow limited liability and maximum capital liquidity.

Vulture capitalism is a common moniker for such actions that take advantage of a dying endeavor for self-enrichment. Some critics see these types of ventures as parasitic on the body of capitalism, leaching out surplus value in ways that suck the blood out of projects to build, house, industrialize, farm, and transport, which can cripple the functioning of capitalism itself. Many of the infrastructure investments discussed in this chapter indeed became dying bodies once foreign capital entered, after which new financial tools were introduced through which global finance could more easily convert nonperforming assets (such as bankrupt shopping malls and office buildings) into liquid assets whose value could be expropriated and circulate elsewhere profitably. Wherever they travel, these investments rarely become responsive to local needs, investors, or communities. The rise of speculative urbanism reflects a tectonic shift in the ways that cities borrow and global finance invests. It is significant enough to merit highlighting a key dimension of the process, that is, financialization, that goes beyond a typical interpretation of capital accumulation (Kaika and Ruggiero 2016).

Instead of focusing on accumulation by dispossession as a singular economic process, I start with the question of what happens in the land-conversion process and observe the multiple transactions and ripples at work. This encompasses the shift in capitalist practices by those who control the flow of capital and the ways in which an assemblage of caste-class-gender power is mobilized by a patrimonial regime of caste-based governance. Here we see the blurring of the role of the state, as state actors take advantage of caste power differentials and ready access to financial backers to produce a system in which government and political-party actors become enriched by land transactions. Unlike what the singular definition of site-based dispossession suggests, these conjunctural moments in rural-urban transformation are much more relationally dependent, unfolding at multiple scales and across borders.

Accumulation in this context of global-city making features investors who channel their capital into assets that can be used as collateral for the circulation of capital, rather than as the foundation for a fixed infrastructural project. In many cities around the globe, from Shanghai to Valencia to Bengaluru, speculative urbanism leads to the proliferation of phantom housing built for speculators, not for end users, which often remains empty, and of ghost cities that have been built but remain largely empty.

As we can see, the productive side of land use in terms of labor's sweat equity does not determine the value of land in cities today (Goldman 2015). In Bengaluru very few ex-farmers have been proletarianized through this process, as few industrial jobs await them. Rather, it is the *rate of dispossession* on the back end and the *rate of financialization* on the front end that create the value that circulates through markets (Levien 2018). Its realization occurs when firms take advantage of, or create opportunities for, value fluctuations across the globe. This chapter shows how these various forms of displacement and disruption do not lead to accumulation in the productivist sense but instead to financialization. Bought and then sold, monopolized values are freed from their earthly fixed locations and circulate through financial firms or their limited liability companies or special project vehicles. These investments in India have generated some of the highest returns in the global economy for global firms through the late 2010s and early 2020s (Alexander and Antony 2018). Using the airport region as an exemplar, I explain in the rest of the chapter how and why global-city projects create displacement and disruption.

The Birth of a Speculative Land Market

Bengaluru is one of the fastest-growing cities in Asia, and its extended reach into the countryside is one of its most attractive features for city boosters and investors. There are three major speculative-urban projects undergirding Bengaluru's recent experiment as a global city: the airport development area in the north; the IT corridor, a privately incorporated entity on the east side; and the Bengaluru-Mysore Infrastructure Corridor to the south, which involves plans to connect Bengaluru to the city of Mysore, some eighty-seven miles away.[2]

Combined, these three global-city projects more than doubled the city's size. They are part of a national experiment in global urbanism, which involves investing in world-class infrastructure and real estate projects to spur economic growth. Eminent domain laws oblige farmers to sell land, and government agencies to convert public lands and rural spaces into an ever-expanding urban landscape. The next section focuses on the financial dimension of the airport project to highlight how it became the catalyst for a rapid-fire process of land conversion, small farmer displacement, and the creation of a speculative and lucrative land market on the city's north side.

Jump-Starting the Financialization Process:
The Airport Investor Contract

The logic of twenty-first-century finance first emerged in the region in the form of a contractual agreement between the Karnataka state government and the firms investing in and building Bengaluru's new airport, first called Bengaluru International Airport and renamed Kempegowda International Airport in 2013.[3] The city had outgrown its old airport, which was built for military planes in what was once the fringe of the city and is now a crowded neighborhood near the burgeoning IT corridor. But the cost of building an international airport was prohibitively expensive for the municipal government, which was unable to collect sufficient funds from property taxes, business taxes, or user fees. As with most public infrastructure proposals in the twenty-first century (in India and globally), the Karnataka government agreed to a public-private partnership, which included Thai, Swiss, and German investors. The contract offered substantial land giveaways and financial enticements. This suggests that the major investors did not anticipate making adequate profits by solely providing airport and transport services (i.e., the productive element of the airport). This business strategy has now become common: to purchase shares in an airport not for its air traffic profitability but for its future rentier value increases from new commercial and real estate projects linked to the airport infrastructure. Although the public was not allowed to see the contract, on the grounds that it was proprietary, it did not take long before the details were leaked and circulated widely on the web (Ministry of Civil Aviation and BIAL 2004).

5.1 A runway at Kempegowda International Airport in Bengaluru, 2016. The runway is known as "the Dalit's graveyard" because the airport was built on what was once a Dalit-majority village. Photo by Pierre Hauser.

When it first opened in March 2008, the airport was a modest structure, with one runway, a café, and a gift shop. But it did have some extraordinary features. It was the first public-private partnership airport in India, and it was built north of the city in the protected green belt that included forest, lakes, pastures, and a wide swath of small farms and villages inhabited primarily by lower-caste and Dalit communities (figure 5.1). As part of the deal, an extra thousand acres were given directly to the investor consortium of Bangalore International Airport Limited, or BIAL, to use as it pleased, and it had to pay only about 1 percent of its annual profits in taxes (BIAL 2016). The original cost of the airport complex was Rs. 1,200 crores (units of ten million), or $146 million, with the government of Karnataka contributing land in exchange for a 13 percent equity share.[4] The engineering firm Larsen and Toubro and the Zurich Airport firm each received a 17 percent share in the company, while Siemens Project Ventures of Germany had a 40 percent stake.

The deal was structured such that the government of Karnataka would deliver cheap land to major investors, who could then enjoy the benefits of escalating land values and spur productive investment on the acquired rural land (Ministry of Civil Aviation and BIAL 2004). The investor consortium received four thousand acres to be used for the international airport and its related services, of which a thousand acres comprised "the gift." Two thousand more acres were set aside for an aerospace SEZ, and ten thousand to twenty thousand acres were earmarked for an IT industrial zone. There were also promises of a Financial City, Science City, and more, much like the speculative projects in and around cities such as Dubai, Kuala Lumpur, and Shanghai. A parastatal agency, the Bengaluru International Airport Area Planning Authority, was created to oversee the expansive development area. The job of the Karnataka Industrial Area Development Board (KIADB) has been to notify farmers and acquire their land, pay a set rate of compensation, and supply very basic infrastructure, such as roads and electricity, for upcoming urban projects surrounding the airport.

According to the airport project contract, approximately two thousand acres of government land were leased to the BIAL corporate consortium at Rs. 1 ($0.01 in 2023 dollars) per acre per year. Yet when the value of the government land contributed to the project was assessed, the land was assigned a market price of Rs. 200,000 ($3,000) per acre. Ten years later, an acre of land not far from the airport sold for approximately $1 million, and at least twice that by 2018, reflecting a substantial rate of appreciation and return on investment. A villa on one-sixteenth of an acre nearby sold in 2015 for a price of $850,000. The villa salesman explained to me that most of the villa buyers in this upscale upper-caste gated community were not end users but speculators. Few would choose to live there since very few industries had emerged around the airport, as had been hoped. But the business model for such gated enterprises anticipates IT professionals from other areas looking for good investments to bank their income, helping them weather the storms of a volatile IT sector forced to compete globally by using periodic layoffs as a signal to their investors that they mean business. Hypercompetition within these professional sectors was the perfect context for producing investors in second homes for upper managers as well as for nonresident Indians living well abroad.

The consortium invested in this airport scheme only on the condition that the state government give them ample rural land at a heavily discounted price, with some free land thrown in as an incentive. Parcels of farmland have changed hands many times since the initial acquisition, and each time the value of the converted land has increased substantially. To some observers, this signaled the project's definitive success. Building an airport far outside the bustling city triggered a high-value land market that enticed investors (especially nonresident Indians) from all over the world and handsomely compensated people from the stagnant primary economic sector of agriculture. But the initial contract also signaled that the construction of a global-city airport would *not* necessarily be a catalyst for large-scale capital infusions into high-value industrial projects and lifestyle communities without heavy subsidies and outright gifts. Therefore, built into the investment model was the necessity of access to cheap land *and* an easy exit from projects, soon after, or even before, the concrete was dry. This looks similar to many other public-private partnerships for infrastructure projects that are driven by financial investors' business models (Glaeser and Joshi-Ghani 2015; Sankhe et al. 2010). It also reminds us of the guarantees the British Parliament offered to financial firms to further its imperial ambitions in colonial India.

According to the contract, foreign investors were allowed to sell off their shares of BIAL within three to seven years of the airport's opening. This gave them the option of pulling out with their profits after the initial phase of airport construction, when land prices had increased and share values had surged. In fact, the original investors did sell off their shares as soon as they could. Their strategy was to profit from the original short-term value appreciation rather than stick around to capture the lower profit rates typically associated with providing and maintaining airport service over the long run. Case in point: In March–April 2012, just four years after opening, the airport was forced to close temporarily for emergency repairs after the runway surface failed prematurely owing to the use of cheap materials that led to buckling. Why build infrastructure to last for generations when you will pull out within a few years? By 2018 the largest shareholder of BIAL became Mauritius Investments Limited. This shell company, based in the double tax-free haven of Mauritius, was owned largely by a Canadian private equity firm with a new business model of building up a revenue-generating portfolio of depressed airport assets globally. They profit from the failures of airport projects, capitalizing on depressed asset values.

Previously, Bengaluru's airport was an old military landing strip within the city, which began to burst at the seams once the IT sector took off. With all this apparent growth, one might ask, why couldn't the new airport pay for itself? After all, airport usage skyrocketed in its first decade. If investors would not have signed without the lure of acquiring discounted and free land, what does this tell us about the value of infrastructure as a stand-alone productive asset under this business model of financialization? How can we assess the metrics of profitability on the global infrastructure market within which these investors work?

Answering these questions helps clarify the logic behind investing in urban infrastructure in emergent land markets. The concession agreement signed in July 2004 and the land lease agreement of January 2005 make it clear that from the investors' perspective, the project's viability—in their eyes—was contingent on a guarantee of undervalued rural land, since the airport itself occupied only a tiny portion of the land associated with the project. It was no accident that the location chosen by the Karnataka chief minister for the airport development region consisted of village commons, government land, and Dalit land. From a local political power perspective, this land could be acquired easily and cheaply. As soon as rumors circulated as to where the airport would be sited, land brokers negotiated with farmers to purchase their land, to combine it with the contiguous land of their neighbors. The larger the assemblage, the more attractive the land is for land aggregators who are hired by developers (Gidwani et al. 2024; Upadhya 2020). With the support of the political and bureaucratic classes, unattended government land—forests, lakes, pastures—would be grabbed in the process. Some deals were allegedly closed after-hours in the local revenue office, with some of the largest grabs benefiting senior political officials. Rumors swirled across the farming landscape that implicated many of the country's major political actors in the secretive process of purchasing farm and government land in this airport-plus project, hoping to cash in on, and contribute to, the skyrocketing-value bonanza. Many of these rumors have since been supported with overwhelming evidence by a series of damning reports commissioned by the state legislature, as noted elsewhere in this chapter.

Turning Farmland and Commons into a Marketable Asset

During the past two decades, major airports, multilane highways, ports, mining-and-energy complexes, and private urban townships across India have required many acres of land, which has displaced millions of people (figure 5.2) (Sainath 2018; Levien 2013; Vasavi 2012). People have responded by launching large-scale protests and starting public discussions about rural land valuation and the way farmers

5.2 New residential complexes arise from the clearing of farmland. Bengaluru, 2017. Photo by Pierre Hauser.

should be compensated and included in this nationwide urbanization project.[5] The debate continues to simmer on the questions of how much compensation is fair, what defines a public purpose for which land can be taken, and what happens to the many rural farmers and laborers who do not own land but occupy or lease land, or depend on public commons land for their basic needs.

Much of the land surrounding the airport in northern Bengaluru is not property *officially* owned by farmers. It comprises forests, pastures, and plowed fields kept verdant by the numerous constructed lakes and reservoirs that capture monsoon rainwater and channel it across the region. The land is primarily occupied by lower-caste and Dalit producers, some of whom do have *pattas*, or land registration records, but many Dalits were denied them; villages in the airport region include a small percentage of upper-caste landowners and village leaders with *pattas*.

According to a leading environmentalist and legal advocate, Leo Saldanha, the government's reform of the legal framework represented a key turning point for land acquisition and commodification, nationally and in Bengaluru. In one of a series of interviews, Saldanha highlighted to me the irony of market mechanisms that were introduced in name but not in practice, by stretching the offer of state subsidies from productive job-creating agriculture and industry to the more ambiguous domain of infrastructure. The latter category includes airports, highways, and gated luxury housing and is an arena in which financial firms have reaped most of the benefit. As he explains it, "The KIADB Act Amendment of 1998 redefined infrastructure as industry and allowed for land to be acquired not at the market rate but at a lower rate, through a new interpretation of the old British notion of eminent domain. Before this amendment, land could only be acquired by the state through eminent domain if it was in the public interest, but now, land can be acquired at below-market rates for private interest. This was the official start of this current period of intensified commodification of land in Bengaluru."[6]

Saldanha further notes how new legal reforms to stimulate land markets were accompanied by shifts in urban governance and an erasure of democratic accountability. New parastatal agencies were created but without any compulsion to regulate or protect: "For every large-scale officially sanctioned land grab for our big infrastructural projects, the state creates a parastatal agency to handle the funds, contractors, land sales, etc. But never does the state create a regulatory agency to oversee it. There are no rules requiring public hearings, no prior consent, no regulatory oversight, nothing. So the democracy side of governance gets completely erased."

It did not take long before state actors within the system realized the lucrative nature of handling land for domestic and foreign investors. They proceeded to collect illegal rents from the many transactions required (in practice, not law) to convert rural land into real estate. When dispossession enables accumulation through extra-economic coercive means, there is little incentive for state actors to ensure that the land they acquire is distributed equitably and used to produce jobs and factories.

A study of land use changes in the airport area depicts the social and ecological consequences of the rise of speculative exuberance on the ground. Scholars analyzed satellite data for the region from 2002 to 2010 and identified some surprising trends (Mayur et al. 2013). Before land acquisition and airport construction, almost half the land had been used in agriculture, and much of the rest was covered with water bodies, forest, shrubbery, and pasture for animal husbandry.[7] Only small clusters of acres were built up in the form of villages and public resources such as schools and marketplaces. But by 2011, after the first round of heady speculative investment swept across the region and led to widespread dispossession of low-income landholding communities, most agricultural activities had ceased. Water bodies were reduced by 53 percent, and forest had shrunk by 37 percent (Mayur et al. 2013). This included the replacement of actively managed biodiverse forests with commercial tree plantations of acacia and eucalyptus that require much less labor and crowd out small farmers. These monocrops also create ecological problems such as depleting soil nutrients and water supplies. Of the land that was under agriculture in the 1990s, only 16 percent was built up by 2011, while 48 percent had been "excavated and kept as barren for further developmental build ups," that is, left fallow purely for speculation (Mayur et al. 2013, 35). Despite the clearing out of farmland and destruction of the agrarian economy, and land prices that skyrocketed beyond anyone's wildest dreams, more than half the land that was to house new infrastructure remained dug up but empty (Mayur et al. 2013). This barrenness amid rocketing land prices on global-city terrain is a clear sign that profitable speculation takes many forms and does not depend on producing high-value jobs or goods for economic development, however that gets defined. The next section explores the social caste dimensions of this phenomenon of speculative displacement.

Mobilizing the Social Technology of Caste

At various times since independence, especially in the 1970s, Dalits in the airport region (e.g., the Devanahalli and Bengaluru Rural districts) had received government land to graze animals, farm, and build their homes, fulfilling long-overdue political promises originating at the dawn of the independence movement. These acts were considered just or fair compensation for the excluded and poorest, who also deserved to benefit from expelling the British, regaining national territory, and achieving independence. At the same time, according to my interviews, village elites who are mostly Vokkaligas—a community of closely related landowning castes—claimed that *their* just compensation for managing the village's well-being should be free access to Dalit labor in the village.[8] As Dalits gradually received legal rights to own land, some Dalits were able to reclaim their labor power, which was otherwise owed to Gowda or Vokkaliga landlords, and to farm their newly acquired land for themselves. The act of returning "land to the tiller," a prominent goal of independence for many, might have been attractive or necessary as a national political promise, but the effects were not taken lightly by elites at the village and district levels (Damle 1989). The compensatory act of allowing the rural majority to possess and till their own soils aggravated upper-caste land-lords and village leaders, and much of this land was taken back from Dalits in violent ways, about which I heard many stories.[9]

A local Dalit legal advocate who works for these and neighboring villagers described to me the arrival of the airport, its prehistory, and the rupture it created for Dalits:

> For the airport and nearby aerospace SEZ, 75 percent of the acquired land was Dalit land, approximately three thousand acres of the four thousand acres. Of three villages acquired for the Aerospace SEZ nearby, 90 percent of the villagers are Dalits. In 1978 the government gave Dalits land, what was called wasteland by the British, but it was land we used as grazing land—and was given as part of the national land-to-the-tillers struggle. We were bonded laborers working for village leaders and land-lords, the [landowning] Patels and Gowdas. We were not bonded in debt, yet we had no other means but to work for them. It created a lot of tension once Dalits received land and were officially free from the Gowdas.[10]

Many Dalits expressed their dismay with the whole discourse of compensation used for the airport real estate project (figure 5.3). They were angry over the minuscule funds they received in exchange for their families' removal from the land, and they were outraged that the whole question of compensation was reduced to a calculation of land prices. "We can fight for the right to the *paisa* [money] but never for the right to land," the legal advocate lamented, capturing the essence of Dalit farmer outrage in the region.[11]

Ground Zero: The Land (and Backs) on
Which the Airport Was Built

To highlight the experiences of those dispossessed from their lands to build the new airport, I share the contents of a series of group interviews con-ducted in the center of a village, which I visited multiple times over two years and which my research assistants revisited on two other occasions for follow-up data collection and discussions. The original village, Arasin-akunte, was named after a sustaining body of water that was paved over

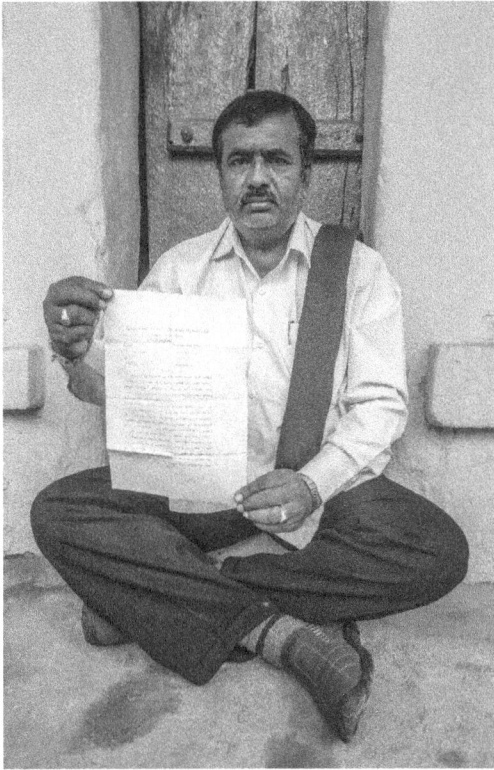

5.3 Farmers displaced by the airport and special economic zone complex argue they have the land deeds and thus deserve fair compensation. Bengaluru, 2017. Photo by Pierre Hauser.

by the airport. Goats and cows were tied to trees to our right and left, and children played around us. When my interlocutors' village had been taken to build the runway, they were resettled on the commons of another village, Ballapura, and the commons was renamed Hosharishinakunte, or New Arasinakunte. These villagers described how their lives were transformed once they lost access not only to their farmland but also to their village commons, their water supply, their houses of worship, and much more. They also revealed the role and false promises of government agencies responsible for the airport's land acquisition.

One interview session started with a few of the older men and women telling the story of their village's displacement and resettlement on another village's common grazing land. As they tell it, this process produced pain, disillusionment, and debt for those who were displaced, and resentment and distrust from their neighbors, whose scarce commons resources then had to be shared. All this sacrifice transpired on a small plot of land that was once the neighboring village's pastureland. Some of the women from the new village were farming a thin strip of grassy land

5.4 Displaced Dalit women illegally occupy and farm a tiny strip of greenery alongside the road. Village adjacent to the Bengaluru airport, 2016. Photo by Pierre Hauser.

abutting the main road, which they acknowledged was a form of illegal squatting, but they claimed they had no choice, as they needed the food (figure 5.4). A few villagers were tempted by city-based land brokers to sell their plots to city folk speculating on the land. They showed their plots, which were marked off by stone pillars, vacant (figures 5.5). There is no village square or common shared land here. However, villagers had been putting away small amounts of money to eventually build a small four-sided shrine on a footpath, a site that could accommodate four different gods sacred to different sets of villagers. This was an innovative compromise that allowed everyone to re-create their lost temples, using a tiny parcel of shared space.

The resettlement and preexisting villages sit adjacent to the international airport and its surroundings of world-class hospitality and amenities. These displaced villagers had been promised fair compensation for their lost land and beneficial resettlement, but those promises were reduced to this tension-producing and inadequate condition. Is this simply the age-old problem of caste-based inequality, or is there more to this unjust process? The following statements came from a few of

5.5 A Dalit resettlement plot that has been sold off to an urban speculator betting that land values will increase and that more Dalits will have no choice but to move again. Bengaluru, 2016. Photo by Pierre Hauser.

those sitting with us on the footpath; they mentioned sums of rupees paid in lakh, or units of 100,000. One man said:

> The Gowda farmers who owned a hundred or fifty acres in our old village sold off immediately and moved on. We are the ones who owned little land, and we have been moved here. We received Rs. 5 lakh per acre [$5,800 in 2025 dollars], not enough to build a home, so once we lost our land, we all fell into debt, and we remain in debt. There were fifty households and 450 acres in our old village; there were plenty of wells with water at less than two hundred feet deep. Here, there isn't even work for coolies. We didn't get any farmland, only money to build a house on a small thirty-by-forty feet site.

Another man chimed in:

> Many of us are illiterate and sign with our thumbs. Before even receiving this small compensation, the government required fourteen different pieces of paper to prove we owned land, and just to get those papers we had to pay Rs. 1 lakh [$1,170 (to the officer)].

Here, in the new village, there is no drinking water, no pump. Three villages around here all share one raised tank and two borewells, but those are based in the other villages, and water tables are at a thousand feet deep. If we work at all, we work elsewhere as laborers. The school is 1.5 kilometers [almost one mile] away, outside of the village.

To survive, we all borrow ration food from a neighboring village's shop on credit, and we work off that credit in their village. All our land—*gomala* [pasture grazing land], *gunthope* [sacred forest], farms, pond—was taken for the airport. In exchange, we weren't given any of our commons back, not even a cemetery or a well. Back there, we all shared common land for agriculture.

A woman added:

Initially, we were promised work at the airport, but only one boy in the whole village works there now. We have no dairy. We used to each have five to ten cows and a house, with plenty of fodder, and the dairy would pay full price for our milk. But now, because there is very little fodder and only a few cows, the dairy pays less for our milk, as it is so weak, so watered down, the dairy tells us. When we resettled, we weren't part of any *panchayat* [representative government]. Now, after protest, we are attached to one, but we have been refused representation or access to it. Our new village was originally *gomala* [pastureland] for the village next door, Ballapura; the government took their forest and ponds and put us on it. So there is resentment from Ballapura and our other neighbors.

Every month, we as a village pay Rs. 350 [$4] per drum of water to supplement the amount of water we get from the borewell we share with two other villages, because it does not produce enough water, and we are always given the least from the well, as our neighbors don't want us here. What kind of life is this? Why should they? We now occupy their *gomala*. The government took their land to relocate us, so of course our neighbors don't like us.

Over a three-year period, my research assistants and I returned for a few more rounds of interviews and data collection at the district revenue office and the courts where several cases on these farmers' behalf had been filed. After one of our discussions in the resettlement village, a woman asked to show us her home, as she wanted to tell us a story. Her home stood apart from the rest, separated by a dusty footpath; it

CHAPTER FIVE

5.6 Dalit families displaced by the airport complex received such poor compensation that some chose to sell off their tiny resettlement plot and instead convert their cowshed into housing to save money. Bengaluru, 2017. Photo by the author.

was perpendicular to the others. It abutted a forested backdrop, side by side with a line of cowsheds. But unlike the cowsheds, her home was built out a bit; an entranceway added to the hut was protected by a blue plastic sheet fluttering in the hot wind (figure 5.6).

She explained, "We sold our [compensation] house plot to someone from Bangalore who then resold it. They leave it empty waiting for the price to go up, just like two others over there," she said, pointing across the village to where the plots were slightly larger. "We moved into our dump plot, a 25 by 20 [feet] plot that we all received to use for cattle and household waste." Then she added, with a laugh, "The funny thing is [that] a neighbor is housing their cow in her former house site, which has been sold to an outsider, while we sold our house and stay in our cow's place."

Adjacent to the airport is a wide swath of 980 acres of village and government land that has been acquired for an Aerospace Park SEZ. This was imagined to be the incubator site for numerous high-end engineering and industrial workplaces, producing airplane parts and supporting the high-growth aerospace sector across Asia. Yet much of the expansive zone lies dormant. We visited a small tea shop on the side of the road on a few occasions, realizing that there is no better place to ask for directions, ask questions, or learn new gossip than from the durable and ever-present *chai walla*, the tea provider (figure 5.7). On our first visit, the tea stall sat on an empty dusty road across from one small construction site, what would become a stand-alone two-story square building (figure 5.8). The tea stall was built from scrap metal, cardboard, and blue tarps that fluttered in the wind. One wall was built up from an old election poster board with images of party-based politicians, all men with ascetic white clothing, uncomfortable smiles, and dyed black hair. Lined up on a shelf were large, fogged jars of biscuits, cookies, and nuts, all well guarded by an army of flies. In the middle of the shelf was enough room for the *chai walla* to place your steaming milky tea when it was ready. Two elderly pastoralists, husband and wife, followed their small herd of goats as they munched on grass and weeds alongside the tea stall (figure 5.9). They, too, were displaced from the common pastures and tended their goats wherever they could.

Outside the blue tarp entrance rested two rickety wooden benches for customers. The first few times we visited, the tea stall was full of itinerant construction workers on a short break from across the road. The construction workers came from northern India and were brought in and employed by a labor broker who lent the men and boys money to help their families pay off some lingering debts back home. They in turn had to repay these loans, at high interest, through their wages, which the contractor kept. They were poor, and the tea stall was their main source of hydration and nutrition; the food choices were limited and simple but affordable. The construction workers lived, bathed, and slept on the work site, sometimes working late into the night.

The tea stall owner and his teenage son told us, on separate occasions, their life stories. The father started:

> My parents were farmworkers, and water was twenty to thirty feet deep, and they grew *paddy* [rice] and *ragi* [millet for flour]. I've done everything from being a cleaner and working in construction. I have three sons and one daughter, including Prashant, who helps me in the tea shop when he is not in school. A while back, we received one acre of land from the government, *gomala* land, which we cultivated for our livelihood. Then the airport came, and the government took it back. I received Rs. 57 lakh compensation, but Rs. 10 lakh [$11,700 of $66,000] went to the brokers. And although I was promised a job at the airport, I never got it.

5.7 Displaced farmer standing in front of a makeshift tea stall. The shop is illegally built along the road inside the airport special economic zone. Bengaluru, 2016. Photo by Pierre Hauser.

5.8 Adjacent to the Bengaluru airport, this IT factory is located on land that the tea stall owner once owned and farmed. Bengaluru, 2016. Photo by Pierre Hauser.

5.9 Pastoralists like this woman were also displaced by the airport and special economic zone complex. She is shepherding a handful of goats on the grassy lands near the tea stall and construction site. Bengaluru, 2016. Photo by Pierre Hauser.

The nearby factories refuse to hire locals. The men in our village tried to come together and put up a protest and demand fair work.

At these new factories, for one day of work, men and women are being brought in from the North and are being paid poorly—men Rs. 400–500 [approximately $6–$8] per day and women Rs. 300–350 [$3–$5] per day. We can't afford to work for that low wage. Because the cost of English-medium school or even Kannada-medium is so high, I can't afford to work for those wages. My wife has a small vegetable shop in the village, and two kids go to the government school, and two go to the private school. But it's so expensive at the [private] English-medium school. A decent education is no longer affordable. So I put up this shop right across from our family's land, which is now part of the aerospace park. I'm not allowed to build this up, it can't be permanent, and I can't make a real business of it, because any day they can come over and tear it down.

That is, the tea shop sits across from their former farmland, where a smattering of small buildings is going up. The government made no provisions for him to, for example, own a small section of his former land to be the landlord for one of these factories, or to put up a small retail shop and perhaps prosper from the new aerospace facilities. Local contractors and land brokers get the land and hold on to it until companies want to buy and build. But over the years very few companies have come.

On my last visit to the tea stall, in 2019, the small construction site across from the stall had been completed, and a few others down the long stretch of empty road were stirring with signs of construction. By this visit, the itinerant construction workers had left, replaced by two young men with button-down shirts and ID badges hanging from their necks. They were young managers overseeing the assemblage of knuckle-sized switches for Boeing jet plane doors.

"Wow," I said, "Boeing jet parts, sounds very high tech and great for the local economy." "No," one of them laughed, "not so high tech." The other explained:

Basically, the tiny [palm-sized] parts for the door switch are flown in from New York City, assembled here, and flown back to New York, where they then continue on to someplace else where doors are assembled—maybe in Europe, maybe in Asia. This could be done anywhere, but for now these switches are made here. The laborers come from northern India; we are engineering graduates from Bengaluru. We are not sure how any of this makes business sense, but we don't mind working up here in the middle of nowhere. It's a long commute for us, but it's a decent first job.

They paused, and the first one added, as he slurped up the last of his tea: "It's empty up here, no people, no businesses. So we don't stay long when we come. We'd rather be working in the city, closer to home and friends. I can't imagine there'll be much opportunity for better jobs for us around here. What do you think?"

The vacant landscape was littered with flattened farmland and felled trees, and there was an occasional wide road with some weather-worn road signs marking a future industrial park, all in anticipation of converting this once-verdant belt into high-value manufacturing and urban real estate. Rumors of major engineering and factory campuses have circulated in political speeches around election time for years. A farming family had been displaced so that cheap switches could be assembled with the tax breaks that a government-sponsored SEZ offers. The farming family is left with an illegal squat where they sell cups of tea and biscuits, not exactly the transformation the coming SEZ promised in which small farmers could become landlords or entrepreneurs.

Back in the town near the airport, Devanahalli, which has a population of twenty-nine thousand, I spent time with members of a well-organized and long-standing farmers organization that represents farmers with ownership rights to land. Although most of these farmers owned land with the right paperwork, they still were required to sell to KIADB at a price that did not reflect the future market value once the farmers had sold it. Nor do nonelite farmers typically get the full amount of the compensation, as illegal rents are extracted from the total compensation. At the time of these interviews, their advocates were filing cases in the courts demanding better compensation. Yet cases languish in the courts for years; meanwhile, the compensation they received only shrinks in purchasing power as land prices continue to rise.

One day we met up with advocates (lawyers) for the Green Brigade, an offshoot of the older Karnataka Rajya Raitha Sangha (Karnataka State's Farmers Association or KRRS), a farmers' movement that was quite powerful thirty years ago. This movement had an international reputation for activism back in the 1980s and 1990s and was famous for torching a Kentucky Fried Chicken outlet and organizing widespread protests against expensive imported GMO inputs and the corporatization of local agriculture. This latest round of displacements has reinvigorated the farmers movement, with members within most villages across Karnataka. I met with ten claimants discussing how to build court cases against KIADB and other state agencies that they insist had stolen their land and cheated them out of fair compensation. The Green Brigade represents a very different clientele than wealthier and powerfully connected elite farmers, even while they may share some caste affiliations.

The following stories reveal how even those with political and social power in the countryside have struggled to make ends meet in this new speculative environment. While most of KRRS's members come from middle-income landowning families of the two dominant farming castes (Lingayats and Vokkaligas), many in these communities were nonetheless thrown into relative precarity. Their stories explain the role of actors working for the state but also within their own political networks, who spun into action to facilitate land grabs in this green-belt area. Collectively, elite factions mobilized close kin and (class-based) caste connections and created alliances with their foreign brethren with bank accounts brimming with cash. Here's what one claimant and Green Brigade activist said:

I had two of five acres taken from me for the road to the airport highway. I was compensated for it and bought some more acres elsewhere, at Rs. 5 lakh [$5,600]/acre, but how much land can you buy with 10 lakhs [$11,000]?! Land prices now are too high nearby, so I used my savings to buy land for Rs. 40 lakhs [$46,000], knowing how important it is to have land. I sold [family] jewelry and borrowed from everyone to buy the land. Fifteen people are in my joint [extended] family. But now we're all divided. Family members could not agree on how to handle the family land, and so, like many other families, we became divided. This process has destroyed families.

Society has changed in other ways. Before the airport came, bribes were quite affordable. We used to pay Rs. 100 here and there. But once land prices shot up, and so much money was involved, it just went crazy. Prices shot up because once news of the airport plans spread, people from all over came to buy land. And people in government wanted a piece of the action. Since our futures depended on the land deal, they knew they could take advantage, and now we are all forced to pay much larger bribes.

The rich Gowda farmers worked with their kin in government and the land mafia to ensure that they can keep their land, but others—like us—were just looted. Government officials created new records and documents and destroyed the older ones. They created a new landownership structure that benefited their own men. Widows were pressured to give over their land rights and were left with little. As we say here, land brokers threw chili powder into our eyes and stole our land.

One of the Green Brigade advocates listening to us chimed in:

As a farmers' association, we have conducted a lot of protests and public meetings to demand transparency. Our main work is to find the original documents for farmers to protect them against these thieves in government and defend their rights to just compensation. But many of their documents held in the Taluk office have clearly been destroyed or forged. We get complaints every day and try to help farmers when their records are manipulated. But we do not have the ability to help farmers when they want to sell, to help them get a fair price and deal. The market is controlled by others.

Another advocate explained his own situation, in which he received compensation, but it was so little he couldn't do much with it except buy a small plot of land in a neighboring district where land is cheaper. He noted, in a tone of resignation:

The profits from farming I spend on household expenses. It's a dry land, and borewell water is already 1,500–2,000 feet deep, which is too expensive to dig for. When I can, I grow a rainfed crop. So basically I'm no more a farmer. I used to grow flowers, and it earned us a living. I had a borewell for cultivation. My old house [separate from the farmland] sits in ruins under the flyover [overbridge] for the airport highway. We can't live in that wretched place, stuck right on the edge of the highway. Instead, I rent it out to waste pickers.

By and large, elite farmers experienced land acquisition differently. We met one while he was farming a plot adjacent to a construction area where a large parking lot was to be built. He farms his family's fields with workers and owns land in different villages, as well as some housing property elsewhere. He confidently told us that he and his Gowda neighbors were challenging the government to get a more attractive compensation package. We spoke with him while standing on a farm plot that had already been acquired by KIADB. He stubbornly, and opportunistically, continued to farm and profit from this plot:

> This land has been in my family for two hundred years and is being acquired by the government for a parking lot and small electric plant and office. This area comprises mostly Gowdas with some Dalits. One hundred and twenty families live here, and we have promised to blockade and take control over the access road to the aerospace park if we don't get fair compensation. The government has already acquired 4.5 acres of my land for Rs. 55 lakhs [$64,000] per acre, and my neighbors and I are still cultivating the land until the construction starts. See, look, even our temples remain. My community [of Gowdas] is demanding compensation for these eighty-five acres we work.
>
> One class action suit has been filed. With the compensation money I received for this land, I bought 1.5 acres six kilometers [3.7 miles] away from here, for Rs. 21 lakh [$24,500] per acre, and there we grow *ragi*, baby corn, and lentils. I also have two houses I rent out. Today I make the same amount of money from those lands as I do from this land here; this land has been notified [for acquisition] and will be taken, but we are still farming and grazing animals in the meantime. And we are protesting. We plan to block the road to stop the development of the SEZ if necessary, to negotiate with the Tehsildar [district-level tax/revenue office]. We have taken the case to higher authorities. It's not right; all they want our land for is a SEZ parking lot!

The next section situates these stories told by Dalit, middle-caste, and upper-caste farmers who were dispossessed from their lands within the context of changing governmental practices in the area.

Extracting Wealth, Fueling a Patrimonial Regime

The dispossession described above has not only created a new market for land but also stimulated a machinery of bureaucratic and political rent seeking (Doshi and Ranganathan 2019, 2017; Piliavsky 2014). Once state officials realized the size of the gap between what farmers, especially Dalits, could be paid for their land and the phenomenal value that land could generate in an urban real estate market, they were quick to exploit these opportunities. The money generated was used for personal gain, for purchasing positions within the state bureaucracy, and for supporting political parties and elections (Ranganathan et al. 2023; Akhil Gupta 2012). Because land is the most lucrative outlet for large amounts of cash, this money invariably finds its way back into the land market, ensuring a steady rise in land prices irrespective of the land's productivity. These practices have created a patrimonial regime of governance, whose different elements are described in this section, starting with the lowest level of rent seeking: the intermediary brokers and officials who facilitate local land sales. This generates substantial sums of wealth for local officials, a percentage of which gets funneled up the hierarchy, ending up in the chief minister's office and the offices of leading political parties. It also consolidates local land banks into fewer hands, mostly those of highly influential and wealthy upper-caste men.

As the largest and most powerful parastatal in the region, KIADB is officially responsible for acquiring and assembling land to sell to firms and supplying basic infrastructure, such as roads and electricity, for industrial development. The documents required to receive compensation for land legally belong to the farmers, and they should not need a middleman or intermediary to retrieve them. Yet KIADB insists that they do, and it has consequently been tagged as the most corrupt parastatal agency in Karnataka, and possibly in all of South India, by the courts and the press. Despite KIADB's criminal reputation, international financial institutions have no problem empowering it with hundreds of millions of dollars of loans to oversee major public projects and infrastructure. In its governing power, KIADB is accountable only to the chief minister of Karnataka and to its creditors, not to democratic institutions such as election-driven city councils, the state legislature, or any public entity.

According to farmers and advocates, KIADB officials stayed out of house-to-house negotiations and never visited villages to survey land. Instead, officials from the parastatal agencies (e.g., KIADB, Bangalore Development Agency) responsible for land acquisition and sale relied on local brokers to do their bidding, keeping at arm's length the series of small transactions. As one Dalit farmer explained to me:

> When the government asked for documents, we had no idea how to assemble them, and KIADB officials said these middlemen would help

collect the papers necessary to prove ownership, use of the land, taxes paid. The brokers promised to get the land records from the Tehsildar office. These brokers knew the local officials well; they worked for them. Many of us had claims to land that the government refused to acknowledge, so the brokers said we needed lawyers to file the cases in court to get the compensation. In the end, broker and lawyer worked together to collect half of the compensation money for themselves.

Dalit villagers from the area had been farming commons land since the 1970s, and some had finally received possession certificates from the government. Just before the airport came, they were told that the paperwork was being processed into property deeds. But once KIADB stepped into the role of acquiring land, the processing stopped. Most of the Dalit farmers in the region never received proof of possession, even though they had been paying taxes on their land for years.

Of the four hundred acres of one village displaced by the airport, half were still under dispute more than ten years after construction had started. Allegedly, KIADB staff had put the compensation money in a bank account while the cases were in the courts. This process takes years, and for the resolved cases, the courts never bothered to increase the value of the compensation amount, even though over time the original amount lost much of its purchasing power. Dispute resolution rarely results in Dalit farmers receiving current urban market prices for their acquired land. With half of court settlement money going to brokers and lawyers, Dalit farmers always lose.

According to my interviewees—whose claims are well documented in court papers—KIADB staff ask for fourteen to sixteen different records from farmers, many of which should be available for free in the Tehsildar office. So it shouldn't be a problem, even for those who cannot read, to acquire these documents. But when they ask, office staff say they will only deal with an intermediary, whom farmers must pay for assistance in government work. Intermediaries then pay the officials for the paperwork to be processed and split the payment with the office workers. In this way, the money quietly flows, with sitting officials rarely seen receiving cash, and the rent-seeking system expands and deepens.

What the revenue and KIADB staff do with their cut of the money reveals the role of land transactions for a wide range of political activities.

As one advocate explained to me in 2016, "KIADB staff have to pay Rs. 25 lakhs [$29,000] in order to get their jobs in the office. And ministers need lots of money for their elections." He concluded our interview with a familiar phrase in the region: "As we say here, the planes fly over the graveyard of the Dalits."

What started out as a contractual obligation that government agencies owed to airport investors—that is, acquiring land from Dalits and converting it into urban real estate—has turned into a set of institutionalized actions, with money extracted from every land and document transaction. A robust revenue stream flows through these bureaucratic government offices up the hierarchy. But some money also pours into political parties to help finance elections (Kapur and Vaishnav 2011). According to the Center for Media Studies in New Delhi, more than Rs. 10,500 crores ($1.2 million), including bribe payments to voters, was spent on the relatively minor May 2018 assembly election in the state of Karnataka. This profligate sum was twice what was spent in the previous election in 2013. It represented "the most expensive election ever" for a state in India, according to the *Indian Express* newspaper (Press Trust of India 2018). Researchers at the Center for Media Studies suggest that the money came largely from real estate transactions.

One senior government official described the depth and extent of this patrimonial regime. Born a Dalit, he became one of the few to work his way up the ranks of state administrative officers and is widely regarded as one of the clean senior officials in the Karnataka government. The first step in this patrimonial regime, he explained to me, involves producing the city's master plan, overseen by the chief minister's office. It involves the zoning of some land as a green belt, where it is protected as land for farms, forests, lakes, and commons and cannot be converted into commercial real estate. Other areas are designated yellow for residential, purple for industrial, and so on. The delineation of zones is big business because it affects where investment and development can go. Consequently, sizable bribes are paid for rezoning certain off-limit areas into new sites for investment.[12] "The master plan has been changed umpteen times," this senior official explained. "Preparing the master plan is itself a huge moneymaker: to first declare a green zone draws in everyone to the office bribing for access or rezoning [of particular plots]. . . . The government runs on the money politics of land. The economy [referring to 2017] is not doing well, so everyone wants to buy land, even foreign investors."[13]

His revelations are not unique and were corroborated by others interviewed. As well, in September 2016, due to public pressure, two special courts were created exclusively to prosecute land encroachment cases. The Karnataka government admitted that more than thirty-five thousand acres of government land in Bengaluru districts, including the airport region, had been stolen with little or no accountability or punishment (*Hindu* 2016). By March 2018 the government had sought even more money to set up new courts just for land-grabbing cases in and around Bengaluru (Shruthi 2018). Illegal land grabs can happen only with the consent and participation of government officials and local politicians. Because land has been the biggest business in Bengaluru during this period and it remains the most financially vibrant sector in India, large sums of cash are offered to and requested by government officials at various levels as incentives. A series of published reports commissioned by the Karnataka legislature documented the encroachment on land and lakes and demonstrated the role—and culpability—of numerous senior politicians and administrative officials (Kumar 2015). These reports have led to few prosecutions, but pressure from civil society groups to demand that private developers return such land in and around public lakes has resulted in new acts, such as the Karnataka Land Grabbing Prohibition Act 2011/2014.[14]

Since the money from these land-based transactions cannot be put into a bank account, as it would be easily traced and taxed, the land market itself has become the most common site for money laundering. The persistent rise in land prices is thus not a simple supply-and-demand phenomenon related to the efficient or profitable use of land for productive purposes. It is a result of the rapid turnover of land for speculative purposes. It is a form of wealth accumulation unrelated to the utility value of land, fed by patrimonial capital, and embedded in extractive caste, bureaucratic, and political technologies of power. The processes of bureaucratic job purchasing and profiteering, money laundering, and election funding depend on a steady flow of cash from the bureaucratic tasks related to land notification, acquisition, conversion, and resale. These micromarket practices undergird the land market and contribute to the phenomenal rise of land prices in Bengaluru and the influx of foreign capital into all large projects of infrastructure and urbanization, regardless of whether such projects ever come to fruition.

Conclusion

In the northern outskirts of Bengaluru, the process of accumulation by dispossession became more accurately a process of dispossession by financialization. It created the conditions that would attract foreign investors to negotiate the airport contract and encourage them to profit from land speculation and value extraction, with some basic guarantees for profitability from the airport infrastructure as well. The contract, the boosterism, and the role of elite politicians grabbing government and Dalit land, with support from the bureaucratic machinery, combined to make land acquisition and turnover the main lever of value creation. This could happen only with support from the evolving caste-based patrimonial regime of governance, which suited the foreign investors' own desire for profitability without commitment, just benefits. What emerges is a business model of no business, as a land grab that becomes much more profitable, offering liquidity for politicians and investors alike. From an investor's or politician's perspective, why bother with the mundane asset-depreciating illiquid problems of manufacturing?

None of this could have happened in Bengaluru without the hand of global finance, and global finance capital couldn't have prospered without the mobilization of Bengaluru's own elite networks. The process required heavy lifting by a wide array of actors within both localized and globalized patrimonial regimes. In Bengaluru they appear to work for their own community's self-interest, mobilizing the vital and sometimes violent social technology of gendered caste power. They work closely with their brethren in global finance. The empire of finance became more emboldened and more aspirational due in part to the widely circulating discourse and aesthetic of global-city making that coalesced around the idea and practices of speculative urbanism. In their entanglements, actors from finance capital and elite quarters of Bengaluru created the conditions for a new market in land, land-based dispossession, land-value escalation, and, as the next chapter illustrates, land-based debt.

Now that we understand what happens to land markets and landed communities under the force of finance-driven urbanization, the next chapter turns to other dimensions of the city's financialization, particularly the role of global private equity and its dance partner, local developers, as they together transform both the city and the world of finance.

REMAKING REAL ESTATE, CAPITAL MARKETS, AND CITY LIFE

PRIVATE EQUITY AND THE NEW LOGICS OF FINANCE

> People say India is neoliberal. But it is not. [Financial firms] don't want a free market; they want government protection, and they want protection from risks. With no domain knowledge, they are pumping money recklessly into the [real estate] sector. Then when things don't go their way, they cry foul. —Indian developer, interview by the author, 2016

One can no longer speak of India as stubbornly backward or intractably poor or underdeveloped, at least not while also acknowledging the tremendous dynamics of its economy, fast-growing cities, and phenomenal IT sector and its talented labor pool. The birth and global dispersion of so many high-tech products, processes, and talents over the past twenty-five years is due in large part to India's cosmopolitan training and research institutes and the ingenuity and hard work of residents of and migrants to Bengaluru, Asia's stellar IT city.

Indian-born and -trained engineers currently (as of 2023) head up numerous large technology companies, from Microsoft and Alphabet/ Google to Adobe and Nokia. Indian IT has spurred the fastest rise in history of a new middle class, numbering 350 million people, more than the total population of the United States. All of this suggests that India is not an isolated or peripheral economy or workforce with a culture averse to innovation, expertise, or so-called normal Western business

6.1 The contrast between old Bangalore and high-rise Bengaluru, 2017. Photo by Pierre Hauser.

practices, as some critics contend (Becker et al. 2010). Indeed, India is now the fifth-largest economy in the world and perched to reach higher in the next decade. Indian software engineers have been co-creating technologies and applications across firms within and outside India, such that it is hard to pinpoint sites of origin. Many of its engineers rotate their job placements as a routine dimension of this profession, working in Minneapolis for Tata as consultants servicing major US companies in the finance, insurance, and real estate sector at one stage of their career, then working in Switzerland or France, and then returning to Bengaluru. The circulation of expertise, intellectual property, investment capital, and products reflects the globalizing domain of multisite IT production. India is deeply implicated in this remarkable phenomenon.

One of the most concrete and physical manifestations of this business trajectory has been the common notion in elite business circles that to maintain such success requires the construction of state-of-the-art infrastructure such as a monorail transport system, amenity-full IT campuses, and the best residential complexes with accoutrements that would keep the talented workforce in town and content. Making Bengaluru into a global city ("out-Shanghaiing Shanghai!") has been the focus of industry leaders over the past two decades (figure 6.1).

Previously, however, neither infrastructure nor real estate was a dynamic sector. One of Bengaluru's premier land bankers told me that when he first entered the land banking and real estate businesses, prime space on MG Road, once the center of the business and shopping district, was being sold at Rs. 25 (less than a US dollar) per square foot. That low rate remained stagnant for years, and there was no profit to be had in real estate. Land prices were not what drove Bengaluru's economy or steered the business sector.

Even when India first liberalized its capital and real estate markets, and there was a great need for a serious upgrade in the quality and quantity of urban infrastructure, Indian developers did not need or want what US financial firms could offer. In their view, sufficient local, trusted capital was available. Mixed-use gated communities and sprawling high-rise apartment complexes appeared only in the late 1990s and didn't become conspicuous and widespread until the first decade of the 2000s. Until then, the Indian real estate sector's appetite for finance capital was modest enough to be met informally and locally.

Developers' costs were largely met through sales, which meant that even the larger projects could be constructed only incrementally: Revenues accrued from the sale of one block of housing units were used to finance the construction of the next. Developers borrowed from local high-net-worth individuals and other moneylenders, who lent at high interest rates but informally, without state oversight, mediation, or accounting, and based on networks of trust. While land was and remains by far the largest cost for developers, India's public banks have never been allowed to lend money for land acquisition, only for construction costs. During the liberalization period from the 1990s until 2005, developers relied on cash flows from buyers. Individual home subscribers would put out money up front to reserve a spot, taking on the risk of early payments to the builder with an expectation that the building would be completed. The earlier one became a subscriber and bought into a residential project, the lower the price one had to pay, and the higher the potential value increase in the future.[1]

All of this began to change slowly starting in the late 1980s, when India began to dismantle the postindependence policy paradigm of self-reliance and economic protectionism. One of the key shifts that affected Bangalore profoundly was the nationwide disinvestment campaign to end government support of the vast terrain of the public sector, which once dominated manufacturing, mining, infrastructural projects, and public goods and services (Mani 2017; Nagaraj 2005). Bangalore's status as a public sector city meant that much of the city's land was under public sector factories and their affiliated housing and public amenities. If one includes land in the hands of the military, a majority of the total acreage of land in the city was in the hands of the government. So, when the liberalizing state declared many public sector factories to be sick and therefore to be sold to the private sector, that primed the pump of the real estate market. It spurred the conversion of public land from having use value to being a tradeable asset (Birch and Ward 2022). The conversion of low-profit but productive industries to real estate became a boon to elites within the patrimonial network and a catalyst for speculative urbanist projects.

A new business model emerged from this pivotal conjuncture, spurred by finance capital from abroad. This particular set of relations overwhelmed the local market of informal lending, which had its own cultural norms, preferential treatment, contractual obligations, and performance expectations. This chapter provides a step-by-step understanding of the often-contentious interactions between this newly arrived finance capital and the well-situated developers in Bengaluru's real estate sector for the first two decades of the twenty-first century.

A Sector Unleashed

A key policy change in the early 2000s allowed foreign direct investment (FDI) to enter the land and real estate sectors. The new decree permitted full foreign ownership in townships, housing, infrastructure, and construction development projects (FICCI 2017). The oldest business federation in India (Federation of Indian Chambers of Commerce and Industry) noted that "the main reason for opening up the real estate sector to 100% FDI was to bridge the huge shortage of housing in the country and to attract new [financial] technologies in the housing sector" (FICCI 2017).

The 2005 Special Economic Zone (SEZ) Act marked another pivotal change. It enabled foreign investors to purchase land, albeit in large quantities that could only be for productive use, such as large-scale industry rather than speculative or nonproductive purposes. The act created benefits for investors in SEZs with expedited one-window approvals, giving foreign investors tax-free access to state-provided land and basic infrastructure. In the first sixteen months after the SEZ

Act's passage, more than 450 sites were approved; however, unlike in China's SEZs, which produced "factories for the world," few industrial sites in India were developed (Cross 2014; Levien 2011). Consequently, the central government eased restrictions on capital by relaxing the requirement that the land be used solely for industrial purposes, to help make SEZ investments more attractive to investors. As noted earlier, from 2008 onward, a high percentage of foreign capital flowed into the finance, construction, and real estate sectors, with only one-fifth going into manufacturing. Less than 0.2 percent was invested in agriculture, the sector that employs most of the Indian population (and where future urban real estate lies) (K. Rao and Dhar 2018, 2011; UN Conference on Trade and Development [UNCTAD] 2017). In fact, the capital invested in the conversion of rural land into urban real estate reflects an alarming national *disinvestment* project that shifts capital out of small-scale agriculture and rural livelihoods and into urban real estate markets.

The largest category of FDI rushing into urban India has been private equity. This is a broad category of what is called *alternative finance capital*, so called because it is not from a deposit-receiving bank; since these firms are privately owned, they are not regulated by state regulators or by shareholders. Instead, they are a financial entity that uses clients' capital to invest in projects or firms from which they can capture future value increases. As of 2024 the global private equity sector's assets under management were valued at about $9.6 trillion total and expected to rise to $15.6 trillion by 2029 (Preqin 2025). Because private equity firms comprise a largely unregulated sector of finance worldwide, they have been allowed to develop aggressive and profitable management strategies over the past few decades without guardrails (UNCTAD 2017; Krippner 2011; Ho 2009).

Private equity by its nature involves risk-taking, but since private equity firms rarely invest their own funds, risk-taking is often done on behalf of their clients. To reduce some of the risks in their ventures, the largest firms tend to not compete in the same markets. They design financial tools to corner specific markets that often enable them to have market-share power and thus have better control of future returns. This was the case for single-family-home rentals in the United States and for India's office space market, which are dominated by a handful of US-based private equity firms (ACCE Institute et al. 2019; P. Sarkar 2019; Anderson 2015; S. Sarkar 2015; Searle 2014; Sabarinath 2014; Sankhe et al. 2010). Once in a market, private equity profits can come from appreciation in the value of the acquired asset or company. Most investments are made with a clear expectation of exiting within five or so years. Private equity firms hope to profit from starting a fund or special project vehicle with limited liability, using clients' money to ignite a spike in share price value in an undervalued asset or firm. Then they exit when prices peak and before they fall.

Scholars K. S. Chalapati Rao and Biswajit Dhar (2011, 10–11) summarize the role of private equity in the post-2005 era in India: "Private equity investors have the overriding objective of large and fast capital gains and revenues in other forms and there is no question/intention of integrating the investee company into their own structures like an MNC [multinational corporation] does. By their very character, these are *not long-term investors*. They do not fall under the motives of FDI, viz., efficiency-seeking, market seeking or resource/strategic asset seeking. . . . . . [T]hey may be categorized as pure return seeking FDI."

In other words, an ever-increasing volume of FDI in India is not concerned with long-term productive investment but committed instead to financial returns that come from quick exits. At investor conferences I attended between 2007 and 2018, talk often focused on how so-called restrictions on land (ease of purchase) and capital (ease of exit) remained the main stumbling blocks for large-scale foreign investment in ambitious government-led projects.

The floodgates to global private equity opened at the same time that the global urbanism discourse gained traction worldwide (Sassen 2014; Ananya Roy and Ong 2011; Ancien 2011; Goldman 2011). Starting in 2015, the government of India's Smart Cities Mission committed to build a hundred smart cities that would be linked by major transport and commercial infrastructure, in theory remaking India's largely rural landscape into a twenty-first-century metropolitan nation.[2] These ambitions have demanded and justified massive infusions of foreign private capital. Unprecedented urban expansion—the construction of a record number of skyscrapers, elite residential enclaves, airports and highways, and high-tech campuses—was already overheating markets and building up unprecedented mountains of debt. City governments, along with real estate and banking firms, were unable to pay their bills (Arvind Subramanian and Felman 2019).

To explain this unpredicted volatility, the following sections dig into the strategies of the newly arrived private equity firms as they interacted with the well-heeled local developers operating in Bengaluru (some of whom got their start elsewhere, such as in Dubai and Kuwait City). These sections shed light on the new volatilities and disruptions experienced locally as a result of this latest wave of urban financialization. The analysis is grounded in two very specific moments of real estate financialization in Bengaluru, two phases with distinct alignments among financiers, consultants, and developers. The role of international finance capital shifted sharply from its *market-making boom phase* (2005–10) to its *market consolidation bust phase* (2011–present). The business logic that defines these two phases reveals the relational dynamics of speculative practices, changing economic authority, and the unique ways that finance capital operates in an out-of-control real estate market. The next sections explain these rapid shifts and the increased volatility that are baked into these two phases of speculative urbanism.

Phase 1: Market Creation and Capital Dumping (2005–10)

The first phase of the financialization of India's urban real estate market was marked by high-volume speculative financing based on the potential of a new market in upscale residential housing projects. From 2005 to 2010, the number of PE deals exploded from a handful to 286. A record $5 billion was committed to real estate projects in 2007 and 2008 alone, leading to a much higher-than-average investment per deal. At that time, one-third of the total PE investments in India poured into real estate firms developing a total of 82,900 acres, twice the area of Chennai, India's fourth-largest city (Annamalai and Doshi 2012). Local developers capitalized on the frenzy at its peak by choosing to list their shares on the stock market, and business magazines published cover stories featuring developers' projects in the most positive light. Shares were issued at a premium, and companies managed to raise millions of dollars while parting with only a small fraction of the total shares. Demand for these shares was high, and for initial public offerings (IPOs) in the sector, oversubscription was common. The country's largest developer, DLF, diluted only 10 percent of its total stock in 2007 and still managed to raise Rs. 9,500 crores ($1.33 billion), which led to a total market capitalization of Rs. 95,000 crores ($13.3 billion), a spectacular tenfold rise for the industry (a crore equals 10 million). Sobha, a major Bengaluru-based company, issued 12 percent of its stock, and the initial issuance was so popular that its stock was quickly oversubscribed.[3]

This aggressive market-making phase was defined by capital-flush private equity rushing into the Indian market alongside a handful of established developers wanting access to this new source of capital. Executives and consultants in real estate and finance described the Indian real estate market between 2005 and 2010 as exuberant, bullish, and euphoric. Private equity funds aggressively invested in real estate projects, and the performance of fund managers was evaluated based on how much capital was dumped into the sector. Thus, private equity firms incentivized reckless investments that reinforced exaggerated expectations. Representatives of global private equity were eager to move profits out of the unstable highs of mortgage-backed securities in the United States and Europe in anticipation of a period of leveling out in those markets. However, India was uncharted territory. The newness of this relationship created welcome opportunities for Indian developers at a time when they wanted more capital to both honor their existing commitments to homebuyers and fuel the acquisition of even more land for speculative possibilities.

A critical aspect of this speculative market was the disincentivizing of the construction and completion of projects. A senior Indian investment broker, acting on behalf of large private equity funds, discussed how international private equity pumped huge amounts of capital into the local market, to the extent that builders were no longer driven to execute projects:

> Private equity [PE] players came in a big way as soon as the gates opened in 2005. They saw it as an emerging market. They thought they would make a quick buck. They love emerging or frontier markets. They came in saying, We want to put in $50 or $100 million, and the developers in India, who were pretty unorganized and unregulated, just told them huge stories with grand promises. So PE funds started dumping their capital, buying 50 percent or 60 percent of stakes. What they never realized is that these projects would never be completed in the proposed time frame and that Indian developers no longer had skin in the game. During the boom period from 2005 to 2008, private equity came in with the money, and developers took the money and cashed out.[4]

He explained that private equity assumed that buying a 50 percent stake in a project would align the interests of the two partners. However, inundated with fresh capital, developers were no longer incentivized to adhere to either traditional or new business plans, expedite approval requests, or, in some cases, carry out project construction. With money in hand, the interests of the local developer and foreign investors diverged, and developers were no longer constrained by the same business logic and temporal pressures as private equity funds. To quote this same private equity representative again (who spoke in Kannada):

> The developer thinks: *Mera paisa to agaya. Agar banega to banega, nahi to nahi.* [My money has come. If it's constructed, it's constructed. If not, then it's not.]. Sticking to the new business plan isn't mandatory. The [local] guy who you had aligned with had already pulled his money out. He was now in no rush. The joke is, when they first came into the business, the PE guys said, "Look, we have the money, you have the experience, together we are a lethal combination." And the developers said, "Well, now we have the money, hope you had a good experience!"

During this first phase of speculation, developers held the upper hand as crucial intermediaries and as points of entry into a potentially lucrative market. They were able to dictate the terms of agreements, persuading investors that the exorbitant land valuations were fair.

Flush with cash, large land assemblers mobilized their on-site brokers and strongmen to find and acquire land from adjacent farmers that they could bundle into sizable plots for future development, a painstaking and time-consuming process.[5] On the urban periphery, land disputes between villagers and land brokers interrupted the life cycle of many projects. There was a surge in court cases as big promises of money were made to family or village members in the hope of creating a fissure between neighbors or families whose members were resistant to selling at the price proposed (Gidwani et al. 2024; *Hindu* 2014).[6] During this post-2005 period, with foreign investors hungry and eager, developers with cash in hand quickly acquired and aggregated land for urban development, assuming that all the farm owners would roll over and forfeit their land claims easily. Many did not (Goldman 2020).

In phase 1, within the urban real estate sector, 50 percent of private equity funds were directed to the residential segment and 26 percent

6.2 Many of these luxury buildings remain partially empty when completed, homes unsold, or else are purchased by speculators who don't move in. Bengaluru, 2017. Photo by Pierre Hauser.

to mixed-use projects (i.e., housing plus retail and office space). Only 1 percent of total foreign investments went to industrial projects. In this period, private equity bet heavily on housing, which contributed to the idea that speculative investments would best accelerate the wealth creation and consumption patterns of a newly globalizing middle class.

Even though housing was a limited market with relatively few buyers, the profit margins on luxury homes, villas, and gated communities were substantial. Consultants explained that the variation in the cost of production across market segments (i.e., low, middle, luxury) was minimal, since the cost of the raw materials, labor, electrical fixtures, and plumbing was more or less comparable across all sectors of the housing market. By adding a few touches at relatively little extra cost—luxury icons such as a clubhouse and a swimming pool, opulent fittings, and upscale flooring—the selling price of these projects would shoot up. The largest developers sold only a fraction of their luxury units yet made a much higher profit than from lower-valued housing schemes (figure 6.2). Unsold inventory was built into their business model, explained an industry consultant. "Why would you be altruistic and build affordable housing on land that can give you much higher profits?" he asked rhetorically.[7]

To sum up the phase between 2005 and 2010, investors offered developers capital, and this capital was spent largely on land acquisition and the promotion of numerous luxury projects, less so on construction and project completion. Funds predominantly flowed into the high-end and upper-caste residential market, and investors sought an exit through IPOs, in which private companies worked with investment banks to become public by selling their shares on the stock exchange. This market-making phase, defined by an abundance of foreign capital, transformed the business practices of the Indian real estate sector by enabling large-scale land acquisition, hoarding, and overproduction.

While private equity players harbored a strong view that they had been cheated by developers, developers often articulated a radically different perspective. One developer, for example, made a trenchant critique of global investors, stating, "Private equity is unwilling to take business risks. Why didn't they assess risk and create solid contracts? Sometimes there are unforeseen delays. What are we supposed to do?"[8]

The subsequent boom in India's real estate sector illustrates the overwhelming power of certain discourses to produce socio-spatial transformations. Narratives of an impending real estate boom produced a frenzy of activity, but the great growth story and its much-anticipated effects were essentially speculative. The story that catalyzed private equity investment started with Goldman Sachs's influential report of 2003, *Dreaming with BRICS: The Path to 2050; How BRICS Will Shape the Next 50 Years*. Despite this salesmanship, private equity funds lost money in the first five years of their involvement in the sector, and projections made at that time were soon exposed as highly unrealistic. To quote the director of a leading real estate consulting firm: "Admittedly, we also bought into the story and fueled it. The story, once born, kept getting bigger, and we were part of that. We gave it more substance. I don't absolve myself. I take blame for fueling it, for miscalculating. Much too rosy a picture was painted of the economy. The BRIC report triggered a massive growth story. But everything rested on shaky ground."[9]

Typically, analyses of speculative cycles foreground the windfall profits of the early financial investors who cash out swiftly. In this instance, capital dumping allowed *the builders* to cash out. Investors found that in the real world, there were just too many obstacles to acquiring land and building luxury residences at the pace they expected to turn over their capital. The series of transaction obstacles they encountered included the difficulty of getting land and holding on to it when land prices sky-rocketed and landowners expected their own share of the profiteering; the perpetual problem of acquiring cement and steel affordably; and the stalling of government agents in licensing and supporting any rapid-paced developments without their own rentier-driven compensation (Gidwani and Upadhya 2022; Searle 2018). These combined to thwart private equity plans and gains.

We should not assume a priori that it is simple for global finance to extract hefty profits in any place and then quickly exit. The balance of power is not that straightforward or static (Halbert and Rouanet 2014). As more people (and institutions) became enamored with the speculative possibilities in and around Bengaluru, they, too, demanded a piece of this speculative pie (Rouanet and Halbert 2016). From the standpoint of private equity players, things did not go according to plan. A new set of logics and financial strategies arose from the crisis generated from these setbacks.

Finance and Real Estate in Crisis: The Short-Lived Bubble Bursts

Wild speculation proved to be unrealistic, and investment funds performed poorly. By 2010 relations between private equity investors and developers soured. A consensus emerged that private equity had "burned its fingers," a recurring phrase in interviews. Many projects were riddled with long delays in construction.

Interviewees from the private equity side explained that in retrospect, equity was terribly overvalued. The collective desire for hypervalued assets overrode the longer-term interest in producing more realistic valuations to prevent future losses. Inflated value is not a simple miscalculation or the outcome of a technical error. In a speculative scenario, a confluence of interests occurs. Third-party rating agencies and property consultants conducting property valuations were, to quote a private equity representative, working hand in glove with developers. The director of a major global consulting firm elaborated on the ways in which converging interests resulted in what he candidly called a "cartel situation."

Consulting agencies performed the allegedly neutral task of property valuations while also brokering the deals between investors and developers, which this director acknowledged was a "conflict of interest."[10] Rating agencies were hired by the same firms they were rating, with the task of legitimizing the speculative imagination.[11] They inflated the value of these investments as well as their prospects, which contributed to a wider public impression that such speculation would be safe, profitable, and enduring.

Meanwhile, in this phase, developers were hit hard by debt, and their share prices fell. An exemplary case comes from the experience of a respected high-end developer in Bengaluru, which we will call Top-Star. Having ridden the high winds of rapid expansion only to become saddled with sizable amounts of debt, Top-Star hired prominent financial analysts to help it raise cash. From 2005 to 2015, the price of an acre of land in Bengaluru rose at many sites from Rs. 10 lakh per acre to Rs. 10 crores (a lakh is a unit of 100,000; Rs. 10 lakh equals $11,700, and Rs. 10 crores equals $1.17 million), representing a 9,900 percent increase over ten years. During this period Top-Star, a family-run business that had started ten years earlier with just one building development, was constructing more than twenty large-scale residential projects covering 3 million square feet. Moreover, it promised another seventy-five projects across eight Indian states, with a land bank of more than three thousand acres. The firm rode the boom and invested big. From 2001 to 2008, growth was phenomenal, and the number of staff increased from a few hundred to ten thousand. "But so did its debt grow," a consultant close to the firm noted. The firm became unwieldy, with too many incomplete projects, too much debt, and anxious lenders and home subscribers nipping at its heels.[12]

Top-Star hired financial analysts to help figure out how to stop the bleeding. Of course, the only option provided was an IPO, a typical tool offered globally by the financial sector, one that heightened global finance's own profits during this period. Top-Star's share price started at Rs. 640 ($10). After the IPO, the share price doubled immediately to Rs. 1,240 but then plummeted to Rs. 65. In short, after the IPO spike in price, the initial foreign investors successfully sold out as planned. This was followed by a crash in the share price, and the original Indian investors and the company were left holding substantially devalued shares. Yet, as written into the contract, the IPO financial advising firm was generously rewarded.

The breakdown of the cozy relationship between developers and investors is best expressed by how foreign private equity (in non-IPO scenarios) tried to recoup their sinking investments. The property consultant Jones Lang LaSalle issued a report that analyzed the methods and strategies of private equity exits at the end of this market phase. It found that private equity would typically exit through the IPO route or via a third party that bought the equity investment at a higher valuation. In this period, however, 70 percent of the private equity funds exited via promoter buybacks. This means that local developers themselves were obliged by agreement with private equity to buy the shares back, even at a loss (Jones Lang LaSalle 2011). The report noted that "the secondary market has no depth," which means there was little demand for the stocks in which firms had invested.

Therefore, most contracts contained what was explained to me as a safety net clause, which stated that if the projections failed to materialize, the promoter/developer would repay the initial investment, with a guaranteed increase in share value, to private equity investors whenever they were ready to sell. These promoter buyback commitments reveal the extent to which projections of asset value appreciation were far off the mark, and the buyback guarantee explains why investors were willing to enter this untested market in the first place. A weak secondary market is a condition that would normally keep private equity away, while a strong secondary market is precisely the condition that allows private equity an easy exit. This situation led to acrimonious battles between the two parties. A private equity representative explained, "Every buyback comes after incessant begging or threatening. The buybacks are forced. Half our deals are in the courts. The buybacks were not profitable; they were a disaster."[13]

He added that the buyback clause violated Indian law since it illegally guaranteed a future price and the purchase of unlisted shares, otherwise known as oligopolistic practices of coercion and price fixing. In some Indian court cases, private equity firms responded to that accusation by claiming that their funds had been mismanaged and/or embezzled by the local developers. In other cases, they threatened builders with personal and firm-level audits. In essence, the fallout between developers and investors became as dramatic as their courtship had been just a few years earlier.

It is possible to interpret this fallout as reflecting the limit of financialization in India. In other words, the limited secondary markets, the downward valuations of local firms, and the growing number of unsold units together indicate an absence of demand and, consequently, an inherent limit to the operation of finance capital. However, I argue against such a reading. As the next section shows, financialized logics were not thwarted but radically reformulated. These discordant dynamics set the conditions for the appearance of new financial strategies and for a second round in the making of India's financialized real estate market. In phase 1, private equity conjured up a market that enticed as well as complemented Indian developers' own expanded agenda. In phase 2, private equity returned with new financial tools and the power to shift out of this plummeting residential housing market of equity into new markets of debt, some of which they themselves created.

Phase 2: From Market Creation to Consolidation in a Bust Cycle (2011–20)

In this second phase of financialization, fewer private equity firms returned, but those that did successfully focused on deploying new strategies and creating noncompetitive markets. The largest ones—GIC-Singapore, KKR, Blackstone, Brookfield Asset Management, and Carlyle Group—came to dominate phase 2. Given the numerous failed investments, weak sales, and paralyzed projects of phase 1, what could possibly maintain private equity's interest in the investment minefields of Indian cities? The basic answer is that new low-risk opportunities were being offered by overleveraged developers and banks in a remade marketplace shaped by fewer dominant players. Phase 2 is marked by a dramatic overhaul of the strategy of foreign finance capital, particularly private equity, which took advantage of the overleveraged real estate sector. Table 6.1 summarizes the key points of comparison between the two phases.

After those earlier days of cat and mouse, private equity firms returned to India with a new set of tools and much more leverage. When asked what was different the second time around, a Mumbai-based investor in 2017 explained, "The euphoria of 2005–8 has not come back. This next phase of the contemporary debt-driven period is marked by a completely different strategy, in a different financial environment. The cats have left and returned as vultures."[14]

After 2010 private equity sought to regain control of the market and secure steady, predictable rates of return by withdrawing from flagging

TABLE 6.1 Two phases of finance-developer relations

PHASE 1: MARKET-MAKING BOOM CYCLE (2005–10)	PHASE 2: MARKET-CONSOLIDATING BUST CYCLE (2011 ONWARD)
Large-scale land acquisition	High rates of unsold inventory
Capital dumping (easy and cheap access to capital)	Capital scarcity/raised costs of capital
Oversubscribed shares of developer firms	Sharp declines in share price: 50 percent of nation's developers go bankrupt
Private equity enters through developers' IPOS and equity investment into special project vehicles	Private equity offers high-interest structured debt and invests in nonperforming assets
High investment in luxury housing	High investment in commercial real estate
Converging interests among private equity, developers, intermediaries, and speculative buyers	Antagonistic relations among developers, private equity, and buyers

Source: Goldman and Narayan (2021).

real estate and construction projects, investing instead in the new market of depressed assets, and issuing structured debt. By offering structured debt to developers, finance firms could reduce their liabilities in the tumultuous world of urban real estate and guarantee a steady rate of return via debt-plus-interest payments and transaction fees (P. Ghosh 2015). Private equity firms began to offer developers loans with fixed interest rates of 20 percent. In short, finance capital turned the tables on developers in phase 2, as they recrafted the rules of the game to off-load the risks of investment in a volatile speculative market.

With a keen eye toward capitalizing on debt, private equity focused on the emergent markets of depreciated assets, underoccupied commercial office space, unfinished housing projects, and unsold real estate inventory (Rathi 2017). Across India, developers' portfolios overflowed with unproductive and unsold assets. Developers were forced to raise funds just to refinance existing loans. India's largest developer, DLF, held outstanding debt of Rs. 26,800 crores ($4 billion) by 2018 and began to sell off major assets at a substantial discount, largely to foreign private equity firms. This new market of troubled firms, insurmountable debt, and asset value collapse appeared to the world as a warning of a major recession. But through the lens of private equity, it looked like a magical moment of opportunity.

"India's Bad Debt Is Looking Better to Investors" declared a headline in the *New York Times*, in an article reporting that India's banks were carrying almost $20 billion worth of bad loans in 2017 (Raghavan 2017). These were dubbed toxic assets by the equity firms buying them up cheaply, just as they did in Spain, Greece, Ireland, and Turkey soon after the 2008 crisis (Smyth and Gittelsohn 2013). Once Indian legislators rewrote bankruptcy laws and insolvency codes in 2016, debtors were held to the fire of stringent payback rules. By early 2019 the amount of nonperforming assets (NPAs), or unrecoverable loans, for India's public banks shot up from $20 billion to $50 billion (S. Ghosh and Pandya 2019; Anup Roy 2018).[15] At the same time that a handful of Wall Street firms were purchasing the toxic NPAs of Indian banks, at pennies on the dollar, they were busy vacuuming up depressed infrastructural assets from the real estate sector, the largest sector (along with construction) in debt to India's banks. This burgeoning market of NPAs was created through a series of bold and fast moves by the central government under the guidance of foreign financial analysts and their network friends at private equity firms, after which these same actors rushed in to capture a piece of this prime market for themselves (Kaul 2018; A. Paul 2018; J. Ghosh and Chandrasekhar 2017).[16]

By 2018 India's nonbanking financial companies, once a major source of capital for builders, had become extremely reluctant to loan money to real estate players, given that their risky foray into real estate in the previous phase had left them dangerously overleveraged. Global private equity gladly filled this gap, becoming one of the sole institutional sources of finance for cash-strapped developers (Babar 2019). Data from consultant reports show that while the amount of private equity flowing into the sector in absolute terms may have declined in the second phase, it accounted for a much larger proportion of inflows.[17] In 2010 private equity funds accounted for 24 percent of total inflows to real estate, while banks accounted for close to 60 percent. By 2016 this pattern had reversed, with such funds accounting for 75 percent of the total, and bank lending only 24 percent (A. Narayan 2019).

To stop the hemorrhaging, India's banks and financial institutions refused to lend any further to builders, creating a void in a market of high demand. In phase 2, we see how quickly private equity capital, which had initially fueled the speculative fires of overvalued markets, consolidated its position as a key source of finance. It helped shape the new market in NPAs, a market that spread across India's business sectors and became the latest and best investment opportunity for the firms' own portfolios. At the largest global private equity firm in India, Wall Street–based Blackstone, in the late 2010s and early 2020s, their Indian portfolio was flush with NPA investments. During this crisis the company earned higher profit rates in India than from its investments in the United States and Europe (Alexander and Antony 2018; P. Sarkar 2019).

This vulture-like tactic of picking the bones of entities drowning in debt exposes the role that monopsony arbitrage can play in private equity's portfolio. We learn from this NPA crisis how a few firms can become the single buyer in a marketplace and, with that power, can control the conditions of both demand and supply. In this case, the product is debt, which gets converted into a liquid asset *through* the sale, discounted by the seller (e.g., the banks and developers) for the buyer's (e.g., the firms') benefit. The new technology of NPAs opened a new profitable revenue stream while private equity's old clients remained under the weight of overleverage caused by private equity's previous bag of financial tricks and expert advice. What I call *monopsony arbitrage* enabled finance capital to set prices, the conditions of its deals, and its exit strategies. It demonstrated the power of finance capital in tumultuous times.

Blackstone jumped on these new opportunities by deploying a record $10.4 billion over ten years, and $6.6 billion in the first four years of phase 2. Blackstone profited enormously from these large deals, extracting and exporting an astounding $4.5 billion from India by 2019 (Nandy 2018). In the process Blackstone became India's largest landlord.[18] Across India, Blackstone owned a record 114 million square feet of office space, albeit with limited liability for the asset's fixed nature.

When Blackstone floated India's first real estate investment trust (REIT), it was met with so much anticipation that shares were oversubscribed and purchased at above-market prices. This REIT generated such a huge inflow of capital from excited Indian investors that it enabled Blackstone to cash out of its own investments in these buildings. As each dollar flowing into the REIT from small and large Indian investors was money Blackstone could export overseas, the company thus turned what was a fixed asset (real estate) into a purely liquid one to exit the Indian marketplace.

These strategies allowed Blackstone to keep its relationship to fixed (illiquid) assets at a minimum regardless of how fixed in place real estate may appear. The size of these deals and the desperate need for so-called scarce capital on the part of large Indian debtors combined to give firms like Blackstone a substantial advantage. In the words of the head of Blackstone's real estate arm, Turin Parikh, in a 2019 interview with *Forbes* magazine: "Our philosophy is, we don't like to do small, discreet deals. If we like a particular thing then we do it in scale and in a concentrated manner so that we can influence the outcome and we spend time and resources to make it work" (P. Sarkar 2019). With this statement, Blackstone's executive neatly articulates the defining strategy of monopoly capital.

Analysis of the financial statements of the top twelve developers across India during this period, including the top developers in Bengaluru, one of India's hottest spots for speculation (Kaul 2018), reveals several clear trends characterizing India's developers during this phase. First, developers faced increased liabilities (i.e., debt) and a rise between 2009 and 2015 in the ratio of total liabilities to total sales (A. Narayan 2019). Second, based on our analysis of firm-level profit-and-loss data, Bengaluru's largest firms have experienced dramatically falling profit margins since 2012. Among the largest developers, the profit margins of Puravankara and Sobha have halved, and that of Prestige has fallen by a third between 2009 and 2015.

Third, there was massive growth in unsold real estate inventory that was not accompanied by a drop in prices. The data reveal that the amounts that firms spent on repaying debt, paying interest, and giving shareholders dividends added up to considerably more than their cash revenues (A. Narayan 2019). Early on, access to capital allowed these firms to expand and set unrealistic prices, but the mounting stock of unsold luxury housing and extremely weak sales did not result in the price corrections that conventional pricing theory would predict (Kaul 2019). Instead, sales and inventory trends reveal a significant disjuncture. Builders continued to produce units at a pace that far exceeded what the market could absorb. Indeed, the growth of inventory measured by both volume and value far exceeded the growth in sales (Aundhe 2019). The oversupply of unsold commercial real estate in India's eight top-ranked cities rose steeply from 346 million square feet in 2009 to 784 million square feet in 2018, at an annual compounded growth rate of 9.5 percent. This mirrors the extremely high volume of unsold residential inventory (1,248 million square feet) across India.

While sales volumes in 2019 were approximately 1.3 times what they were in 2009, inventory volumes more than tripled (to approximately 3.3 times). When measured by value, the divergence is even starker. Sales value increased only approximately 1.6 times, while inventory value had ballooned to approximately 4.7 times what it was a decade earlier (Annamalai and Doshi 2012). The value of unsold stock rose to four times the value of sold stock in India's top eight cities (*Financial Express* 2019). In the larger cities, such as Chennai and Bengaluru, and in smaller ones, such as Cochin/Kochi, new buildings in the center of the city were only 70 percent occupied, while along the fast-growing periphery only 20–30 percent of homes were apparently occupied.[19] This occupancy problem for high-end housing came at a time of surging unmet demand for truly affordable housing for lower socioeconomic groups left out of (and in some cases dispossessed by) this construction boom (Basole 2019).

Weak sales and rising inventory would cause companies to be alarmed in virtually any other segment of the economy. Unsold stock is typically a reflection of wasted investment and hence a drain on profits, and capitalist enterprises strive to closely track and predict demand to avoid such pile-ups. The real estate sector seems peculiarly indifferent to these pressures. External sources of finance and large land bank owners—as well as intimate fraternal links to movers and shakers in the political world who could bail them out if necessary—allowed developers to remain impervious to the actual purchasing ability of consumers. Large developers relied on expensive private equity to buttress their staying power in the face of low sales. This trend of builders setting high prices and sitting on inventory resulted in popular protest at the glaring lack of affordable housing, eliciting a tepid government directive to reduce prices.

TABLE 6.2 Consolidation and rapid decline in the number of developers across India

CITY	2011–12 (N)	2017–18 (N)	CHANGE (%)
Bengaluru	646	251	−61.10
Mumbai	364	248	−31.90
Calcutta/Kolkata	235	83	−64.70
Gurgaon/Gurugram	82	19	−76.80
Pan-India	3,538	1,745	−50.70

Source: Aundhe (2019).

A final trend defining phase 2 is consolidation among developer firms. While developers' untenable burden of debt and liability created an exploitable opportunity for large financial firms, smaller developers by contrast were being squeezed out of their market, resulting in greater consolidation among the few remaining developers (Aundhe 2019). By 2018 more than 50 percent of the developers in nine of India's largest cities had folded—a shocking collapse and reconfiguration of the industry.

A longtime employee of a land-aggregating firm explained the pressure on and risks for smaller enterprises as follows: "We are the biggest land banker in Bangalore, and yet even for us, it has gotten difficult, with such high interest on the borrowed capital, to still make enough money. Most players have dropped out; the business has become too risky. Many of the local players can no longer compete. The drive to acquire land for future luxury projects keeps private equity interested, but it only raises the stakes for developers, forcing them to consolidate or disappear."[20]

Industry consolidation of developers and land bankers narrowed the possibilities for small and medium-sized companies to produce affordable housing, even as the demand for basic housing continues to rapidly grow (table 6.2). Indeed, this dichotomy has exacerbated the already existing homelessness problem in Indian cities.

Alongside these major shifts affecting real estate developers, some significant changes were occurring in the financial sector, especially once the Indian state intervened to help global private equity firms profit from toxic assets. Here we see a new business model emerge. By 2018 distressed-asset purchases became financial investors' biggest business in India. As soon as one of the largest nonbanking financial companies, IL&FS (Infrastructure Leasing and Finance Services), collapsed, alarm bells rang and triggered the pincer-grip conditions of sky-high credit lending rates alongside a paucity of credit that ultimately undercut most sectors of the national economy (*Economic Times* 2018). Small and medium-sized domestic finance and real estate firms fell into deep trouble. As early as 2016, the central government stepped in with life preservers in the form of new bankruptcy laws and the creation of asset reconstruction companies that brought together public banks and private equity firms to buy these toxic assets at reduced prices and then securitize them as high-risk/high-reward assets on the international markets.

In other words, the state actively bailed out the largest banks and their bad loans, hoping to reboot the real estate market by clearing the banks' books of nonperforming and unpayable debt and thus allow them to start anew with a fresh tranche of loans. Debt forgiveness seems to exist only for the largest players in society. (By contrast, many of Bengaluru's construction workers cope with endless debt; see figure 6.3). Once enacted, this bailout maneuver attracted a group of elite vultures—the same characters who had advised governments on how to turn bad bank loans into investable assets—to feed on the carcass of the debt-burdened economy. Remarkably, the media, government officials, and the financial community were able to artfully present this reincarnation act as an innovative business technology to the public, which was blindsided by these revelations of bank failure.

Quickly, the global private equity firm Brookfield jumped into the fray, partnering with the State Bank of India to launch a $1 billion distressed-asset fund. They were soon followed by India's Piramal and the United States' Bain Capital (also with a $1 billion fund), Apollo Global Management, and the Caisse de dépôt et placement du Québec (a Canadian pension fund) coupled with the Mumbai-based Edelweiss Group, with Wall Street's Carlyle Group as its minor owner. With this new synthetic

6.3 Many construction workers are young male migrants from poorer regions of North India who borrow money at usurious rates from labor contractors to pay off debts back home. Near the suburb of Varthur on the eastern outskirts of Bengaluru, 2017. Photo by Pierre Hauser.

business model, we see the blurring of distinctions between credit and debt, public and private, domestic and foreign, North and South. A high percentage of these distressed assets originated in the very same sectors that the World Bank and Asian Development Bank had promoted two decades earlier as the key sectors that could help India build its twenty-first-century global cities: real estate, construction-related industries, and finance (Goldman 2014).

These complex, multisite, and often-hidden shifts affirm the utility of using the optics of finance to follow their actions, movements, and behavior (wherever they take us) rather than restricting analysis to a single scale, sector, or site. For example, I initially thought I was researching the financing of world-class urban infrastructure; instead, I ended up observing a nationwide bailout that maximized private equity capital. This switch, and the relationship across these seemingly disparate phenomena, taught me how investments in fixed assets like infrastructure can be a catalyst for capturing rents in and beyond that sector, rather than the end goal. The love affair between finance capital and developers started with an ebullient courtship to work together to build the world-class infrastructure and housing needed for the much-desired global city. This urban imaginary was conjured by a host of actors, including the Asian Development Bank, McKinsey and Company, USAID, Global Cities policy networks, Goldman Sachs, and scores of Indian government agencies keen on reaping the benefits of a more prosperous city.

These actors were also keen to become rentier intermediaries in this new cash-flush environment. Once the expected returns failed to materialize, however, the techniques, tools, and strategies of private equity rapidly changed. The preceding analysis captures the fragile, relational, and interscalar aspects of financialization and the remarkable speed and force with which transformations in the strategies of finance capital occurred during this period, much to the disadvantage of the population in need of housing. The logic and dominance of private equity requires that its investments remain liquid and mobile. Its modus operandi is to seek out and create opportunities of scarcity and distress through arbitrage, upend stable business models, and then capture and monopolize future asset value increases as they circulate *through* infrastructure and the various financial instruments under its immediate control. The effects ripple unevenly across cities and governance structures around the globe.

Conclusion: New Financial Logics of Arbitrage and the Speculative State

Global finance did not have a problem shifting gears on a dime in its dealings with developers once their Indian counterparts became overleveraged. Within just a few years, private equity went from recklessly dumping capital and creating a speculative frenzy to doubling down and leveraging the liquidity crunch and depressed markets it left in its wake. These patterns and trends are symptomatic of the latest turn in speculative urbanism in many cities around the world, a phenomenon that urban scholars are only beginning to fully understand. This chapter has highlighted the particular dynamics that led to a rapid shift in relations between financiers and developers in India, resulting in the consolidation of power for a select few. It revealed how and why finance moves from one sector to another, strategically bouncing from housing to office space, from equity to debt, from fixed to liquid shares in infrastructure and then in toxic debt. These tactics, largely unmapped or acknowledged in the media or in political discussions, benefit oligopolistic actors in finance and receive strong support from state administrators, regulators, and legislators.

These same private equity firms are redirecting their Indian earnings to indebted and vulnerable infrastructural opportunities in Spain, Germany, Turkey, the United States, and China. Indian cities fuel and finance speculative projects elsewhere. Profits are made through the circulatory process of their capital, moving freely in and out of fixed assets, across sectors, borders, and discourses, overturning conventions and rules in its path.

Thus, it doesn't make sense to invoke the notion of India as a singular case isolated from other financialization processes elsewhere. Interscalar nodes of speculation have become deeply entwined in global networks of finance capital. Urban sites and spaces in many parts of the world have become more unstable due to finance capital's increasing ability to off-load its liabilities and risks onto others (Tooze 2018). The dynamics of debt borrowing for developers and consumers have invoked a caustic speculative urban strategy that compels cities and investor classes to acquire more public and private land as incentives—and collateral—for speculative markets. Tensions arising with the scarcity of public and private land for affordable housing and the speculation-fueled costs of land and housing have intensified across metropolitan and rural regions worldwide (Rolnik 2019).

The logic of finance capital thrives on these monopolistic, interscalar, and arbitrage-driven practices, enabling global finance to drive down values in one place and drive them up elsewhere, pitting sites and people against each other. These practices wreak havoc on our cities and our institutions as finance searches for new grounds on which to expropriate and exploit. As asset devaluation attracts the world's largest financial firms, it sparks cyclical up-and-down valuations with greater frequency and intensity. This emergent wild market started in Bengaluru with the tumultuous love affair between real estate and global private equity, a tryst, it turns out, common to many other cities pursuing the dream of global urbanism.

This chapter has documented the actors pivotal to this high-stakes game. Urban transformations driven by speculative capital have been endorsed by states willing—and sometimes eager—to support the most robust financial firms to ply their trade in all sectors of society to which they can gain access. In twenty-first-century India, and in most other neoliberal settings across the Global North and South, state institutions have developed their own speculative stance by requiring municipalities and local agencies to borrow from capital markets and reorient their priorities away from building, distributing, and managing public goods. This has meant austerity, deprivation, and discipline for city denizens, while offering prosperity and freedom for transient global investors and their local elite brethren.

As states have become more intimately involved in institutionalizing the logic of speculative urbanism, they have mobilized the new public management discourse and embraced the role of rentier intermediary, encouraging capital markets to take over their money-raising responsibilities and enabling finance to remain liquid and exit its commitments and responsibilities at a moment's notice, for the good of their transnational band of investor clients (Christophers 2019). Consequently, finance has assiduously off-loaded most risks and liabilities onto those who build, use, and manage public infrastructure and space. These endeavors have heightened the power asymmetries among state agents, financiers, and the urban majority.

Arbitrage practices are not simply a technique of taking advantage of price differences across uneven geographies. They are also predicated on the ability of finance to abruptly move and change its form and technique of operation as it works with new and established power network geometries. Although this chapter has focused on the logics mobilized by global finance, I am not suggesting that large developers or national banks are somehow victims of finance's arbitrage practices. Far from being victims, the largest developers and banks benefit from the unanticipated consolidation occurring as small and medium-sized players get pushed out and new rentier benefits are secured from this less competitive marketplace.

Our story is less about the overwhelming power of Global North actors and the peripheralization of the South, and more about the variegated institutionalization of finance and its unpredictable ability to shift, on a dime, its speculative urban logics. This process has become dispossessive for a widening range of actors globally—not just for the lower-caste and outcaste land users described in the previous chapter—while enriching others positioned in the upper echelons of social hierarchies in India and elsewhere.

A cross-national and intercity approach is important to help us crack open the hidden mysteries of the empire of finance. It reveals the ways that private equity thrives in India while based elsewhere, succeeding by flowing into and out of unanchored equity and debt vehicles. Capital often originates in special project vehicles that are logistically housed within the cavernous cracks of a broken twentieth-century model of nation-states. They are neither in the core nor in the periphery but wherever they can work unencumbered, such as in tax havens in the Cayman Islands, Singapore, Panama, and Mauritius. The fact that these global private equity funds are managed in India by Indian managers, many of whom had previous careers in local real estate companies, and many others who worked for global firms in Singapore, Dubai, and New York City, makes it even more difficult to impose a neat paradigm of a Northern victor and a Southern victim. In other words, this method and theory suggest new forms of politics emerging within this brave new world of twenty-first-century finance.

Finally, this chapter demonstrates that finance capital reflects a contingent set of processes that actively produce urban spaces through adaptive and speculative relationships. Global financial firms work within an interconnected set of marketplaces that contract and re-emerge, bouncing from one fiery crisis to another, under conditions that they themselves help to configure. The rapidly shifting financial dynamics in Indian real estate have provided a vantage point from which to see the interscalar, relational, and conjunctural dimensions of speculative urbanism. Over a short period, the entrance of private equity into the urban landscape destabilized social and spatial relations, forcing out an older, locally rooted way of doing business and cementing a financialized model fundamentally rooted in the idea of grow, grow, grow, harnessed to the mandate to dispossess, dispossess, dispossess.

While the previous chapter explored the foundational nature of dispossession affecting those living on the urban periphery, this chapter has revealed how even elite wealthy leaders of the Indian economy, such as the CEOs and investors in banking, real estate, and construction, can suffer under the power and authority of global finance capital. Some profit, many fail, but all must change. Bankruptcies and crippling debt negatively impact employment and wages, housing access for the working class, and the operation of small-scale artisanal and commercial enterprises (Chowdhury 2011). Government budgets must prioritize bailouts and usurious interest payments over the distribution of public goods and services.

In addition to this retrenchment and austerity, waves of financialization have also influenced the ways that people imagine an alternative politics—one that seeks to definancialize structures of power and everyday social-natural relations, while also envisioning realms of just sociality, supportive care, and restorative ecology. The conclusion explores the question of a postspeculative urban future: We will hear from agents of change in Bengaluru and beyond, as they consider a postspeculative agenda for us all.

CONCLUSION

> Reorganizing the economy around publicly created money is not utopian. It simply requires recognizing and reorienting what exists, and what underpins our money system today. In the wake of the financial crisis of 2007–8, the sovereign power to create public money was made clear when governments used it to rescue the banks and other large businesses, such as auto manufacturers and insurance companies. Let it now be used to provision the people. —Fred Block and Robert Hockett, *Democratizing Finance: Restructuring Credit to Transform Society*, 2022

Translating Critique into Meaningful Action

After I gave a public talk in Bengaluru on the role of finance capital in the increasing volatility in the city, a working-class activist raised his hand and said, "This all makes sense to me, but how can I possibly communicate this to people on the streets? What would be the slogan we can put on a placard?" I came up with some feeble response like "Get Wall Street Off Our Backs!" but I understood his concern. Financialization of the city is a rather abstract concept and mysterious target for protest; moreover, the media won't typically address such a complex issue that requires a deep dive into the tools and relationships and cultures that finance creates to profit from projects, including the unbuilt ones.

The obsession in political and media discourses is to blame the mafias, which are imagined to be nasty rent-grabbing parasites. But that finger-pointing assumes that there exists an otherwise well-functioning machinery of capital investment and circulation on which the parasite attaches. Most news media have a business and finance section reporting on financial transactions and voice enthusiasm over the heightened role of international investors in cities in India and around the world. Global finance's workings are opaque, and yet the practices are lauded for finance's ability to enter new markets, promising riches and progress for all.

I followed up this question at my talk with a short reminder of their own local accomplishments: Remember, I told them, you had already effectively kept this type of rapacious foreign finance capital out of your city and nation for decades after independence. It was only after the 1990–91 US war in Iraq and Kuwait that the Indian economy collapsed under the weight of foreign debt and geopolitics, which kicked off a decade of neoliberal policies of disinvestment, austerity, and incentives for foreign capital to enter India. It was only in 2005, not that long ago, that foreign financial investors were invited to invest in land, property, and real estate. So it should be possible to bring back those anti-imperial and pro-public sentiments of the twentieth-century independence movement and implement strict regulations against these destructive practices. Prior regulations and public disdain for global finance existed for a reason.

But as so many people have emphasized to me, the goal is to *not* revert to a more restrictive era for finance capital and bring back the prefinancialized economy but to set out on a new course of urban and rural development that foregrounds justice and equity for the majority who had already been marginalized by racialized, classed, and gendered forms of exploitation and expropriation.

Dalit Activists' Vision

A leading Bengaluru slum dweller and activist, Narasimhamurthy, used the term *financialization* in a series of interviews my colleagues and I had with him.[1] He is the state convenor of Slum Janandolana Karnataka based in Bengaluru, where he lives in what he affirms as a slum: "You can see financialization in all the projects coming from OnMs [State government's Operations and Maintenance]. We find them in the MoU [memorandum of understanding] documents between KUIDFC and KDB [Karnataka Development Board] and banks like World Bank and Asian Development Bank." He understands clearly the tools and strategies of finance, and the role of the handmaiden state, when he makes a sharp distinction between the way slum dwellers were negatively treated in the past and the way they are abused today. In other words, he uses what I call a *relational-conjunctural approach.*

Elaborating on the complexity of the issue, Narasimhamurthy says:

> The culture of providing houses for the urban poor is a recent trend— in practice for the past twenty years only. Before that, land sites were being allocated instead. People back then, depending on their financial situation, would build a hut or a house of their dreams on that allotted land. This dream has been taken away by the government. We ask for a site, they insist on giving us [flats in tenements]. Why? Because they have profits to make. There are contractors and political parties that benefit from this arrangement [of undertaking construction of multi-story buildings under redevelopment or rehabilitation schemes]. They lobby a lot for this [housing schemes]. . . . The government's housing plans are a business. It is a business of poverty. They are not interested in our development.
>
> More recently, [government leaders] have shifted their arguments. They are now claiming that there is no land in [central] urban areas. But we know there is land. . . . The government is hesitating to let certain castes access these lands and give them ownership.
>
> In a way, the politicians themselves do not want to give us any rights— they need a hook to bait us so they can win elections—so they promise us new houses elsewhere. Their idea is like this—"If we give them [slum residents] land rights and houses, they won't be in our control anymore." That is why there is no political will for them to solve this issue.[2]

He explains that in Bengaluru about twenty-seven thousand acres of government land were identified by the 2006 AT Ramaswamy Committee report (commissioned by the Karnataka legislature to document land grabbing) as illegally stolen and encroached on by a cabal of interconnected elites within and outside of government. It is a huge amount of land that could easily satisfy the needs of the houseless, poorly housed, displaced, and evicted; instead, this land grabbing—during this era of speculative urbanism—upends the lives of minoritized communities such as his:

> When we demanded land for slum dwellers [from this stolen land bank], they gave us 248 acres [but spread out in isolated sites across the city's periphery]. Initially, the government said that they would cover 50 percent of the market value of the land while the residents must pay for the rest. We fought against this requirement and managed to have [the 50 percent payment] waived. [Beyond this stolen land,] there is government land in every city. [Some of it] is absorbed by private elite educational societies that politicians have taken up [as a legal means to acquire government land and start a tax-free private business]. There are many such instances, and we have records to support this claim. The government must acquire some of this land and give it to people—such revolutionary policies are yet to happen. Be it revenue land or land on the outskirts of the city—there is a lot of government land there. What the state always does is, they give us houses [flats in multistory buildings] in these [peripheral] areas but not land.[3]

He argues that all the daily problems they face—threat of eviction, lack of access to basic amenities, poor housing, poor wages, lack of health care, humiliating discriminatory caste-based treatment—occur because the state (and the courts) does not view them as citizens; hence, they do not have the same rights as most other citizens. A way of attaining these rights, and by extension solving their problems, would be to get land rights. "Because in India," he argues, "no one can contest your citizenship if you own a piece of land." He says that these barriers and obstacles put before Dalits and other minorities are part of a larger pattern of what he explained to me as *government speculation*.

Narasimhamurthy articulates well the linkages across government policies and actions, the ways that financial institutions encourage shifts in urban land governance, and the discursive scaffolding built to support this financialized, caste-based urban turn. One of the first successful campaigns of the Slum Janandolana Karnataka, formed in 2010, was to force a change in the name of the official slum agency of the state—from the Slum Clearance Board to the Slum Development Board. Words matter, he notes. So do the deep-seated affect and emotion behind the role of land for urban and rural Dalits (Sharma 2017).

Slum dwellers refuse to be cleared out; what they want is land on which to build their future.

Clearing slums, which often happens in the middle of the night with large bulldozers and a lathi-swinging police force, dismembers city life for the low-waged poor. As political scientist Supriya RoyChowdhury (2021) shows, many of Bengaluru's slum dwellers were once government employees in those now-dismantled public sector units working as maintenance workers, garbage collectors, security guards, clerks, and sweepers. However poorly they were paid, they had relatively secure employment with a modicum of social welfare protections and benefits. Self-constructed slum housing was the way that communities of rural migrants could afford to live in the city on such low wages and in a context of deeply discriminatory rental markets. Informal settlements overflow with workshops, storage sites, and informal markets in which extended families ply their trades while living side by side, sharing resources and more. To clear a slum for the good of the global city destroys more than shoddy housing. It upends existing networks of care, sociality, and economy for the OBC (Other Backward Classes), Muslim, and Dalit communities. To live in a tiny box on a floor high off the ground in newly built high-rise tenements creates an atomized space suitable only for the bare minimum of members of an extended family (i.e., with two small bedrooms at most) that cannot alone sustain themselves. Networks are a survival strategy and the essence of city life (Simone 2004).

New homes offered to displaced slum dwellers are typically far from their home, work, play, and social networks. They are disconnected from what poor neighborhoods provide. Slum evictions are a nationwide (and global) policy formulated based on already existing institutional disdain for the lower castes and poor by state and market actors. But as Narasimhamurthy argues, these policies of dispossession are only worsened today due to the intrusive forces of speculative urbanism undermining multiple dimensions of city life.

A similar perspective can be heard from Dalit farmer activists and advocates, some of whom I interviewed on several occasions. Here is Siddhartha, from a farming community displaced by the airport and SEZ complex: "For the past twenty-five years, we've been fighting for the rights of farmers. But now the entire structure has been dismantled; now everyone has either become a land broker or a victim. Once people lose their land, they lose their sense. . . . They are destroyed. Women face the burden of their husbands who struggle with fatalism and alcoholism. . . . This is the new Bangalore."[4]

His response to these evictions imposed on rural Dalit communities is not to concede failure but instead to organize on two fronts: One is to work with legal advocates to challenge elite patrimonial networks grabbing land, winning small victories now and then for the most egregious cases of theft. In some rare but meaningful cases, land has been returned to the rightful Dalit owner. With the recovery of this farmland, he has developed a small business of Dalit land brokerage. As an advocate, he helps dispossessed Dalit farmers win their cases in court and regain land. But since the overall condition of state disinvestment from the agrarian economy has left them with little hope as farmers, he and his colleagues accept that land in the countryside alone cannot improve the lives of underresourced and unsupported farmers. Deprived of possibilities and a livable income as farmers, Dalits and other evictees are figuring out ways to conduct themselves that align with speculative governmentality—to become gamblers with land and challenge the patrimonial regime of actors that can at any time impose danger and violence.

Siddhartha became an advocate and a land broker who negotiates the best price for land that Dalit farmers are willing to sell and that urban investors are willing to buy. He attempts to cut out the rent-seeking maneuvers that undercut Dalit futures while also brokering land deals for them. Taking control of the profitable land market for the benefit of the community is a quite radical step toward Dalit justice, he and his colleagues contend, even if it commoditizes land and alienates farmers from their land. With rural resources for most poor farmers becoming prohibitive—as inputs, water, electricity, schooling, and transport have skyrocketed once the government stopped subsidizing them—Siddhartha reasons that he can help some Dalits benefit from their land in much the way the upper- and middle-caste communities have throughout history.

His other organizing strategy has been to strike at the heart of this soulless transformation of the rural by tapping into the long tradition of the Ambedkarite movement. He's actively introducing Hindu outcastes to the power and possibilities of becoming casteless Buddhists. He has used profits from his land-brokering business to set up a stunning Buddhist temple amid farmland, with an attached school and community gathering place in the rural periphery of the city. There, he and his colleagues offer a soulful alternative to the depredation and humiliation of caste-based technologies of power and hate so prevalent in this phase of deruralization.

I heard and observed a range of similar sentiments and articulations from other city dwellers. For example, street vendors and auto rickshaw drivers have been organizing to defend their rights to the city's footpaths and streets (Sreenivasa 2024). They, too, are being evicted and dispossessed by elite and middle-class opponents who believe that these situated entrepreneurs and workers are despoiling the streets and reducing property values. Ironically, of course, they provide essential services—as cobblers, barbers, recyclers, fruit and vegetable vendors, leather workers, chai and snack vendors, booksellers—to the people who revile them. Those who depend on urban public space to ply their trade and provide services to the public also demand basic rights to the volatile city.

Here is yet another space where the contradictions of the attraction of city life emerge. These street vendors provide inexpensive food and services conveniently along the footpath between the middle-class home and office, yet these providers are condemned for clogging up the circulation of speculative capital and depressing property values. Or so the aspirational middle class believes.

Another choke point common to most Bangaloreans is traffic, as the city was built for a modest-sized population, not fourteen million and growing, thus making life in this city of commuters untenable. Instead of building up transit based on the needs of the urban majority, whose work and home have become separated by an ocean of pricey real estate, raised state-of-the-art Metro rail lines have been built. A bus riders' campaign has emerged with the goal of reversing the trend of underfunding buses, the main transit option for the urban majority. The financialized Metro rail system is based on substantial loans of up to $7 billion, forcing ticket prices to be too high for most denizens. As of 2023, ridership for the Metro was one-sixth of the ridership for the bus lines even though the bus budget is a small fraction of the Metro's. The buses are routinely overcrowded and in great need of repair and replacement (U. Rao 2024).

The financial logic of the Metro system requires that the city sell off the rights to build and maintain the major Metro stations to speculators. The incentive to developers was that they could design the stations to their liking, with privatized real estate ventures in and alongside the so-called public stations (U. Rao 2024). As a result, at each location numerous homes, small shops, and footpaths were bulldozed so that enough real estate could become available to make the investment in a station feasible for a private firm (U. Rao and Sonti 2014).

Deep-seated tensions delineated by structures of power based on geography, language, caste, and class have created a difficult context for the emergence of a coalitional social movement that could coordinate across overlapping campaigns and concerns in Bengaluru and globally. But at critical moments, a common language of taking back the city does materialize. The following sections highlight these connections and identify a path forward toward a postspeculative future.

Speculative Urbanism, Its Negation, and an Alternative Future

The previous chapters offered a relational-conjunctural approach—a theory, method, and politics—for understanding what's happening to our cities. This approach has helped me understand the key features of speculative urbanism. My research project reflects, in part, my interactions with numerous actors steeped in this world-altering process. My conclusions are also deeply informed by the ideas of critics and activists, in other words, organic intellectuals (Gramsci 1971). Their critique delineates a loose and evolving agenda for a postspeculative future.

As I have described throughout the book, speculative urbanism comprises a set of key features. The first and paramount feature is the power and tools of finance, which has been a topic of considerable debate, confusion, and concern. The dark arts of high finance remain in the shadows, while its reputation, despite a bevy of crises, continues to soar. I have documented how global financial firms gain power and authority over city life through their instruments and tactics, contributing to the shrinking of the productive side of national economies and the rise of their financialization. For the urban and rural majorities, this developing tension translates into the downsizing of small farming and other rural resource-based production. It leads to the elimination of public social space and the conviviality and commerce of street life. Public ecological space, such as watersheds, aquifers, and wetlands, has become a tradeable asset deprived of its vitality.

These financial tools are the result of a concerted effort not just from Wall Street actors but also from the hard work of a transnational policy network and its discourse of global urbanism. The resurgence of the

power of finance capital since the 1970s has led to an agenda of investments in urban infrastructure, land markets, and public space. It is no
coincidence that local city planners speak a language similar to that of
the consultants of PricewaterhouseCoopers and the World Bank, who
have come to mimic the business strategies and goals of Wall Street's
megafirms, such as Blackstone and Citibank. The outing of local actors
who parrot global newspeak while tailoring it to local conditions has become a common strategy of critique from urban activists who denounce
the prevalence of this dangerous echo chamber.

Buttressed by these global influencers and by the aggressive practices of global finance, the state manifests its catalytic role in speculative urbanism in three ways: as an avid supporter, as fertile ground
for self-interested speculative agents using their state authority, and as
a stimulus for the population-wide conduct of risk-taking and future
divining, or speculative governmentality. That is, the financialization
process has enabled financial actors to intervene in, and at times replace, the state's governing practices related to lending and borrowing,
and managing and distributing access to public goods and services,
as well as the mundane tasks of fee collection, taxation, and budget
decision-making.

At the same time, the state does not merely act as a singular actor
but comprises a multitude of state agents with their own networked interests, identities, and side hustles. For many campaigns in the city and
countryside, it is the state agent whom most people see and experience
as the main actor collecting rents and undermining rights, even if financiers and developers are working the backrooms of state policymaking
and implementation. Often these state actors work both for the benefit
of their government agency and also for themselves and the fraternal
network in which they collaborate to create new types of rents, challenging the well-being of the nonelite majority.

Beyond the workings of the formal state in governance is the more
insidious and pervasive phenomenon of *speculative governmentality*.
This term refers to the types of conduct, rationalities, and subjectivities that emerge from the tensions of speculation with which urban and
rural denizens must engage to keep up with spiraling global-city ambitions and rents in the context of dwindling state provisioning of public
goods, services, and spaces.

A key element of speculative urbanism—speculative ecologies—
reflects the centrality of nature and the environment for human life as

well as for finance's goal of total assetization. This is an underlying element of my argument because it represents the stripping away of the intrinsic use values of nature and its essential dimensions of water, land, wetlands, watersheds, forests, and aquifers, without which there would be no livable city or countryside (for people at least). Major investors can move forward with their grand plans of extracting wealth from real estate only if they are able to manipulate nature so that it becomes the basis for future exchange-value production and circulation as a tradeable liquid asset.

This analytic framework arises from my long-standing engagement with critical minds working in research labs, government offices, farm villages, slum activist offices, and protect-the-lakes nongovernmental organizations (NGOs), and even with business consultants who spoke frankly of the contradictory implications of their own actions. Collectively, these voices described how, today, *finance capital rules*. It is a modality of rule that is stealthy yet widespread and highly consequential. Sadly, its rules are not easy to discern.

These interlocutors argue that we need a better understanding of finance's opaque workings and must carefully document its intended and unintended consequences. One lesson stood out for me. Many activists explained in various ways how dispossession and racialization have become fundamental to the processes of speculative urbanism. But they also noted, like the Indigenous scholars Glen Coulthard and Leanne Betasamosake Simpson (2016), that the opposite of dispossession is not necessarily property ownership. It is what Coulthard and Simpson call *grounded normativity*, or the alternative realities and worldviews in which oppressed communities have lived over time.

Although many urban ills cannot be directly attributed to the workings of finance capital, the concept of speculative urbanism is useful as it reveals threadlike connections across many of the structural issues noted above and thus sheds light on the complex power of finance in these domains. The types of finance power noted in these pages have contributed to linked conditions of indebtedness, sucked value from our cities and our countryside, intensified social inequities and hierarchies, undermined civic participation, and accelerated ecological degeneration (Brand and Wissen 2021). They have contributed to the consolidation of corporate power, the bankruptcy of many nonfinancial firms and the diminishing of work, the defunding of public services, and the decline of democratic practices. Global finance has accrued so

C.1 Occupy movements across Spain demanded a more just postspeculation future. This image shows a 15-M rally in Valencia, Spain, in 2012. Photo by the author.

much power in so many different spheres that it has become the global leader in these new forms of capital extraction, exploitation, and dispossession. It is the hegemonic actor weaving global imaginaries about how to turn urban, financial, political, and ecological crises into profitable opportunities. The effects pile up and contribute to expanding authoritarian practices, and thus a lack of hope, especially among the marginalized (Coelho et al. 2020).

Bengaluru is not alone in cultivating activism and resistance under these conditions of speculative urbanism (RoyChowdhury 2005). Millions of people in city squares and streets around the world, including Spain and the United States, but also Egypt and Tunisia, Argentina and Brazil, have been mobilizing against the grief of financialization, the dwindling of public goods, and the transformation of governance and democracy (figure C.1). This is the final topic to which I now turn to illustrate, in brief, the transnationally relational and conjunctural nature of resistance. And the opportunities that have sprung from such concerted thought and action.

Around the world, 2011 was a momentous year reflecting a collective outcry arising in part from the 2008 financial crisis but primarily from the explosive injustices built up over time and related to the persistence of state authoritarianism and unbridled capitalism. Calls for democracy reflected the worsening nature of class inequalities, with young people seeing no hope for their future. Revolts first erupted in Tunisia, Egypt, Morocco, Syria, Libya, Bahrain, the Palestinian territories, and Yemen. Protesters of the Arab Spring, many of whom were young and deeply disillusioned, pressed for an end to harsh and undemocratic patrimonial regimes of governance that ruled by political cronyism, police brutality, and state repression, while denouncing increasing income inequality and the wealth of elites controlling state power (Bayat 2021). Luxury yachts, colossal cruise ships, and opulent residential complexes sat in the shadows of worsening poverty and helplessness in Cairo, Tunis, and other port cities of the Middle East and North Africa. Millions challenged the post–financial crisis austerity policies that were imposed on them while observing elite splendor and wealth arise across the gleaming exclusivity of their city's skyline.

Protest sentiments travel fast and furiously. Soon after the Arab Spring, protests in Spain erupted over the financialization of housing and subsequent rent hikes and mass evictions. Long-lasting street mobilizations that became known as the Movimiento 15-M (and the Indignados Movement) marked the start of Spain's Occupy movement on May 15, led by activists whose reference point was the bursting sentiments of the Arab Spring. Across Spain, people suffered from extreme cutbacks in public services, which the state deemed necessary as the economy collapsed from the financial crisis. The mass movement involved more than seven million Spaniards, one-seventh of the total population, who actively participated in street rallies and plaza occupations. It called attention to how the banks and corporations were getting bailed out while the public suffered with record high unemployment, evictions, and cutbacks in basic public goods and services. Occupiers mobilized supporters by making the connections between austerity and wealth accumulation affecting all aspects of city life, feeding on a collective anger over how the rich continued to prosper during the worst of times.

The movement started with a union-directed general strike and then blossomed into multiple occupations of squares in Madrid and other Spanish cities, borrowing the organizing tools of the Arab Spring and calling for the remaking of society based on horizontal, consensus-based structures of power and provisioning. The leaderless movement experimented with ideas of anarchy, deliberative democracy, and a moneyless economy of barter and care in the public squares they occupied and "freed." A similar movement emerged in many of Portugal's cities, where protesters occupied vacant land and buildings, blockaded hospitals to prevent privatization, and created neighborhood assemblies and community gardens in hopes of democratizing the politics of, and rights to, the city.

After municipal economies collapsed across Europe, elite financial advisers gave city governments little choice but to sell their public goods, such as a once-robust stock of affordable social housing, at a huge discount to global private equity firms. In Germany, after a few years, Blackstone, BlackRock, Goldman Sachs, Morgan Stanley, and their German associates became some of Germany's largest landlords. This incensed the urban majority of Berlin, where 80 percent of Berliners were renters, not owners, with a solid history of low rents and available apartments. Within a few years, the Preventing Forced Evictions campaign grew in response to private equity firms' business model of forcing evictions, charging excessive rents, and securitizing rent payments into global rental housing bonds. After a decade of organizing, occupations, and strategic campaigns, Berlin voters passed a referendum that asked the city council to freeze rents and buy back the once-affordable social housing properties from the city's two largest landlords, Vonovia and Deutsche Wohnen (in which Blackstone was a major shareholder). These acquisitions happened at the same time as these firms acquired a large number of housing units across Denmark, Sweden, Germany, and the United States. Here we learn how robust and sustained protest can pursue and disrupt finance wherever it travels, but, sadly, we also see how unfettered finance can find fresh new opportunities in the wake of protest. It's a beast that is hard to cage.

In Spain the evicted, immigrant rights organizations, and right-to-the-city activists joined together to combat bank-related evictions by creating the Plataforma de Afectados por la Hipoteca (Platform for People Affected by Mortgages). It was organized horizontally by assembly and spread across Spain, with 220 local groups by 2017. They organized resistance campaigns against evictions and in support of a social rent and aid for people unable to pay their mortgages. One of its founders, Ada Colau, was elected mayor of Barcelona in June 2015, and the left political party Podemos ("We Can") sprouted across the nation as a legitimate contender in the dominant two-party system, adopting concerns about finance capitalism and promoting alternatives that foster noncapitalist, or at least much tamer capitalist, practices (García-Lamarca 2022).

The Occupy movement also swept across US cities and set off public conversations about austerity policies and the riches of finance. This activism introduced into the public lexicon the gross differences between the richest 1 percent, who benefit from status quo politics, and the 99 percent who do not. It also helped to forge solidarity coalitions across concerns around housing, underemployment and miserly wages, high tuition costs and oppressive student loan debt, the climate crisis, police brutality against people of color, and more. Protesters questioned the humanity and sustainability of a capitalist economy that prioritizes financialized profits over human needs and planetary health. In Los Angeles, New York City, and Boston, activists called for rent controls and more public housing, the right for the houseless to receive housing, and greater access to social services. They advocated for a decommodified approach to housing rather than the typical liberal notion of affordability, which does not work for the urban majority who cannot afford median-derived rents or a bank mortgage, when the calculation determining affordability leaves housing inaccessible to most city dwellers.

A key point that emerges from this fertile period of confrontative politics is that global circuits for capital are less feasible if reentry becomes riddled with hostility and barricades. Successful resistance occurs when rebellious actors work together within and across cities, making finance's global strategy of arbitrage—playing one investment site off another for the best deal—a friction-filled and expensive slog. Much like communities around the world that boycotted apartheid South Africa and its supportive corporations in the 1970s and 1980s, mobilized groups are successful when they coordinate to delegitimate and boycott Wall Street. Part of the challenge is to offer an alternative to hot capital, as cities and municipalities do need money (Mellor 2022). People everywhere need socially useful infrastructure. Hence, activists in these movements argue for alternative economic strategies that are embedded in, and subservient to, the needs of society and nature, and not the reverse.

Bengaluru's working-class laborers have engaged in bus riders' activism to bring down bus fees and increase the accessibility of public transit. Some organizers have worked closely with middle-class environmentalists demanding new restrictions on fossil-fuel-burning cars (Gidwani et al. 2024). Some Occupy movements have formed their own parties, and some activists have run for office, combining an electoral strategy with their movement-based one. They have expanded their efforts to build cross-class solidarities inside and outside the electoral process.

Farmer activists note that the massive protest led by small-holder farmers in New Delhi in 2021 was due in part to the unwavering support they received from those in cities and other villages, from people who see their futures inextricably linked to the well-being of these food producers and land protectors (Jain 2021). Similarly, urbanites need affordable food, protected water catchments, and the wetlands that are cared for by farmers (figures C.2 and C.3). To tackle speculative urbanization, people are imagining ways to extricate local economies, land, labor, and ecosystems from speculative business practices and convert those energies into providing what most people and surrounding environments need to thrive.

Bengaluru's activists working to revitalize the lakes are now encouraging ward-level oversight power, devolving control to the community level to oversee and revitalize their currently toxic and desiccated neighborhood lakes (*Financial Express* 2017). Some community leaders see this victory as a turning point for the local control of essential urban commons. They argue that if they can stop the residential sewage from flowing into the water system and stop developers from grabbing lake land and water channels, and proactively work to regenerate the ecosystems that allow the lakes to flourish, they can invigorate local democratic practices. These efforts could be a catalyst for a new, democratizing way to manage cities and reduce, if not remove, power from the patrimonial network of elites. If water-justice activists can collaborate with those fighting for housing, alongside itinerant workers and groups demanding fair access to land, the commons, sidewalks, and parks, they imagine a powerful coalition to redefine the city through a postspeculative lens (Gago 2020; Federici 2014).

Structures of power have been rearticulated, realigned, and transnationalized in new ways to harness new forms of value creation and destroy older forms, in ways that intensify already existing social hierarchies. The political challenge, I have come to understand, therefore is to confront the ways that processes of speculative urbanism strip people of

C.2 Karnataka's farmers' movement comes alive to challenge the encroachment of the city's real estate sector. Bengaluru urban district. Source: Wikicommons.

C.3 Karnataka's slum dweller's movement demanding land for homes and livelihoods. The banner shows Ambedkar's image and the words, in Kannada, "Stop the discrimination meted out against slum people; Organized by the platform for deprived city dwellers [Nagara vanchitara vedike]." Bengaluru rural district. Source: Wikicommons.

their dignity as well as conditions of social reproduction and to envision a feasible alternative. Forever growth has not translated into better lives for the majority under speculative urbanism. The idea of economies of mutual care and reciprocity is completely antithetical to finance capital's success (Schor 2010).

Some activists based in major European cities have articulated their plan forward as based in the idea of degrowth, reimagining a society based on need and care and *not* on gross national product and the compulsion to grow, grow, grow, and accumulate, accumulate, accumulate (Latouche 2009; Kallis et al. 2020; Schmelzer et al. 2022). They advocate *not* growing merely for the sake of growing profits but seeking to thrive sustainably on what we, on a shared planet, have. The politics of degrowth requires an institutional shift from capitalist plutocratic and patrimonial regimes to radical forms of democracy and social and ecological reciprocity, with priorities based on what people and the ecosystem need rather than on what corporations need for their survival and growth. It means moving away from what Ashish Kothari calls the "imperial mode of living," which is an impossible way of being for the world's population without destroying the rest of the planet (Kothari et al. 2019; Brand and Wissen 2021).

Up until the early twentieth century, rural land was the most important source of wealth (Piketty 2014). Capital morphed, as Thomas Piketty has explained, during the wild times of unfettered speculation in the late nineteenth century when the global economy was ruled by the leaders of Wall Street and their equivalents in Europe. The actions of the hidden empire of finance precipitated the global financial crisis of the late 1920s. For the first time in history, corporate shares, bonds, urban housing, and many other financial assets outpaced rural land for surplus value creation in the capitalist economy, creating immeasurable global suffering. Ninety years later, the 2008 global financial crisis produced a disturbing array of inequalities and expulsions but also the consolidation of finance power and its emergence as a source of governmental power.[5]

And yet a new vision has risen from the ruins of these disastrous crises. Listen to the prime minister of Barbados, Mia Mottley, speaking before the World Trade Organization and during an interview afterward, in 2022, making it clear that business as usual is unacceptable and dangerous (Lustgarten 2022). To fight the climate crisis, to fight the COVID-19 pandemic, and to meet development goals, Mottley said, Global South countries are still fighting for a platform. "You will realize that in almost every instance, we're fighting our old struggles on the same basis," she explained. "What is its underlying cause? The inequity in the world in which we live, and the inequity is preserved fundamentally because we've not changed the power structure." "The world," Mottley argued, "is segregated regrettably between those who came first and, in whose image the global order is now set," a global order that is itself "simply the embalming of the old colonial order that existed at the time of the establishment of these institutions. We have therefore to ask ourselves *whether we can live in this global order*. That we are more concerned with generating profits than saving people is perhaps the greatest condemnation that can be made of our generation." This sounds a lot like the young Greta Thunberg before the United Nations Summit on Climate Action, when she proclaimed, "We are in the beginning of a mass extinction. And all you can talk about is money and fairytales of eternal economic growth. How dare you!" (quoted in Higgins 2019).

Just as people can shut down the city for a day or a week, and millions of farmers encircled India's capital for months, they could also see the potential of reopening the city with alternative paradigms of shared living based on new ways to socially reproduce. The world is getting much too hot—in many ways—to think otherwise. This hothouse is already spawning imaginaries and practices of liberation that should give us hope (Táíwò 2022; Thunberg 2022; Burkhart et al. 2020). As the current ideal among financial elites and their fellow travelers is to make everything liquid, mobile, borderless (except for poor migrants escaping violence), unregulated, and transcendent of any social or ecological obligation, it is refreshing to see how many others caught in their crossfire focus their sights on an opposite world, one in which the future of a stable planet and the long-term well-being of people matter. We are confronted with a historic opportunity, much like the eras of nineteenth-century colonial resistance and the independence struggles of the mid-twentieth century. Activists argue that we must break through the shackles of finance capitalism and start anew with humanistic and ecological imaginaries in which the planet and our own socio-ecological living spaces are no longer an asset that alienates people in a world of cities on fire. The chaos engulfing us is offering us one clear message: There is no alternative but to definancialize in ways that lead to socially just institutions of care and mutual support for the environment and society, forever.

NOTES

Introduction. Through the Looking Glass
of Global-City Making

1 All dollar amounts are in US dollars.

2 An alternative asset is one that does not fall within the conventional categories of equity or income or cash. Examples include actors that are called private equity and venture capital, which invest in hedges, real estate, commodities, and tangible assets like urban infrastructure. Private equity firms investing in real estate and infrastructure are the main focus of this book, for reasons that will become quite clear.

3 Once called Bangalore, the city's official name was changed to Bengaluru in 2014. I will use *Bangalore* when discussing times before 2014 and *Bengaluru* when discussing the post-2014 city.

4 The idea of an overaccumulation crisis is that any given productive sector comes up against the limits to rising profit rates in their sector. Such a crisis leads capital—in theory—to search for new outlets and arenas to realize profits (O'Connor 1984). Urban space and infrastructure became that temporary "spatial fix" to the falling rate of profit, an idea argued by critical urban theorists starting in the 1970s.

5 The post–World War II era of what scholars call Fordism reflects how the innovations of the Ford Motor Company—industrial mass production and standardization coupled with a Keynesian state that supported mass consumption by providing infrastructure, services, and stable fiscal policy—became normalized for leading industrialized societies.

6 The term *Dalit* has a political history and translates as "oppressed and broken." Dalit is the self-designation referring to the community whose members are placed outside the hierarchical Hindu caste system; they were formerly called "Untouchables." Although the constitutional term is Scheduled Caste, Dalit is the chosen name of many fighting against systemic oppression.

7   For more on the question of caste as race that transcends reductive interpretations, see Khilnani (2020). On the complex nature of caste as a stratified hierarchy that includes the odd-sounding category of Other Backward Classes (OBCs), see Somanaboina (2022) and A. Rao (2009). For excellent coverage of the two dominant rural-based communities in Karnataka that defy easy classification, see Janaki Nair's series of articles in the media over the past decade, including her 2021 piece in *India Forum* on the Lingayats and Vokkaligas, where she explains how these two landed castes in Karnataka maintain significant power despite being officially part of the OBC category. Caste hierarchies differ from one region to another in India, and even non-Hindu communities have adopted their own version of a caste system.

8   This definition is different from the one used by historical sociologists, who highlight kinship and the familial and patriarchal nature of early modern patrimonial states.

9   Geographer Louis Moreno (2014, 2018) mobilizes the concept for his study of capital accumulation as it affects the built environment and living conditions in Global North cities, especially in Spain.

10   According to Atlas Arteria's disclosure statement (2022) in acquiring a majority interest in the Chicago Skyway, it promises to its shareholders that it will raise the toll prices annually over the remaining eighty-eight years on the lease. The report also offers a diagram of the numerous entities that are different owners of the Skyway, all of which were once part of the mother company, Macquarie. These diagrams, typical of private equity shareholder reports, reflect the complexity of ownership—and liquidity—that might, for one, make it quite difficult for someone in Chicago to follow the money or even express their concern about a bumpy ride and rising tolls. Even though Atlas Arteria acquired a majority interest in a public good, stamped on every page is the notice that Americans are not allowed to read the document: "Not for Distribution or Release in the U.S." It is widely available online.

11   Scholars continue to refine the concept. See Shih and de Laurentis (2022) on Taiwan; Sood (2019) on India; Nam (2017) on Cambodia; Zappa (2022) on Vietnam; Shin and Kim (2016) on South Korea; Z. Li et al. (2014) on China; Leitner and Sheppard (2018, 2023) and Colven (2023) on Indonesia; Juan Zhang (2017) on Southeast Asia; Barasa (2021) on Kenya; and Knuth (2014) on the United States.

12   For example, China and Japan have invested widely in infrastructure projects in and around Jakarta, Indonesia, supporting their own construction firms as major contractors, and their financiers as investors collecting rents from each project (Anguelov 2023).

Chapter 1. The Making of the Global Urban Turn: Transnational Policy Networks Redefine the City

1   The following argument comes from my long-standing research on the World Bank since the early 1990s, interviews with key actors in and around the Bank since 2007, interviews with global-city consultants, document analysis, participant observation, and interviews from 2007 to 2019 at a few of these exclusive global-city conferences (in India, Spain, and the United States) as well as my work co-organizing conferences that carefully scrutinized this agenda with academics, government officials, and activists (in Jakarta, Shenzhen, Bengaluru, and Minneapolis).

2   The term *international financial institutions* typically refers to the World Bank (based in Washington, DC), the International Monetary Fund (based in Paris and Brussels), and regional development banks, such as the Asian Development Bank.

3   McNamara was the secretary of defense commanding the US war in Southeast Asia, always obsessed with fighting the red wave of rural revolution. He brought this mentality to the World Bank, a position President Lyndon Johnson gave him as a soft landing after he was fired from his secretary post.

4   When McNamara launched the Urban Department in 1973, its first four country loans averaged just $6 million each. Adjusting for inflation, this $6 million would be worth $35 million today, a far cry from the $500 million loans for urban development being made at the turn of the millennium.

5   Interview with a former senior urban policy director at the World Bank, New York City, May 2016.

6   The quotation in the heading is from *Cities in Transition: World Bank Urban and Local Government Strategy* (World Bank 2000, 79).

7   The C40 joined a partnership with the Cities Program of the Clinton Climate Initiative in 2015 (C40 2015).

8   With offices in more than 150 countries and hundreds of thousands of employees, PwC mobilized its vast network in support of this larger transnational network, bringing together mayors with corporate executives and institutional investors.

9   The survey on which this report is based was done in cooperation with the Economist Intelligence Unit.

10   These UN reports are now called *Financing for Sustainable Development*. For a list of reports, see United Nations, Department of Economic and Social Affairs, Financing for Sustainable Development, https://financing.desa.un.org/iatf/reports.

Chapter 2. The Gathering Storm: Urban Transformation Across Three Continents

1   Another major factor in the financialization in the US economy was the rise of hostile takeovers, in the 1980s, of major corporations by Wall Street firms. From the late 1950s on, the US economy had become an economic superpower in large part due to huge contracts from the US government to rebuild war-devastated Europe and expand the US military, as well as the national highway system, electric grid, and water systems via major dams, in addition to the wild expansion of the suburban landscape. These triggered the birth of widespread consumer credit and mass consumerism. In the 1980s an iconoclastic group of raiders decided to take on these "fattened" and productive firms and dediversify them by selling off their many parts as liquid assets in the marketplace, making enormous profits from their sale. In the process, finance gained the reputation of a moneymaker, which enabled it to redefine, via disruption, corporate business models across the economy. For the purposes of this book, I primarily focus on the dimensions of disruption that directly affected the city and the ways that these corporations benefited from, and changed as a result of, their deepening relations with cities and city governance structures.

2   "In plain language, a special district is a separate local government that delivers a limited number of public services to a geographically limited area" (California Senate Local Government Committee 2010, 2).

3   After years of ruinous outcomes, then California Governor Jerry Brown dissolved redevelopment agencies in 2011, arguing they were siphoning revenues away from government and restricting the ability for government to invest/build. Meanwhile, the model travels and spreads around the world.

4   "The supertall towers were built with subsidies including a 30-year deal on property taxes that lasts until 2044 and saved more than $50 million off the towers' theoretical property-tax bill of $150 million last year, according to the New York City Industrial Development Agency. The cost to Hudson Yards developer The Related Cos. for lobbying city officials was $120,000 [in 2022] . . . Hudson Yards' property-tax exemption is called a payment in lieu of taxes, or PILOT. These deals were created about 40 years ago so large tax-exempt organizations such as universities would pay something for government services" (Elstein 2023).

5   A system originally created by Citigroup in 1988, SIVs raise capital and then leverage it through the issuance of short-term securities such as ABCPs, at lower rates, and then use that money to buy

longer-term securities, such as mortgage-backed securities, and earn on the net credit spread.

6   According to the intergovernmental agency, the Financial Stability Board, as well as the IMF (Kodres 2013), the shadow banking system plays the self-proclaimed role of credit intermediation. As an employee of the IMF, Laura Kodres breaks down their work into four categories: "maturity transformation: obtaining short-term funds to invest in longer-term assets; liquidity transformation: a concept similar to maturity transformation that entails using cash-like liabilities to buy harder-to-sell assets such as loans; leverage: employing techniques such as borrowing money to buy fixed assets to magnify the potential gains (or losses) on an investment; credit risk transfer: taking the risk of a borrower's default and transferring it from the originator of the loan to another party" (Kodres 2013, 1). These financial firms do not, however, acknowledge the "shadow" part of the moniker, which describes the fact that federal and international agencies are unable to track nor require accountability for these new financial practices. It is the shadowy dimension that is most worrisome for democracy and that is explored throughout this book.

7   LPG also refers to the essential gas used in homes, whose price fluctuations deeply affect household pocketbooks. By using this reference in their campaigns, critics are building on a commonly named and experienced crisis—price inflation in the world of a common and necessary energy source—to also note the underlying cause of such a painful experience for the average consumer.

*Chapter 3. "The Bubble on a Whirlpool of Speculation":
Afterlives of the Financial Crisis and the New Urban
Imaginary*

1   The Skyway Deal is an example of how private equity can extract value from an otherwise mediocre profit generator (Ashton et al. 2016), as these Chicago-based scholars explain it:

> The large prices fetched by brownfield-asset leases reflect new techniques for mining value out of infrastructure investment, even in situations where the underlying asset produces low or even negative returns. One approach evident in the Skyway deal was the use of structured finance products to increase its book value. For instance, Cintra-Macquarie employed interest-rate "swaps" to fix the interest payments on variable-rate bonds. As this lowered the risk of interest-rate variations to investors'

returns, Macquarie changed the internal risk-weighted cost of the capital it used to value the Skyway concession, increasing its book value from $882 million in 2004 to $1.2 billion by the end of 2007 (a 37% increase) (Zhang 2008). It then refinanced the project based on the higher valuation, replacing $1.1 billion in short-term financing used to pay for the concession with $1.5 billion in long-term bonds. . . . This generated a $373 million windfall that it paid out as a distribution to equity investors. These approaches helped Macquarie generate a 21% internal rate of return for its Skyway equity investors (Macquarie Infrastructure Group, 2011, 10). (Ashton et al. 2020, 1385)

2   The local weekly newspaper, the *Chicago Reader*, and journalist Ben Joravsky in particular, covered this issue extensively and doggedly, using materials sought through the Freedom of Information Act process, which revealed the troubling bidding process and some details of the contract (Joravsky 2018).

3   For excellent analyses of the long history of racialized injustices in Black city life, with a focus on housing, see Jenkins and Leroy (2021); Rothstein (2017); and Taylor (2019).

4   Apollo was founded by the notorious CEO Leon Black, who left his job after a series of allegations of sexual harassment and questionable business relations with his predatory friend Jeffrey Epstein.

5   This is based on eviction tracking data on the Eviction Lab's website as of March 15, 2023. The lab is a leader in national-level data collection on evictions and houselessness, run by sociologist Matthew Desmond, author of *Poverty, by America* (2023) and *Evicted: Poverty and Profit in the American City* (2016).

6   In 2021 rent control measures were passed in both Minneapolis and its sister city, St. Paul, despite large sums of money spent by corporate landlords to prevent their passage.

7   Lee Enterprises' report (2022) to the US Securities and Exchange Commission explains the attempt by Alden Global to acquire its newspapers and Alden's job-slashing, asset-selling, and value-extracting work across the media industry.

Chapter 4. *"A Picture of the Future": Urbanization and the Challenges to Democracy in Bengaluru*

1   As the story goes, British colonial officials changed the original name Bengaluru to Bangalore, as with so many other Indian city names, because they had trouble pronouncing it. The name was

changed back to Bengaluru in 2014 due to pressure from, among others, Kannada linguistic nationalists. This occurred within the context of a national wave of name changes attributable to local linguistic demands, primarily, and Hindu nationalist sentiments as well. I use the designator Bangalore for the period prior to 2014 and Bengaluru for the period after 2014.

2   Based on an interview conducted in 2010 and then follow-up discussions over the years with these experts. This quotation and the next few come from interviews conducted and transcribed by my former research assistant, Jake Carlson, now a professor; this quotation was also used in his article "Model Employers and Model Cities?" (2018).

3   Interview, Bengaluru, 2016.

4   Interview, Bengaluru, 2016.

5   The Public Affairs Centre published Dr. Samuel Paul's *Making Voice Work: The Report Card on Bangalore's Public Service* (1998) and several more "citizen's report cards" subsequently, to publicly shame government agencies and make them (voluntarily) accountable to complaints from the public. The BDA was the focus of these early reports, as the people surveyed were most vociferous about the BDA. Dr. Paul was a longtime World Bank employee who retired in Bangalore and started this accountability project, with World Bank funding; the Bank and Paul then reproduced the report card model in many other countries in the Global South that borrowed from the Bank. Although it was very much an elite approach to the notion of voluntarism, accountability, and reform, it did spur activist organizations to take on the mantle of shaming these agencies, backed by widespread street protests and numerous court cases demanding that officials give over their powers to locally elected governing bodies.

6   James Heitzman (2004, 61–62) offers a vivid contrast between government agencies—the Bangalore City Council office, sleepy and casual, versus the parastatal BDA, equipped with armed guards and a bank within the premises.

7   These statements are based on commissioned reports from the state legislature as well as a series of reports and articles from scholars and nongovernmental organizations (NGOs) on the disappearance of the city's water infrastructure, including my personal communications with many of the authors of these reports.

8   In the 1960s Torekadanahalli pump station sent 19 million cubic feet of water per day from the Kaveri/Cauvery River along sixty-two miles through a very expensive pumping system that pumps the water uphill to the city—sitting on a plateau three thousand feet above sea level—with an electricity bill that once formed the city's biggest annual expenditure.

9   Interview, July 2016.

10   Interview, June 2018.

11   Interview, June 2018.

12   The Japanese are the biggest national sources of loan capital, through JBIC and JICA; DHV Netherlands and a Singapore firm consult on sewerage; and AusAid paid to produce a master plan for the sewage system. Based on author interview with USAID consultant, March 2009.

13   Prof. Trilochan Sastry at the Indian Institute of Management-Bengaluru explained to me (June 2016): "Most of our money is going to foreign firms. Why not try what they do in Surat: float municipal bonds with local shareholders at 5 to 6 percent interest, and locals demanding and shaping how the actual waterworks are built—isn't this democracy? Well, this scares the hell out of the bureaucrats!"

14   Interview, February 2009.

15   Interviews, June 2016 and July 2018.

*Chapter 5. The Making of an Urban Land Market:
Dispossession, Financialization, and the Emergence
of Bengaluru as a Global City*

This chapter uses some material from a published article of mine (Goldman 2020).

1   My interviews and calculations, 2013–18.

2   This ambitious private toll highway and township project has been stalled over the past twenty-five years due to concerted protest from farmers, especially by the powerful Lingayats and Vokkaligas communities, in regard to the paltry compensation promised and the way they were being treated. (These two represent contentious political-caste factions that do not agree on the merit of this project.) Only a small portion of the toll highway has been built, circumventing the city, with only a minimum of farmers, mostly Dalit and lower caste, thus far displaced. Commuters and truckers protest the continuous toll fee increases as the operators insist that the contract guarantees them an annual 10 percent fee hike.

3   Bengaluru is in the state of Karnataka. The most powerful government agencies and the largest business deals and public works projects are overseen at the state level, with the most valuable portfolios in the chief minister's office. City government has historically been weak.

4   All dollar amounts are in 2025 US dollars unless otherwise noted.

5   In the 2010s widespread political agitation erupted across the country for more equitable land acquisition and farmer support policies. The Mahatma Gandhi National Rural Employment Guarantee Act of 2005 had promised that the state would provide a minimum wage to one laborer in each farming household during bad times, but the promised wages were limitedly distributed. Protesters also called for updating the 1894 Land Acquisition Act to increase compensation for lands taken under eminent domain and allow for communities to vote against government acquisition. The 2013 legislation (Right to Fair Compensation and Transparency in Land Acquisition, Rehabilitation and Resettlement), a response to widespread discontent, was shaved down soon after it was passed.

6   Interview with Leo Saldanha, Bengaluru, July 2015. This was one of dozens of interviews and discussions with him; the Environment Support Group's dedicated and insightful codirector, Bhargavi Rao; and their colleagues.

7   See Goldman and Narayan (2019) for an analysis of the link between the rapid urbanization of this ecological landscape and the current water crisis in Bengaluru.

8   The term used by Dalit villagers for village headmen and leaders is Gowda, according to my interviews. The term *Gowda* locally often refers to self-appointed village decision-makers, due to their power as major landowners and landlords. See also Srinivas (1994) on this process in South India, and Gidwani (2008) in West India. Most of the Gowda community come from the dominant farming castes of the region, Vokkaligas (typically from South Karnataka and most common in rural Bengaluru). Some of the same dynamics described here for the northern periphery of the city can be found on the rural eastern and southern periphery, with the dominant landowning caste, and surname, being the Reddys (see Gidwani et al. 2024). The name Gowda is a prominent surname in Karnataka used by Vokkaligas. When negotiations started as to where the international airport would go, Deve Gowda (a Vokkaliga) was chief minister of Karnataka, then briefly prime minister of India, and his son became chief minister a decade later. His name popped up in my interviews with farmers, displaced and advantaged, as key to enabling his kin and community to benefit from the decision to locate the airport and the tens of thousands of acres for business parks and luxury enclaves in this Vokkaliga region. The region is also marked by a large Dalit population and by Dalit activism, as caste divisiveness remains stark. Dr. B. R. Ambedkar defined Dalits in his fortnightly publication *Bahishkrut Bharat*: "Dalithood is a kind of life condition that characterizes the exploitation, suppression and marginalization of

Dalit people by the social, economic, cultural and political domination of the upper castes" (as cited in Guru 2005, 69). Such oppression is central to Ambedkar's notion of Brahminical ideology; the idea of Dalithood or Dalitness is therefore controversial to dominant communities and essential to anticaste politics and resistance.

9   The literature on caste politics, oppression, and subjectivity is vast and fruitful, including Omvedt (1994, 2011); Bairy (2010); Ajantha Subramanian (2015); Dirks (2001); Jaffrelot (2003); and Deshpande (2003, 2013).

10   Interview, New Arasinakunte, June 2015. To clarify, the farmer is saying they were bonded by obligations and threats from elite villagers and thus obliged to give up their labor power when asked. They were not all bonded by financial debt.

11   Interviews, Bengaluru Rural district, July 2016.

12   The director of the European spatial mapping firm originally hired in the mid-2000s to create Bengaluru's first comprehensive plot-by-plot mapping of land use described to me in several interviews over three years how often his carefully studied and precisely drawn maps were changed by the chief minister's office to include certain plots of land for speculative investments.

13   Interview, July 2017.

14   See Joint House Committee report on land grabbing (Ramaswamy 2007a, 2007b); Koliwad Committee on Lakes (Karnataka Legislature 2017); and Task Force for Recovery of Public Land and Its Protection, Greed and Connivance, Chairman's Report (Balasubramanian 2011).

Chapter 6. Remaking Real Estate, Capital Markets, and City Life: Private Equity and the New Logics of Finance

This chapter draws on a published article coauthored as a collaborative effort with Devika Narayan (Goldman and Narayan 2021).

1.   This narrative and analysis come from a series of interviews with people in the field of real estate and finance that I conducted between 2007 and 2019 and that Devika Narayan conducted in 2018–19.

2.   Smart Cities Mission website, accessed May 21, 2025, https://smartcities.gov.in/.

3.   From a series of interviews in 2017–18.

4.   Interview, September 2017.

5.   Interviews, 2015–18. Also, see Gidwani et al. (2024).

6.   Based on interviews, 2010–18.

7.   Interview, September 2017.

8. Interview, June 2016.
9. Interview, September 2017.
10 Interview, September 2017.
11 Interviewees explained that this is a common practice in the industry.
12 Based on interviews, 2016–18.
13 Interview, September 2017.
14 Interview, June 2017.
15 Interview, investment banker, July 2019.
16 Two investigative books (Kaul 2020; Bandyopadhyay 2021) map out the important role of India's public banks and their intimate links to politicians and oligarchs in establishing a banking system that flew out of control during this period—rife with corruption, political misdeeds, and rentierism on steroids. It was a perfect storm that contributed to the conditions for the NPA debt crisis described here. I chose not to add this dimension into the narrative so as not to further complicate the story, but their findings confirm the value of a relational approach to show how a global elite network can tap into the opportunities presented by a local elite network. Their research shows how the mounting debt occurring in India's public banks created a rupture and opportunity to exploit for private equity firms from elsewhere. Their research carefully documents how the power of the Indian patrimonial regime of governance works. Although I underplay this local angle here, these authors fail to explicate the important role of foreign finance capital and policy powerbrokers in this phase of Indian finance—hence the value of shared knowledge.
17 This analysis of national- and firm-level data was conducted by Amay Narayan (2019), an economist hired to support this research.
18 Indeed, by 2020 the company had become the world's largest corporate landlord, despite having started to acquire real estate only as far back as 2010, with no prior experience in the sector.
19 Based on interviews, 2016–18.
20 Interview, land banker and developer, June 2016.

Conclusion. The Turn to a Postspeculative Future

1 We collectively interviewed him in 2019 and 2022. I shared lengthy conversations with him at workshops we organized at the National Institute of Advanced Studies, Bengaluru, on housing rights and the right to the city.
2 This quotation comes from an interview conducted by two colleagues and myself, for our National Science Foundation–funded

project on speculative urbanism; it has been published in our collective book project, in the chapter titled "Why Not Us?" written by Swathi Shivanand (2024). Other quotations come from my interviews with him.

3   You can find the report here: http://www.savekarnataka.in. It documents the whole land-grabbing process in Karnataka including the names of developers, politicians, and other elites involved.

4   Interview, Devanahalli, July 2016.

5   In the 2019 book *The Code of Capital*, legal scholar Katharina Pistor argues that backing those financial assets are a series of laws and legal codes supported by legislatures and courts to ensure that the rocky road of speculation and risk is smoothed out by legal protections for elite investors.

REFERENCES

Aalbers, Manuel B. 2008. "The Financialization of Home and the Mortgage Market Crisis." *Competition and Change* 12 (2): 148–66. https://doi.org/10.1179/102452908X289802.

Aalbers, Manuel B. 2016. *The Financialization of Housing: A Political Economy Approach.* Oxford: Routledge.

Aalbers, Manuel B. 2017. "The Variegated Financialization of Housing." *International Journal of Urban and Regional Research* 41 (4): 542–54. https://doi.org/10.1111/1468-2427.12522.

Aalbers, Manuel B. 2019a. "Financial Geographies of Real Estate and the City: A Literature Review." Financial Geography Working Paper 21. Financial Geography Network and KU Leuven/University of Leuven.

Aalbers, Manuel B. 2019b. "Financial Geography III: The Financialization of the City." *Progress in Human Geography* 44 (3): 595–607. https://doi.org/10.1177/0309132519853922.

ACCE Institute, Americans for Financial Reform (AFR), and Public Advocates. 2019. *Wall Street Landlords Turn American Dream into a Nightmare.* Los Angeles: ACCE Institute. https://www.acceinstitute .org/wall_street_landlords_turn_american_dream_into_american _nightmare.

Alexander, George, and Anton Antony. 2018. "Blackstone India: How Blackstone Turned India into Its Most Profitable Market." *Economic Times*, March 12.

Álvarez, Nacho. 2012. "The Financialization of the Spanish Economy: Debt, Crisis and Social Cuts." Working paper. Department of Applied Economics, University of Valladolid.

Amaral, Rodrigo. 2010. "The Road to Latin America." *Professional Pensions*, September 3. https://www.professionalpensions.com/feature /1731078/-road-latin-america.

Ambedkar, Bhimrao Ramji. 2016. *Annihilation of Caste.* Annotated ed. London: Verso.

Anand, Nikhil. 2017. *Hydraulic City: Water and the Infrastructures of Citizenship in Mumbai.* Durham, NC: Duke University Press.

Ancien, Delphine. 2011. "Global City Theory and the New Urban Politics Twenty Years On: The Case for a Geohistorical Materialist Approach to the (New) Urban Politics of Global Cities." *Urban Studies* 48 (12): 2473–93. https://doi.org/10.1177/0042098011411945.

Anderson, Bendix. 2015. "Single-Family Rental Companies Cash in on Wall Street." *National Real Estate Investor*, June 22. https://www.proquest.com/docview/1690359534?sourcetype=Trade%20Journals.

Angelo, Hillary, and David Wachsmuth. 2015. "Urbanizing Urban Political Ecology: A Critique of Methodological Cityism." *International Journal of Urban and Regional Research* 39 (1): 16–27. https://doi.org/10.1111/1468-2427.12105.

Anguelov, Dimitar. 2023. "Financializing Urban Infrastructure? The Speculative State-Spaces of 'Public-Public Partnerships' in Jakarta." *Environment and Planning A: Economy and Space* 55 (2): 445–70. https://doi.org/10.1177/0308518X221135823.

Annamalai, Thillai, and Maulik Doshi. 2012. "Beyond Capital: Private Equity and Real Estate Development in India." *Journal of Private Equity* 15 (3): 62–76. https://doi.org/10.3905/jpe.2012.15.3.062.

Anthony, Cara, and Liz Szabo. 2020. "The Nation's 5,000 Outpatient Surgery Centers Could Help with the COVID-19 Overflow." KFF Health News, March 27. https://kffhealthnews.org/news/the-nations-5000-outpatient-surgery-centers-could-help-with-the-covid-19-overflow/.

Ash, Jordan. 2023. *Blackstone Comes to Collect: How America's Largest Landlord and Wall Street's Highest Paid CEO Are Jacking Up Rents and Ramping Up Evictions*. N.p: Private Equity Stakeholder Project and Alliance of Californians for Community Empowerment. https://pestakeholder.org/wp-content/uploads/2023/03/PESP_Report_Blackstone_March2023_v4.pdf.

Ashton, Philip, Marc Doussard, and Rachel Weber. 2016. "Reconstituting the State: City Powers and Exposures in Chicago's Infrastructure Leases." *Urban Studies* 53 (7): 1384–400. https://doi.org/10.1177/0042098014532962.

Ashton, Philip, Marc Doussard, and Rachel Weber. 2020. "Sale of the Century: Chicago's Infrastructure Deals and the Privatization State." *Metropolitics*, November 24. https://metropolitics.org/IMG/pdf/met-ashton-doussard-weber-en.pdf.

Asian Development Bank. 2007. *Managing Asian Cities: Sustainable and Inclusive Urban Solutions*. Mandaluyong: Asian Development Bank.

Atlas Arteria. 2022. *Acquisition of Majority Interest in Chicago Skyway: Acquisition and Equity Raising Investor Presentation*. N.p.:

Atlas Arteria. https://d3ar6irj6sybdw.cloudfront.net/stores/
_sharedfiles/Investor_Resources/Investor_Presentations/Acquisition
_of_Majority_Interest_in_Chicago_Skyway_Presentation_-_14
_September_2022.pdf.

Aundhe, Sanjiv. 2019. "Financialisation of Real Estate in Bangalore."
Working Paper. NSF research project, NIAS-Bengaluru.

Ayyathurai, Gajendran. 2021. "It Is Time for a New Subfield: 'Critical
Caste Studies.'" *South Asia @LSE* (blog), July 5. https://blogs.lse
.ac.uk/southasia/2021/07/05/it-is-time-for-a-new-subfield-critical
-caste-studies/.

Azim Premji University. 2021. *State of Working India 2021: One Year of
Covid-19.* Bengaluru: Centre for Sustainable Employment, Azim
Premji University.

Babar, Kailash. 2019. "PEs Enter Realty Space Vacated by Cash-Starved
NBFCs." *Economic Times* (Mumbai), April 17. https://economictimes
.indiatimes.com/industry/banking/finance/pes-enter-realty-space
-vacated-by-cash-starved-nbfcs/articleshow/68914733.cms?from=mdr.

Baindur, Vinay, and Lalitha Kamath. 2009. *Reengineering Urban Infra-
structure: How the World Bank and Asian Development Bank Shape
Urban Infrastructure Finance and Governance in India.* New Delhi:
Bank Information Centre, South Asia.

Bairy, Ramesh T. S. 2010. *Being Brahmin, Being Modern: Exploring the
Lives of Caste Today.* New Delhi: Routledge.

Balachandran, G. 2003. *India and the World Economy, 1850–1950.* Oxford: Oxford University Press.

Balakrishnan, Sai. 2019. *Shareholder Cities: Land Transformations Along
Urban Corridors in India.* Philadelphia: University of Pennsylvania
Press.

Balakrishnan, Sai, and Narendar Pani. 2021. "Real Estate Politicians
in India." *Urban Studies* 58 (10): 2079–94. https://doi.org/10.1177
/0042098020937917.

Balasubramanian, V. 2011. *Task Force for Recovery of Public Land and Its
Protection: Greed and Connivance: Chairman's Report.* Karnataka:
Government of Karnataka, Bengaluru.

Ball, Stephen. 2012. *Global Education, Inc.: New Policy Networks and the
Neoliberal Imaginary.* New York: Routledge.

Bandyopadhyay, Tamal. 2021. *Pandemonium: The Great Indian Banking
Tragedy.* New Delhi: Roli Books.

Banerjee-Guha, Swapna. 2013. "Accumulation and Dispossession: Contradictions of Growth and Development in Contemporary India." *South
Asia: Journal of South Asian Studies* 36 (2): 165–79. https://doi.org/10
.1080/00856401.2013.804026.

Bangalore International Airport Limited (BIAL). 2016. *16th Annual Report 2016–17.* Bengaluru: BIAL.

Bank for International Settlements. 2009. *OTC Derivatives Market Activity in the Second Half of 2008*. Basel: Bank for International Settlements, Monetary and Economic Department. https://www.bis .org/publ/otc_hy0905.pdf.

Barasa, Topista N. 2021. "Speculative Urbanism and the Urban Planning Process of Nairobi Kenya: A Case Study of the Southern Bypass." MA thesis, Miami University.

Basole, Amit. 2019. *State of Working India 2019*. Bengaluru: Centre for Sustainable Employment, Azim Premji University.

Bates, Crispin. 1995. "Race, Caste and Tribe in Central India: The Early Origins of Indian Anthropometry." In *The Concept of Race in South Asia*, edited by Peter Robb, 219–59. New Delhi: Oxford University Press.

Baucom, Ian. 2005. *Specters of the Atlantic: Finance Capital, Slavery, and the Philosophy of History*. Durham, NC: Duke University Press.

Bayat, Asef. 2021. *Revolutionary Life: The Everyday of the Arab Spring*. Cambridge, MA: Harvard University Press.

BBC News. 2018. "Is India's Bangalore Doomed to Be the Next Cape Town?" BBC News, March 6.

Bear, Laura. 2015. *Navigating Austerity: Currents of Debt Along a South Asian River*. Stanford, CA: Stanford University Press.

Bear, Laura. 2017. "Anthropological Futures: For a Critical Political Economy of Capitalist Time." *Social Anthropology* 25 (2): 142–58. https://doi.org/10.1111/1469-8676.12412.

Bear, Laura. 2020. "Speculation: A Political Economy of Technologies of Imagination." *Economy and Society* 49 (1): 1–15. https://doi.org/10 .1080/03085147.2020.1715604.

Bear, Laura, Ritu Birla, and Stine Simonsen Puri. 2015a. "Speculation: Futures and Capitalism in India." *Comparative Studies of South Asia, Africa and the Middle East* 35 (3): 387–91. https://doi.org/10 .1215/1089201X-3426241.

Bear, Laura, Karen Ho, Anna Lowenhaupt Tsing, and Sylvia Yanagisako. 2015b. "Gens: A Feminist Manifesto for the Study of Capitalism." *Cultural Anthropology*, Editors' Forum, March 30. https://culanth.org /fieldsights/gens-a-feminist-manifesto-for-the-study-of-capitalism.

Becker, Joachim, Johannes Jäger, Bernhard Leubolt, and Rudy Weissenbacher. 2010. "Peripheral Financialization and Vulnerability to Crisis: A Regulationist Perspective." *Competition and Change* 14 (3–4): 225–47. https://doi.org/10.1179/102452910X12837703615337.

Benjamin, Solomon. 2008. "Occupancy Urbanism: Radicalizing Politics and Economy Beyond Policy and Programs." *International Journal of Urban and Regional Research* 32 (3): 719–29. https://doi.org/10 .1111/j.1468-2427.2008.00809.x.

Benjamin, Solomon, and Bhuvaneswari Raman. 2011. "Illegible Claims, Legal Titles, and the Worlding of Bangalore." *Revue Tiers Monde*

206 (2): 37–54. https://shs.cairn.info/revue-tiers-monde-2011-2
-page-37?lang=en.

Bhasthi, Deepa. 2017. "City of Burning Lakes: Experts Fear Bangalore
Will Be Uninhabitable by 2025." *Guardian*, March 1.

Bigger, Patrick, and Sophie Webber. 2021. "Green Structural Adjustment in the World Bank's Resilient City." *Annals of the American
Association of Geographers* 111 (1): 36–51. https://doi.org/10.1080
/24694452.2020.1749023.

Birch, Kean, and Callum Ward. 2022. "Assetization and the 'New Asset
Geographies.'" *Dialogues in Human Geography* 14 (1): 9–29. https://
doi.org/10.1177/20438206221130807.

Birla, Ritu. 2015. "Speculation Illicit and Complicit: Contract, Uncertainty, and Governmentality." *Comparative Studies of South Asia,
Africa and the Middle East* 35 (3): 392–407. https://doi.org/10.1215
/1089201X-3426253.

BlackRock. 2015. *Infrastructure Rising: An Asset Class Takes Shape.* New
York: BlackRock Infrastructure.

Block, Fred, and Robert Hockett, eds. 2022. *Democratizing Finance:
Restructuring Credit to Transform Society.* London: Verso.

Bombay First–McKinsey. 2003. *Vision Mumbai: Transforming Mumbai into
a World-Class City.* Mumbai: McKinsey. https://mumbaifirst.org/wp
-content/uploads/2020/11/McKinsey-Report-on-Vision-Mumbai.pdf.

Bonizzi, Bruno, Annina Kaltenbrunner, and Jeff Powell. 2019. "Subordi-
nate Financialization in Emerging Capitalist Economies." Greenwich
Papers in Political Economy 23044 (GPERC69). Greenwich Political
Economy Research Centre, University of Greenwich. https://core.ac
.uk/download/pdf/189394133.pdf.

Boston Consulting Group. 2021. *Global Asset Management 2021: The
$100 Trillion Machine.* N.p.: Boston Consulting Group.

Brand, Ulrich, and Markus Wissen. 2021. *The Imperialism Mode of Living:
Everyday Life and the Ecological Crisis of Capitalism.* London: Verso.

Breman, Jan. 2010. "India's Social Question in a State of Denial." *Economic and Political Weekly* 45 (23): 42–46. https://www.jstor.org
/stable/27807105.

Breman, Jan. 2013. *At Work in the Informal Economy of India: A Perspective from the Bottom Up.* New Delhi: Oxford University Press.

Brenner, Neil, ed. 2014. *Implosions/Explosions: Towards a Study of Planetary Urbanization.* Berlin: JOVIS.

Brenner, Neil, and Christian Schmid. 2015. "Towards a New Epistemology of the Urban?" *City* 19 (2–3): 151–82. https://doi.org/10.1080
/13604813.2015.1014712.

Brenner, Robert. 2006. *The Economics of Global Turbulence: The Advanced Capitalist Economies from Long Boom to Long Downturn,
1945–2005.* London: Verso.

Brown, Dana. 2023. "How Private Equity Is Swallowing Up Health Care—and What to Do About It." *Non Profit Quarterly*, April 19. https://nonprofitquarterly.org/how-private-equity-is-swallowing-up -health-care-and-what-to-do-about-it/.

Buck, Tobias. 2013. "Spain Threatened by Resurgent Credit Crunch." *Financial Times*, April.

Buck, Tobias. 2014. "Spain's Banks Reap Billions from Sovereign Bond Holdings." *Financial Times*, January 29.

Buckley, Michelle, and Adam Hanieh. 2014. "Diversification by Urbanization: Tracing the Property-Finance Nexus in Dubai and the Gulf." *International Journal of Urban and Regional Research* 38 (1): 155–75. https://doi.org/10.1111/1468-2427.12084.

Buckley, Robert M., and Jerry Kalarickal. 2006. *Thirty Years of World Bank Shelter Lending: What Have We Learned?* Washington, DC: World Bank.

Bugbee, Mary. 2022. *Envision Healthcare: A Private Equity Case Study.* Chicago: Private Equity Stakeholder Project. https://pestakeholder.org/wp -content/uploads/2022/12/Envision_CaseStudy_Final_Dec2022.pdf.

Burkhart, Corinna, Matthias Schmelzer, and Nina Treu. 2020. *Degrowth in Movement(s): Exploring Pathways for Transformation.* Winchester: Zero Books.

Byrne, Michael. 2016. "'Asset Price Urbanism' and Financialization After the Crisis: Ireland's National Asset Management Agency." *International Journal of Urban and Regional Research* 40 (1): 31–45. https://doi.org/10.1111/1468-2427.12331.

Byrnes, Dave. 2022. "Federal Judge Dismisses Antitrust Suit over Chicago Parking Meters." Courthouse News Service, January 24. https://www.courthousenews.com/federal-judge-dismisses-antitrust -suit-over-chicago-parking-meters/.

c40. 2015. "Press Release: President Clinton and Mayor Bloomberg Join Forces to Combat Climate Change." c40 Cities, March 4. https:// www.c40.org/news/press-release-president-clinton-and-mayor -bloomberg-join-forces-to-combat-climate-change-8c6d9d2f-8686 -4f57-b406-e6bf02f8bcee/.

California Senate Local Government Committee. 2010. *What's So Special About Special Districts? A Citizen's Guide to Special Districts in California.* 4th ed. Sacramento: Senate Local Government Committee.

Call, Rob, Denechia Powell, and Sarah Heck. 2014. *Blackstone: Atlanta's Newest Landlord.* N.p.: Occupy Our Homes Atlanta and the Right to the City Alliance Homes for All Campaign.

Campbell, John L. 2010. "Neoliberalism in Crisis: Regulatory Roots of the US Financial Meltdown." In *Markets on Trial: The Economic Sociology of the U.S. Financial Crisis*, edited by Michael Lounsbury and Paul M. Hirsch, 65–101. Bingley: Emerald.

Carlson, H. Jacob. 2018. "Model Employers and Model Cities? Bangalore's Public Sector and the Rise of the Neoliberal City." *Urban Geography* 39 (5): 726–45. https://doi.org/10.1080/02723638.2017.1388734.

Cháirez-Garza, Jesús F. 2022. "Moving Untouched: B. R. Ambedkar and the Racialization of Untouchability." *Ethnic and Racial Studies* 45 (2): 216–34. https://doi.org/10.1080/01419870.2021.1924393.

Cháirez-Garza, Jesús F., Mabel Denzin Gergan, Malini Ranganathan, and Pavithra Vasudevan. 2022. "Introduction to the Special Issue: Rethinking Difference in India Through Racialization." *Ethnic and Racial Studies* 45 (2): 193–215. https://doi.org/10.1080/01419870.2021.1977368.

Chandra, Kanchan. 2015. "The New Indian State: The Relocation of Patronage in the Post-Liberalisation Economy." *Economic and Political Weekly* 50 (41): 46–58. https://www.jstor.org/stable/44002714.

Chang, David. 2010. *The Color of the Land: Race, Nation, and the Politics of Landownership in Oklahoma, 1832–1929.* Chapel Hill: University of North Carolina Press.

Charnock, Greig, Thomas F. Purcell, and Ramon Ribera-Fumaz. 2014. "City of Rents: The Limits to the Barcelona Model of Urban Competitiveness." *International Journal of Urban and Regional Research* 38 (1): 198–217. https://doi.org/10.1111/1468-2427.12103.

Chhabria, Sheetal. 2023. "Where Does Caste Fit in a Global History of Racial Capitalism?" *Historical Materialism* 31 (2): 136–60. https://www.historicalmaterialism.org/article/where-does-caste-fit-in-a-global-history-of-racial-capitalism/.

Chislett, William. 2014. *Spain Leads the World Market for Infrastructure Development.* ARI 52. Real Instituto Elcano, November 5. https://www.realinstitutoelcano.org/en/analyses/spain-leads-the-world-market-for-infrastructure-development/.

Chowdhury, Subhanil. 2011. "Employment in India: What Does the Latest Data Show?" *Economic and Political Weekly* 46 (32): 23–26. https://www.epw.in/journal/2011/32/commentary/employment-india-what-does-latest-data-show.html. Christophers, Brett. 2018. "Financialisation as Monopoly Profit: The Case of US Banking." *Antipode* 50 (4): 864–90. https://doi.org/10.1111/anti.12383.

Christophers, Brett. 2019. "The Rentierization of the United Kingdom Economy." *Environment and Planning A: Economy and Space* 55 (6): 1438–70. https://doi.org/10.1177/0308518X19873007.

Christophers, Brett. 2020. *Rentier Capitalism: Who Owns the Economy, and Who Pays for It?* London: Verso.

Christophers, Brett. 2022. "Mind the Rent Gap: Blackstone, Housing Investment and the Reordering of Urban Rent Surfaces." *Urban Studies* 59 (4): 698–716. https://doi.org/10.1177/00420980211026466.

Christophers, Brett. 2023. *Our Lives in Their Portfolios: Why Asset Managers Own the World*. New York: Verso.

Coelho, Karen, Lalitha Kamath, and M. Vijayabaskar. 2020. *Participolis: Consent and Contention in Neoliberal Urban India*. London: Routledge.

Collins, Chuck, Omar Ocampo, Sara Myklebust, et al. 2021. *Cashing In on Our Homes: Billionaire Landlords Profit as Millions Face Eviction*. Report. Bargaining for the Common Good, March 17. https://www.bargainingforthecommongood.org/report-cashing-in-on-our-homes-billionaire-landlords-profit-as-millions-face-eviction/.

Colven, Emma. 2023. "A Political Ecology of Speculative Urbanism: The Role of Financial and Environmental Speculation in Jakarta's Water Crisis." *Environment and Planning A: Economy and Space* 55 (2): 490–510. https://doi.org/10.1177/0308518X221110883.

Coq-Huelva, Daniel. 2013. "Urbanisation and Financialisation in the Context of a Rescaling State: The Case of Spain." *Antipode* 45 (5): 1213–31. https://doi.org/10.1111/anti.12011.

Coulthard, Glen. 2014. *Red Skin, White Masks: Rejecting the Colonial Politics of Recognition*. Minneapolis: University of Minnesota Press.

Coulthard, Glen, and Leanne Betasamosake Simpson. 2016. "Grounded Normativity/Place-Based Solidarity." *American Quarterly* 68 (2): 249–55. https://doi.org/10.1353/aq.2016.0038.

Cowan, Thomas. 2018. "The Urban Village, Agrarian Transformation, and Rentier Capitalism in Gurgaon, India." *Antipode* 50 (5): 1244–66. https://doi.org/10.1111/anti.12404.

Cowen, Deborah. 2020. "Following the Infrastructures of Empire: Notes on Cities, Settler Colonialism, and Method." *Urban Geography* 41 (4): 469–86. https://doi.org/10.1080/02723638.2019.1677990.

Cross, Jamie. 2014. *Dream Zones: Capitalism and Development in India*. London: Pluto.

Cunningham, Benjamin. 2025. "Madrid's Biggest Landlord? U.S. Investment Firms." *New York Times*, April 25. https://www.nytimes.com/2025/04/25/realestate/spain-rents-prices-homes.html.

Damle, C. B. 1989. "Land Reforms Legislation in Karnataka: Myth of Success." *Economic and Political Weekly* 24 (33): 1896–906. https://www.epw.in/journal/1989/33/special-articles/land-reforms-legislation-karnataka-myth-success.html.

Dastidar, Riddhi. 2021. "India's Suffering Female Dalit Farmers Have the Most to Lose." *Foreign Policy*, April 13. https://foreignpolicy.com/2021/04/13/indias-suffering-female-farmers-have-the-most-to-lose/.

Davis, Gerald. 2009. *Managed by the Markets: How Finance Re-Shaped America*. New York: Oxford University Press.

Davis, Gerald, and Suntae Kim. 2015. "Financialization of the Economy." *Annual Review of Sociology* 41:203–21. https://doi.org/10.1146/annurev-soc-073014-112402.

De Cecco, Marcello. 1974. *Money and Empire: The International Gold Standard, 1890–1914.* Oxford: Basil Blackwell.

Deloria, Vine, Jr. 1988. *Custer Died for Your Sins.* Norman: University of Oklahoma Press.

Derenoncourt, Ellora, Chi Hyun Kim, Mortiz Kuhn, and Moritz Schularik. 2022. "Wealth of Two Nations: The U.S. Racial Wealth Gap, 1860–2020." Working paper. Program for Research in Inequality, Princeton University. https://www.nber.org/papers/w30101.

Derickson, Kate, Michael Goldman, Kevin Ehrman-Solberg, Robin Wonsley Worlobah, Ross Abram, and Sydney Shelstad. 2021. "Private Equity Firms: The New Landlord." *Market Failure*, June 12. https://marketfailure.substack.com/p/private-equity-firms-the-new-landlord.

Deshpande, Satish. 2003. "Caste Inequalities in India Today." In *Contemporary India: A Sociological View*, by Satish Deshpande, 98–124. New Delhi: Viking by Penguin Books India.

Deshpande, Satish. 2013. "Caste and Castelessness: Towards a Biography of the 'General Category.'" *Economic and Political Weekly* 48 (15): 32–39. https://www.epw.in/engage/article/51-years-epw-caste-and-castelessness-towards-biography-%E2%80%98general-category%E2%80%99-6.

Desmond, Matthew. 2016. *Evicted: Poverty and Profit in the American City.* New York: Broadway Books.

Desmond, Matthew. 2023. *Poverty, by America.* New York: Crown.

de Soto, Hernando. 2000. *The Mystery of Capital: Why Capital Triumphs in the West and Fails Everywhere Else.* New York: Basic Books.

Development Planning Unit (DPU). 2002. "The History of the Cities Alliance." In *Cities Alliance, Cities Without Slums: Independent Evaluation, an Assessment of the First Three Years*, 1–16. London: DPU, University College London. https://www.citiesalliance.org/sites/default/files/CA_Docs/members-pages/independent_evaluations/annex-2.pdf.

DiNapoli, Thomas P., and Kenneth B. Bleiwas. 2012. *The Securities Industry in New York City.* Albany, NY: Office of the State Comptroller.

Dirks, Nicholas. 2001. *Castes of Mind: Colonialism and the Making of Modern India.* Princeton, NJ: Princeton University Press.

Dobbs, Richard, Sven Smit, Jaana Remes, James Manyika, Charles Roxburgh, and Alejandra Restrepo. 2011. *Urban World: Mapping the Economic Power of Cities.* New York: McKinsey Global Institute.

Dobbs, Richard, Herbert Pohl, Diaan-Yi Lin, et al. 2013. *Infrastructure Productivity: How to Save $1 Trillion a Year*. New York: McKinsey Global Institute.

Doshi, Sapana, and Malini Ranganathan. 2017. "Contesting the Unethical City: Land Dispossession and Corruption Narratives in Urban India." *Annals of the American Association of Geographers* 107 (1): 183–99. https://doi.org/10.1080/24694452.2016.1226124.

Doshi, Sapana, and Malini Ranganathan. 2019. "Towards a Critical Geography of Corruption and Power in Late Capitalism." *Progress in Human Geography* 43 (3): 436–57. https://doi.org/10.1177/0309132517753070.

Dowsett, Sonya. 2014. "Special Report: Why Madrid's Poor Fear Goldman Sachs and Blackstone." *Reuters*, October 24. https://www.reuters.com/article/business/special-report-why-madrids-poor-fear-goldman-sachs-and-blackstone-idUSKCN0ID0GP/.

D'Souza, Rohan. 2014. "When Lakes Were Tanks." *Down to Earth*, August 31. https://www.downtoearth.org.in/environment/when-lakes-were-tanks-45815.

D'Souza, Rohan. 2024. "The Importance of Bengaluru's Lakes and Their Associated Land." *The Hindu*, October 28.

Dumke, Mick. 2015. "While the City Is Strapped for Cash, the Private Parking Meter Company Makes Millions of Dollars More." *Chicago Reader*, May 6. https://chicagoreader.com/blogs/while-the-city-is-strapped-for-cash-the-private-parking-meter-company-makes-millions-of-dollars-more/.

Economic Times. 2018. "IL&FS: The Crisis That Has India in Panic Mode." October 3. https://economictimes.indiatimes.com/industry/banking/finance/banking/everything-about-the-ilfs-crisis-that-has-india-in-panic-mode/articleshow/66026024.cms?from=mdr.

Elstein, Aaron. 2023. "The Tax Zombies of New York." *Crain's New York Business*, May 23. https://www.crainsnewyork.com/politics/new-york-tax-breaks-cost-residents-10b-annually.

Environment Support Group. 2007. *Water Bodies of Bangalore*. Bangalore: Environment Support Group.

Epstein, Gerald. 2005. *Financialization and the World Economy*. Northampton, MA: Edward Elgar.

Express News Service. 2018. "JICA Inks Rs 2,500 Crore Deal for Water Project in Bengaluru." *New Indian Express*, January 25. https://www.newindianexpress.com/cities/bengaluru/2018/Jan/25/jica-inks-rs-2500-crore-deal-for-water-project-in-bengaluru-1763081.html.

Fairbairn, Madeleine. 2020. *Fields of Gold: Financing the Global Land Rush*. Ithaca, NY: Cornell University Press.

Farrell, Diana, Eric Beinhocker, Ulrich Gersch, Ezra Greenberg, Elizabeth Stephenson, Jonathan Ablett, Mingyu Guan, and Janamitra Devan. 2006. *From "Made in China" to "Sold in China": The Rise of the Chinese Urban Consumer.* New York: McKinsey Global Institute.

Federation of Indian Chambers of Commerce and Industry (FICCI). 2017. *Economy of Jobs.* New Delhi: FICCI.

Federici, Silvia. 2014. "From Commoning to Debt: Financialization, Microcredit, and the Changing Architecture of Capital Accumulation." *South Atlantic Quarterly* 113 (2): 231–44. https://doi.org/10.1215 /00382876-2643585.

Fernandez, Rodrigo, and Manuel B. Aalbers. 2020. "Housing Financialization in the Global South: In Search of a Comparative Framework." *Housing Policy Debate* 30 (4): 680–701. https://doi.org/10 .1080/10511482.2019.1681491.

Fields, Desiree. 2017. "Unwilling Subjects of Financialization." *International Journal of Urban and Regional Research* 41 (4): 588–603. https://doi.org/10.1111/1468-2427.12519.

Fields, Desiree. 2018. "Constructing a New Asset Class: Property-Led Financial Accumulation After the Crisis." *Economic Geography* 94 (2): 118–40. https://doi.org/10.1080/00130095.2017.1397492.

Financial Express. 2017. "Bengaluru Water Crisis: Karnataka Faces Severe Scarcity, 160 of 176 Taluks Declared Drought-Hit." March 2. https://www.financialexpress.com/india-news/bengaluru-water -crisis-karnataka-faces-severe-scarcity-160-of-176-taluks-declared -drought-hit/572048/.

Financial Express. 2019. "Real Estate Crisis: Indian Lenders Sleepwalking to Trouble on Builder Debt." February 17.

Financial Stability Board. 2023. *Promoting Global Financial Stability: 2023 FSB Annual Report.* Basel: Financial Stability Board. https://www.fsb. org/uploads/P111023.pdf.

Finel-Honigman, Irene. 2009. *A Cultural History of Finance.* London: Routledge.

Fischer, Stanley. 1998. *The Asian Crisis: A View from the IMF.* Washington, DC: International Monetary Fund.

Fisher, Bridget, and Flávia Leite. 2020. "How Risk Undermines TIF's Self-Financing Premise: A Case Study of Hudson Yards." Working Paper Series 2020-2. Schwartz Center for Economic Policy Analysis and Department of Economics, New School for Social Research, New York.

Fisher, Max. 2010. "Why Does Abu Dhabi Own All of Chicago's Parking Meters?" *Atlantic*, October 19.

Fix LA Coalition. 2014. *No Small Fees: LA Spends More on Wall St. Than Our Streets.* Los Angeles: Fix LA Coalition. https://www.seiu721.org /wp-content/uploads/2014/07/No-Small-Fees-A-Report-by-the-Fix -LA-Coalition-2014-07-28-2.pdf.

Fligstein, Neil, and Adam Goldstein. 2010. "The Anatomy of the Mortgage Securitization Crisis." IRLE Working Paper No. 200-10. Institute for Research on Labor and Employment, University of California, Berkeley.

Fligstein, Neil, and Jacob Habinek. 2014. "Sucker Punched by the Invisible Hand: The World Financial Markets and the Globalization of the US Mortgage Crisis." *Socio-Economic Review* 12 (4): 637–65. https://doi.org/10.1093/ser/mwu004.

Foucault, Michel. 1979. *The Birth of Biopolitics: Lectures at the College de France, 1978–1979.* Edited by Michel Senellart. London: Palgrave.

Foucault, Michel. 1991. "Governmentality." In *The Foucault Effects: Studies in Governmentality*, edited by Graham Burchell, Colin Gordon, and Peter Miller, 87–104. London: Harvester Wheatsheaf.

Foucault, Michel. 2004. *Security, Territory, Population: Lectures at the Collège de France, 1978–1979.* New York: Picador.

Fumagalli, Andrea, and Sandro Mezzadra, eds. 2010. *Crisis in the Global Economy: Financial Markets, Social Struggles, and New Political Scenarios.* Los Angeles: Semiotext(e). Distributed by MIT Press.

Gago, Verónica. 2020. *How to Change Everything.* London: Verso.

García, Marisol. 2010. "The Breakdown of the Spanish Urban Growth Model: Social and Territorial Effects of the Global Crisis: Debates and Developments." *International Journal of Urban and Regional Research* 34 (4): 967–80. https://doi.org/10.1111/j.1468-2427.2010.01015.x.

García-Lamarca, Melissa. 2022. *Non-Performing Loans, Non-Performing People: Life and Struggle with Mortgage Debt in Spain.* Athens: University of Georgia Press.

García-Lamarca, Melissa, and Maria Kaika. 2016. "'Mortgaged Lives': The Biopolitics of Debt and Housing Financialisation." *Transactions of the Institute of British Geographers* 41 (3): 313–27. https://doi.org/10.1111/tran.12126.

Ghertner, Asher. 2015. *Rule by Aesthetics: World-Class City Making in New Delhi.* New Delhi: Oxford University Press.

Ghosh, Jayati, and C. P. Chandrashekhar. 2017. "A Crisis Is Building Up in India's Real Estate Sector." *Hindu Business Line*, September 25. https://architexturez.net/pst/az-cf-184841-1506489898.

Ghosh, Priyanka. 2015. "Structured Debt Preferred PE Route for Realty Investment." *Financial Express*, April 13. https://www.financialexpress.com/market/structured-debt-preferred-pe-route-for-realty-investment/63134/.

Ghosh, Suvashree, and Dhwani Pandya. 2019. "$63 Billion of Zombie Buildings Sound Warning for Indian Banks." *Economic Times*, October 3. https://economictimes.indiatimes.com/industry/banking/finance/63-billion-of-zombie-buildings-sound-warning-for-indian-banks/articleshow/71434585.cms?from=mdr.

Gidwani, Vinay. 2008. *Capital Interrupted: Agrarian Development and the Politics of Work in India*. Minneapolis: University of Minnesota Press.

Gidwani, Vinay, and Amita Baviskar. 2011. "Urban Commons." *Economic and Political Weekly* 46 (50): 42–43. https://urbanforensics .wordpress.com/wp-content/uploads/2012/09/gidwani_baviskar _urbancommons.pdf.

Gidwani, Vinay, Michael Goldman, and Carol Upadhya, eds. 2024. *Living the Speculative City*. Minneapolis: University of Minnesota Press.

Gidwani, Vinay, and Carol Upadhya. 2022. "Articulation Work: Value Chains of Land Assembly and Real Estate Development on a Peri-Urban Frontier." *Environment and Planning A: Economy and Space* 55 (2): 407–27. https://doi.org/10.1177/0308518X221107016.

Gilbert, Paul, Clea Bourne, Max Haiven, and Johnna Montgomerie, eds. 2023. *The Entangled Legacies of Empire: Race, Finance and Inequality*. Manchester: Manchester University Press.

Gillespie, Tom. 2016. "Accumulation by Urban Dispossession: Struggles over Urban Space in Accra, Ghana." *Transactions of the Institute of British Geographers* 41 (1): 66–77. https://doi.org/10.1111/tran.12105.

Glaeser, Edward, and Abha Joshi-Ghani. 2015. *The Urban Imperative: Towards Competitive Cities*. Washington, DC: World Bank.

Goldman, Michael, ed. 1998. *Privatizing Nature: Political Struggles for the Global Commons*. Newark, NJ: Rutgers University Press.

Goldman, Michael. 2005. *Imperial Nature: The World Bank and the Struggles for Social Justice in the Age of Globalization*. New Haven, CT: Yale University Press.

Goldman, Michael. 2007. "How 'Water for All!' Policy Became Hegemonic: The Power of the World Bank and Its Transnational Policy Networks." *Geoforum* 38 (5): 786–800. https://doi.org/10.1016/j .geoforum.2005.10.008.

Goldman, Michael. 2011. "Speculating on the Next World City." In *Worlding Cities: Asian Experiments and the Art of Being Global*, edited by Ananya Roy and Aihwa Ong, 229–58. Oxford: Blackwell.

Goldman, Michael. 2014. "Development and the City." In *Cities of the Global South Reader*, edited by Faranak Miraftab and Neema Kudva, 54–65. Oxford: Routledge.

Goldman, Michael. 2015. "With the Declining Significance of Labor, Who Is Producing Our Global Cities?" *International Labor and Working-Class History* 87:137–64. https://doi.org/10.1017/ S0147547915000034.

Goldman, Michael. 2020. "Dispossession by Financialization: The End(s) of Rurality in the Making of a Speculative Land Market." *Journal of Peasant Studies* 47 (6): 1251–77. https://doi.org/10.1080/03066150 .2020.1802720.

Goldman, Michael. 2021. "Speculative Urbanism and the Urban-Financial Conjuncture: Interrogating the Afterlives of the Financial Crisis." *Environment and Planning A: Economy and Space* 55 (2): 367–87. https://doi.org/10.1177/0308518X211016003.

Goldman, Michael, and Devika Narayan. 2019. "Water Crisis Through the Analytic of Urban Transformation: An Analysis of Bangalore's Hydrosocial Regimes." *Water International* 44 (2): 95–114. https://doi.org/10.1080/02508060.2019.1578078.

Goldman, Michael, and Devika Narayan. 2021. "Through the Optics of Finance: Speculative Urbanism and the Transformation of Markets." *International Journal of Urban and Regional Research* 45 (2): 209–31. https://doi.org/10.1111/1468-2427.13012.

Goldman, Michael, Nancy Peluso, and Wendy Wolford, eds. 2024. *The Social Lives of Land*. Ithaca, NY: Cornell University Press.

Goldman Sachs. 2003. *Dreaming with BRICs: The Path to 2050; How BRICs Will Shape the Next 50 Years*. New York: Goldman Sachs. https://www.goldmansachs.com/insights/goldman-sachs-research/brics-dream.

Goldstein, Matthew. 2015. "Equity Firms Are Lending to Landlords, Signaling a Shift." *New York Times*, March 3.

Gonick, Sophie. 2021. *Dispossession and Dissent: Immigrants and the Struggle for Housing in Madrid*. Stanford, CA: Stanford University Press.

Gorton, Gary, and Andrew Metrick. 2012. "Securitized Banking and the Run on Repo." *Journal of Financial Economics* 104 (3): 425–51. https://doi.org/10.1016/j.jfineco.2011.03.016.

Goswami, Manu. 2004. *Producing India: From Colonial Economy to National Space*. Durham, NC: Duke University Press.

Gotham, Kevin Fox. 2009. "Creating Liquidity out of Spatial Fixity: The Secondary Circuit of Capital and the Subprime Mortgage Crisis." *International Journal of Urban and Regional Research* 33 (2): 355–71. https://doi.org/10.1111/j.1468-2427.2009.00874.x.

Gottfried, Miriam. 2022. "Blackstone Earnings Nearly Double as Firm Enjoys Record Cash Haul." *Wall Street Journal*, January 27.

Government of India. 1996. *The India Infrastructure Report: Policy Imperatives for Growth and Welfare*. New Delhi: Ministry of Finance.

Graeber, David. 2011. *Debt: The First 5000 Years*. Brooklyn, NY: Melville House.

Gramsci, Antonio. 1971. *Selections from the Prison Notebooks*. New York: International Publishers.

Gupta, Akhil. 2012. *Red Tape: Bureaucracy, Structural Violence, and Poverty in India*. Durham, NC: Duke University Press.

Gupta, Atul, Sabrina Howell, Costantine Yannelis, and Abhinav Gupta. 2021. "Owner Incentives and Performance in Health Care: Private

Equity Investment in Nursing Homes." Working Paper 28474. National Bureau of Economic Research, Cambridge, MA. https://www.nber.org/papers/w28474.

Guru, Gopal. 2005. *Atrophy in Dalit Politics*. Mumbai: Vikas Adhyayan Kendra.

Gururani, Shubhra. 2020. "Cities in a World of Villages: Agrarian Urbanism and the Making of India's Urbanizing Frontiers." *Urban Geography* 41 (7): 971–89. https://doi.org/10.1080/02723638.2019.1670569.

Hackett, David. 2023. "Redevelopment for Who? How TIF Redistributes Public Funds to the Wealthy." *Chicago Policy Review*, April 13. https://chicagopolicyreview.org/2023/04/13/redevelopment-for-who-how-tif-redistributes-public-funds-to-the-wealthy/.

Hackworth, Jason. 2007. *The Neoliberal City: Governance, Ideology and Development in American Urbanism*. Ithaca, NY: Cornell University Press.

Halbert, Ludovic, and Hortense Rouanet. 2014. "Filtering Risk Away: Global Finance Capital, Transcalar Territorial Networks and the (Un)Making of City-Regions: An Analysis of Business Property Development in Bangalore, India." *Regional Studies* 48 (3): 471–84. https://doi.org/10.1080/00343404.2013.779658.

Hall, Derek. 2013. "Primitive Accumulation, Accumulation by Dispossession and the Global Land Grab." *Third World Quarterly* 34 (9): 1582–604. https://doi.org/10.1080/01436597.2013.843854.

Hall, Stuart. 2021. *Selected Writings on Race and Difference*. Edited by Paul Gilroy and Ruth Wilson Gilmore. Durham, NC: Duke University Press.

Hall, Stuart, Chas Critcher, Tony Jefferson, and Brian Roberts. 1978. *Policing the Crisis: Mugging, the State, and Law and Order*. London: Macmillan.

Hart, Gillian. 2018. "Relational Comparison Revisited: Marxist Postcolonial Geographies in Practice*." *Progress in Human Geography* 42 (3): 371–94. https://doi.org/10.1177/0309132516681388.

Hart, Gillian. 2023a. "Enabling Connections: Relational Comparison in a Global Conjunctural Frame." In *Routledge Handbook on Comparative Urban Studies*, edited by Patrick Le Galès and Jennifer Robinson, 289–99. London: Routledge.

Hart, Gillian. 2023b. "Modalities of Conjunctural Analysis: 'Seeing the Present Differently' Through Global Lenses." *Antipode* 56 (1): 135–64. https://doi.org/10.1111/anti.12975.

Harvey, David. 2001. *Spaces of Capital: Towards a Critical Geography*. New York: Routledge.

Harvey, David. 2003. *The New Imperialism*. New York: Oxford University Press.

Harvey, David. 2005. *A Brief History of Neoliberalism*. New York: Oxford University Press.

Harvey, David. 2007. "Neoliberalism and the City." *Studies in Social Justice* 1 (1): 1–12. https://www.researchgate.net/publication/26637301 _Neoliberalism_and_the_City.

Heitzman, James. 2004. *Network City: Planning the Information Society in Bangalore.* New York: Oxford University Press.

Higgins, Eoin. 2019. "'How Dare You!': Greta Thunberg Rages at 'Fairytales of Eternal Economic Growth' at UN Climate Summit." Commondreams, September 23. https://www.commondreams.org/news /2019/09/23/how-dare-you-greta-thunberg-rages-fairytales-eternal -economic-growth-un-climate.

Hildreth, W. Bartley, and C. Kurt Zorn. 2005. "The Evolution of the State and Local Government Municipal Debt Market over the Past Quarter Century." *Public Budgeting and Finance* 25 (4s): 127–53. https:// doi.org/10.1111/j.1540-5850.2005.00007.x.

Hindu. 2014. "Special Courts to Be Set Up to Try Land Grabbing Cases." February 5. https://www.thehindu.com/news/national /karnataka/special-courts-to-be-set-up-to-try-land-grabbing-cases /article5654141.ece.

Hindu. 2016. "Special Courts to Try Land-Grab Cases Inaugurated." September 1. https://www.thehindu.com/news/cities/bangalore/Special -courts-to-try-land-grab-cases-inaugurated/article14617515.ece.

Hindustan Times. 2017. "Drought-Hit Tamil Nadu Farmers Hold Mock Funeral in Delhi." March 26. https://www.hindustantimes.com/delhi /drought-hit-tamil-nadu-farmers-hold-mock-funeral-in-delhi/story -5EggoM5Ebq9Huey8GZkWuI.html.

Ho, Karen. 2009. *Liquidated: An Ethnography of Wall Street.* Durham, NC: Duke University Press.

Hoang, Kimberly Kay. 2022. *Spiderweb Capitalism: How Global Elites Exploit Frontier Markets.* Princeton, NJ: Princeton University Press.

Hobsbawm, Eric. 1987. *The Age of Empire: 1875–1914.* New York: Vintage Books.

Hudson Yards Infrastructure Corporation. 2017. *Hudson Yards Infrastructure Corporation Second Indenture Revenue Bonds.* New York: Hudson Yards Infrastructure Corporation. https://www.nyc.gov /assets/hyic/downloads/bond-statements/2017/hyic-2017a-b.pdf.

Immergluck, Dan, and Jonathan Law. 2014. "Speculating in Crisis: The Intrametropolitan Geography of Investing in Foreclosed Homes in Atlanta." *Urban Geography* 35 (1): 1–24. https://doi.org/10.1080 /02723638.2013.858510.

Ismi, Asad. 2004. *Impoverishing a Continent: The World Bank and the IMF in Africa.* Ottawa: Canadian Centre for Policy Alternatives.

Iyer, Radhika. 2014. "Bangalore Crumbles as Civic Body Goes Bankrupt." NDTV, February 25. https://www.ndtv.com/bangalore-news /bangalore-crumbles-as-civic-body-goes-bankrupt-552005.

Jaffrelot, Christophe. 2003. *India's Silent Revolution: The Rise of the Lower Castes in North India.* New York: Columbia University Press.

Jain, Sanket. 2021. "How Indian Farmers Led One of the Largest Protests in History—and Won." *Progressive*, December 18. https://progressive.org/latest/indian-farmers-led-protests-jain-211218/.

Jenkins, Destin, and Justin Leroy, eds. 2021. *Histories of Racial Capitalism.* New York: Columbia University Press.

Jenks, Leland Hamilton. 1927. *The Migration of British Capital to 1875.* New York: Alfred A. Knopf.

Jones Lang LaSalle (JLL). 2011. *Reaping the Returns: Decoding Private Equity Exits in India.* Accessed December 1. https://research .jllapsites.com/.

Joravsky, Benjamin. 2018. "With Bill Daley Running for Mayor, It's Good to Remember What Happened the Last Time We Turned Chicago over to the Daleys." *The Reader*, September 17. https://chicagoreader.com/blogs/with-bill-daley-running-for-mayor-its -good-to-remember-what-happened-the-last-time-we-turned -chicago-over-to-the-daleys/.

Kaika, Maria, and Luca Ruggiero. 2016. "Land Financialization as a 'Lived' Process: The Transformation of Milan's Bicocca by Pirelli." *European Urban and Regional Studies* 23 (1): 3–22. https://doi.org /10.1177/0969776413484166.

Kallis, Giorgos, Susan Paulson, Giacomo D'Alisa, and Federico Demaria. 2020. *The Case for Degrowth.* Medford, MA: Polity.

Kannan Sneha, Joseph Dov Bruch, and Zirui Song. 2023. "Changes in Hospital Adverse Events and Patient Outcomes Associated with Private Equity Acquisition." *Journal of the American Medical Association* 330 (24): 2365–75. https://doi.org/10.1001/jama .2023.23147.

Kaplan, Steven N., and Joshua Rauh. 2010. "Wall Street and Main Street: What Contributes to the Rise in the Highest Incomes?" *Review of Financial Studies* 23 (3): 1004–50. https://doi.org/10.1093/rfs/ hhp006.

Kapur, Devesh, and Milan Vaishnav. 2011. "Quid Pro Quo: Builders, Politicians, and Election Finance in India." Working Paper 276. Center for Global Development, Washington, DC. https://www.files.ethz .ch/isn/142897/1425795_file_Kapur_Vaishnav_election_finance_India _FINAL.pdf.

Karnataka Legislature. 2017. *Koliwad Committee Report on Lake Encroachments.* Bengaluru: Government of Karnataka. https://data .opencity.in/dataset/bangalore-rural-urban-tanks-report/resource /koliwad-committee-report-on-lake-encroachments-in-bengaluru.

Kaul, Vivek. 2018. "The Great Indian NPA Mess: Banks, Govt and Industrialists Worked Together to Kick Bad Loans Can down the

Road." *Firstpost*, September 21. https://www.firstpost.com/business
/the-great-indian-npa-mess-banks-govt-and-industrialists-worked
-together-to-kick-bad-loans-can-down-the-road-5220771.html.

Kaul, Vivek. 2019. "India's Real Estate Sector Is Tied Up in Knots." *Deccan Herald*, October 27. https://www.deccanherald.com/india/india
-s-real-estate-sector-is-tied-up-in-knots-771415.html.

Kaul, Vivek. 2020. *Bad Money: Inside the NPA Mess and How It Threatens the Banking System*. Noida: Harper.

Keynes, John Maynard. 1935. *The General Theory of Employment, Interest and Money*. London: Palgrave Macmillan.

Khanna, Sundeep. 2019. "Indian Hospitals in ICU, Private Equity to the Rescue." *Mint*, January 3. https://www.livemint.com/Opinion
/zKcsYI5SsF0KMxcdT2hfdM/Opinion--Indian-hospitals-in-ICU
-private-equity-to-the-res.html.

Khilnani, Sunil. 2020. "Isabel Wilkerson's World-Historical Theory of Race and Caste." *New Yorker*, August 17. https://www.newyorker
.com/magazine/2020/08/17/isabel-wilkersons-world-historical
-theory-of-race-and-caste.

Kirkpatrick, L. Owen, and Michael Peter Smith. 2011. "The Infrastructural Limits to Growth: Rethinking the Urban Growth Machine in Times of Fiscal Crisis." *International Journal of Urban and Regional Research* 35 (3): 477–503. https://doi.org/10.1111/j.1468-2427.2011
.01058.x.

Knuth, Sarah. 2014. "Seeing Green: Speculative Urbanism and the Green Economy." PhD diss., University of California, Berkeley.

Kocieniewski, David, and Caleb Melby. 2020. "Private Equity Lands Billion-Dollar Backdoor Hospital Bailout." *Bloomberg*, June 2.
https://www.bloomberg.com/news/features/2020-06-02/private
-equity-lands-billion-dollar-backdoor-hospital-bailout.

Kodres, Laura. 2013. "What Is Shadow Banking?" *Finance and Development* 50 (2): 42–43. https://www.imf.org/external/pubs/ft/fandd
/2013/06/basics.htm.

Kothari, Ashish, Ariel Salleh, Arturo Escobar, Federico Demaria, and Alberto Acosta, eds. 2019. *Pluriverse: A Post-Development Dictionary*. New Delhi: Tulika Books.

KPMG International. 2009. *Bridging the Global Infrastructure Gap: Views from the Executive Suite*. London: Economist Intelligence Unit. https://impact.economist.com/perspectives/sites/default/files
/Bridging_global_infrastructure_gap.pdf.

Krippner, Greta. 2011. *Capitalizing on Crisis: The Political Origins of the Rise of Finance*. Cambridge, MA: Harvard University Press.

Kumar, Satish. 2015. "List of 56 Encroachments Released." *Hindu*,
May 16. https://www.thehindu.com/news/cities/bangalore/list-of-56
-encroachments-released/article7212334.ece.

Kundu, Amitabh. 2010. "Urban System in India: Trends, Economic Base, Governance, and a Perspective of Growth Under Globalization." In *India's New Economic Policy: A Critical Analysis*, edited by Waquar Ahmed, Amitabh Kundu, and Richard Peet, 90–110. New York: Routledge.

Kundu, Amitabh. 2013. "Making Indian Cities Slum-Free: Vision and Operationalisation." *Economic and Political Weekly* 48 (17): 15–18. https://www.jstor.org/stable/23527179.

Langley, Paul. 2020. "The Financialization of Life." In *The Routledge International Handbook of Financialization*, edited by Philip Mader, Daniel Mertens, and Natascha van der Zwan, 68–78. Oxford: Routledge.

Lapavitsas, Costas. 2014. *Profiting Without Producing: How Finance Exploits Us All*. London: Verso.

Lapavitsas, Costas, and Jeff Powell. 2013. "Financialisation Varied: A Comparative Analysis of Advanced Economies." *Cambridge Journal of Regions Economy and Society* 6 (3): 359–79. https://doi.org/10.1093/cjres/rst019.

Latouche, Serge. 2009. *Farewell to Growth*. Hoboken, NJ: Wiley.

Lee, Marissa, and Kainoa Blaisdell. 2021. "Why Indian Buyouts Are Well Positioned for Growing Private Capital Support." Preqin, April 28.

Lee Enterprises. 2022. *Building Long-Term Value—Investor Presentation*. February 22. Davenport, IA: Lee Enterprises. https://www.sec.gov/Archives/edgar/data/58361/000110465922025705/tm222792d16_defa14a.htm.

Lefcoe, George, and Charles W. Swenson. 2014. "Redevelopment in California: The Demise of TIF-Funded Redevelopment in California and Its Aftermath." *National Tax Journal* 67 (3): 719–44. https://doi.org/10.17310/ntj.2014.3.09.

Lefebvre, Henri. 1991. *The Production of Space*. Oxford: Blackwell.

Leitner, Helga, and Eric Sheppard. 2018. "From Kampungs to Condos? Contested Accumulations Through Displacement in Jakarta." *Environment and Planning A: Economy and Space* 50 (2): 437–56. https://doi.org/10.1177/0308518X17709279.

Leitner, Helga, and Eric Sheppard. 2020. "Towards an Epistemology for Conjunctural Inter-Urban Comparison." *Cambridge Journal of Regions, Economy and Society* 13 (3): 491–508. https://doi.org/10.1093/cjres/rsaa025.

Leitner, Helga, and Eric Sheppard. 2021. "Global Urbanism Inside/Out: Thinking Through Jakarta." In *Global Urbanism: Knowledge, Power, and the City*, edited by Michele Lancione and Colin McFarlane, 107–15. London: Routledge.

Leitner, Helga, and Eric Sheppard. 2023. "Unleashing Speculative Urbanism: Speculation and Urban Transformations." *Environment and*

Planning A: Economy and Space 55 (2): 359–66. https://doi.org/10
.1177/0308518X231151945.

Levien, Michael. 2011. "Special Economic Zones and Accumulation by Dispossession in India." *Journal of Agrarian Change* 11 (4): 454–83. https://doi.org/10.1111/j.1471-0366.2011.00329.x.

Levien, Michael. 2012. "The Land Question: Special Economic Zones and the Political Economy of Dispossession in India." *Journal of Peasant Studies* 39 (3–4): 933–69. https://doi.org/10.1080/03066150 .2012.656268.

Levien, Michael. 2013. "Regimes of Dispossession: From Steel Towns to Special Economic Zones." *Development and Change* 44 (2): 381–407. https://doi.org/10.1111/dech.12012.

Levien, Michael. 2018. *Dispossession Without Development: Land Grabs in Neoliberal India.* New York: Oxford University Press.

Li, Tania Murray. 2014. "What Is Land? Assembling a Resource for Global Investment." *Transactions of the Institute of British Geographers* 39 (4): 589–602. https://doi.org/10.1111/tran.12065.

Li, Zhigang, Xun Li, and Lei Wang. 2014. "Speculative Urbanism and the Making of University Towns in China: A Case of Guangzhou University Town." *Habitat International* 44:422–31. https://doi.org /10.1016/j.habitatint.2014.08.005.

Lin, Ken-Hou, and Donald Tomaskovic-Devey. 2013. "Financialization and U.S. Income Inequality, 1970–2008." *American Journal of Sociology* 118 (5): 1284–329. https://doi.org/10.1086/669499.

López, Isidro, and Emmanuel Rodríguez. 2011. "The Spanish Model." *New Left Review*, no. 69, 5–28. https://newleftreview.org/issues/ii69 /articles/isidro-lopez-emmanuel-rodriguez-the-spanish-model.

Luby, Martin J., and Tima Moldogaziev. 2014. "Tax Increment Debt Finance and the Great Recession." *National Tax Journal* 67 (3): 676–96. https://doi.org/10.17310/ntj.2014.3.07.

Lucarelli, Stefano. 2010. "Financialization as Biopower." In *Crisis in the Global Economy: Financial Markets, Social Struggles, and New Political Scenarios*, edited by Andrea Fumagalli and Sandro Mezzadra, 119–38. Cambridge, MA: MIT Press.

Lustgarten, Abrahm. 2022. "Caribbean Nations Are Trapped Between the Global Financial System and a Looming Climate Disaster. One Country's Leader Has Been Fighting to Find a Way Out." *New York Times Magazine*, July 27. https://www.nytimes.com /interactive/2022/07/27/magazine/barbados-climate-debt-mia -mottley.html.

Macquarie Infrastructure Group. 2011. *Macquarie Atlas Roads Annual Report 2011.* https://d3ar6irj6sybdw.cloudfront.net/stores /_sharedfiles/Investor_Resources/Annual_Reports/mqa-annual -report-2011.pdf.

Mamdani, Mahmood. 2020. *Neither Settler nor Native: The Making and Unmaking of Permanent Minorities.* Cambridge, MA: Harvard University Press.

Mammen, David. 2001. "Roundtable discussion for the International Division of the American Planning Association." *Interplan* (June):2–9.

Mani, Anjana. 2017. "The Disinvestment Programme in India: Impact on Efficiency and Performance of Disinvested Government Controlled Enterprises (1991–2010). *Dharana—International Journal of Business from M. P. Birla Institute of Management, Bengaluru* 11 (2): 32–41. https://www.mpbim.com/manage/images/pioneersuploads/_Disinvestment%20Programme%20in%20India%20-%20Impact%20_%20Anjana%20Mani.pdf.

Manor, James. 2007. "Change in Karnataka over the Last Generation: Villages and the Wider Context." *Economic and Political Weekly* 42 (8): 653–60. https://www.jstor.org/stable/4419280.

Marx, Karl, and Frederick Engels. 1997. *Marx and Engels Collected Works.* Vol. 36, London: Lawrence and Wishart.

Mathur, Anuradha, and Dilip da Cunha. 2006. *Deccan Traverses: The Making of Bengaluru's Terrain.* New Delhi: Rupa.

Mawdsley, Emma. 2018. "Development Geography II: Financialization." *Progress in Human Geography* 42 (2): 264–74. https://doi.org/10.1177/0309132516678747.

Mayur, A. M., S. Hattappa, M. Mahadevamurthy, and A. K. Chakravarthy. 2013. "The Land Use Pattern Changes due to Establishment of Bangalore International Airport." *Global Journal of Agriculture, Biology and Health Services* 2 (2): 34–37. https://www.walshmedicalmedia.com/open-access/the-land-use-pattern-changes-due-to-establishment-of-bangalore-international-airport-bia.pdf.

McKinsey. 2022. *McKinsey Global Private Markets Review* 2022. New York: McKinsey.

McNamara, Robert. 1981. *The McNamara Years at the World Bank: Major Policy Addresses of Robert S. McNamara, 1968–1981.* Baltimore: Johns Hopkins University Press.

Mehta, Uday Singh. 1999. *Liberalism and Empire: A Study in Nineteenth Century British Liberal Thought.* Chicago: University of Chicago Press.

Mehta, Vishal K., Rimi Goswami, Eric Kemp-Benedict, Sekhar Muddu, and Deepak Malghan. 2014. "Metabolic Urbanism and Environmental Justice: The Water Conundrum in Bangalore, India." *Environmental Justice* 7 (5): 130–37.

Melamed, Jodi. 2015. "Racial Capitalism." *Critical Ethnic Studies* 1 (1): 76–85. https://doi.org/10.5749/jcritethnstud.1.1.0076.

Mellor, Mary. 2022. "Democratizing Finance or Democratizing Money?" In *Democratizing Finance: Restructuring Credit to Transform Society*, edited by Fred Block and Robert Hockett, 233–42. London: Verso.

Merchant, A., M. S. Mohan Kumar, P. N. Ravindra, P. Vyas, and U. Manohar. 2014. "Analytics Driven Water Management System for Bangalore City." *Procedia Engineering* 70:1137–46. https://doi.org/10.1016/j.proeng.2014.02.126.

Ministry of Civil Aviation and Bangalore International Airport Limited (BIAL). 2004. *Concession Agreement for the Development, Construction, Operation and Maintenance of the Bengaluru International Airport.* N.p.: Ministry of Civil Aviation.

Ministry of Urban Employment and Poverty Alleviation and Ministry of Urban Development. 2005. *Jawaharlal Nehru National Urban Renewal Mission.* Government of India. https://mohua.gov.in/upload/uploadfiles/files/1Mission%20Overview%20English(1).pdf.

Mirowski, Philip, and Dieter Plehwe, eds. 2015. *The Road from Mont Pèlerin: The Making of the Neoliberal Thought Collective.* Cambridge, MA: Harvard University Press.

Mitchell, Timothy. 2002. *Rule of Experts: Egypt, Techno-Politics, Modernity.* Berkeley: University of California Press.

Montaner, Josep Maria. 2010. "The Barcelona Model Reviewed: From the Beginning of Democracy to Now." *Transfer* 7:48–53. https://docs.llull.cat/IMAGES_175/transfer07-foc03.pdf.

Moreno, Louis. 2014. "The Urban Process Under Financialised Capitalism." *City* 18 (3): 244–68. https://doi.org/10.1080/13604813.2014.927099.

Moreno, Louis. 2018. "Always Crashing in the Same City: Real Estate, Psychic Capital and Planetary Desire." *City* 22 (1): 152–68. https://doi.org/10.1080/13604813.2018.1434295.

Morran, Chris, and Daniel Petty. 2022. "What Private Equity Firms Are and How They Operate." *ProPublica*, August 3. https://www.propublica.org/article/what-is-private-equity.

Moser, Whet. 2012. "How Much Do TIFs Cost the Chicago Public Schools?" *Chicago Magazine*, April 12. https://www.chicagomag.com/city-life/april-2012/how-much-do-tifs-cost-the-chicago-public-schools/.

Moser, Whet. 2013. "The Truth About TIFs: A New Study Suggests Chicago's Massive Use of the Controversial Tax-Financing Program Doesn't Benefit the City." *Chicago Magazine*, December 18. https://www.chicagomag.com/chicago-magazine/january-2014/the-truth-about-tifs/.

Mosse, David. 2018. "Caste and Development: Contemporary Perspectives on a Structure of Discrimination and Advantage." *World Development* 110:422–36. https://doi.org/10.1016/j.worlddev.2018.06.003.

Mundoli, Seema, B. Manjunatha, and Harini Nagendra. 2016. *Losing the Commons: Rapid Changes in Gunda Thopes in Bangalore*. Bangalore: National Institute of Advanced Studies.

Mundoli, Seema, B. Manjunatha, and Harini Nagendra. 2018. "Lakes of Bengaluru: The Once Living, but Now Endangered Peri-Urban Commons." Working Paper Series 10. Azim Premji University.

Munro, William. 2017. "Analyzing Transnational Policy Networks: Outline of a Research Strategy." Unpublished manuscript.

Murthy, Prabha. 1997. "Report of Court Appointed Commissioner Prabha Murthy on Green Belt Violations." Bangalore: Karnataka Legislature.

Nagaraj, R. 2005. "Public Sector Performance Since 1950: A Fresh Look." *Economic and Political Weekly* 41 (25): 2551–57.

Nagendra, Harini. 2016. *Nature in the City: Bengaluru in the Past, Present, and Future*. New Delhi: Oxford University Press.

Naiman, Robert, and Neil Watkins. 1999. *A Survey of the Impacts of IMF Structural Adjustment in Africa: Growth, Social Spending, and Debt Relief*. Center for Economic and Policy Research. https://www.cepr.net/documents/publications/debt_1999_04.htm.

Nair, Janaki. 2005. *The Promise of the Metropolis: Bangalore's Twentieth Century*. New Delhi: Oxford University Press.

Nair, Janaki. 2021. "Subverting Reservations in Karnataka." *India Forum*, May 27. https://www.theindiaforum.in/article/subverting-reservations-karnataka.

Nam, Sylvia. 2017. "Urban Speculation, Economic Openness, and Market Experiments in Phnom Penh." *positions: asia critique* 25 (4): 64567. https://doi.org/10.1215/10679847-4188350.

Nandy, Madhurima. 2018. "The Rise and Rise of Blackstone in India." *Mint*, March 26. https://www.livemint.com/Companies/sAmeIFH75FWRKJTPbXKwyK/The-rise-and-rise-of-Blackstone-in-India.html.

Naoroji, Dadabhai. 1888. *Poverty of India: Papers and Statistics*. London: W. Foulger.

Narayan, Amay. 2019. "A Brief Survey of the Real Estate Sector in India: Aggregate and Firm-Level Financial Trends." Working paper. Speculative Urbanism Project, Bangalore: National Institute of Advanced Studies.

Narayan, Devika. 2022. "Platform Capitalism and Cloud Infrastructure: Theorizing a Hyper-Scalable Computing Regime." *Environment and Planning A: Economy and Space* 54 (5): 911–29. https://doi.org/10.1177/0308518X221094028.

NewsGuild–Communications Workers of America. 2020. "Fear the Vulture: Alden Destroys News Organizations While Promising to Save Them." *Hedge Clippers* (blog), September 10. https://hedgeclippers

.org/fear-the-vulture-alden-destroys-news-organizations-while
-promising-to-save-them/.

New York City Independent Budget Office. 2004. "West Side Financing's
Complex, $1.3 Billion Story." Fiscal Brief, August. https://www.ibo
.nyc.ny.us/iboreports/WestsidefinanceFB.pdf.

Nichols, Robert. 2020. *Theft Is Property! Dispossession and Critical Theory.* Durham, NC: Duke University Press.

Nicolaou, Anna, and James Fontanella-Khan. 2021. "The Fight for the
Future of America's Local Newspapers." *Financial Times,* January 20. https://www.ft.com/content/5c22075c-f1af-431d-bf39
-becf9c54758b.

Norris, Michelle, and Michael Byrne. 2015. "Asset Price Keynesianism,
Regional Imbalances and the Irish and Spanish Housing Booms
and Busts." *Built Environment* 41 (2): 227–43. https://doi.org/10
.2148/benv.41.2.227.

Nowak, Samuel. 2023. "The Social Lives of Network Effects: Speculation
and Risk in Jakarta's Platform Economy." *Environment and Planning A: Economy and Space* 55 (2): 471–89. https://doi.org/10.1177
/0308518X211056953.

O'Connor, James. 1984. *Accumulation Crisis.* New York: Basil Blackwell.

O'Connor, James. 1988. "Capitalism, Nature, Socialism: A Theoretical
Introduction." *Capitalism, Nature, Socialism* 1 (1): 11–38. https://doi
.org/10.1080/10455758809358356.

Omvedt, Gail. 1994. *Dalits and the Democratic Revolution: Dr. Ambedkar and the Dalit Movement in Colonial India.* New Delhi: Sage.

Omvedt, Gail. 2011. *Understanding Caste: From Buddha to Ambedkar
and Beyond.* New Delhi: Orient BlackSwan.

Organisation for Economic Cooperation and Development. 2002. *Foreign
Direct Investment for Development.* Paris: OECD Directorate.

Organisation for Economic Cooperation and Development. 2009.
Benchmark Definition of Foreign Direct Investment. Paris: OECD
Directorate.

Ouma, Stefan. 2016. "From Financialization to Operations of Capital:
Historicizing and Disentangling the Finance–Farmland-Nexus."
Geoforum 72:82–93. https://doi.org/10.1016/j.geoforum.2016.02.003.

Pacewicz, Josh. 2013. "Tax Increment Financing, Economic Development
Professionals and the Financialization of Urban Politics." *Socio-
Economic Review* 11 (3): 413–40. https://doi.org/10.1093/ser/mws019.

PAH (Plataforma de Afectados por la Hipoteca). N.d. "Qué es la PAH."
Accessed May 19, 2025. https://afectadosporlahipoteca.com/que-es
-la-pah/.

Palomera, Jaime. 2014. "How Did Finance Capital Infiltrate the World
of the Urban Poor? Homeownership and Social Fragmentation
in a Spanish Neighborhood." *International Journal of Urban and*

Regional Research 38 (1): 218–35. https://doi.org/10.1111/1468-2427 .12055.

Palter, Robert, and Herbert Pohl. 2014. *Money Isn't Everything (but We Need $57 Trillion for Infrastructure).* New York: McKinsey Global Institute.

Pandian, M. S. S. 2007. *Brahmin and Non-Brahmin: Genealogies of the Tamil Political Present.* Delhi: Permanent Black.

Pani, Narendar, and Chidambaran G. Iyer. 2013. *Evaluation of the Processes in the Implementation of Jawaharlal Nehru National Urban Renewal Mission in Karanataka.* Report, Karnataka Evaluation Authority, Planning Programme Monitoring and Statistics Department. Bangalore: National Institute of Advanced Studies.

Parsons, Richard, and James Nguyen. 2017. "Bank Consolidation Before and After the 2008 Crisis." *Applied Economics Letters* 24 (2): 98–101. https://doi.org/10.1080/13504851.2016.1164815.

Patil, N. K. 2011. *Preservation of Lakes in the City of Bengaluru: Report of the Committee Constituted by the High Court of Karnataka to Examine the Ground Realities and Prepare an Action Plan for Preservation of Lakes in the City of Bengaluru.* Bangalore: High Court of Karnataka. http://static.esgindia.org/campaigns/lakes/legal/A1_HC _Lakes_Report_WP_817_2008_HC_Feb_2011.pdf.

Pattem, Leah. 2021. "Evictions Are State Violence and Institutional Theft." *Madrid No Frills*, July 15. https://madridnofrills.com /evictions-are-state-violence-and-institutional-theft/.

Paul, Ahita. 2018. "Examining the Rise of Non-Performing Assets in India." *PRS Legislative Research*, September 13. https://prsindia.org /theprsblog/examining-the-rise-of-non-performing-assets-in-india.

Paul, Samuel. 1998. *Making Voice Work: The Report Card on Bangalore's Public Service.* Bengaluru: Public Affairs Centre. https:// opac.igidr.ac.in/cgi-bin/koha/opac-detail.pl?biblionumber =132389&shelfbrowse_itemnumber=433660.

Pearl, Robert. 2023. "Private Equity and the Monopolization of Medical Care." *Forbes Magazine*, February 20. https://www.forbes.com/sites /robertpearl/2023/02/20/private-equity-and-the-monopolization-of -medical-care/.

Peck, Jamie. 2012. "Austerity Urbanism: American Cities Under Extreme Economy." *City* 16 (6): 626–55. https://doi.org/10.1080/13604813 .2012.734071.

Peck, Jamie. 2017. "Transatlantic City, Part 1: Conjunctural Urbanism." *Urban Studies* 54 (1): 4–30. https://doi.org/10.1177 /0042098016679355.

Peck, Jamie. 2024. "Practicing Conjunctural Methodologies: Engaging Chinese Capitalism." *Dialogues in Human Geography* 14 (3): 461–82. https://doi.org/10.1177/20438206231154346.

Pereira, Alvaro Luis Dos Santos. 2017. "Financialization of Housing in Brazil: New Frontiers." *International Journal of Urban and Regional Research* 41 (4): 604–22. https://doi.org/10.1111/1468-2427.12518.

Peterson, George. 2008. "Unlocking Land Values to Finance Urban Infrastructure: Land-Based Financing Options for Cities." *Gridlines*, August. https://documents1.worldbank.org/curated/en/209711468316175525/pdf/462640BRI0Box31nlocking1Land1Values.pdf.

Pike, Andy, Peter O'Brien, and Tom Strickland. 2019. *Financialising City Statecraft and Infrastructure*. Northampton, MA: Elgar.

Piketty, Thomas. 2014. *Capital in the Twenty-First Century*. Cambridge, MA: Belknap Press of Harvard University Press.

Piliavsky, Anastasia, ed. 2014. *Patronage as Politics in South Asia*. New Delhi: Cambridge University Press.

Pistor, Katharina. 2019. *The Code of Capital: How the Law Creates Wealth and Inequality*. Princeton, NJ: Princeton University Press.

Polanyi, Karl. 1957. *The Great Transformation: The Political and Economic Origins of Our Times*. 2nd ed. Boston: Beacon.

Poznar, Zoltan, Tobias Adrian, Adam Ashcraft, and Hayley Boesky. 2010. *Shadow Banking*. New York: New York Federal Reserve Bank.

Pratley, Nils. 2024. "Cheap Sales, Debt, and Foreign Takeovers: How Privatisation Changed the Water Industry." *Guardian*, July 10. https://www.theguardian.com/business/article/2024/jul/10/cheap-sales-debt-and-foreign-takeovers-how-privatisation-changed-the-water-industry.

Preqin. 2025. *Preqin 2025 Global Report: Private Equity*. London: Preqin. https://www.preqin.com/insights/global-reports/2025-private-equity.

Press Trust of India. 2018. "Karnataka Elections Most Expensive Ever in Terms of Expenditure by Parties, Candidates: Survey." *Economic Times*, May 14. https://economictimes.indiatimes.com/news/politics-and-nation/karnataka-state-polls-most-expensive-ever-in-terms-of-expenditure-by-parties-and-candidates-survey/articleshow/64159293.cms?from=mdr.

PricewaterhouseCoopers (PwC). 2005. *Cities of the Future: Global Competition, Local Leadership*. London: PricewaterhouseCoopers.

PricewaterhouseCoopers (PwC). 2007. *Cities of Opportunity*. London: PricewaterhouseCoopers.

PricewaterhouseCoopers (PwC). 2019. *Creating the Smart Cities of the Future: A Three-Tier Development Model for Digital Transformation of Citizen Services*. London: PricewaterhouseCoopers.

PricewaterhouseCoopers and Global Infrastructure Facility. 2020. *Increasing Private Sector Investment into Sustainable City Infrastructure*. London: PricewaterhouseCoopers and Global Infrastructure Facility, January 1. https://www.pwc.com/gx/en/industries/capital-projects-infrastructure/publications/making-cities-investable.html.

Private Equity Stakeholder Project (PESP). 2018. "KKR, Bain Capital, Vornado Repeatedly Rewarded Themselves for Adding Debt to Toys'R'Us." Private Equity Stakeholder Project, May 29. https://pestakeholder.org/news/kkr-bain-capital-vornado-repeatedly-rewarded-themselves-for-adding-debt-to-toys-r-us/.

Public-Private Infrastructure Advisory Facility (PPIAF). N.d. "Results." Accessed May 10, 2023. https://www.ppiaf.org/results.

Raghavan, Anita. 2017. "India's Bad Debt Is Looking Better to Investors." *New York Times*, May 29.

Raj, Krishna. 2013a. "Sustainable Urban Habitats and Urban Water Supply: Accounting for Unaccounted for Water in Bangalore City, India." *Current Urban Studies* 1 (4): 156–65. https://doi.org/10.4236/cus.2013.14017.

Raj, Krishna. 2013b. "Where All the Water Has Gone? An Analysis of Unreliable Water Supply in Bangalore City." Working Paper 307. Institute for Social and Economic Change, Bangalore.

Rajashekar, Anirudh V. 2015. "Do Private Water Tankers in Bangalore Exhibit 'Mafia-Like' Behavior?" Master's thesis, Massachusetts Institute of Technology. http://hdl.handle.net/1721.1/99090.

Ramachandra, T. V., et al. 2015. *Wetlands: Treasure of Bangalore.* ENVIS Technical Report 101. Bangalore: Energy and Wetlands Research Group, Centre for Ecological Sciences, Indian Institute of Science.

Ramachandra, T. V., Bharath Setturu, K. S. Rajan, and M. D. Subash Chandran. 2016. "Stimulus of Developmental Projects to Landscape Dynamics in Uttara Kannada, Central Western Ghats." *Egyptian Journal of Remote Sensing and Space Science* 19 (2): 175–93. https://doi.org/10.1016/j.ejrs.2016.09.001.

Ramaswamy, A. T. 2007a. *Joint House Committee Report on Land Grabbing.* Bengaluru: Karnataka Legislature.

Ramaswamy, A. T. 2007b. *Joint Legislature Committee on Encroachments in Bengaluru Urban District: Interim Report Part II.* Bengaluru: Karnataka Legislature.

Ramsamy, Edward. 2006. *World Bank and Urban Development: From Projects to Policy.* Abingdon: Routledge.

Ranganathan, Malini. 2010. "Fluid Hegemony: A Political Ecology of Water, Market Rule, and Insurgence at Bangalore's Frontier." PhD diss., University of California, Berkeley.

Ranganathan, Malini. 2014. "Paying for Pipes, Claiming Citizenship: Political Agency and Water Reforms at the Urban Periphery." *International Journal of Urban and Regional Research* 38 (2): 590–608. https://doi.org/10.1111/1468-2427.12028.

Ranganathan, Malini. 2022. "Caste, Racialization, and the Making of Environmental Unfreedoms in Urban India." *Ethnic and Racial Studies* 45 (2): 257–77. https://doi.org/10.1080/01419870.2021.1933121.

Ranganathan, Malini, Lalitha Kamath, and Vinay Baindur. 2009. "Piped Water Supply to Greater Bangalore: Putting the Cart Before the Horse?" *Economic and Political Weekly* 44 (33): 53–62. https://www .epw.in/journal/2009/33/special-articles/piped-water-supply-greater -bangalore-putting-cart-horse.html.

Ranganathan, Malini, David L. Pike, and Sapana Doshi. 2023. *Corruption Plots: Stories, Ethics, and Publics of the Late Capitalist City*. Durham, NC: Duke University Press.

Rao, Anupama. 2009. *The Caste Question: Dalits and the Politics of Modern India*. Berkeley: University of California Press.

Rao, K. S. Chalapati, and Biswajit Dhar. 2011. *India's FDI Inflows: Trends and Concepts*. New Delhi: Institute for Studies in Industrial Development. https://isid.org.in/wp-content/uploads/2022/09/WP138 .pdf.

Rao, K. S. Chalapati, and Biswajit Dhar. 2018. *India's Recent Inward Foreign Direct Investment: An Assessment*. New Delhi: Institute for Studies in Industrial Development.

Rao, Usha. 2024. "Metro Mutations." In *Chronicles of a Global City: Speculative Lives and Unsettled Futures in Bengaluru*, edited by Vinay Gidwani, Michael Goldman, and Carol Upadhya, 123–38. Minneapolis: University of Minnesota Press.

Rao, Usha, and Gautam Sonti, dirs. 2014. *Namma Metro/Our Metropolis*. Documentary film. https://www.ourmetropolis.in/.

Rath, Sharadini. 2017. "The City as Dichotomy." *Seminar*. https://www .india-seminar.com/2017/694/694_sharadini_rath.htm.

Rathi, V. 2017. *Analysis of Institutional Funding in Real Estate*. Mumbai: Knight Frank.

ReFund and ReBuild. 2013. *The Looting of Oakland: How Wall Street's Predatory Practices Are Costing Oakland Communities Millions and What We Can Do About It*. Oakland, CA: Oakland Coalition. https://d3n8a8pro7vhmx.cloudfront.net/reinvestinoakland/pages/13 /attachments/original/1372215628/The_Looting_of_Oakland-Wall _St_Predatory_Practices_June_2013.pdf?1372215628.

Robertson, Benjamin, and Beata Wijeratne. 2021. "Private Equity Is Smashing Records with Multi-Billion M&A Deals." *Bloomberg*, September 17. https://www.bloomberg.com/news/articles/2021-09-17 /private-equity-is-smashing-records-with-multi-billion-m-a-deals.

Robinson, Cedric J. 1983. *Black Marxism: The Making of the Black Radical Tradition*. London: Zed.

Robinson, Jennifer. 2011. "Cities in a World of Cities: The Comparative Gesture." *International Journal of Urban and Regional Research* 35 (1): 1–23. https://doi.org/10.1111/j.1468-2427.2010.00982.x.

Robinson, Jennifer. 2022. *Comparative Urbanism: Tactics for Global Urban Studies*. Oxford: John Wiley and Sons.

Rodrigues, João, Ana C. Santos, and Nuno Teles. 2016. "Semi-Peripheral Financialisation: The Case of Portugal." *Review of International Political Economy* 23 (3): 480–510. https://doi.org/10.1080/09692290 .2016.1143381.

Rolnik, Raquel. 2019. *Urban Warfare: Housing Under the Empire of Finance*. London: Verso.

Rose, Nikolas. 1999. *Powers of Freedom: Reframing Political Thought*. Cambridge: Cambridge University Press.

Rothstein, Richard. 2017. *The Color of Law: A Forgotten History of How Our Government Segregated America*. New York: Liveright.

Rouanet, Hortense, and Ludovic Halbert. 2016. "Leveraging Finance Capital: Urban Change and Self-Empowerment of Real Estate De-velopers in India." *Urban Studies* 53 (7): 1401–23. https://doi.org/10 .1177/0042098015585917.

Roy, Ananya, and Aihwa Ong. 2011. *Worlding Cities: Asian Experiments and the Art of Being Global*. Oxford: Blackwell.

Roy, Anup. 2018. "Year Ender 2018: NPAs of Indian Banks Surged Past Rs. 10 Trillion." *Business Standard*, December 25. https://www .business-standard.com/article/economy-policy/year-ender-2018-npas -of-indian-banks-surged-past-rs-10-trillion-118122500654_1.html.

Roy, Satyaki. 2020. *Contours of Value Capture: India's Neoliberal Path of Industrial Development*. New York: Cambridge University Press.

RoyChowdhury, Supriya. 2005. "Labour Activism and Women in the Unorganised Sector: Garment Export Industry in Bangalore." *Economic and Political Weekly* 40 (22/23): 2250–55.

RoyChowdhury, Supriya. 2021. *City of Shadows: Slums and Informal Work in Bangalore*. New Delhi: Cambridge University Press.

Ruparelia, Sanjay, Sanjay Reddy, John Harris, and Stuart Corbridge, eds. 2011. *Understanding India's New Political Economy: A Great Trans-formation?* New York: Routledge.

Sabarinath, M. 2014. "US Private Equity Firm Kohlberg Kravis Roberts to Invest Rs 750 Crore in 2 Realty Projects in Metros." *Economic Times*, October 3. https://economictimes.indiatimes.com/wealth/personal -finance-news/us-private-equity-firm-kohlberg-kravis-roberts-to -invest-rs-750-crore-in-2-realty-projects-in-metros/articleshow /44146942.cms?from=mdr.

Sainath, P. 2018. "In India, Farmers Face a Terrifying Crisis." *New York Times*, April 13.

Sankhe, Shirish, Ireena Vittal, Richard Dobbs, et al. 2010. *India's Urban Awakening: Building Inclusive Cities, Sustaining Economic Growth*. New York: McKinsey Global Institute.

Sanyal, Kalyan. 2007. *Rethinking Capitalist Development: Primitive Accumulation, Governmentality and Postcolonial Capitalism*. New Delhi: Routledge.

Sarkar, Pooja. 2019. "How Blackstone Made India Its Largest Market in Asia." *Forbes India*, June 7. https://www.forbesindia.com/article /boardroom/how-blackstone-made-india-its-largest-market-in-asia /53849/1.

Sarkar, Swagato. 2015. "Beyond Dispossession." *Comparative Studies of South Asia, Africa and the Middle East* 35 (3): 438–50. https://doi .org/10.1215/1089201X-3426289.

Sassen, Saskia. 1991. *The Global City: New York, London, Tokyo.* Princeton, NJ: Princeton University Press

Sassen, Saskia. 1998. *Globalization and Its Discontents: Essays on the New Mobility of People and Money.* New York: New Press.

Sassen, Saskia. 2014. *Expulsions: Brutality and Complexity in the Global Economy.* Cambridge, MA: Belknap Press of Harvard University Press.

Schmelzer, Matthias, Aaron Vansintjan, and Andrea Vetter. 2022. *The Future Is Degrowth: A Guide to a World Beyond Capitalism.* London: Verso.

Schor, Juliet. 2010. *Plentitude: The New Economics of True Wealth.* New York: Penguin Books.

Schulte, Fred. 2022. "Sick Profit: Investigating Private Equity's Stealthy Takeover of Health Care Across Cities and Specialties." *Kaiser Health News*, November 14. https://kffhealthnews.org/news/article /private-equity-takeover-health-care-cities-specialties/.

Searle, Llerena Guiu. 2014. "Conflict and Commensuration: Contested Market Making in India's Private Real Estate Development Sector." *International Journal of Urban and Regional Research* 38 (1): 60–78. https://doi.org/10.1111/1468-2427.12042.

Searle, Llerena Guiu. 2016. *Landscapes of Accumulation: Real Estate and the Neoliberal Imagination in Contemporary India.* Chicago: University of Chicago Press.

Searle, Llerena Guiu. 2018. "The Contradictions of Mediation: Intermediaries and the Financialization of Urban Production." *Economy and Society* 47 (4): 524–46. https://doi.org/10.1080/03085147.2018.1538638.

Searle, Llerena Guiu. 2020. "Fragile Financialization: The Struggle for Power and Control in Indian Real-Estate Investment." *Metropolitics*, November 27. https://metropolitics.org/Fragile-Financialization -The-Struggle-for-Power-and-Control-in-Indian-Real.html.

Sell, Zach. 2021. *Trouble of the World: Slavery and Empire in the Age of Capital.* Chapel Hill: University of North Carolina Press.

Shah, Esha. 2008. "Telling Otherwise: A Historical Anthropology of Tank Irrigation Technology in South India." *Technology and Culture* 49 (3): 652–74. https://doi.org/10.1353/tech.0.0054.

Shah, Esha. 2012. "Seeing Like a Subaltern—Historical Ethnography of Pre-Modern and Modern Tank Irrigation Technology in Karnataka, India." *Water Alternatives* 5 (2): 507–38.

Sharma, Mukul. 2017. *Caste and Nature: Dalits and Indian Environmental Politics*. New Delhi: Oxford University Press.

Shatkin, Gavin. 2017. *Cities for Profit: The Real Estate Turn in Asia's Urban Politics*. Ithaca, NY: Cornell University Press.

Shaxson, Nicholas. 2018. *Treasure Islands: Tax Havens and the Men Who Stole the World*. New York: Vintage Books.

Shelton, Tracey, Christina Zhou, and Ning Pan. 2018. "China's Eerie Ghost Cities a 'Symptom' of the Country's Economic Troubles and Housing Bubble." ABC News, June 27. https://www.abc.net.au/news/2018-06-27/china-ghost-cities-show-growth-driven-by-debt/9912186.

Sheppard, Eric, Vinay Gidwani, Michael Goldman, Helga Leitner, Ananya Roy, and Anant Maringanti. 2015. "Introduction: Urban Revolutions in the Age of Global Urbanism." *Urban Studies* 52 (11): 1947–61. https://doi.org/10.1177/0042098015590050.

Shih, Mi, and Cecille de Laurentis. 2022. "Social Governance for Value Creation: State-Led Land Assembly, the Property Mind, and Speculative Urbanism in Taiwan." *Urban Geography* 43 (5): 784–92. https://doi.org/10.1080/02723638.2022.2054582.

Shin, Hyun Bang, and Soo-Hyun Kim. 2016. "The Developmental State, Speculative Urbanisation and the Politics of Displacement in Gentrifying Seoul." *Urban Studies* 53 (3): 540–59. https://doi.org/10.1177/0042098014565745.

Shivanand, Swathi. 2024. "Why Not Us?" In *Chronicles of a Global City: Speculative Lives and Unsettled Futures in Bengaluru*, edited by Vinay Gidwani, Michael Goldman, and Carol Upadhya, 176–87. Minneapolis: University of Minnesota Press.

Shruthi, H. M. 2018. "Officials Urge Government to Set Up Additional Anti-Land Grabbing Courts." *Hindu*, March 21. https://www.thehindu.com/news/cities/bangalore/officials-urge-government-to-set-up-additional-anti-land-grabbing-courts/article23314787.ece.

Simone, AbdouMaliq. 2004. "People as Infrastructure: Intersecting Fragments in Johannesburg." *Public Culture* 16 (3): 407–29. https://doi.org/10.1215/08992363-16-3-407.

Simpson, Leanne Betasamosake. 2017. *As We Have Always Done*. Minneapolis: University of Minnesota Press.

Singh, Yashswini, Ziriu Song, Daniel Polsky, Joseph D. Bruch, and Jane M. Zhu. 2022. "Association of Private Equity Acquisition of Physician Practices with Changes in Health Care Spending and Utilization." *JAMA Health Forum* 3 (9): e222886. https://doi.org/10.1001/jamahealthforum.2022.2886.

Smyth, Sharon R., and John Gittelsohn. 2013. "Blackstone Begins Rental Housing Empire in Spain." *Bloomberg*, November 7. https://www.bloomberg.com/news/articles/2013-11-07/blackstone-begins-rental-housing-empire-in-spain.

Somanaboina, Simhadri. 2022. "The Other Backward Classes: Pre-
and Post-Mandal India." In *The Routledge Handbook of the Other
Backward Classes in India: Thought, Movements and Development*,
edited by Simhadri Somanaboina and Akhileshwari Ramagoud,
215–53. Oxford: Routledge.

Sood, Ashima. 2019. "Speculative Urbanism." In *Wiley Blackwell Ency-
clopedia of Urban and Regional Studies*, edited by Anthony Orum.
Hoboken, NJ: Wiley. https://doi.org/10.1002/9781118568446.eurs0317.

Spielman, Fran. 2020. "Parking Meter Deal Chicagoans Love to Hate
Gets Worse—Again." *Chicago Sun-Times*, August 2.

Spielman, Fran. 2022. "Parking Meter Deal Gets Even Worse for Chicago
Taxpayers, Annual Audit Shows." *Chicago Sun-Times*, May 26.

Sreenivasa, Vinay. 2024. "Whose Streets?" In *Chronicles of a Global
City: Speculative Lives and Unsettled Futures in Bengaluru*, edited
by Vinay Gidwani, Michael Goldman, and Carol Upadhya, 207–16
Minneapolis: University of Minnesota Press.

Srinivas, M. N. 1994. *The Dominant Caste and Other Essays*. Delhi: Oxford University Press.

Sriram, M. 2023. "Indian Hospitals Set Investors' Pulses Racing in Post-
COVID Boom." *Reuters*, June 30. https://www.reuters.com/business
/healthcare-pharmaceuticals/indian-hospitals-set-investors-pulses
-racing-post-covid-boom-2023-06-30/.

Stiglitz, Joseph. 2019. "Nobel Laureate Economist Joseph Stiglitz: It's
Time for Congress to Do Something About the Economic Mess
That Private-Equity Giants Have Created." *Business Insider*, December 7. https://www.businessinsider.com/joseph-stiglitz-private
-equity-impact-us-economy-jobs-wages-2019-12.

Stockhammer, Engelbert. 2012. "Financialization, Income Distribution
and the Crisis." *Investigación Económica* 71 (279): 39–70. https://doi
.org/10.22201/fe.01851667p.2012.279.37326.

Strange, Susan. 1997. *Casino Capitalism*. Manchester: Manchester University Press.

Strathmann, Cynthia, Joe Donlin, Rachel Laforest, Tony Romano, and
Sarah Heck. 2014. *Renting from Wall Street: Blackstone's Invitation
Homes in Los Angeles and Riverside*. Los Angeles: Home for All
Campaign of the Right to the City Alliance. https://www.saje.net/wp
-content/uploads/2021/04/SAJE_RentingfromWallstreet_2014.pdf.

Structural Adjustment Participatory Review International Network
(SAPRIN). 2004. *Structural Adjustment: The SAPRI Report; The Policy
Roots of Economic Crisis, Poverty and Inequality*. Boston: Zed Books.

Subramanian, Ajantha. 2015. "Making Merit: The Indian Institutes of
Technology and the Social Life of Caste." *Comparative Studies
in Society and History* 57 (2): 291–322. https://doi.org/10.1017/
S0010417515000043.

Subramanian, Ajantha. 2019. *The Caste of Merit: Engineering Education in India*. Cambridge, MA: Harvard University Press.

Subramanian, Arvind, and Josh Felman. 2019. "India's Great Slowdown. What Happened? What's the Way Out?" CID Faculty Working Paper 370. Harvard Center for International Development, December. https://www.hks.harvard.edu/centers/cid/publications/faculty -working-papers/india-great-slowdown.

Sud, Nikita. 2014. "The Men in the Middle: A Missing Dimension in Global Land Deals." *Journal of Peasant Studies* 41 (4): 593–612. https://doi.org/10.1080/03066150.2014.920329.

Sudhira, H. S. n.d. *Bengaluru's Infrastructural Landscapes: Understanding the Historical Landscape of Water and Energy Infrastructure in Bengaluru*. Gubbi Labs, Bengaluru. Accessed May 20, 2025. https://gubbilabs.in/bengaluruscape/.

Swyngedouw, Erik, and Callum Ward. 2024. "Producing Assets: The Social Strife of Land." In *The Social Lives of Land*, edited by Michael Goldman, Nancy Peluso, and Wendy Wolford, 269–88. Ithaca, NY: Cornell University Press.

Táíwò, Olúfẹ́mi O. 2022. *Reconsidering Reparations*. New York: Oxford University Press.

Taylor, Keeanga-Yamahtta. 2019. *Race for Profit: How Banks and the Real Estate Industry Undermined Black Homeownership*. Chapel Hill: University of North Carolina Press.

Thorner, Daniel. 1950. *British Railway and Steam Shipping Enterprise in India, 1825–1849*. Philadelphia: University of Pennsylvania Press.

Thunberg, Greta. 2022. *The Climate Book: The Facts and the Solutions*. London: Penguin.

Tomaskovic-Devey, Donald, and Ken-Hou Lin. 2011. "Income Dynamics, Economic Rents, and the Financialization of the U.S. Economy." *American Sociological Review* 76 (4): 538–59. https://doi.org/10.1177 /0003122411414827.

Tooze, Adam. 2018. *Crashed: How a Decade of Financial Crises Changed the World*. New York: Penguin Books.

Torrance, Morag I. 2008. "Forging Glocal Governance? Urban Infrastructures as Networked Financial Products." *International Journal of Urban and Regional Research* 32 (1): 1–21. https://doi.org/10.1111/j .1468-2427.2007.00756.x.

Torrance, Morag I. 2009. "The Rise of a Global Infrastructure Market Through Relational Investing." *Economic Geography* 85 (1): 75–97. https://doi.org/10.1111/j.1944-8287.2008.01004.x.

Tremlett, Giles. 2012. "Valencia's Hopes Remain Grounded as It Bids for Bailout." *Guardian*, August 29. https://www.theguardian.com /world/2012/aug/29/valencia-hopes-remain-grounded-bailout.

Turner, John F. C., and Robert Fichter, eds. 1972. *Freedom to Build: Dweller Control of the Housing Process.* New York: Macmillan.

UN Conference on Trade and Development (UNCTAD). 2017. *Trade and Development Report, 2017, Beyond Austerity: Towards a Global New Deal.* Geneva: UNCTAD. https://unctad.org/publication/trade-and -development-report-2017.

Upadhya, Carol. 2016. *Reengineering India: Work, Capital, and Class in an Offshore Economy.* New Delhi: Oxford University Press.

Upadhya, Carol. 2020. "Assembling Amaravati: Speculative Accumulation in a New Indian City." *Economy and Society* 49 (1): 141–69. https://doi.org/10.1080/03085147.2019.1690257.

Upadhya, Carol, Vinay Gidwani, and Michael Goldman, eds. 2017. Special Issue on "The Great Transformation: Bangalore." *Seminar,* no. 694.

Upadhya, Carol, and Sachinkumar Rathod. 2021. "Caste at the City's Edge: Land Struggles in Peri-Urban Bengaluru." *South Asia Multidisciplinary Academic Journal*, no. 26. https://doi.org/10.4000/samaj.7134.

Urs, Anil. 2018. "Nearly One-Fifth of Lake Area in Bengaluru Encroached." *Hindu*, January 9. https://www.thehindubusinessline .com/news/national/nearly-onefifth-of-lake-area-in-bengaluru -encroached/article9969980.ece.

Vasavi, A. R. 2012. *Shadow Space: Suicides and the Predicament of Rural India.* Gurgaon, Haryana, India: Three Essays Collective.

Vasudevan, Ramaa. 2008. "Accumulation by Dispossession in India." *Economic and Political Weekly* 43 (11): 41–43.

Viswanath, Rupa. 2014. *The Pariah Problem: Caste, Religion, and the Social in Modern India.* New York: Columbia University Press.

Walton, John K., and David Seddon. 1994. *Free Markets and Food Riots: The Politics of Global Adjustment.* Cambridge, MA: Wiley-Blackwell.

Ward, Callum, and Erik Swyngedouw. 2018. "Neoliberalisation from the Ground Up: Insurgent Capital, Regional Struggle, and the Assetisation of Land." *Antipode* 50 (4): 1077–97. https://doi.org/10.1111/anti.12387.

Weber, Barbara, Mirjam Staub-Bisang, and Hans Wilhelm Alfen. 2016. *Infrastructure as an Asset Class: Investment Strategy, Sustainability, Project Finance and PPP.* 2nd ed. Hoboken, NJ: John Wiley and Sons.

Weber, Rachel. 2010. "Selling City Futures: The Financialization of Urban Redevelopment Policy." *Economic Geography* 86 (3): 251–74. https://doi.org/10.1111/j.1944-8287.2010.01077.x.

Weber, Rachel. 2015. *From Boom to Bubble: How Finance Built the New Chicago.* Chicago: University of Chicago Press.

Weisbrot, Mark, and Rebecca Ray. 2011. *Latvia's Internal Devaluation: A Success Story?* Washington, DC: Center for Economic and Policy Research.

Woetzel, Jonathan, Nicklas Garemo, Jan Mischke, Martin Hjerpe, and Robert Palter. 2016. *Bridging Global Infrastructure Gaps*. New York: McKinsey Global Institute.

Wolfson, Martin, and Gerald Epstein. 2013. *The Handbook of the Political Economy of Financial Crises*. New York: Oxford University Press.

World Bank. 1991. *Urban Policy and Economic Development: An Agenda for the 1990s*. Washington, DC: World Bank.

World Bank. 1994. *Infrastructure for Development*. New York: Oxford University Press.

World Bank. 2000. *Cities in Transition: World Bank Urban and Local Government Strategy*. Washington, DC: World Bank.

World Bank. 2009. *Systems of Cities: Harnessing Urbanization for Growth and Poverty Alleviation (English)*. Washington, DC: World Bank Group.

World Bank. 2012. *Rethinking Cities*. Washington, DC: World Bank.

World Bank. 2015. *India Land Governance Assessment: National Synthesis Report*. Washington, DC: World Bank.

World Bank. 2020. "City Creditworthiness Initiative: A Partnership to Deliver Municipal Finance." Accessed December 6, 2020. https://www.worldbank.org/en/topic/urbandevelopment/brief/city-creditworthiness-initiative.

World Cities Summit. 2010. "World Cities Summit 2010." Accessed May 22, 2023. https://www.worldcitiessummit.com.sg/about-us/past-editions/world-cities-summit-2010.

World Economic Forum. 2019. *The World Is Facing a $15 Trillion Infrastructure Gap by 2040. Here's How to Bridge It*. Davos: World Economic Forum.

World Resources Institute Ross Center for Sustainable Cities (WRI). n.d. "About." Accessed May 15, 2023. https://www.wri.org/cities/about.

Wu, Fulong. 2021. "The Long Shadow of the State: Financializing the Chinese City." *Urban Geography* 44 (1): 37–58. https://doi.org/10.1080/02723638.2021.1959779.

Wu, Fulong. 2022. "Land Financialisation and the Financing of Urban Development in China." *Land Use Policy* 112:104412. https://doi.org/10.1016/j.landusepol.2019.104412.

Yengde, Suraj. 2019. *Caste Matters*. New Delhi: Penguin Random House India.

Zappa, Marco. 2022. "'Greening' Speculative Urbanism? Space Politics and Model Circulation in South Korea and Vietnam's Special Economic Zones." *Nuovi Autoritarismi e Democrazie: Diritti, Istituzioni, Società* 4 (2): 68–86. https://doi.org/10.54103/2612-6672/19468.

Zérah, Marie-Hélène, Vèronique Dupont, and Stéphanie Tawa Lama-Rewal, eds. 2011. *Urban Policies and the Right to the City in India: Rights, Responsibilities and Citizenship*. New Delhi: UNESCO and CSH.

Zhang, Juan. 2017. "Introduction: Integrated Mega-Casinos and Speculative Urbanism in Southeast Asia." *Pacific Affairs* 90 (4): 651–74.
https://doi.org/10.5509/2017904651.

Zhang, Xin. 2008. "An Analysis of the Current Investment Trend in
the US Toll Road Sector." MS thesis, Massachusetts Institute of
Technology. https://dspace.mit.edu/bitstream/handle/1721.1/45620
/320453281-MIT.pdf.

Zoellick, Robert. 2010. "Remarks for Launch of the Infrastructure Finance Center of Excellence and Signing of MOUs for Singapore Hub
Projects." World Bank, November 10. https://documents1.worldbank
.org/curated/en/892801521628685358/pdf/Remarks-for-the-launch-of
-the-infrastructure-finance-center-of-excellence-and-signing-of-MOUs
-for-Singapore-hub-projects-by-Robert-B-Zoellick.pdf.

Zuloaga, Jorge. 2014. "Deutsche Bank Purchases Europe's Largest NPL
Portfolio from BBVA." AURA Real Estate Experts, Madrid. November
24. https://www.auraree.com/real-estate-news/deutsche-bank
-purchases-europes-largest-npl-portfolio-from-bbva/.

INDEX

Page numbers in italics indicate figures; those followed by "t" indicate tables.

Asian Development Bank: Bengaluru and, 141, 154, 233; BWSSB and, 8, 21, 163, 165; global urban turn and, 53, 225–26; Indian liberalization policies endorsed by, 95–97; India's payment commitments to, 94; JNNURM policies and, 99; *Managing Asian Cities* (report 2007), 96; World Cities Summit and, 65

Asian financial crisis (1997), 22, 24, 33

asset-backed commercial paper (ABCP) market, 80, 253n5

asset-manager society, 4, 13–14

asset values, 16, 227; collapse in Bengaluru, 21, 215, 219, 221; private value capture, 91; property value capture, 69; Wall Street's goal to increase in 1970s, 6–7. *See also* Bengaluru, financialization and emergence as global city

Atlanta, 110–11

Atlas Arteria, 250n10

AusAid, 163, 256n12

authoritarianism, 241–42

AXA (French fund), 91

Ayyathurai, Gajendran, 18

Bain Capital, 6–7, 224

Ballapura (dispossessed villagers from Arasinakunte moved to), 185, 188

Banco del Sur (Brazil), 58

Bangalore Development Agency (BDA), 153, 155–57, 161, 168, 198, 255nn5–6

Bangalore (former name of Bengaluru). *See* Bengaluru

Bangalore International Airport Limited (BIAL), 177–79. *See also* Bengaluru International Airport and surrounding area

Bangalore Water Supply and Sewerage Board (BWSSB), 8–9, 21, 153, 155; antiprivatization campaign against, 8, 11; brain drain and loss of employees, 165–66; caste and class in distribution of water supply, 160–61; shift in local governance and priorities for

water distribution, 158–68; World Bank and, 8, 21, 159, 163

Bangalore Woolen Factory, 146

banking-and-finance sector: capital reserve ratios and, 76; deregulation of, 5, 15, 75; GDP share, 30; Glass–Steagall Act repeal and, 76; in India, 198, 219–20, 259n16. *See also* finance (global finance capital); private equity firms and funds; Wall Street finance

Bank of America, 6, 82

Bank of England, 94

bankruptcy, 75, 81, 104, *105*, 106, 120, 219, 224, 229, 240

Barcelona, 39, 45–46, 88–92; destruction of history and heritage, 90–91; finance-driven infrastructure, 90–91; knowledge-based economy, 91–92; lack of affordable housing, 91; Olympics (1992), 89–91; property boom until 2008 financial crisis, 91; 22@ project, 91–92

Bates, Crispin, 18

Baucom, Ian, 3

Bayview Asset Management (Blackstone affiliate), 110

BBVA (Spanish bank), 91, 121–22

BDA. *See* Bangalore Development Agency

Bear, Laura, 33

Bellandur (Bengaluru lake), 144

Bengaluru (generally): construction workers, 34, 40, 190, 193, 224, *225*; environmental casteism and, 19; FDI in land and real estate sectors, 206; floods, 34, 162; IT Park, 9–11, *10*; IT professional class's growth in, 9–11, 151–52; land grabbing by officials, 11, 16–17, 19, 37, 152, 156–57, 172, 180, 182, 188, 194–95, 199–202, 233, 236, 245; luxury complexes, *137, 167,* 171, *204,* 205, 212, *212,* 222; Metro rail system, 99, 153, 237–38; neoliberalism in, 152; patrimonial regimes of governance and, 38, 157, 171, 197–202,

233; public bus transit, 237–38, 245; research in, 36–40; residential housing partially completed or partially empty, 135–36, *204*, 222; slum dwellers, 232–35, *246*; speculative urbanism and, 8–12, 131–32, 137, 141, 171, 176, 202, 234; street vendors, 10, 237; taking back the city, 238–48; transportation projects, 99, 101, 136 (*see also* Metro rail system, *above*); water shortage and lakes, 140–42, 144, 157–68, 245. *See also* Bengaluru, background and history of; Bengaluru, financialization and emergence as global city; Bengaluru International Airport and surrounding area

Bengaluru, background and history of, 38, 40, 139–68; BDA and growing power of parastatal agencies, 155–57, 168; Blackpetty (old Indian marketplace), 144; BWSSB (*see* Bangalore Water Supply and Sewerage Board); Cauvery River hydraulic system, 158–61; colonial era, 139–41, 143–47; conversion to European-style global city, 97; earliest settlements and precolonial era, 142–43; ecological stewardship, 142–43, 162; eminent domain of colonial era, 19, 145; exploitation of public works in colonial era, 146, 179; financialization replacing public sector development, 158–68; as global city, 141, 156; global financial crisis (2008) and, 12; gold mines, 145–46; government by layout, 156; government disinvesting, 152; greenspace sold illegally for housing and resorts, 157; housing shortage, 152, 155–56; hydro dams, 146; industrial growth, 141, 148–50; international finance institutions and, 141, 153–55, 158; IT economy and, 151–52; Karnataka's refusal of self-governance to, 153–54, 256n3; Land Acquisition Act (British Raj, 1894), 145; large-scale infra-

structure projects, influx of (1990s), 153; liberalization period, 140, 153–55; multinodal urbanism, 141, 151; name change from Bangalore (2014), 249n3, 254–55n1; neoliberal agenda and, 152; postindependence era, 141, 147–53; public goods as false binary, 145–46; as public sector city, 148–51, 206; public sector governance, demands for return to, 167–68; racialized economy of colonial era, 145–46; speculative urbanism and, 8–12, 141; union strikes, 152; water supply and access, 140–42, 158–68

Bengaluru, financialization and emergence as global city, 40, 141, 156, 169–202, 204, 209; Bengaluru-Mysore Infrastructure Corridor, 175–76, 256n2; burst of bubble (2010), 214–17; buyback commitments and court cases, 216; caste and land dispossession, 183–97, 202 (*see also* Bengaluru International Airport and surrounding area); comparison of boom and bust phases, 217, 218*t*; consolidation and decline in number of developers, 223*t*; conversion of public land into tradeable asset, 206; court cases to prosecute land grabbing, 156–57, 188, 194–95, 199, 201; developers' debt load and collapse of asset value, 21, 215, 219, 221; dispossession by financialization, 40, 172–75; eminent domain and, 19, 176, 182; family and social structure destroyed by, 195, 235–36; IT corridor, 151–52, 161, 166, 175; market consolidation bust phase (2011–present), 40, 209, 217–23, 218*t*; market-making boom phase (2005–10), 40, 209–14, 218*t*; master plan of city, corruption involved in changes to, 200; patrimonial regimes of governance and, 197–201; speculative land market, 11, 170, 175–76, 180–83, 198, 201–2, 209; toxic growth, 224–26, 225; zoning of land, 200

250n7; racialization of, 18; speculative land markets and, 16–17, 234; violence and, 171, 184. *See also* Dalits; Reddys; Vokkaligas

Catalonia, Spain, 89–90

Cauvery Water Supply Project (India), 158–61, 164–66, 168, 255n8

Center for Media Studies (New Delhi), 200

Cerberus Capital Management, 110, 116, 123

C40 Cities Climate Leadership Group, 39, 61, 67

chains of rentiership, 34, 214, 226, 228

Chandra, Kanchan, 169

Chang, David, 19

Chennai, India, 222

Chhabria, Sheetal, 18

Chicago: foreclosed homes in, 111; parking meter scandal in (2009), 105–10; Skyway toll road, 26, 28, 106, 108–9, 250n10, 253–54n1; tax increment financing, 79, 109

China: Belt and Road Initiative, 2; car manufacturing in India and, 128; ghost cities, 2; greenfield investment projects, 128; private equity firms and, 227; special economic zones (SEZs), 100–101, 207; transnational policy network funding cities in, 71; Twenty-First-Century Silk Road, 2

Christophers, Brett, 4, 125

Cintra-Macquarie, 108, 253n1

Cisco, 39, 129

Citibank, 79, 82, 239

Cities Alliance, 39, 61, 67

Citigroup, 6, 82, 252n5

climate change: activism as source of hope, 248; Bengaluru's water shortage and, 161–62; C40 Cities Climate Leadership Group, 39, 61, 67; climate-smart infrastructure projects, 60; Global South and, 247; infrastructure improvements needed due to, 103; transnational policy network including

strategists of, 53; urban growth linked to reversal of, 63, 66; World Bank and, 61

Clos, Joan, 47–48

cloud computing, 127

Coalition for Urban Transitions (CUT), 67

Cohen, Michael, 58

Colau, Ada, 244

collaboration. *See* elite networks; patrimonial regimes of governance

Colonial Capital, 110

colonial expropriation, effects of, 68, 145–46, 179, 248

company agency, 154

consulting firms, 62–65, 214–15

contracts for deeds, 112–13

Cornwallis, George, 143

corruption and clientelism, 20, 156, 169, 180, 195, 198–201, 259n16

Coulthard, Glen, 240

COVID-19 pandemic: bailout money for US health care companies, 116; evictions related to, 112–13; Global South and, 247; in India, 129–31; US nursing homes, 117

Credit Suisse, 91, 121

critical urban theorists, 249n4

Daley, Richard M., 106

Daley, William, Jr., 106

Dalits: activism of, 21, 232–38, 257n8; BWSSB distribution of water supply and, 160–61; in colonial Bangalore, 144–45; discrimination based on biological falsehoods, 18; dispossession and expropriation of land of, 16–19, 21, 157, 171, 177, 180–81, 197–201; experiences of the Bengaluru dispossessed, 19, 38, 184–97, *185–87, 189, 191–92,* 235–37; as farmworkers and farm owners, 170–71, 199; Gowda term used for village headmen and leaders, 257n8; in independent Bangalore, 141, 148; as self-designation of community, 249n6; as slum residents, 232–35, *246*

Facebook/Meta, 83, 129
Fannie Mae, 115
farms and farmers. *See* agricultural land and farmers
FDI. *See* foreign direct investment
Federal Reserve, 4, 81
Federation of Indian Chambers of Commerce and Industry (FICCI), 206
Ferrovial, 108
finance (global finance capital): British imperial history and, 35–36; capital recycling, 69; challenges created by, 3, 239; definancialization as the future, 248; elite networking of (*see* elite networks; patrimonial regimes of governance); enthusiasm for, 232; global networks of (*see* transnational policy network); high-risk borrowing and, 31; hoarding assets and profiting as goals, 127; hostile takeovers, 252n1; linked conditions of, 240; optics of, 22–30; relational dynamics in moments of crisis and, 22; right to demand national reforms as prerequisite to, 68; role in city life, 13–22, 240 (*see also* financialization of the city); in twenty-first century, 5–8; user fees and tolls, 4, 26, 28–29, 69, 87, 92, 94, 96, 103, 105, 121
financialization of the city, 5, 21, 24, 29, 34; as abstract concept, 231; Bengaluru and (*see* Bengaluru, financialization and emergence as global city); circulation of capital to create profits, 13; competition of world governments and, 48; defined, 13; dispossession by financialization, 17, 40 (*see also* dispossession); negatives of, 7, 9–10, *10*, 13, 15, 108, 119, 162–63, 226, 238; oversupply of unsold commercial real estate in Indian cities, 222; racial capitalism's historical agency and, 17–18; state falling in line with and acting on behalf of financiers and developers, 239

FIRE (finance, insurance, and real estate) sector, 5, 13, 92, 97, 123
floods, 34, 162
Fordism and US manufacturing, 14, 73, 75, 249n5
foreign currency to repay loans, 154, 163–65
foreign direct investment (FDI), 86–87, 93–94, 97, 100–102, 126–28, 206–7. *See also* private equity firms and funds
Foucault, Michel, 33, 49
franchising, 127
Franco, Francisco, 85–86, 90, 92
Friedman, Milton, 75
Front Yard Residential, 113–14
future. *See* postspeculative future

gender, 10, 170
General Atlantic, 130
General Electric, 146
General Motors, 128–29
Germany, 227, 243
ghost cities and towns, 2, 88–89, 120, *120*, 175
GIC-Singapore, 217
Gidwani, Vinay, 37–38
global cities and global-city making: China's Belt and Road Initiative and, 2; conference on (Barcelona 2012), 45–48, *46*; elite experts of, 20; formation of, 15; global urban turn and, 31–32, 35; India and, 51–52, 98–99, 138, 203; investment and spending priorities of, 20; original goals for, 225–26; world-class infrastructure, 1, 34, 47, 52. *See also* Bengaluru, financialization and emergence as global city
global civil society, 66
global consulting industry, 62–66, 99
global financial crisis (2008), 12–13; activists reacting to, 242; aftermath of, 2–3, 27, 46, 49, 104–32, 219, 247; causes of, 49, 82; financialization of

international financial institutions
(IFIs), 54, 57–58, 65, 95, 98–99;
Bengaluru economy and, 153–55,
158, 168; BWSSB local governance
and priorities for water distribution,
158–68. *See also* Asian Development
Bank; International Monetary Fund;
World Bank
International Monetary Fund (IMF):
debt relief/loan packages from, 33;
global urban turn and, 71; Indian
economic crisis and, 95; on shadow
banking system, 4, 82, 253n6; Spanish
financial crisis and, 122; staffing of
former colonial officers, 154; structural adjustment programs, 57
Invitation Homes (Blackstone subsidiary), 110–11, 113–15
IPOs (initial public offerings), 209, 215
Iraq, US invasion of (1991), 94, 232
Ireland, 120, 122, 219
IT corridor (India): Bengaluru and,
151–52, 161, 166, 175; growth of,
203–4; tech companies and, 129;
wetlands loss attributed to, 35

J. Nehru National Urban Renewal
Mission (JNNURM), 98–99
Jaipur, India, 52
Jakarta, Indonesia, 250n12
Japan Bank for International Coopera-
tion (JBIC), 158, 163–65, 256n12
Japan International Cooperation
Agency (JICA), 21, 95, 256n12;
Bengaluru and, 141, 154
Jenks, Leland Hamilton, 36
John Taylor and Sons (electrical com-
pany), 146
Jones Lang LaSalle (property
consultant), 216
JPMorgan Chase, 6, 82

Kaplan, Steven, 83
Karnataka (Indian state): Bengaluru
International Airport investment and,

176–78; Bengaluru water infrastructure and, 159–60; court cases against,
over illegal land grabs, 200–201;
flows from JNNURM implementation, 99; IFI debts of, 164; industries
given land by, 150; refusal of self-
governance to Bengaluru, 153–54,
256n3; Town and Country Planning
Act (1961), 155
Karnataka Development Board (KDB),
233
Karnataka Industrial Area Development Board (KIADB), 156, 178, 195,
197–200
Karnataka Industrial Area Develop-
ment Board Act Amendment (1998),
182
Karnataka Land Grabbing Prohibition
Act (2011/2014), 201
Karnataka Rajya Raitha Sangha (KRRS,
farmers' movement), 194–95
KDB (Karnataka Development Board),
233
Kempe Gowda I (Indian chieftain),
142
Kempegowda International Airport. *See*
Bengaluru International Airport and
surrounding area
Keynes, John Maynard, 103–4
Keynesianism, 14, 73, 75, 87, 249n5
KIADB. *See* Karnataka Industrial Area
Development Board
Kim, Suntae, 75
KIMS Hospitals (India), 130
KKR (investment firm), 6–7, 29, 112,
116, 130, 217
Kodres, Laura, 253n6
Kothari, Ashish, 247
KPMG, 62–64; *Bridging the Global
Infrastructure Gap* (report 2009), 66
Krippner, Greta, 13
Krishnaraja Wodeyar III (Mysore king),
143
KRRS (Karnataka Rajya Raitha Sangha),
194–95

public goods: in colonial India, 145–46; as finance capital, 4; financiers' role in, 32, 74, 104, 152; global urban turn and, 72, 152; as monopolies, 29; national and municipal governments defunding, 33, 152, 239–40; negatives of financialization of urban infrastructure, 108, 168, 172, 239; tolls and user fees on (*see* user fees and tolls)

public land: Bengaluru's conversion into tradeable asset, 11, 16–17, 97, 124, 148, 171–73, 175–83, 206; Dalits seeking to live on, 233–34; revenues from sale of, 8, 97, 167; Spain's conversion into tradeable asset, 91

public-private partnerships, 47, 98, 179; Bengaluru International Airport construction as, 176–77; IFIs promoting, 154

public vs. private capital, 68–70

Puravankara (Indian developer), 221

PwC. *See* PricewaterhouseCoopers

racialization: of caste in Indian history, 18, 235, 250n7 (*see also* caste and class); colonial Bengaluru and, 144–46; contracts for deeds and, 112–13; defined, 17–18; dispossession and, 19, 110–15; elite networks targeting acquirable land by, 20; racial capitalism's historical agency and, 17–18; speculative urbanism and, 19, 34, 240; use of theory of, 18–19; water access in colonial Bengaluru, 144; wealth gap between Black and white households, 111

Radiant Life Care, 130

Ramachandra, T., 144

Ramsamy, Edward, 54

Ranganathan, Malini, 19

Rao, K. S. Chalapati, 128, 208

Rao, P. V. Narasimha, 95

Rath, Sharadini, 167

Rauh, Joshua, 83

Reagan, Ronald, 75, 85

real estate investment trusts (REITs), 113, 221

Reddys (landowning caste), 141, 257n8

relational-conjunctural approach, 12, 21, 23–30, *25*, 39, 233; in aftermath of 2008 global financial crisis, 104–5, 125; in years leading to 2008 global financial crisis, 73, 84, 102

rent control, 96, 113–14, 244, 254n6

rentier capitalism's rise, 34, 125–31, 214, 226, 228

rent-seeking practices, 105, 129, 155, 157, 197–99, 236

Rethinking Cities: Framing the Future (Barcelona conference 2012), 45–48, *46*

risk-taking norms, 10, 33–34, 207

road tolls. *See* toll roads

Robinson, Cedric, 17–18

Rodríguez, Emmanuel, 85–86, 122

Ross Center for Sustainable Cities (WRI), 61

Rothschilds, 27

RoyChowdhury, Supriya, 235

rule by contract, 108

rural-urban migration, 54–55, 84, 156, 235

Saldanha, Leo, 181–82

Saldanha, Michael, 157

Sánchez, Pedro, 124

Santander Bank, 121

Sanyal, Kalyan, 40

Sareb (Spanish government agency), 122–23

Sassen, Saskia, 13

Sastry, Trilochan, 256n13

Schmid, Christian, 13

securitization, 82–83

SEZs. *See* special economic zones

shadow banking system, 4, 82, 253n6

shadow or hidden empire, 36. *See also* optics of financial capital

Shah, Esha, 143

Shanghai, 15, 178

shareholder capitalism, 13–15

www.ingramcontent.com/pod-product-compliance
Lightning Source LLC
Chambersburg PA
CBHW032343280326
41935CB00008B/434